Mediating
Canadian
Politics

edited by

shannon sampert
UNIVERSITY OF WINNIPEG

linda trimble
UNIVERSITY OF ALBERTA

Mediating Canadian Politics

Pearson Canada
Toronto

Library and Archives Canada Cataloguing in Publication

Mediating Canadian politics/[edited by] Shannon Sampert, Linda Trimble.

Includes index.
ISBN 978-0-13-206864-2

1. Mass media—Political aspects—Canada.   2. Canada—Politics and government—
Press coverage.   3. Press and politics—Canada.   I. Trimble, Linda, 1959–
II. Sampert, Shannon, 1961–

P95.82.C3M44 2010   302.230971   C2008-905391-5

ISBN-13: 978-0-13-206864-2
ISBN-10: 0-13-206864-8

Vice President, Editorial Director: Gary Bennett
Editor-in-Chief: Ky Pruesse
Editor, Humanities and Social Sciences:
  Joel Gladstone
Executive Marketing Manager: Judith Allen
Senior Developmental Editor: Patti Altridge
Production Editor: Patricia Jones

Copy Editor: Margaret Burgess
Proofreaders: Sally Glover, Lisa LaFramboise
Production Coordinator: Avinash Chandra
Compositor: Integra
Art Director: Julia Hall
Cover and Interior Designer: Jennifer Stimson
Cover Image: Getty Images/ Peter Dazeley

For permission to reproduce material on pages 17, 93, 169, and 239, the publisher gratefully
acknowledges the copyright holder, Artizans.com.

For permission to reproduce copyrighted material, the publisher gratefully acknowledges the
copyright holders listed under the figures and tables in the book, which are considered an
extension of this copyright page.

Statistics Canada information is used with the permission of Statistics Canada. Users are forbidden
to copy the data and redisseminate them, in an original or modified form, for commercial purposes,
without permission from Statistics Canada. Information on the availability of the wide range of
data from Statistics Canada can be obtained from Statistics Canada's Regional Offices, its World
Wide Web site at http://www.statcan.ca, and its toll-free access number 1-800-263-1136.

1 2 3 4 5   13 12 11 10 09

Printed and bound in the United States of America.

Contents

Preface

It is 7 a.m. on a Wednesday morning in the summer of 2008 and a CBC reporter is following up on a rumour that Prime Minister Stephen Harper is ready to call a fall election. She logs on to a university website, finds the contact information for academics in her city who are experts in Canadian politics, and starts calling for reaction. She reaches a professor on his cellphone and arranges to do a live phone interview just after the 8 a.m. news. The reporter then starts to do research in preparation for the interview by downloading the local ridings featuring close races in 2006 from the Elections Canada website and accessing the latest polling numbers from an online polling company. At the same time, political party activists log in to their blogs to ruminate on the implications of the timing of the election call for their parties. An email from organizers in party "war rooms" urges party members to write letters to the editors of their local papers either praising or criticizing the decision to call the election early. Individuals can send their comments in a heartbeat, via email, by simply hitting the "enter" key. Meanwhile, local candidates begin to upload their personal details onto their campaign websites and Facebook as a way of gaining even more access to voters as they prepare for the expected call. Party organizers download their latest campaign advertisement on YouTube as a way of discerning whether the ad will "sell" or whether it needs to be revised. This flurry of activity is accomplished before many of us have even finished our first cup of coffee at work. None of this would have been possible even five years ago.

Writing in the late summer of 2008 as we sit poised on the brink of yet another Canadian federal election, it becomes clear that how we come to understand our world has changed dramatically because of the rise of the internet. Change within the media environment is, of course, not unusual. Technological advances have always had an impact on how news is produced and consumed. For instance, the rise of television in the late 1950s and early 1960s greatly influenced the look and content of newspapers. Now, with the immediacy of the internet, we are seeing yet another dramatic shift in how we obtain our information, and, perhaps as importantly, how it is presented to us as citizens, voters, activists, and political spectators. What impact is the internet revolution having on the actual content of election reporting? Is our media world revolving faster, with an even greater emphasis on the "now"? Does the internet give citizens and activists alternatives to mainstream news? Is mainstream news more entertaining, more opinionated, and more negative?

THE APPROACH AND ORGANIZATION OF THIS TEXT

Mediating Canadian Politics explores this new environment by looking at what happens when political actors, events, issues, and ideas are presented through the intermediary of the mass media, including new and old media technologies. In particular, we pay attention to "media logic"—the frames of reference employed by the media to construct meanings—and the role media logic plays in the selection and presentation of political events, personalities, and public policies. Fundamentally, this book is about the styling of politics through and by the media. While several chapters address the shifting technologies and political economy of the media, the central focus of this volume is the role of news mediation in democratic political engagement by political elites and citizens. In addition to traditional political communication topics such as the impact of technological and regulatory trends on the relationships between media and politics, media coverage of elections, the role and impact of opinion polling, and government control of advertising and access to information, authors address the discursive construction by the press of issues of race, gender, and identity. Case studies examining media representations of politicians, racialized citizens, civil-society groups, and public-policy issues are presented in this volume.

Our introductory chapter, **"Mediations: Making News About Politics,"** stresses the importance of news mediations of political life, arguing that most aspects of Canadian political life are performed, communicated, understood, and contested by and through the mainstream mass media. The chapter outlines the key filters shaping the selection, production, and presentation of political news to the public, identifying the complex power relationships within which political "realities" are constructed. In particular, the increasing concentration of ownership in the hands of a few corporations that control news content across several media platforms (from radio and newspapers to television and the internet) leads many critics to worry about the independence and vibrancy of the news media in Canada. Moreover, the proliferation of entertainment and media choices leads newsmakers and news producers to try to consolidate fragmented markets and capture inattentive audiences with ever more entertaining "products."

Part I, **"Politainment,"** explores what the rise of "infotainment" means for political news. Chapters in Part I look at the intersection of political news and entertainment in radio programming, in newspaper coverage of "celebrity" politicians, and in government advertising. These chapters ask whether citizens can be both informed and entertained at the same time.

Part II, **"Contests, Conquests, and Coronations: Elections as Media Events,"** takes a fresh look at the Olympic event of political reporting—election news coverage. Chapters in this section investigate the implications of mediation for engaged and informed citizen participation in the electoral process by examining the crucial role of opinion polling, debating the pros and cons of horse-race coverage, and analyzing newspaper treatment of Muslim Canadians over the course of three national election campaigns.

Part III, **"Intersections: Citizens, Media, Politics,"** examines the interrelated roles of citizens and new media. Chapters in Part III analyze the ways in which citizens and social-movement groups use traditional media to communicate with like-minded activists and reach new publics, and raise some difficult questions about the capacity of groups to challenge dominant media filters and frames. This section also investigates the potential of new, alternative media to empower citizen groups and democratize political communication.

Part IV, "Wagging the Dog? Media and Public Policy," the final section of the book, discusses the struggle to control a key aspect of the mediation process—the "spin," or the ways in which issues or policies are conceptualized and presented to the public. Chapters included in this section illustrate the power of "spin," or issue framing, to shape what is regarded as "real" and what is seen as possible. They also highlight troubling limitations on media independence and critical journalism posed by government control of access to information and the dominance of particular discourses in the post-9/11 political environment.

THE PRACTITIONERS AND THE ACADEMICS

Mediating Canadian Politics is designed as primary reading for courses on media and politics in Canada, political communication, and mass media and society. As indicated, the book is organized into four sections, each of which is prefaced by an introduction outlining its impetus and logic and summarizing the key points of each chapter. **Unique to this volume, each section of the book begins with the insights and experiences of a media practitioner.** Based on reflections about their own careers as radio jocks, reporters, columnists, and bloggers, these four media experts offer opinions about the organizational dynamics and structural constraints of news industries, and their chapters set the stage for the ideas and debates presented in the academic chapters. Our practitioners, all of whom have years of experience in the mediation of politics, invite readers to scrutinize their arguments, contest their evidence, and look for new examples.

Complementing and expanding on the practitioners' introductions to the main issues, the chapters written by academics offer a wide range of topics, approaches, theories, and methodologies, but all feature primary research based on original source material, including government documents, websites, and news items. Our view as scholars and teachers is that intensive, systematic, rigorous media analysis is essential to understanding political communication in Canada, and we wanted this book to illustrate the benefits of this type of research, as well as to assist in the presentation and discussion of its objectives and techniques in the classroom.

FEATURES

Media Journal Exercises: Each of the academic chapters includes **media journal exercises,** which are designed to allow students the opportunity to test, in a direct "hands-on" way, the central themes and arguments posed by these chapters.

Appendix: Putting It into Practice: A Primer on Content and Discourse Analysis To help understand how media analysis is conducted, we have included, in an **Appendix,** a brief overview of content and critical discourse methods. Students are encouraged to refer to this primer as they complete the media journal assignments. The Appendix is also intended for anyone interested in employing content and discourse analysis methodologies to generate quantitative and qualitative data. It provides a step-by-step approach to content analysis, includes sample coding frames for content-analysis projects, introduces discourse analysis, and offers tips about what works and what doesn't.

COURSESMART

CourseSmart is a new way for instructors and students to access textbooks online anytime from anywhere. With thousands of titles across hundreds of courses, CourseSmart helps instructors choose the best textbook for their class and give their students a new option for buying the assigned textbook as a lower cost eTextbook. For more information, visit www.coursesmart.com.

CHANGING TIMES

These are exciting times to study Canadian politics and media. It is our hope that this book will provide our students with some tools to understand the complex ways in which news mediations of Canadian politics shape understandings of our political environment. We know we can't provide the most up-to-date information, as by the time a book on media is published, it is already outdated. Because the business of media changes quickly, with mergers and sales having an impact on the media environment, we recommend that students regularly consult a number of websites to keep abreast of the current media conditions. We suggest as a starting point the following sites:

www.cbc.ca, the Canadian Broadcasting Corporation (CBC), Canada's public broadcaster
www.crtc.ca, the Canadian Radio-television and Telecommunications Commission (CRTC), the regulatory agency for radio, television, and telecommunications
www.cbsc.ca, the Canadian Broadcast Standards Council (CBSC), which sets standards for industry self-regulation
www.ccna.ca, the Canadian Community Newspapers Association (CCNA)
www.cna-acj.ca, the Canadian Newspaper Association (CNA)
www.rtnda.org, the Association of Electronic Journalists (RTNDA = Radio-Television News Directors' Association)

As well, most Canadian newspapers are available online, as are websites posted by local television stations.

Author and Contributor Biographies

TEXT EDITORS

Shannon Sampert is Assistant Professor of Politics at the University of Winnipeg. Before entering the world of academe, Shannon was an award-winning television producer, news reporter, writer, and communications consultant, and because old habits die hard, she still writes the occasional column for the *Winnipeg Free Press*. She is currently working on an analysis of the media representation of sexual assault crimes for publication by UBC Press. Her recent publications include: "More Than Just Cowboys with White Hats: A Demographic Profile of Edmonton and Calgary," in Caroline Andrew et al., eds., *Electing a Diverse Canada: The Representation of Newcomers and Minorities in Canadian Cities* (UBC Press, 2008); and "King Ralph: The Ministry of Truth and the Media in Alberta," in Trevor Harrison, ed., *The Return of the Trojan Horse: Alberta and the New World (Dis)order* (Black Rose, 2005).

Linda Trimble is Professor and Chair of the Department of Political Science at the University of Alberta. Her teaching and research interests focus on women's electoral and legislative representation and media coverage of women politicians. Her books include *Representing Women in Parliament* (Routledge, 2006, co-edited with Marian Sawer and Manon Tremblay); *Still Counting: Women in Politics across Canada* (Broadview Press, 2003, co-authored with Jane Arscott); and *Women and Electoral Politics in Canada* (Oxford University Press, 2003, co-edited with Manon Tremblay). Professor Trimble's most recent journal article is "Gender, Political Leadership and Media Visibility: *Globe and Mail* Coverage of Conservative Party of Canada Leadership Contests," *Canadian Journal of Political Science* 40 (4) (2007).

CONTRIBUTING AUTHORS

Yasmeen Abu-Laban is Professor in the Department of Political Science at the University of Alberta. Her research interests centre on the Canadian and comparative dimensions of gender and ethnic politics, nationalism and globalization, immigration policies and politics, and citizenship theory. In addition to publishing over 40 articles and chapters, she is the co-author of *Selling Diversity: Immigration, Multiculturalism, Employment Equity and Globalization* (Broadview Press, 2002), the co-editor of *Politics in North America: Redefining Continental Relations* (Broadview Press, 2007), and the editor of *Gendering the Nation-State: Canadian and Comparative Perspectives* (UBC Press, 2008).

Christopher Adams is Senior Research Director at Probe Research and Adjunct Professor at both the University of Winnipeg and the Department of Politics at the I.H. Asper

School, where he teaches marketing-research methods. He began his career in 1995 with Goldfarb Consultants, before becoming Vice President of the Angus Reid Group. His latest research includes *The Politics of Manitoba: Parties, Leaders and Voters* (University of Manitoba Press, 2008) and his analysis has appeared in the *American Review of Canadian Studies, The Innovation Journal,* and *Inroads: The Journal of Opinion.* He holds a Ph.D. from Carleton University and regularly provides polling results and analysis to the CBC, GlobalTV, and the *Winnipeg Free Press.*

Blake Andrew is a Ph.D. candidate in the Department of Political Science at McGill University. His dissertation compares the news content of mass-media headlines with the content of the stories they lead. Blake was the Donner Doctoral Fellow from 2005 to 2007 for the Media Observatory at the McGill Institute for the Study of Canada (MISC). His fields of research include political communication, Canadian politics, and comparative politics. Recent publications include: "Media-Generated Shortcuts: Do Newspaper Headlines Present Another Roadblock for Low-information Rationality," *Harvard International Journal of Press/Politics* 12 (2) (2007); "From Ink-Stained Wretches to Talking Heads: A Short History of the Press Gallery," *Policy Options* 27 (6) (2007), with Stuart Soroka; and "Just When You Thought It Was Out, Policy is Pulled Back In," *Policy Options* 27 (3) (2006), with Antonia Maioni and Stuart Soroka.

Robert Bragg became a member of the Journalism faculty at Mount Royal College's Centre for Communication Studies in August 1999. Robert has a B.A. and M.A. in English Literature from the University of Calgary. He has 26 years of journalism experience, 2 at CKUA Radio and 24 at the *Calgary Herald,* including 13 years on the *Herald* editorial board as an editorial writer and columnist. As a reporter at the *Herald,* Robert covered municipal, provincial, and federal politics. As an editorial writer he specialized in political and social commentary. Robert was a member of a *Calgary Herald* team that won a National Newspaper Award (NNA) in 1992 for a Special Project publication on the Canadian Constitution and the Charlottetown Accord. In 1995, he was a Nuffield Press Fellow at Wolfson College, Cambridge University, U.K. From 1997 to 1999, Robert was a member of the Calgary advisory committee of the World Psychiatric Association's (WPA) campaign to combat the stigma against schizophrenia. In 1998, he won the Alberta Communications Award from the Canadian Mental Health Association.

Lisa Brandt has been a broadcaster since 1981 and has worked across the country, with stops in British Columbia, Alberta, and Ontario. As a radio announcer and program host, she has interviewed major politicians, world-renowned music stars, and other famous figures. She reached the pinnacle of her radio-broadcasting success as a co-anchor of the all-news morning show on Canada's highest-rated radio station, 680 News in Toronto. Lisa has taught broadcast studies at Humber and Mohawk Colleges, and presents a media-training course to groups and organizations wishing to attract more positive coverage from the news media. She is also a published author. Her first book, *Celebrity Tantrums: The Official Dirt* was published in 2003 (ECW Press). She has been a columnist with Sun

Media Corporation newspapers since 2007 and has frequently been a guest in other magazines and papers, in addition to her monthly stint as an advice columnist for *Real Women Magazine* and her daily online blog. Lisa contributes her pop-culture expertise to the television series *Whatever Happened To*, on air since 2005.

Curtis Brown is a Manitoba-based blogger, journalist, commentator, and student of political science. A graduate of the University of Regina School of Journalism, Mr. Brown began his reporting career in Saskatchewan before shifting to the political beat with the *Brandon Sun*. Mr. Brown later served as the *Sun's* editorial-page editor, and in the spring of 2005 launched a political blog, Endless Spin Cycle (http://endlessspin.blogspot.com), which he continues to update as this book goes to press. Mr. Brown also writes regular columns for the *Winnipeg Free Press* and *Brandon Sun*, and is currently working on a Master's thesis at the University of Manitoba that explores how partisan blogs frame media coverage of the federal Conservative government.

Bob Cox is the publisher of the *Winnipeg Free Press*. He has spent 25 years working in Canadian daily journalism, after starting as a summer student at the *Globe and Mail* in 1983. Since then he has taken a long and winding road. He has worked at several newspapers, at jobs including general reporter for the *Cobourg Star*, court reporter for the *Winnipeg Free Press*, city editor of the *Edmonton Journal*, and national editor of the *Globe and Mail*. He also spent 10 years at The Canadian Press news agency, including six on Parliament Hill in Ottawa covering national politics. In May 2005, Cox was appointed editor of the *Winnipeg Free Press*, a role he held until July 2007, when he became publisher of the newspaper.

Joanna Everitt is Professor of Political Science and Chair of the Department of History and Politics at the University of New Brunswick in Saint John. Her research interests include gender and politics, media studies, public opinion and voting, social capital, and political behaviour. She is a member of the 2004, 2006, and 2008 Canadian Election Study Team and was a co-investigator of the 2003 New Brunswick Social Capital Survey. She has written extensively on the interaction between gender, media, and public opinion. She is a co-author of *Advocacy Groups* (UBC Press, 2004) and co-editor of *Citizen Politics: Research and Theory in Canadian Political Behaviour* (Oxford University Press, 2002). Her work has appeared in the *Canadian Journal of Political Science*, *Political Communication*, *Women & Politics*, the *Harvard Journal of Press/Politics*, the *Canadian Review of Sociology and Anthropology*, *Atlantis*, and *Canadian Ethnic Studies*, as well as in several edited books on women and politics, public opinion, and elections.

Angela Failler is Assistant Professor of Sociology and Women's and Gender Studies at the University of Winnipeg in Manitoba. Her general areas of teaching and research include feminist and queer theory, cultural studies, and psychoanalysis. Currently, she is interested in questions emerging from the politics of memory and loss, memorial/counter-memorial practices, and the field of psychodermatology. She has published in scholarly journals including the *International Journal of Gender and Sexuality Studies*, *Journal for the*

Psychoanalysis of Culture and Society, and *Eating Disorders: The Journal of Treatment and Prevention*. She also has a chapter in the forthcoming edited collection *Embodiment and Agency* (Penn State University Press).

Anne-Marie Gingras is Professor in the Department of Political Science at Université Laval (Quebec City). Her field of research is political communication: she has written on the public sphere, on trash radio and freedom of expression, on electronic government, on cultural diversity, and on political language. She also works on social representations of democracy and is director of a special edition of *Politique et Sociétés* on "constructing legitimacy in the public sphere" (2008). She is the author of *Media et démocratie: Le grand malentendu* (2nd ed., PUQ, 2006) and was director of *La communication politique: État des savoirs, enjeux et perspectives* (PUQ, 2003), and of *Démocratie et réseaux de communication* (*Politique et Sociétés* 18 [2]), among other publications. Anne-Marie Gingras has taught at the Institut d'études politiques in Bordeaux and has been Invited Researcher at Centre de recherches politiques de Sciences Po (Paris), Concordia University (Montreal), and the University of Florida (Gainesville).

Yasmin Jiwani is Associate Professor in the Department of Communication Studies at Concordia University, Montreal. Her doctorate in Communication Studies, from Simon Fraser University, examined issues of "race" and representation in Canadian television news. Prior to her move to Montreal, she was the Executive Coordinator and principal researcher at the BC/Yukon FREDA Centre for Research on Violence against Women and Children. Her recent publications include *Discourses of Denial: Mediations of Race, Gender and Violence* (UBC Press, 2006) and an edited collection with Candice Steenbergen and Claudia Mitchell titled *Girlhood: Redefining the Limits* (Black Rose Books, 2006). Her work has appeared in *Social Justice, Violence Against Women, Canadian Journal of Communication, Journal of Popular Film & Television*, and the *International Journal of Media and Cultural Politics*.

Graham Longford is Assistant Professor in the Department of Politics at Trent University. Dr. Longford's research interests revolve around the social and political implications of new information and communication technologies. He has published on a range of subjects, including democracy and the internet, e-government, the digital divide, telecommunications policy, and citizenship and technology. Prior to teaching at Trent he held postdoctoral fellowships in the Faculty of Information Studies at the University of Toronto and the Division of Social Science at York University. Dr. Longford holds a Ph.D. in Political Science from York University.

Hugh Mellon is Associate Professor of Political Science at the University of Western Ontario's King's University College. Hugh has published in such journals as *Canadian Public Administration*, the *British Journal of Canadian Studies*, and *Constitutional Forum*. His most recent published article was "Charter Rights and Public Policy: The Supreme Court and Public Finance" (*Constitutional Forum*, 2006). He also has an essay on prime ministerial power in the upcoming *Cross-Currents* text edited by Barker and Charlton (2008).

With his UWO colleague Martin Westmacott he has co-edited three works on Canadian politics: *Challenges to Canadian Federalism* (Pearson Education, 1997), *Public Administration and Policy: Governing in Challenging Times* (Pearson Education, 1998), and *Political Dispute and Judicial Review* (Nelson Education, 2000). In 2005 he served a term as Visiting Professor of Canadian Studies at Kwansei Gakuin University in Nishinomiya, Japan. At present he is working on research related to notions of state branding among various jurisdictions.

Steve Patten is Associate Professor of Political Science at the University of Alberta. As is evident from his contribution to this volume, an important aspect of Steve's teaching, research, and political work has focused on citizenship, democracy, and democratization. He is a member of Public Interest Alberta's Task Force on Democracy and teaches an undergraduate course on Citizenship for Democracy. His research and writing on democracy has focused on two themes: (1) the implications of neo-liberal culture and governance for citizenship and democracy, and (2) civic education and the politics of extending democracy. In addition to his contribution to this volume, his publications on democratic themes include: "Democracy in the Age of the Internet" (with Graham Longford), *University of New Brunswick Law Journal* 56 (2007); "Valuing Civics: Political Commitment and the New Citizenship Education in Australia" (with Cosmo Howard), *Canadian Journal of Education* 29 (2) (2006): 454–75; "The Democratic Deficit: Neo-liberal Governance and the Undermining of Democracy's Potential," in J. Brodie and L. Trimble, eds., *Re-Inventing Canada: Politics in the 21st Century* (Scarborough: Prentice-Hall, 2003); and "Democratizing the Institutions of Policy-making: Democratic Consultation and Participatory Administration," *Journal of Canadian Studies* 35 (4) (2001).

David G. Pelletier is an M.A. student in the Political Science Department of Laval University in Quebec City. He also acts as coordinator for ZAP Québec, a non-profit organization devoted to the development of free hot spots throughout the Metropolitan Area. He has worked as coordination and research assistant for the centre of expertise and research on lifelong learning, La Société pour l'Apprentissage à Vie (SAVIE) and has assisted Louis Villardier of TELUQ (UQAM) in various research projects on e-learning. He has also had the pleasure of collaborating on research projects with Anne-Marie Gingras of Laval University, who is the supervisor of his Master's thesis. His main areas of interest are related to political communication, alternative media, digital citizenship, and the democratization of communication.

Alasdair Roberts is Rappaport Professor of Law and Public Policy at Suffolk University Law School in Boston. He received his law degree from the University of Toronto and his Ph.D. in Public Policy from Harvard University. He is a Fellow of the U.S. National Academy of Public Administration and an Honorary Senior Research Fellow of the School of Public Policy, University College London. His books include *Blacked Out: Government Secrecy in the Information Age* (Cambridge University Press, 2006) and *The Collapse of Fortress Bush: The Crisis of Authority in American Government* (New York University Press, 2008).

Jonathan Rose was educated at Queen's and the University of Toronto. He teaches Canadian politics, political communication, and mass media at Queen's University, where he is Associate Professor. His research is in the area of Canadian politics and mass media, including studies of the impact of political advertising. He is the author of a book and several articles on government or political advertising. He is also the lead author of *The Art of Negotiation* (2002), a federalism simulation published by Broadview Press that has been translated into three languages. Rose served as consultant for the federal Office of the Auditor General when it examined government advertising. He is a member of the Advertising Clearance Group for the Auditor General of Ontario, the body that reviews all provincial government ads in that province. From 2006 to 2007 he was seconded from Queen's to be the Academic Director of the Ontario Citizens' Assembly on Electoral Reform, an experience that only confirmed his assumptions about the capacity of ordinary citizens to reason about complex political problems. He is writing a book with Ken Carty, André Blais, Patrick Fournier, and Henk VanderKolk on citizens' assemblies in British Columbia, Ontario, and the Netherlands.

Stuart Soroka is Associate Professor and William Dawson Scholar in the Department of Political Science at McGill University. He is also Adjunct Professor at the School of Policy Studies at Queen's University, where he is Director of the Canadian Opinion Research Archive. Stuart's research focuses on the relationships between mass media, public opinion, and policy. His book *Agenda-Setting Dynamics in Canada* was published by UBC Press in 2002. Subsequent work has been published in a wide range of edited volumes and journals, including the *Journal of Politics*, the *British Journal of Political Science*, and the *Harvard International Journal of Press and Politics*.

Miriam Smith is Professor in the School of Public Policy and Administration at York University. Her fields of interest include Canadian and comparative politics and public policy, public law, human rights, social movements, and lesbian, gay, bisexual, and transgender politics. Her recent publications include *Critical Policy Studies* (UBC Press, 2007, co-edited with Michael Orsini), *Group Politics and Social Movements in Canada* (Broadview Press, 2008, edited) and *Political Institutions and Lesbian and Gay Rights in the United States and Canada* (Routledge, 2008). Her work has recently appeared in journals such as *Economy and Society*, *Politics and Society*, and *Social and Legal Studies*.

Chapter 1

Mediations: Making News about Politics

Shannon Sampert and Linda Trimble

INTRODUCTION

To say politics are mediated is to state the obvious; modern politics cannot exist without mass communication. Communication technologies are so ubiquitous and so enthusiastically embraced that they increasingly shape all human experiences. Consider the impact of mobile phones and internet networking sites such as Facebook and YouTube. There is no doubt that Canadians live in a news-saturated society (Allan, 2004, p. 1; Bennett, 2007, p. 19). As a result, "mediated political communication has become central to politics and public life in contemporary democracies" (Bennett & Entman, 2001, p. xxiv). Canadian politics are performed, communicated, understood, interrogated, and contested through the mass media, particularly radio, television, print, and web-based mediums. Castells (1996, p. 311) goes so far as to argue that the media "create and control the space in which politics now chiefly happens for most people" and that "in order to engage in the political debate we must now do so through the media." Since the media, especially news media, are crucial agents of representative democracy, the fact of mediated communications is of concern to students of politics.

Stuart Allen (2004, p. 4) describes news mediation as a dynamic process in which a news item is selected, constructed, produced, and consumed. The content and structure of news is shaped by a wide range of factors, including commercial forces in the news business, the ways in which political actors employ technologies of mass communication, and the news preferences and personal entertainment habits of citizens (Bennett, 2007, p. 19). As such, mediation does not end with the production of news; rather, it continues as citizens decide whether or not to consume the news, and, if they do, how to react to these versions of "reality." Audience reactions shape the news that is created, bringing the process full circle. However, processes of mediation are rarely neutral. "The news account, far from simply 'reflecting' the reality of an event, is effectively providing a codified definition of what should count as the reality of the event" (Allen, 2004, p. 4). Even on those rare occasions when the news media publish a government document verbatim or broadcast a political event "live" without editing, mediation is occurring. The media have decided that the document or event are important or interesting enough to be the focus of such attention; governments or political actors have undoubtedly kept media requirements and audiences in mind when formulating their messages; and media consumers can ignore, digest, interpret, and argue with the story.

As we were writing this chapter, the Maxime Bernier–Julie Couillard story broke in the Canadian news media. At the time, Maxime Bernier was Minister of Foreign Affairs in the Harper government, but his political career began to unravel on May 7, 2008, when ex-girlfriend Julie Couillard was linked with the biker underworld. Couillard's relationships with two members of the Hells Angels gang were raised as an issue of public security. Initially the Prime Minister snapped at the press for pursuing the story, saying it was nobody's business who his cabinet ministers dated and calling opposition leaders "gossipy old busy-bodies" for asking questions about Couillard's past.[1] The story gained momentum when, on a Quebec television show, Couillard revealed that Bernier had left confidential cabinet documents at her home. Bernier resigned on May 26, 2008, but opposition parties kept the narrative alive by prompting an inquiry by the House of Commons Public Safety Committee. We raise this example because it illustrates the central point of this book: Canadian politics are invariably mediated by the press. The "scandal"—the media branded it as such—may well have been the subject of water-cooler or Facebook gossip, but what Canadians know of the Bernier–Couillard affair comes not from first-hand information, but rather from news reports on mainstream media. As a result, the story has been selected, interpreted, evaluated, and packaged for presentation to the public.

The Bernier affair illustrates three central elements of news mediation of politics: the selection and framing of stories by the press; the instrumental use of mass media by political actors; and the ways in which the structure and organization of media shape news stories. The initial "Minister's ex-girlfriend associated with criminal underworld" story was selected and indeed rendered highly visible by the press because of its considerable news value. It featured personalities, drama, intrigue, and, thanks to revealing photos of Couillard's décolletage snapped at Maxime Bernier's swearing-in ceremony and resurrected when the story broke, it also had sex appeal. Opposition leaders, recognizing the allure of the story to the news media, adapted their behaviour accordingly, and their voices of outrage fuelled spectacularization of the news narrative. Application of the scandal frame, coupled with the infamous and oft-published photos of Couillard in a revealing sundress, rendered the story entertaining enough for international media, illustrating the commercial logic of the press. According to a media watchdog, Julie Couillard was the subject of thousands of news articles and 821 television reports in 61 countries, even capturing 6 percent of U.S. news coverage in a 72-hour time period.[2]

Were the media merely entertaining the public in an effort to recapture audience share and improve profits, or were they performing their legitimate function of bringing important matters to the attention of citizens? Were politicians trying to spin the story to suit their political agendas, or were they truly interested in promoting political transparency and government legitimacy? According to a letter writer to the *Globe and Mail*, media exposure of the facts of the Bernier situation demonstrated the value of a free and open press, as it informed the public and eventually prompted appropriate government action.[3] *Globe and Mail* columnist Lysiane Gagnon offered a more cynical interpretation of media attention to the scandal. For the press, she said, Couillard "embodies the mixture of sex, motorbikes and shady dealings that sells tabloids," and for opposition politicians, "this juicy soap opera" was exploited to undermine the Harper government and deflect attention from their own political vulnerabilities.[4] Who is right, the columnist or the reader? Can citizens be amused and informed at the same time? More importantly, what does the Bernier story reveal about the power relationships embedded in mass-mediated politics? Whose truth has been presented, and whose construction of events is now considered "real"?

The Bernier–Couillard example illustrates that dichotomizing "media" and "politics" is problematic because each is deeply embedded in the other. The symbiotic nature of media and politics generates both productive tensions and damaging silences, and nowhere are these dynamics more evident than in the production of political news. We begin this chapter by discussing news selection and framing. How do the news media decide what is news? Once news items are elected, how are they presented? Whose stories are told and whose perspectives are presented as authoritative? The second part of the chapter puts the news production process in the context of the increasingly concentrated and converged media environment. We close the chapter with a final narrative that punctuates the profound implications of news mediations for democratic political ideals, practices, and outcomes.

MAKING NEWS: SELECTION AND FRAMING

The *New York Times*'s motto, "All the news that's fit to print," acknowledges the newspaper's role in news selection. Indeed, all news organizations have to filter the raw material of news because they simply cannot print or broadcast stories about every political event and issue. Even if they could, their audiences would not be able to cope with, never mind digest, all of the political information that is available. The public relies on the press to decide what we need (or want) to know about. How do news media choose which of the plethora of news releases and media events are important? Whose interests are considered interesting enough to be "fit to print"? News selection reflects dominant news values, those elements of a story that are thought to make it important or appealing to news audiences. Events or issues have value to news media when they feature conflict, drama, novelty, timeliness, and vividness (Cook, 1997, p. 6). Graber suggests that "the news tend to contain information that is timely, often sensational (scandals, violence, and human drama frequently dominate the news), and familiar (stories often drawing on familiar people or life experiences that give even distant events a closer-to-home feeling)" (quoted in Bennett, 2007, p. 11). But how do news media decide that these values are in accordance with public interests and tastes? And how do these values direct the format and content of political news stories?

Political events are rarely narrated in their entirety, and thus are subjected to further filtering to render them easily digestible by audiences. Once stories have been chosen, journalists must decide which elements are included and which are left out of the narrative. News frames generate easily described and packaged stories "with two distinct sides, terseness, good visuals, pithy sound bites" (Cook, 1997, p. 6). Framing the story according to dominant ideas about news and news storytelling makes the task much easier. News frames are the "interpretive structures that journalists use to set particular events within their broader context" (Norris et al., 2003, p. 10). Framing allows reporters and editors to fit complex events into familiar categories by activating knowledge and tapping into cultural norms and social assumptions (Entman, 1993, p. 53). Frames are indicated by words, phrases, or images that guide a reader's approach to reading and interpreting a story. However, framing is rarely a neutral instrument, as a news frame "determines what is included and excluded, what is salient and what is unimportant" (Cappella & Jamieson, 1997, p. 38). Moreover, framing positions certain versions of reality as common sense, or, as Allen (2004, p. 5) puts it, as "what everyone knows to be true." For instance, a scandal frame emphasizes wrongdoing and may therefore obscure evidence of conscientious or appropriate political action. The game (or horse race) dominates election coverage, and, as discussed in detail in Part II of this volume, calls attention to the strategic elements of a campaign, focusing on leaders rather than candidates, on who is winning and losing rather than on the ideas they represent. Framing of contemporary policy issues is analyzed in Part IV of this book, with Chapters 16 and 17 examining the scripts conveyed by coverage of the Gomery Commission and the 9/11 terrorist attacks.

Understanding processes of news selection and news framing leads media analysts to question the possibility of journalistic objectivity. News frames invariably promote a particular impression or interpretation of events but, as Norris et al. (2003, p. 14) argue, the use of conventional news frames breeds journalistic complacency. Frames such as the game frame for election coverage or the law-and-order frame for crime reporting are so pervasive and dominant that journalists employ them without question, assuming they are offering objective and balanced reporting (Norris et al., 2003, p. 14). A truly objective news report is impossible to produce, yet it is an aspiration (to borrow from Hackett and Zhao, 1998) that just won't die. Indeed, in journalism textbooks, the issue of objectivity is widely discussed, usually in terms of providing balance and fairness. The meanings of "objective journalism" vary, but the assumption that somehow journalists can be detached and neutral in their work is problematic. As critics have suggested, the "rhetoric of news constructs its authority as accounts of the Real at the expense of other accounts" (Hackett & Zhao, 1998, p. 232).

News selection and framing are in many respects products of the power relationships governing the political economy of news production. According to Herman and Chomsky's "propaganda model," a series of interrelated elements or "filters" influences news selection and presentation, moulding the news according to the ideological context within which it is produced (1988, pp. 1–35). One does not need to accept Herman and Chomsky's assertion that the agenda-setting news media function as instruments of propaganda to appreciate the importance of the factors they identify as central to the manufacture of political news. The first two filtering agents, ownership and advertising, reflect the corporate logic of media. The most dominant influential media organizations are privately owned, and thus "market-profit-oriented forces" lead them to filter the events and issues they report according to commercial norms and interests (Herman & Chomsky 1988, p. 14). For example, *Ottawa Citizen* publisher Russell Mills was fired by the CanWest Global media conglomerate for printing an editorial critical of then Prime Minister Jean Chrétien. Critics maintained that the owners of CanWest, the Asper family, were close friends of Mr. Chrétien, and this both influenced the company's editorial policy and led to undue interference in the content of the newspapers in its chain (Shade, 2005, p. 103). A larger concern about ownership is that the proliferation of electronic communication platforms and the opening up of media markets fosters intense competition for audiences, leading critics to worry that the increasingly competitive and fragmented news marketplace cannot, or will not be able to, supply the information citizens need for effective democratic participation (Bennett & Entman, 2001, p. 12). The importance of advertising to the success of for-profit media is a second factor. Because advertising is the primary income source of most news-media organizations, including the internet, news organizations are essentially "selling" audiences to advertisers. The need to capture audience share and secure advertising profits means news choices are influenced directly by advertisers as well as indirectly by entertainment values. Part I of this volume, titled "Politainment," illustrates what happens when the "market-profit" logic of news production is buffeted by the proliferation of media and entertainment choices. Is it possible for the corporate news media to address people as consumer audiences *and* as citizen publics (Bennett & Entman, 2001, p. xxv)?

The third filter discussed by Herman and Chomsky, the reliance by news media on information provided by government and business elites, is well documented in the literature on political communication. Not only do political and corporate elites provide prepackaged news, but they also offer credibility and authority as news sources. For journalists, the most important news sources are those who represent the "society's chief political, economic, intellectual and control institutions" (Martin, 1997, p. 243). Because of the power and perceived legitimacy of these officials and experts, they are sought as news sources and often allowed to define what a news story is all about (Martin, 1997, p. 243). Elites further facilitate the news-gathering process by employing public-relations consultants and offering the media "ready-for-broadcast" news items (speeches, press releases, staged media events). As a result, elites enjoy privileged access to the media, while the ordinary citizen is excluded or marginalized. Or, to put it somewhat differently, "the subordinate group has to work harder to be heard, while the favoured group is invited to argue its own case" (Brown, 1989, p. 258). As an outcome, news becomes highly formulaic and repetitive, offering access to only "certain storylines—and to those political actors who anticipate the recurring preferences of the news media" (Cook, 1997, p. 5). The challenges posed by this aspect of news selection and framing are explored in Part III of this volume, which looks at the use by citizens and social-movement organizations of mainstream news media and new media and assesses the capacity of new media technologies and platforms, such as the internet, to facilitate citizen communication unmediated by corporate media or the state.

Herman and Chomsky call the fourth filter "flak," meaning that dominant social institutions, especially governments, have the power and resources to "discipline" the media, often encouraging right-wing bias in news selection. One of the many tools political actors employ to control the media is access. A good politician can, "with skill in the management of access, leaks, plants and other techniques," launch pre-emptive strikes against potential bad press and cultivate good press (Nesbitt-Larking, 2007, p. 339). Canada's current prime minister's often acrimonious relationship with the Ottawa press gallery is a case in point. The first Conservative prime minister to be elected since 1993, Stephen Harper felt the Ottawa press gallery was biased against him, and soon after he was elected in 2006 declared his plan to avoid them by going directly to less hostile local reporters. With several manoeuvres likened to the American approach to media relations adopted during George W. Bush's presidency, Harper signalled his desire to discipline the press by controlling access and choosing the messenger. A key aspect of the American approach is control of access by journalists to the president, and the Harper government has embraced this strategy. Prior to the election of the Conservative government, government press conferences in the national press theatre were monitored by press gallery executive members and not by political staff. Now the Prime Minister's staff members decide who gets to ask the PM questions. The national press corps has strenuously objected to this approach (MacCharles, 2007), and has also complained that press-gallery scribes have been prevented from accessing the inner workings on the Hill. Journalists are no longer informed when cabinet meetings are taking place, and are no longer allowed to congregate outside the hallway of the cabinet room, where they used to be able to pounce on ministers walking in and out of meetings (Crocker, 2007). As Robert Bragg discusses in Chapter 14, Harper is taking a page from Ronald Reagan's media-relations book by controlling the message. Spontaneous scrums with cabinet ministers are not permitted.

The Harper media team has attempted to bypass the Ottawa press gallery altogether. If the press gallery insisted on acting like the official opposition, criticizing the government's every move, Harper said, he would bypass them by taking his message "out on the road" (CTV Online, 2007). This decision to give preference to the local reporters may have been the impetus behind a story the *Toronto Star* broke in early 2007 suggesting Harper would further sidestep the national press theatre and press gallery executive by building a new media centre featuring direct satellite access to local television stations. According to the *Star*'s Tonda MacCharles, planning for the new $2-million media centre, code-named "The Shoe Store Project," was in the works for more than a year (MacCharles, 2007). In response to rumours about the project, the Prime Minister's Director of Communications told the Canadian Press that there were no plans to pursue the media centre; however, MacCharles maintains the project has not yet been cancelled (MacCharles, 2007). The Ottawa press gallery was worried the new media centre would operate much like the system in place in the United States presidential press office under

George W. Bush. Until the fallout from Hurricane Katrina and the Iraq war took its toll, Bush kept the Washington press at bay, and his approval ratings high, by speaking directly to local audiences. As Chapters 3 and 15 of *Mediating Canadian Politics* show, Canadian governments have both formal and informal strategies of discipline at their disposal, including control over access to politicians and officials, and the legislative capacity to regulate media structure, ownership, and content. Whether these approaches actually suppress the capacity of news media to dig for and publicize information politicians and governments want to hide is another question. For instance, *Toronto Star* columnist Susan Delacourt (2008) believes the Harper government's "communications-management machine" may be showing signs of wear and tear because "one can only keep the lid on information so long in government before the effort explodes in strange and unexpected ways." This was certainly the case with the Maxime Bernier affair discussed earlier in the chapter. Despite the Prime Minister's attempts to manage the story, it took on a life of its own and ended in Harper's capitulation and Minister Bernier's resignation.

Finally, Herman and Chomsky's fifth filter shaping news selection and content, "anticommunism," is passé in the post–Cold War era. As an alternative to this filter, we suggest that "war on terrorism" discourses serve as significant selection and framing devices in the aftermath of the terrorist attacks perpetrated on September 11, 2001. The events of 9/11 fit the pattern of a "political wave," which is "marked by a dramatic increase in media coverage about an issue, an increase in public reactions by political leaders and activists concerning the topic, and an increase in discussions about the issue among the general public" (Wolfsfeld, 2001, p. 226). As such, the "war on terror" has influenced news selection and, as Chapters 8 and 17 of this volume point out, the discursive frame for the "war" shapes particular narrative structures and approaches to issue definition. This "war on terror" filter also illustrates the two primary effects of news mediation on political attitudes and behaviours: agenda setting and priming. Agenda setting refers to the impact of news selection, as the more attention given to a topic by the news media the more likely it is to be considered important by the public (Cappella & Jamieson, 1997). While the news media did not initiate the events of 9/11 or the subsequent "war on terror," they certainly amplified the debate. As Wolfsfeld (2001, p. 229) notes, "once a wave has been identified, the news media become massive search engines looking for any information and events that can be linked to the story." News selection, then, helps set priorities for political discussion and deliberation.

Agenda setting and framing can work in concert to prime audiences; that is, to influence the ways in which citizens attribute responsibility for political problems and evaluate political leaders. Framing provides important cues for understanding and evaluation, as news frames activate prior knowledge, stereotypes, and assumptions (Cappella & Jamieson, 1997, pp. 40–42). For example, as Yasmin Jiwani shows in Chapter 17, binaries of "us" and "them" construct Canadian Muslims and Arabs as threatening in the post 9/11 political environment. Cappella and Jamieson (1997, p. 44) note the serious consequences of frames for "what is recalled, how messages are interpreted, and how people and policies are judged." However, the work of those who study the ways in which audiences deconstruct the news shows that priming is rarely straightforward or simple (Allen, 2004, pp. 98–117). Social context, experience, and ideology, as well as patterns of news consumption, can affect the ways people interpret the news. Mediated politics are, therefore, a product of complex power relationships, increasingly shaped by new technologies and new demands from media-savvy publics and situated within a political economy of convergence and corporate concentration.

CONCENTRATION AND CONVERGENCE: THE CANADIAN NEWS-MEDIA ENVIRONMENT

As a 2006 report by the Canadian Senate emphasized, "No real democracy can function without healthy, diverse and independent news media to inform people about the way their society works, what is going well and, perhaps most important, what is not going well or needs to be improved" (Canada, 2006, p. 1). The most profound threats to this vision of the news media are concentration of ownership and convergence of media formats. Concentration means fewer and fewer owners control news production, and convergence means these mass-media conglomerates own a wide range of media assets and platforms. In other words, while it seems there are more and more media choices, in fact the newspaper you read, television station you watch, radio channel you tune in to, and internet service provider you use for email and web access may be owned by the same company.

Any attempt to chronicle the ownership map for Canadian media is doomed to be outdated by the time the document is published. The media market in Canada (and elsewhere) is volatile, with media companies being bought and sold with surprising alacrity. Winseck (2002, p. 797) documents some of the convoluted processes of corporate concentration and convergence that occurred in the late 1990s:

> Canwest took over Western International Communications and a chain of newspapers stretching from Vancouver to Halifax that had previously been owned by Conrad Black's Hollinger Inc. Quebecor absorbed Videotron. Rogers Communications aligned itself with global media titans Microsoft and AT&T, and formed an alliance with Shaw Communications to divide Canada's cable industry into Cable Monopoly East and Cable Monopoly West. Shaw Communications–based Corus Entertainment bought Nelvana, the premier creator of animated programs in Canada. And, of course, Bell Canada parlayed its dominance in telecommunications across the vast Canadian mediascape by launching ExpressVu and Sympatico, in 1994 and 1995, respectively, and over the last year acquiring CTV and the *Globe and Mail*.

As the foregoing suggests, Canada has one of the most consolidated media markets in the world (see Skinner and Gasher, 2005). This is particularly true of the newspaper industry. Despite the fact that two Royal Commissions have undertaken to study the problem and recommend solutions, little has been done to stall the momentum toward increasing concentration of ownership. The Davey Commission, which held hearings in 1970, pointed out that newspaper ownership was largely in the hands of big newspaper chains. The Kent

Commission opened its 1981 report about media ownership with a straightforward assertion: "Concentration engulfs Canadian daily newspaper publishing" (Kent, 1981, p. 1). Matters have not improved since then; in 2006, five media conglomerates controlled close to 80 percent of newspaper circulation in Canada (Nesbitt-Larking, 2007, p. 100).

Concentration in Canada's media is amplified by the phenomenon of convergence. Many media analysts have expressed concerns that Canadians now have "one of the most consolidated media systems in the developed world and an unrivalled scale of cross-media ownership" (Winseck, 2002, p. 798), resulting in declining diversity of opinions and perspectives. Prior to the early 1980s, Canada's media watchdog, the CRTC, restricted cross-media ownership, but pressures of neo-liberal globalization have led the regulator to ignore overlaps in market penetration (Hildebrandt et al., 2005, p. 89). Taras (2001, p. 61) identifies the key features of convergence as the union of corporations, technologies, information, and cultures. Large corporations own several different types of news and telecommunications mediums, from radio and television stations to newspapers and internet search engines, and are able to speak with one voice across multiple technologies. Indeed, convergence has become the watchword for media critics concerned that large-scale media-platform companies control media markets in cities and potentially control the type of information being provided by all news genres.

The effects of concentration and convergence, and the erosion of public media such as the Canadian Broadcasting Corporation, are hotly debated, but they certainly shape the context and nature of mass-mediated politics in Canada. As fewer and fewer corporations form bigger and bigger media conglomerates, there is increasing homogeneity of news topics, sources, information, and analysis. This means news audiences find the same stories and the same approach to news-telling whether they listen to radio, read newspapers, or search for news online. Those looking for unmediated material about a political issue can type their search terms into an internet search engine, but chances are the top results will be websites produced by dominant news organizations. Citizens may have more, and more varied, news sources available to them, but do they have the time or the inclination to Google their way through a myriad of weblinks to find the information they are seeking? Is this proliferation of information simply giving the illusion of vibrant civic engagement in politics, or (to paraphrase Jenson, 2005) is "the free press killing democracy"?

Moreover, as the Senate Committee report documents, concentration and convergence have placed material constraints on the news-gathering process by mainstream news media. For the time being, foreign ownership rules keep control of Canadian newspapers and television stations in Canadian hands, but the consolidation of ownership within Canada has wrought worrisome trends. Canada's major media companies have expanded, buying up media organizations in an effort to aggregate audiences across mediums and increase their market shares, and have suffered increasing debt burdens as a result of these spending sprees (Skinner & Gasher, 2005, pp. 53–55). The consequence has been budget cuts and layoffs, resulting in closures of foreign, national, and local news bureaus, and increasingly centralized news coverage (Canada, 2006, pp. 9–13). The closure of foreign news bureaus is a matter of concern for national identity as "Canadians need to have their own eyes and ears to report on world news from a Canadian perspective" (Canada, 2006, p. 10). Closer to home, cuts to national and provincial news bureaus and the resultant decline in the number of journalists currently reporting full-time from provincial and federal legislatures are a matter of concern. The *Winnipeg Free Press* is one of the last Canadian dailies to dedicate a full-time legislative reporter to the Ottawa press gallery (Samyn, 2008). Coverage at provincial legislatures is also diminished, with fewer reporters covering the daily question periods in provincial capitals (Lett, 2008). Simply put, it is much easier for government spin doctors to control one reporter than four. Increasingly, news production is centralized in the headquarters of media conglomerates such as CanWest Global, the largest daily newspaper provider in Canada, which also owns radio stations, the Global Television Network, and Canada.com. An example of this process occurred when a controversial editorial policy that combined centralized content with acts of discipline and censorship was implemented (Shade, 2005). Newspapers in the CanWest chain had their editorial independence curtailed when they were forced to print "national" editorials crafted by head office. However, as Shade (2005) documents, these policies prompted a firestorm of protest by journalists and citizens and condemnation by other media organizations.

Some say the result of consolidation and convergence is media coverage of politics that is vapid and superficial. As *Inside Ottawa* columnist John Chenier complains,

> Lots of attention is paid to the actions (or non-actions) of the players during the theatrics of Question Period; meanwhile, the motivations or consequences of certain acts and sometimes even the substance of the issues are relegated to footnote status, at best. It is acceptable for the news to be event-driven; but what about those pundits counted on to provide context and meaning to events? Why does this commentary dwell on whether or not there will be an election this week or next or not at all? (Chenier, 2008)

Is hyper-commercialism of news media in Canada diminishing the quality of democratic discourse by promoting "infotainment" and attenuating aggressively independent journalism? After all, as Schudson (2007) argues, democracies need an "unlovable press"; that is, media organizations capable of challenging and even subverting established power. We believe that media independence is at risk because of corporate consolidation, but we argue that the Canadian news media has not lost its "unlovable" qualities of cynicism, inquisitiveness, and obsession with conflict and "bad news." The story of the *Globe and Mail* and Maher Arar, recounted below, makes this point.

THE *GLOBE AND MAIL* AND "THE ALARMING CASE OF MAHER ARAR"[5]

On September 26, 2002, Maher Arar, a Syrian-born Canadian citizen, was detained by the United States on suspicion of terrorist links. Mr. Arar was on a stopover in New York, en route to Montreal from a family vacation in Tunisia. The then 32-year-old telecommunications engineer was held without charge for 12 days by U.S. officials and interrogated about alleged links to al Qaeda before being chained, shackled, and flown to Syria, where he was beaten, tortured, and forced to make a false confession (see www.maherarar.ca). During his imprisonment, Arar's wife, Monia Mazigh, campaigned relentlessly on his behalf until he was returned to Canada over 10 months later, in October 2003. Her efforts were buttressed by media attention. Arar credits several Canadian newspapers, including the *Globe and Mail*, for pressuring the Canadian government to bring him home, and, after his return, to investigate the circumstances that led to his extraordinary rendition to Syria (Arar, 2007). Continuous calls for a public investigation led, in January 2004, to the creation of the Commission of Inquiry into the Actions of Canadian Officials in Relation to Maher Arar. In the Commission's report, released in 2006, Mr. Justice Dennis O'Connor cleared Arar of all terrorism allegations, stating he was "able to say categorically that there is no evidence to indicate that Mr. Arar has committed any offence or that his activities constitute a threat to the security of Canada" (www.maherarar.ca). With the innocence of Maher Arar confirmed and the complicity of the Canadian state laid bare by the Commission, the RCMP and the Government of Canada issued formal apologies to Arar and his family.

News mediation of the events shaping Mr. Arar's life put the issue in the public eye and undoubtedly kept it on the agenda of the Canadian government. The *Globe*'s editorial position was resoundingly on Mr. Arar's side, and the paper did not hesitate to dig for information that disputed the Canadian government's account of events and revealed the role of Canadian security services, especially the RCMP, in the U.S. government's decision to dispatch Mr. Arar to Syria, where he was imprisoned and tortured, rather than send him home to Canada. Moreover, in its editorials, the *Globe* declared and emphasized Mr. Arar's "Canadianness" rather than focusing on his Muslim identity and casting him as the "other" threatening the "us" in the wake of the 9/11 terrorist attacks (see Chapter 17 for a discussion of the implications of such characterizations). In its editorials about the Arar case, the *Globe* raised troubling questions about state secrecy, democracy, and citizenship, drawing attention to the constraints on civil liberties posed by the post-9/11 security environment. This example illustrates the crucial role of an independent and inquisitive press in revealing government wrongdoing and ensuring state accountability.

"A Canadian has disappeared."[6] This was the opening sentence of a *Globe and Mail* editorial titled "The alarming case of Maher Arar," printed on October 19, 2002, just a few weeks after Maher Arar's rendition to Syria, and it was the first of many *Globe* editorials about the Arar situation. That a citizen had disappeared was profoundly disturbing, but the reasons why this particular Canadian had vanished were even more disquieting. After relating the few facts known at that time about Mr. Arar's circumstances, the *Globe and Mail* said: "when a Canadian in the hands of U.S. justice disappears into a distant land, and U.S. officials are silent on the particulars, this country must ask some hard questions."[7] The editorial ended with the words: "A Canadian passport should mean something." Indeed, most Canadians see their passports as symbols of cherished citizenship rights and liberties, as shields against harm. "A Canadian traveller is no less Canadian because he is of Muslim or Arab background," said the *Globe*, serving notice to Canadians that the passport doesn't protect everyone equally. A Canadian disappeared, passport in hand, and ideas about citizenship in the wake of 9/11 were disrupted.

After Maher Arar's release and return to Canada, *Globe and Mail* editorials persisted in asking (as one headline put it) "Troubling questions in the Arar case" (October 8, 2003, p. A24), accusing the government of "Needless opacity" (September 27, 2003, p. A28) and documenting the responsibility of Canadian officials and police services for Arar's plight. "Don't say Arar's case conformed to the law" (November 21, 2003, p. A18), "Canada's role in Arar's ordeal" (June 26, 2004, p. A24), and "Arar and the RCMP" (September 30, 2004, p. A22) were among the headlines of the editorials the paper printed. Faced with this disquieting information about the willingness of Canadian security services to run roughshod over a Canadian's civil liberties by colluding with U.S. officials, the *Globe* (along with other news organizations) pleaded for a public inquiry into the affair. "Hold an inquiry into the Arar case" (November 5, 2003, p. A24), "Call an Arar inquiry" (December 23, 2003, p. A20), and "At last, an inquiry in to the Arar case" (January 29, 2004, p. A 18), said its editorial headlines. "No Canadian should be dehumanized in this fashion without the country asking why," declared the *Globe*'s editorial writers.[8] Then, as the O'Connor inquiry unfolded, *Globe and Mail* editorials reported its revelations with these headlines: "Canada's role in Arar's ordeal" (June 26, 2004, p. A24), "What Canada knew about Arar's treatment" (August 29, 2005, p. A12), and "How Canada failed to protect Maher Arar" (September 19, 2006, p. A18).

As the *Globe and Mail* editorial writers argued, the story of Maher Arar "has much to tell us about the dark side of the democratic world," which accepts "barbarism as part of the war on terrorism."[9] The *Globe* revealed that democracies, including Canada, have outsourced torture, reinforced hierarchies of citizenship, and implemented counterterrorism measures that are inimical to the rule of law and to the protection of fundamental human rights. The *Globe and Mail*'s account stressed the importance of protecting freedom, democracy, and civil liberties for all Canadians. To be sure, one could accuse the *Globe and Mail* of sensationalizing the story by emphasizing its most shocking aspects, and of reporting it in a manner that was unduly critical of the government of the day. Negativity and cynicism, detachment from politics, and passivity are bred by such reportage, some would argue. But, as Martin (2008) demonstrates, "bad news about issues is good news for participation," as it cues citizens to pay closer attention to the activities of governments and can even mobilize them into social and political action. As we have emphasized in this chapter, because most citizens engage with politics through mass-mediated presentations of political reality, the power of the press to shape these perceptions can curtail or embolden democratic citizen participation.

CONCLUSION

In Frank L. Baum's *The Wonderful Wizard of Oz*, the Wizard is inadvertently exposed as a common man and not the "Great and Terrible" creature Dorothy, the Tin Man, the Scarecrow, and the Cowardly Lion believed him to be. The Wizard's supremacy was the product of an elaborate illusion; his ordinariness shrouded by curtains, his voice magnified by machines, he convinced his subjects he could perform feats of magic and might. In an exchange with Dorothy after his unveiling, the Wizard of Oz admitted that because he was never seen by his subjects he was accorded enormous power. The narrative of the Wizard of Oz can serve as an analogy for contemporary political communication. Like the Wizard, politicians and governments operate behind a curtain of mass-media technologies, giving people what they think they want (Hearn, 1983, p. 105). However, while the Wizard of Oz controlled his image and his messaging, Canadian leaders do not have unencumbered access to the media, nor do they command the news agenda. The media industry has an important role to play in providing the Canadian public with information about politics and government. As we have argued in this chapter, there is considerable power in the news selection and news presentation process, and the struggle to determine and define the political agenda of the mainstream media features complex power relations between the state, political actors, and media organizations. The four sections of this book explore the effects of such mediations on the public good and the health of democratic political engagement.

Media Journal Assignments

1. Over a five-day period, from Monday to Friday, identify the lead stories published by your local daily newspaper *or* carried on the suppertime television news broadcast. What are the top five stories about? Why do you think they have been selected—which news values do they display? Who are the primary sources for the story—the authoritative voices whose views define the story? Why do you think these sources have been chosen?

2. Outline the extent of corporate concentration and convergence in your city (or nearest city). Apart from the CBC, how many corporations control the available radio, television, and newspaper outlets?

3. Using a news database such as Factiva, gather the editorials printed by the *Globe and Mail* and the *National Post* newspapers about the Maher Arar case between October 1, 2002 and December 31, 2006. Compare the headlines for the editorials. What are the similarities and differences? Do some research on the ownership and the editorial positions of these newspapers over this time period. Do you think the editorials illustrate the ideological or partisan interests of the ownership?

Endnotes

1. Tu Thanh Ha, Julian Sher, and Daniel LeBlanc, "Bernier's ex-girlfriend is nobody's business: PM," *Globe and Mail*, May 8, 2008.

2. John Barber, "Thousands of articles, 821 TV shows, 61 countries and one breast," *Globe and Mail*, May 31, 2008, p. F3.

3. Giselle Déziel, "Aw shucks," letter to the editor, *Globe and Mail*, June 16, 2008, p. A14.
4. Lysiane Gagnon, "MPs must have better things to do," *Globe and Mail*, June 9, 2008, p. A15.
5. "The alarming case of Maher Arar," *Globe and Mail*, October 19, 2002, p. A24.
6. "The alarming case of Maher Arar," editorial, *Globe and Mail*, October 19, 2002, p. A24.
7. "The alarming case of Maher Arar," editorial, *Globe and Mail*, October 19, 2002, p. A24.
8. "Hold an inquiry into the Arar case," editorial, *Globe and Mail*, November 5, 2003, p. A24.
9. "At last, an inquiry into the Arar case," editorial, *Globe and Mail*, January 28, 2004, p. A18.

References

Allen, Stuart. 2004. *News Culture*. 2nd ed. Berkshire: Open University Press.

Arar, Maher. 2007. "Civil Liberties and National Security." Distinguished Annual Lecture, Department of Political Science, University of Alberta. Edmonton, April 18.

Arar, Maher. Available at www.maherarer.ca (accessed June 28, 2008).

Bennett, W. Lance. 2007. *News: The Politics of Illusion*.7th ed. New York: Pearson.

Bennett, W. Lance & Robert M. Entman. 2001. "Preface," and "Mediated Politics: An Introduction." In *Mediated Politics: Communication in the Future of Democracy*, ed. Lance W. Bennett and Robert M. Entman, xxiii–29. New York: Cambridge University Press.

Brown, M. 1989. "Soap Opera and Women's Culture: Politics and the Popular." In *Doing Research on Women's Communication: Perspectives on Theory and Method*, ed. K. Carter and C. Spitzack, 192–258. New Jersey: Ablex Publishing.

Canada. 2006. *Final Report on the Canadian News Media*.Standing Senate Committee on Transport and Communications. Senate of Canada. June 2006. Available at www.parl.gc.ca/39/1/parlbus/commbus/senate/Com-e/TRAN-E/rep-e/repfinjun06vol1-e.htm (accessed September 21, 2008).

Cappella, Joseph N. & Kathleen Hall Jamieson. 1997. *Spiral of Cynicism: The Press and the Public Good*. New York: Oxford University Press.

Castells, Manuel. 1996. *The Rise of the Network Society*. Oxford: Basil Blackwell.

Chenier, John. 2008. "Media coverage contributes to childish depths of this Parliament." *The Hill Times*, May 19.

Cook, Timothy. 1997. *Governing with the News: The News Media as a Political Institution*. 2nd ed. Chicago: University of Chicago Press.

Crocker, Nathan. 2007. "The case of the abandoned shoe store." *Ryerson Review of Journalism*, December 3. Available at www.rrj.ca (accessed June 7, 2008).

CTV Online. 2007. "No plans to pursue government media centre: PMO." CTV online, October 15. Available at www.ctv.ca (accessed June 8, 2008).

Delacourt, Susan. 2008. "The big stuff gets away from PM." *Toronto Star* Online, May 30. Available at www.thestar.com (accessed August 17, 2008).

Entman, Robert M. 1993. "Framing: Toward Clarification of a Fractured Paradigm." *Journal of Communication* 43 (34): 41–58.

Hackett, Robert & Yuezhi Zhao. 1998. *Sustaining Democracy? Journalism and the Politics of Objectivity*. Toronto: Garamond Press.

Hearn, Michael Patrick, ed. 1983. *The Wizard of Oz*. New York: Schocken Books.

Herman, Edward S. & Noam Chomsky. 1988. *The Manufacturing of Consent: The Political Economy of the Mass Media*. New York: Pantheon.

Hildebrandt, Kai, Walter C. Soderlund, & Walter I. Romanow. 2005. "Media Convergence and CanWest Global." In *Canadian Newspaper Ownership in the Era of Convergence*, ed. Walter C. Soderlund and Kai Hildebrandt, 89–108. Edmonton: University of Alberta Press.

Jenson, Robert. 2005. "Prologue: Has a Free Press Helped to Kill Democracy?" In *Converging Media, Diverging Politics*, ed. David Skinner, James R. Compton, and Michael Gasher, 1–5. Latham and Oxford: Rowman & Littlefield.

Kent, Tom. 1981. *Royal Commission on Newspapers*. Ottawa: Minister of Supply and Services Canada.

Lett, Dan. 2008. Personal Correspondence with Shannon Sampert, January 27.

MacCharles, Tonda. 2007. "PM plans own media centre." *Toronto Star* Online, October 15. Available at www.thestar.com (accessed August 17, 2008).

Martin, Michèle. 1997. *Communication and Mass Media: Culture, Domination and Opposition*. Scarborough: Prentice Hall.

Martin, Paul. 2008. "The Mass Media as Sentinel: Why Bad News about Issues is Good News for Participation." *Political Communication* 24: 180–93.

Nesbitt-Larking, Paul. 2007. *Politics, Society and the Media*. Peterborough: Broadview Press.

Norris, Pippa, Montague Kern, & Marion Just. 2003. "Framing Terrorism." In *Framing Terrorism: The News Media, the Government and the Public*, ed. Pippa Norris, Montague Kern, and Marion Just, 3–23. New York: Routledge.

Samyn, Paul. 2008. Personal Correspondence with Shannon Sampert, January 27.

Schudson, Michael. 2007. "Why Democracies Need an Unlovable Press." In *Media Power in Politics*, 5th ed., ed. Doris A. Graber, 36–47. Washington: CQ Press.

Shade, Leslie Regan. 2005. "Concentration, Convergence and Censorship." In *Converging Media, Diverging Politics*, ed. David Skinner, James R. Compton, and Michael Gasher, 101–16. Latham and Oxford: Rowman & Littlefield.

Skinner, David & Mike Gasher. 2005. "So Much by So Few: Media Policy and Ownership in Canada." In *Converging Media, Diverging Politics*, ed. David Skinner, James R. Compton, and Michael Gasher, 51–76. Latham and Oxford: Rowman & Littlefield.

Taras, David. 2001. *Power and Betrayal in the Canadian Media*. Peterborough: Broadview.

Winseck, Dwayne. 2002. "Netscapes of Power: Convergence, Consolidation and Power in the Canadian Mediascape." *Media, Culture and Society* 24: 795–819.

Wolfsfeld, Gadi. 2001. "Political Waves and Democratic Discourse: Terrorism Waves During the Oslo Peace Process." In *Mediated Politics: Communication in the Future of Democracy*, ed. Lance W. Bennett and Robert M. Entman, 226–251. New York: Cambridge University Press.

Rupert Murdoch
→ founder, CEO and chair of News Corp
→ this the world's largest media conglomerate
→ By 2000, he owned over 800 companies
in more than 50 countries.
→ Some examples of companies he owns are:
the wall street Journal, century Fox and
Harper collins.
→ Murdoch is considered the 38th richest
person in the US w/ a net worth of
$7.6 billion

Geosynchronous orbit satellites (GSO)
- rotates with an orbit period the same as
the Earth's rotation period
- there are approx 180 satellites, about
2 degrees apart surrounding the earth
- these satellites have antennas that
can be fixed in place and are much
less expensive than tracking antennas.
- they have permanent fixation in the sky,
which means that ground based antennas
do not need to track them. This type
of satellites is used often for communication
purposes

Media Synergy
- In media, synergy is the promotion and sale of
production throughout various subsidies of a
media conglomerate.
- For example: walt Disney pioneered synergistic
techniques in the 1930s by granting dozens of
firms the right to use his mickey mouse characte
in products and ads, and continued to
market Disney media through lincensing
arrangements.

Part I

Politainment[1]

These products can help advertise the film itself and thus help to increase the film's sales.

In her book *Entertaining the Citizen*, Liesbet van Zoonen (2005, p. 1) asks, "Can politics be combined with entertainment? Can political involvement and participation be fun? Can citizenship be pleasurable?" These are important questions to ponder as politics and popular culture converge. As van Zoonen notes, citizens "do politics" in their leisure time, and the news media are compelled to compete with the growing number of possibilities for entertainment. People can consume political news—or they can watch a DVD, play a video game, surf the web, update their Facebook status, or listen to a podcast. For those who want political news, there are many different forms and genres from which to select, including newspapers (in both print and online format), television, radio, and blogs. There are also plenty of choices within mediums; television watchers, for instance, can choose between the traditional newscast and the comic version—*The Daily Show* and *The Colbert Report* in the United States, and the *Rick Mercer Report* in Canada. Intense competition for audiences among the many media seeking to deliver political information to citizens fosters the presentation of news as entertainment, termed "politainment" by van Zoonen, and "infotainment," "tabloidization," or "Newzak" by others (Allen, 2004, p. 203). As the term suggests, politainment is the presentation of politics through the mass-mediated lenses of entertainment and popular culture.

This section of the book explores the practical impacts of politainment on the performance of politics by media, politicians, and governments (the effects on citizen politics are discussed in Part III of this volume). As Chapters 2 and 3 illustrate, contemporary political news is marked by sensationalization, personalization, celebritization, and popularization. Politicians speak in 10-second sound bites, instigate media spectacles, and maximize photo ops and, as Chapter 4 discovers, some emerge as full-blown celebrities. That governments engage in branding and present policies as populist rhetoric through colourful advertising is detailed in Chapter 5. What does it all mean for active citizenship and democratic political engagement? Many commentators see the trend toward politainment as harmful to democracy, as they fear it promotes style over substance, thereby dumbing down political information and breeding cynicism, disaffection, and alienation (see Postman, 1985; Allan, 2004, pp. 202–05). But, as van Zoonen (2005, p. 4) argues, the intersection of politics and entertainment presents an "important sign that politics is part of everyday culture and not above it." Politics cannot, and perhaps should not, be presented as "purely informational, rational and deliberative," or it would rapidly lose touch with its audiences (van Zoonen, 2005, p. 2).

This debate is taken up in the practitioner chapter, "On-Air Sizzle: Selling News as Entertainment," which suggests that political news can be both entertaining and informative. **Lisa Brandt** knows all about entertaining audiences. She has been a radio broadcaster since 1981, working as a radio announcer and program host, most recently as co-anchor of the all-news morning show on Canada's highest-rated radio station, 680 News in Toronto. Lisa has interviewed major politicians, world-renowned music stars, and other famous figures, and these experiences inspired her book *Celebrity Tantrums: The Official*

Dirt (ECW Press, 2003). In addition to delivering political news on air, she is a columnist, blogger, and novelist, and contributes her expertise on popular culture through public-speaking engagements and several television programs. In her chapter, Lisa explains how radio has changed since she entered the business. The explosion of new media has led traditional media outlets like radio to blur the line between news and entertainment in an effort to keep old audiences and attract new ones. However, she argues that entertainment and information are not mutually exclusive; political news may be truncated, dressed up in sensational language, and introduced with a zippy "hook," but it still delivers a message. Brandt is not sanguine about the impact of new news formats, for she highlights the risks of "infotainment": the danger of emphasizing the sensational and superficial while neglecting the relevant and meaningful; the problems with the shock-radio tactics of the ideologues; and the damage that can be done by broadcasting a story before all the facts are in. Critics may argue that "McNews" is a junk-food diet, starving the citizen of crucial informational nutrients, but Brandt insists that the fast-food version of political information is better than no information at all.

In Chapter 3, **Shannon Sampert** disagrees, asserting that convergence and corporate concentration is limiting the quality and quantity of radio news. While most analysts ignore radio or consider it unimportant, Sampert establishes radio as a crucial news source. Most Canadians tune in to some form of radio, and many listen a lot. That they are listening to fewer voices owned by fewer companies is a concern for Sampert, as is the type of news being delivered. "Jock Radio/Talk Radio/Shock Radio" maps the radio environment in Canada and elaborates the technological, regulatory, economic, and cultural trends shaping radio news. Shannon Sampert asserts that the mass-produced quick-and-dirty format of jock radio, the babble of talk radio, and the provocative and sometimes defamatory logic of shock radio illustrate the ascendance of market logic and the impotence of the regulatory environment. Despite the fact that the shock-radio tradition has yet to establish a strong toehold in the Canadian market, Sampert believes its ascendance will be governed by audience preferences, not by government intervention. As a result, the political news Canadians receive via the radio waves will likely become even more superficial, trivial, and vulgar.

Chapter 4 raises another emerging feature of politainment—celebritization—which reflects the important role of entertainment in politics. In "Belinda Stronach and the Gender Politics of Celebrity," **Linda Trimble** and **Joanna Everitt** illustrate the intersections of news media, gender, and popular culture through a case study of newspaper portrayals of Canadian Member of Parliament Belinda Stronach. Stronach's celebrity status accounts for much of her high-volume and often hyperbolic media coverage, they argue, and reflects the gender politics of mediated celebrity. By examining newspaper coverage of two phases of Stronach's political career, her bid for the leadership of the fledgling Conservative Party of Canada in 2004 and her political defection to the (then-governing) Liberal Party in 2005, Trimble and Everitt show that Stronach's celebrity reflected media intrigue with her youth, femininity, sexuality, and glamour. As a result, Stronach's entertainment value was exploited at the expense of her political credibility. While the celebrity frame may amuse readers, its intensely personalizing and sexualizing gaze is dangerous for female politicians seeking legitimacy in a male-dominated political environment.

John Street (2004, pp. 439–40) argues that style and symbolism have long been essential elements of political representation. Popular culture, he says, can help symbolize politics in ways that are immediate or evocative, thereby stimulating links between politicians (or politics) and citizens. Chapter 5, "When the Message Is the Meaning: Government Advertising and the Branding of States," by **Jonathan Rose** and **Hugh Mellon**, discusses government's mediation of its own messages through advertising and branding campaigns. While government advertising is not new, its volume is increasing, its intensity evident in state attempts to brand their identity via popular slogans, logos, or symbols. Rose and Mellon ask whether such techniques actually enhance representation or merely serve as political marketing tools for the parties in power. State legitimacy, they argue, is eroded when marketing techniques are exposed as crass political manipulations. For example, Rose and Mellon discuss the "advertising chill" produced by the Gomery Inquiry's revelations of massive improprieties in the Government of Canada's advertising and sponsorship politics. Their chapter also reflects this volume's interest in the dialectics of mediation by reflecting on citizen engagement with government advertising and branding; Rose and Mellon analyze the difficulty of convincing an amorphous and diverse audience to "buy" a consistent identity.

Can politics be combined with entertainment? Of course they can; that governments themselves are interested in blending politics and entertainment by communicating with citizens through advertisements, slogans, and logos is illustrated in Chapter 5. The chapters in this section debate the implications. Brandt, in Chapter 2, feels politainment can enhance democracy by delivering pithy and enticing messages about pressing political issues to citizens. But, as Chapters 3 and 4 suggest, when politics are presented in the language of popular culture, mediated by industries more interested in entertaining than enlightening, important messages may be lost in translation, leaving citizens bemused, confused, under-informed, or even outraged.

Endnote

1. van Zoonen, 2006.

References

Allan, Stuart. 2004. *News Culture*. 2nd ed. London: Open University Press.

Postman, Neil. 1985. *Amusing Ourselves to Death*. New York: Viking.

Street, John. 2004. "Celebrity Politicians: Popular Culture and Political Representation." *British Journal of Politics and International Relations* 6: 435–452.

van Zoonen, Liesbet. 2005. *Entertaining the Citizen: When Politics and Popular Culture Converge*. New York: Rowman & Littlefield.

———— 2006. "The Personal, the Political and the Popular: A Woman's Guide to Celebrity Politics." *European Journal of Cultural Studies* 9 (3): 287–301.

Chapter 2

On-Air Sizzle: Selling News as Entertainment

Lisa Brandt

INTRODUCTION

Imagine if your clock radio went off each morning at 7:30 to the same news story. You would quickly change the dial to find a station that offered something you hadn't heard before. This is the challenge of broadcast news organizations. If an ongoing story is still "alive," it must be presented in a new and different way or else the audience will remark, "That is old news," as they turn the dial to find a competitor. The news story has to grab the listener's attention by offering something new, unusual, or compelling, or by presenting an intriguing twist on an old story. "Sex sells"—who among us hasn't heard that phrase? And in the media, sex doesn't necessarily mean, literally, sex. It means sizzle or cachet. It means novelty or drama or excitement, or something to which the listener or viewer can instantly relate.

Here is an example. A reporter notices that Reform Party leader Preston Manning is doing his hair differently, and this becomes a topic of radio, television, and print media stories about the party. Manning's image makeover in the late 1990s garnered much more attention than many serious newshounds thought it deserved. Manning evolved from a staid and unadventurous-looking country bumpkin into a sophisticated executive with a slick of hair gel and some new fitted suits. Was the hairstyle an important story? Probably not, but it was a change that everybody recognized. Now, the story didn't sizzle because it was about a politician's attempt to appear more mainstream and appealing. It was intriguing because everybody was talking about it. Who doesn't care about their own image? And to what lengths do we go to fit into somebody else's idea of what it takes to belong? While the discussion of Manning's Lasik surgery and new "do" may have seemed superficial, the story carried some important messages. Pundits and voters had a reaction to the image makeover in part because it signalled Manning's seriousness about pursuing his political goals. It gave the average Canadian a glimpse into the sausage-making machine that is the political system, which can churn out candidates who look a certain way in order to attract more votes. Manning's physical makeover was the hook on which a lot of dry and unsexy political information was hung.

The idea that sex sells certainly isn't new; it's always been a cornerstone of advertising. Similarly, the argument that political events and leaders need some form of "sizzle" to make the news isn't new, either. However, in the early days of broadcast media, "news" was more narrowly defined. It was a natural disaster or a political scandal or what the president or prime minister or other political or public figure said or did that day. Today, not only is news edited and tailored for a specific demographic, but you will be hard pressed to find a universal definition of what constitutes a legitimate news story. On the new-music station, whose audience is comprised mostly of savvy 20-somethings, a survey of condom users' favourite flavours is the lead story. On the classic-rock station, a Led Zeppelin reunion tops the newscast. On the classical-music station, the lead is a story about a property-tax increase. If pop tart Britney Spears runs over a photographer's foot it may actually play higher in the minds of some listeners than a confidence vote in the House of Commons.

I've been in the radio business for 25 years now and see two related trends developing. The first is the impact of new media. There is a virtual explosion of sources attempting to offer the same timely, fresh, and authoritative news that was once the exclusive territory of broadcast news, especially radio. New technologies, including websites, weblogs, email, instant messaging, and text messaging, allow individuals and news organizations to spread information in nanoseconds. Instant news used to be the domain of radio; now other media sources present news in a flash. The second trend is widely observed and commented upon, and that is entrenchment of the entertainment factor in news content and delivery. News has always been, at some level, entertaining, but the need to amuse audiences has become an imperative for traditional news formats like radio and television. Indeed, it is increasingly difficult to draw a line between news and entertainment. Also, under-30s are as likely to find out what is going on from YouTube or the *Rick Mercer Report* as from *The National*. So the trend toward "infotainment" is aided and abetted by the need to cater to audiences who do not see the news as the exclusive domain of formal news organizations.

My chapter discusses these trends from the vantage point of someone whose work has been shaped by them. I provide my own insights into the evolution of radio news with the intention of posing the following questions. Is the rise of instant "infotainment" undermining the value of radio news? Or is a merging of news with entertainment creating a more relevant and competitive type of information under the banner of "news"?

RADIO NEWS AND THE IPOD GENERATION

The proliferation of new media sources and vehicles has implications for traditional news outlets. The impatient iPod age bracket, the one that is currently developing the means and producing the disposable income to become a coveted advertising target, sees little value in waiting through commercials on radio to finally hear music they may or may not like, programmed by someone who is likely their mom or dad's age. They are their own programmers, who download their own choices of songs and search the internet to decide which news items are of interest to them. What impact is this trend having on the content and format of radio news? To answer this question, we need a glimpse back to the era before the emergence of new information technologies.

Before television and long before me, radio was seen as incredibly reliable and credible, so much so that it spawned the "War of the Worlds" incident in 1938. Orson Welles's reading of an adaptation of H.G. Wells's classic novel as a series of news bulletins, performed as a Halloween special, frightened thousands of listeners into believing a real Martian landing had taken place. Such was the power of radio. Later, with the development of television, the broadcast media became even more powerful. The big three U.S. broadcast networks battled it out with each other over which would reign supreme across the continent. If legendary news anchor Walter Cronkite said it on the air, people believed it almost entirely without question. Then came the all-news channels. Ted Turner launched the genre in 1980 with CNN, which spawned many imitators. They are ravenous beasts that require constant feedings of news and news-related items. Gone were the brief top-of-the-hour newscasts and daily hour-long presentations of television news. In Canada, journalists and producers leapt onto the 24-hour news bandwagon with the launch of CBC Newsworld in 1989 and CTV News 1 (now Newsnet) less than a decade later. Initially, both relied heavily on international news supplied by affiliates with bigger budgets and reporters stationed around the globe. The all-news format is expensive to staff and produce, and importing prepackaged material is cheaper and more efficient. Eventually, as revenues and budgets allowed, staff sizes increased and more original content was produced.

Radio went in this direction, too. I watched the profitable hit radio station CFTR morph into 680 News, a pioneer in the "new" all-news format in Canadian radio, a format put in motion by Rogers Broadcasting. Following a few lean years, during which millions of dollars were lost, the station began to hold its own and then, finally, make money—a lot of money! How did they do it? Well, 680's staff is required to forget preconceived notions about what constitutes news and how it is supposed to be presented. Sometimes referred to by detractors as the "fast food of news," 680's fast-paced format does not allow much lingering on a single topic. Its attention span is short to reflect that of its busy listeners. The long-form interview has almost entirely vanished from the radio landscape, replaced by ever quicker and snappier sound bites. If a story can't be explained in a few brief sentences, it might be considered not "radio friendly," and therefore not worthy of coverage because it would take up too much time.

Other complex stories are distilled down to one core point to save airtime and simplify them for harried listeners, who are undoubtedly multi-tasking as they ingest information. The rampant and ongoing genocide in Darfur became more about a rising death toll than an explanation of the tragedy of a long-term conflict in a part of the world most of us will never visit, and perhaps can't even point out on a map. In its lowest form, this would be called "dumbing down" stories, but that is not our aim. We boast that we'll bring you what's going on in your world with one newscast, and a little squeezing and jostling of stories is required. More news is always being created, but the clock still only provides 60 minutes in an hour. As political analyst John Stall, who has covered national politics as a reporter, talk show host, and analyst for more than three decades, argues, coverage of politics must be "short, sweet, tight, and [offered] in little wee bits." Stall says this is the result of new technologies and formats, including "all of the specialty channels, 24/7 news on radio, television, newspapers going 24 and all of their online versions and BlackBerries and all of the personal communication devices" (personal interview, February 6, 2007).

Does the rise of new technology mean radio is obsolete? I may be biased, as my livelihood depends on the success of private radio, but I think radio remains relevant. Although many consumers say they tune in to television news for most of their information, radio, and specifically all-news and news/talk radio, continues to offer an immediacy that other media cannot match. Certainly radio has something commuters want and need. Three-quarters of news followers use their radio for news while travelling to and from work and one-third continue to rely on the radio for information while they're on the job. For those who are stuck in their cars and want to stay informed, there is still no substitute for the instant reaction of radio. Listeners don't have to wait for pictures or text to get information. All they need is a receiver and they're set. It's not surprising, then, that the Radio and Television News Director's Association found that news ranks second only to music as the reason why listeners choose to tune in to a particular radio station (for more on this, see Chapter 3). Most news junkies depend on their local news/talk radio station during an emergency situation and half of listeners tune in for weather and breaking events.

Long gone are the days when newscasters saw only each other as the competition. We now know we live in a very fragmented world where people are not all doing the same thing at the same time. For example, the traditional dinner time no longer exists. With flex hours in workplaces, families in flux, and children involved in an endless variety of activities, there is no longer a single universal routine. The *Leave It to Beaver* lifestyle—if it ever truly was real—isn't real anymore. As well, every semi-literate person with access to a computer can decide for him or herself what "news" is. It is estimated that one-quarter of all Americans rely solely on the internet for their news, and internet accessibility is comparable for Canada. Not only are those of us in traditional broadcast media having to compete with an explosion of radio, television, and satellite programming, but we also have to out-think and out-entertain people who are gathering their own information and provide a worthy alternative. Competition isn't just fierce; it's also unpredictable and constantly evolving. Staying ahead of it— and sometimes managing only to keep up with it—is extremely challenging and some competitors are indeed being left behind. Our task as broadcasters is to make sure that we are not rendered voiceless by our greatest fear: a lack of ratings. It is the newsperson's job to hang on to a listener or viewer despite the lure of the PlayStation or music-video channel or any number of other rivals. She or he has a mandate to out-entertain them all.

NEWS AS ENTERTAINMENT

In the early 1980s I ventured out to find my first full-time broadcasting job with a stack of resumés and tapes of my best newscasts from the campus radio station. My first job offer came following an audition as a so-called "jock" for a country-music radio station in Alberta. This was my first real break in the radio business and although it didn't involve news, which had been my career goal, it was actual work in my chosen field that would put me on the air every day. As an inexperienced newbie, I was in no position to turn the offer down. For the next 12 years I "jocked" at various stations, and eventually—when the time and my level of experience were right—I worked my way back to news, via talk and entertainment reporting. Back then, the dividing line between a newscaster and a music jock, or "deejay," was thick and nearly impenetrable. We, the jocks, didn't understand what the newscasters did, and thought they were uptight and too serious. They didn't understand what we did, and thought our work was merely simple and fun; all we had to do was play some records and tell listeners the song titles and artist names. We were both right and we were both wrong. Newscasters tended to rely on sources that told them what was important: the newswire, the news director and the assignments he or she gave to reporters, and local newspapers. The anchors generally reported news, sports, and weather twice an hour, spending their in-between time writing stories, gathering tape, making phone calls, and chasing newsmakers. They made value judgments on story content within the framework of their news directors' guidelines, and this aspect of the job has not changed. In contrast, the jocks had structure in their formats from their program and music directors, but they were given more leeway in their presentations. They could ad lib, joke, and explore ways of injecting their individual personalities into their shows, as long as they got the required musical, promotional, and commercial content on the air. Occasionally the two would meet on the airwaves, but more often than not the music presenter and the newscaster existed in separate worlds that collided only for a major story of general interest, a sports score that needed to get on the air right away, or the on-air hand-off from the music portion of the show to news—if a particular station allowed that sort of kibitzing. Most did not.

Today, interaction from hosts on either end of a newscast—and sometimes in the middle of it—is often encouraged. News isn't a break from regular programming anymore; now it is part of the entire entertainment package. A newscaster is a sidekick who is involved in fun parts of programming, especially on morning shows. Robin Quivers, news anchor on the wildly successful Howard Stern Show, weaves seamlessly in and out of comedy skits and interviews while maintaining her role as the voice of the so-called serious stuff. Listeners understand that newscasters and reporters are people with senses of humour, and the credibility of a journalist doesn't seem to suffer if he or she enjoys a laugh once in a while.

There have been a lot of changes. The traditional announcer position has been replaced in many instances by a voice track, a pre-recorded show programmed to sound live. One announcer can voice track several shows for many stations, eliminating each of those individual jobs. As FM's superior signal for music rendered the AM signal nearly obsolete, many wise AM programmers turned to information-based formats. These required personnel, and many of former announcers and journalists wishing to continue their radio careers evolved into news and talk presenters. When there is a choice between a seasoned newscaster and a former music presenter, the latter may get the job because of his or her more entertaining delivery and propensity toward injecting more "show" into the show-business aspect of broadcasting. Examples abound of former television stars and music deejays who have become celebrated news anchors, bringing their particular sensibilities with them. CNN *American Morning* news anchor John Roberts is a former MuchMusic veejay. Actress Andrea Thompson wanted more time with her family and left the drama *NYPD Blue* to anchor news on CNN *Headline* News. Marcia Clark, a crown prosecutor who came to prominence as part of the team that lost the O.J. Simpson murder trial, got a makeover and became a celebrated and sought-after analyst who continues to contribute to *Entertainment Tonight* whenever there's a high-profile court case involving a music, television, or movie star. Lawyer Greta Van Susteren came to prominence in a similar way. Their legal expertise is now spun as entertainment news. Clearly, their star quality enhances the sizzle of the news.

A news director under whose supervision I once worked governed her all-news radio station staff with this motto: We have no right to bore our listeners! In many ways, that saying cemented the merging of news with entertainment and encapsulated for us, as gatherers, writers, editors, and anchors, the genre of "infotainment." Previous to this, news didn't aim to be boring, but it did aim to be seen as "important." As altruistic and artistic as we all may think ourselves to be, in the final analysis the news business is a *business*, and, whether it's the powerful CBC or a 1,000-watt radio station in rural Saskatchewan, it needs listeners and ratings to justify its existence, either to taxpayers or to shareholders or to advertisers. Mere survival requires of each station a certain amount of intelligently designed pandering to its audience. The presentation of the product has had to evolve along with listener and viewer expectations. The traditional long-form interview has largely given way to the 10-second sound bite in an effort to cater to the shortened attention spans of the MuchMusic generation, raised on quick edits and constant motion. When I first started in the business, it wasn't uncommon to interview a politician for the news and provide a news clip of him or her speaking that lasted 20 or 30 seconds. Now, that news clip is 10 seconds long. Think of it this way. In today's radio market, Martin Luther King's famous speech would be edited down to just one pithy line: "I have a dream." We are reduced to slogans.

Those of us on the inside do feel pressure to entertain as we inform. But entertaining the audience and informing the audience aren't mutually exclusive options. Within the realm of news, entertainment is defined as the angle or approach to a story that makes it come alive and truly relate to the listener. It doesn't mean adding details that are not fact. It doesn't mean creating wild speculations in order to make it more interesting. It doesn't mean blowing the story out of proportion. It does mean finding the stories that will make the listener want to stay tuned longer. For example, if a traveller with a shoe bomb gets through screening at an airport in another city, sending a reporter to the local airport to ask questions about screening procedures and to discover, "Could that happen here?" brings the story home and makes it more relevant to the local listener. Our main challenge is to worm away at a story until we find its essence and relevance to our listeners. It's not enough sometimes to present a story straight up, and that is where we draw fire from traditional newscasters. We dare to claw at it until we reveal the human aspect—what it truly means.

We don't aim to sensationalize in order to fill the many hours of time laid before us for news, news, and more news, although we are accused of that. For instance, in the world of 24-hour news, the person-on-the-street interview is more prominent than ever before. If a reporter is unable to locate an expert, he or she can always rely on a gaggle of bystanders who are more than happy to step up to a microphone and bid for their own 15 minutes of fame. The input from the "average citizen" is more important to news broadcasts than ever before. They can be counted on to spew opinions—sometimes intelligently—and fill those relentlessly needy hours of airtime with local content that is entertaining.

Aiming for a healthy balance between information and entertainment has pitfalls. The most obvious consequence is the emphasis on the sensational and superficial. Stories that may be important are passed over for those that can be explained more simply or that news gatherers believe have a more direct impact on the lives of listeners and viewers. Newscasters of previous decades are lamenting the loss of so-called "real news" in radio today, as information gives way to titillation, and a story's importance can now be judged by the familiarity of its subject, not its relevance to the audience. Troubled pop singer and actress Lindsay Lohan has become a household name not only because of her ability to entertain but also because of her antics in and out of rehab. Even those who claim not to care about her or what she has done now know who she is, and this is enough to convince an editor that her exploits are worth covering again and again and again. There is a tangible increase in entertainment-based programming, and a deliberate approach to looking for the entertainment value within news.

Another problem is the tendency toward capturing audience share with overtly ideological or biased approaches to telling the news. Charles Adler is Canada's only nationally syndicated talk-show host. While he is decidedly conservative, emulating in many ways his American counterparts, his lone voice is in stark contrast to the sheer numbers heard on American radio. On television, we have well-known political commentators like Craig Oliver and Mike Duffy. Neither rivals the ideological vitriol of American commentators like Bill O'Reilly of The O'Reilly Factor, a right-wing commentator who presents his program in the guise of a news show. Despite the fact that this is American television, Canadians watch this programming and are exposed to Fox News Network's consistently hawkish slant on politics.

In Canada, most media attempt to avoid political branding, although favouritism is tolerated more and more and even welcomed as all-news formats attempt to fill their time. On the one hand, we are kept accountable through comparisons to each other, and that can be a good thing. On the other, we are more susceptible than ever before to the possibility of losing our unique voices in the marketplace as listeners gravitate toward other options of satellite radio and American television to get their news fixes.

The competition to be first with a story also plays a role in the contemporary media environment. Some journalists find it tempting to play fast and loose with the facts in order to be perceived as "first" on a story. Watch the unfolding of any type of news story while it occurs live on television. As reporters and anchors desperately try to provide as much up-to-date information as possible, facts on the first iteration may be classified as unconfirmed, but within minutes that disclaimer is removed. While it is generally unacceptable to go to air with an unconfirmed item, it does happen, and part of this is because reporters, particularly in highly stressful news moments, are pressured to "feed the beast" and fill airtime. Reporters are pressured to gather information that may simply not yet be available. Anchors and editors are monitoring the competition and scrambling to beat them to the whole story or a yet-to-be revealed fact. On-air talent sometimes needs to be reined in and reminded that it is better to be correct than first—although being correct *and* first is the ultimate goal. Leading the market on a story garners bragging rights for the station. By comparison, being the only outlet to have the facts right merely inspires an inner sense of pride, something much harder to sell to shareholders who are interested only in increasing the value of their portfolio.

It is widely understood in the news-radio business that elections—and politics in general—are not big ratings grabbers. "But how can that be?" you may ask. Everybody has a stake in politics. Everybody has an opinion about the state of their community, their country, and the world, and a political point of view. All of that may be true, but experience tells us that news-radio ratings do not shoot up during times of heavy political coverage. They increase during a natural phenomenon or a deliberate disaster, like 9/11. They grew during the first days of the U.S.-led invasion of Iraq. They spiked when Princess Diana was killed in a Paris car crash and political figures emerged, one by one, to offer condolences to the Royal Family.

But politics in general isn't considered to be a scintillating topic. That requires us to search for the sexiness within the genre of political coverage. Sometimes we have to search very hard indeed, and what ends up on the air as news may not fit under the traditional definition of news at all. In the JFK era, the charismatic American president's suspected extramarital dalliances were simply off-limits for the press. But in 2007, when MP Belinda Stronach began dating former Maple Leaf hockey player Tie Domi, the story was kept alive for weeks in virtually all types of media, with reported sightings of the couple and scintillating details of Domi's messy pending divorce. Consider the coverage of a federal election campaign, which lasts a minimum of 36 days. Candidates and spin doctors know very well that they must continue to create events each and every day if they are to remain in the news (see Chapter 6). If a modern newscaster's aim is to entertain as well as inform, he or she will not be satisfied to fill out a newscast with a day-by-day account of where the leaders are campaigning and what they are saying about planks in the party platforms, because that's boring. There must be a hook upon which to hang each day's election coverage story. The hook, or the sizzle, could come from a surprising voter poll, a candidate's faux pas, or any number of unexpected turns of events that set the day's proceedings apart from the day before, and the day before that.

Let's look at my station's coverage of the recent Quebec election as an illustration. At 680 News, an Ontario-based radio station, we realized that if not handled correctly, the Quebec vote could easily slide into mere irrelevant chatter to our listeners. Delivered straight up, the election results were inconsequential to a Toronto audience. The outcome required analysis. The Parti Québécois had been all but decimated at the polls, which, we realized, had reverberations in Ottawa. If not dead, separatism was clearly on life support, and that boded well for the minority Harper Conservative government, which needed the support of Quebec for its future aspirations of gaining a majority. We explored the impact of the election on the national political landscape and mused about whether Gilles Duceppe might leave the federal Bloc Québécois to lead the PQ. The result, we found, was an approach to a potentially dry story that had relevance to our audience because it centred on power struggles and political aspirations.

Outside of election campaigns, politicians—especially those who do not form the government—learn very quickly how to keep their names in the news. Some attempt to do it through sheer volume and a possible wearing down of the media. This approach can backfire on the person it is meant to assist. One Ontario provincial opposition leader's camp sends out a flurry of emails each and every day. These emails point to a supposed litany of the premier's inadequacies concerning various issues, sometimes with a continuing theme that centres on a topic before the provincial legislature. The approach is well directed and obviously deliberate, but ultimately futile because of its frequency. Instead of attracting the desired coverage and the attention they so desperately crave, they have become the party that "cries wolf." Forcing editors and newscasters to wade through and evaluate so much information (most of it useless to them) makes it more difficult to distinguish between manipulative hype and an actual, airtime-worthy issue or event. This approach is an irritating pebble in the tight shoe of a busy editor.

Other opposition politicians make an effort to cultivate individual contacts within media organizations, which appears somewhat wise in principle. Some go so far as to try to woo certain pundits and hosts with offers of "friendship" through gifts of things like invitations to golf tournaments on exclusive courses, swanky party passes, and perhaps even a free airline flight. These can be dangerous propositions for both parties. A news reporter is supposed to remain free of overt bias and should therefore refuse gifts. However, columnists and talk-radio hosts do not have the same requirement and are much more likely to be cultivated by publicists from every type of organization and business. Many commentators proudly wear their allegiances on their collars and happily jet off to Florida to play a round on the back nine. But their star treatment does not guarantee positive media coverage. Moreover, in the volatile business of broadcasting, the person with whom a politician may have developed a rapport might have switched jobs (or careers) during the times that they are needed, and that private golf session will have been wasted.

CONCLUSION

The radio business is about attracting and keeping listeners, generating advertising revenue, and, in some cases, keeping shareholders happy. There is the additional pressure of technological changes that mean people can gather their own news with the click of a mouse, and so it's paramount that we set ourselves apart by entertaining as well as informing. For that reason, the information news radio presents aims to be what people are talking about or what they will be talking about. Finding the "sexiness" or entertainment value of a news story is becoming more crucial as every second counts, literally, given the many choices on the dial and in the airwaves. A competitor is just a button punch away. Technological advances are changing the way news is generated and gathered. It is now lightning quick, with instant analysis and sometimes obvious partiality peppered within. Twenty-four-hour news coverage requires a constant stream of information, and stretching the definition of news is needed in order to fill the time. These are the realities of entertaining and informing the citizen. Whether it's what citizens ultimately want is uncertain, but their preferences will show up in the ratings, and, if they're smart, broadcasters will govern themselves accordingly.

It is no longer enough to deliver the news the way our predecessors did, with consistently serious and authoritative voices reading dry and mildly condescending copy. Newscasters of old didn't face the onslaught of competition that my peers and I must now try to fend off. We are mandated to find the entertainment value in our source material—and in our imaginations—in order to grow ratings, attract ad revenue, and, ultimately, survive. We are informers, and that's important, but we are performers, too. Otherwise, who would listen?

Chapter 3
Jock Radio/Talk Radio/Shock Radio
Shannon Sampert

INTRODUCTION

Radio was my first love. As a teenager living in small-town Alberta, I used to stay up late in my bedroom listening to the CBC and marvelling at voices originating from places like Poland, England, and Germany. When I began my career in radio, reading the news, I was told to pretend I was talking to one person. Like all good radio broadcasters at that time, I would try my best to form a bond with my audience by pretending I was talking to just one person. Because of this, I felt radio was a truly intimate experience for newscasters and listeners alike. This intimate business has changed dramatically in the past 30 years. Technological, regulatory, and market changes have influenced how radio conducts its business over the airwaves, with important consequences for the style and format of radio news. Jock radio, which features music introduced by on-air hosts, now offers a minimalist, "rip and read" version of a newscast, often produced elsewhere. Much of private talk radio, which should be all about information, presents news as babble—chatter by radio hosts and endless call-in shows—while the publicly funded CBC faces budget cutbacks and layoffs. Shock radio has also made its way onto the Canadian airwaves, with industry self-regulation and government oversight holding off the worst excesses of the shock-radio trend, which attracts audiences with deliberately provocative and titillating, even defamatory and demeaning, broadcasts. As it stands, Canadians have a radio market that is markedly different from the American model, and that provides us with a distinctive voice. How long it will last is open for debate, as the regulatory agencies that oversee broadcasting are increasingly pressured to let the market determine what acceptable free speech is and what it is not.

Little has been written about the state of radio in Canada, particularly private radio, and radio has rarely been a topic of investigation by political scientists. As Michele Hilmes suggests, the academic study of radio was largely frowned upon, particularly during the 1960s and 1970s, mostly because radio was viewed as culturally marginal and technologically inferior to television (Hilmes, 2002). In the first section of this chapter, I argue that radio remains popular and relevant for many Canadians who are seeking news and information. I provide an overview of audiences and formats, thus mapping the radio terrain in Canada. The second section of the chapter focuses on corporate concentration and media convergence and their impact on the radio industry. While there may be more channels on the dial, fewer and fewer players dominate the industry, and these players own everything from the local radio station (or stations) to television stations, cable companies, magazines, cellphone systems, and video outlets. These trends are shaping what we hear and how we hear it, and have particularly serious implications for the comprehensiveness of radio news. Third, I examine radio regulation, by broadcasters themselves and by the Canadian government's regulatory body, the Canadian Radio-television and Telecommunications Commission, and show that attempts to censor radio have not been particularly successful. Finally, I examine talk and information radio in Canada and determine that American-style conservatism and U.S. talk-radio formats have influenced this media genre.

RADIO: WHO IS LISTENING?

On September 11, 2001, when terrorists attacked New York and Washington, D.C., many Canadians at work found they were unable to access television and instead turned to the radio for the latest updates. Indeed, I first heard about the planes crashing into the Twin Towers as I lay in bed awakening to the alarm-clock radio. While I relied on television to truly bring home the story, when I went to work that day I found the internet to be an inadequate backup. The vast number of people trying to access information online created system crashes, and websites of major news organizations froze. I remember walking down the hallway at the University of Alberta listening to the sound of CBC Radio coming out of professors' offices as they tried to get a sense of what was happening. Radio was a reliable and important source of information in a time of crisis and confusion.

Who listens to radio and for what reason? Radio has been referred to as a "secondary medium" because "no one cares whether you listen to radio so long as you do not turn it off" (Berland, 1990, p. 179). In fact, many Canadians listen to radio regularly, and for many different reasons. Overall, 92.1 percent of Canadians over the age of 12 listened to radio for at least 15 minutes per week in fall of 2005. Trends indicate that the length of time we listen to radio is decreasing. On average, Canadians listened to 20.4 hours of radio per week in 2006, down 20 minutes from the previous year (CRTC, 2007, p. 10). A survey of Prairie Canadians conducted by the Canada West Foundation indicates that, while the majority of those surveyed relied on television and newspapers for information about current events, 30 percent still turned to radio for information (Berdahl, 2006, p. 9). Moreover, respondents living in "urban fringe and rural communities, and respondents with either a college or trade diploma, a bachelor's degree or a graduate/professional degree are more likely to report getting information from radio," and there is a correlation between increased income and age and increased reliance on radio for information (Berdahl, 2006, p. 9). The Radio Marketing Survey indicates that 77 percent of Canadians listened to the radio while driving or while at work or school. Overall, Canadians spend "one-third of their daily media time with radio, second only to TV"

(Radio Marketing Bureau, 2007). According to the "Foundation Research Study 2007" conducted for the Radio Marketing Bureau, radio is seen "as a perfect fit for modern life; it's effortless, easy to listen to during other activities; entertains and informs throughout the day; is compatible with other media and provides a soundtrack for life" (Radio Marketing Bureau, 2007).

Distinct radio formats dominate commercial radio stations in North America because they provide a way for radio stations to differentiate themselves from other stations and to attract listeners (Berland, 1990). In essence, there are two main types of radio formats in Canada: music formats and information (or talk) formats. Music stations run the gamut from adult top-40 to rock and jazz to "oldies" music. Information or talk stations provide information around the clock. David Taras suggests that "the key to radio survival" is the use of formats that will help "locate and appeal to a 'super core' of ardent listeners: people who will not only listen to the station but identify with the lifestyle and hence the products that it promotes" (Taras, 2001, p. 103).

Relying on the CRTC's Broadcasting Policy Monitoring Report for 2007, it becomes clear that private commercial radio stations have the biggest audience, with the highest percentage of hours tuned in to during an average week. The most popular music format on AM and FM stations is adult contemporary, with 126 stations broadcasting in English (15.2 percent of English stations), and 37 broadcasting in French (29.4 percent of French stations). Country, adult standards, classical, and adult rock, among others, round out the rest of the music formats on AM and FM. Of interest is the size of the radio market that provides news or talk-radio formats. These stations make up 11.1 percent of the English-language market (35 stations), and 12.8 percent (8 stations) of the French-language market (CRTC, 2007). However, when you combine the number of CBC stations with commercial private stations that also feature news or talk-radio formats, the overall percentage of stations that offer information 24 hours a day in Canada is quite high. In total, 20 percent (26 CBC stations and 35 private radio stations) of the English-language stations and 23.6 percent (16 CBC stations and 8 private stations) of the French-language stations are talk/news formats, suggesting that talk or information radio is a salient component of Canada's radio-station formats (CRTC, 2007).

The growth of talk radio in Canada and the U.S. is a result of deregulation and the expansion of technology in the 1980s. Beginning in the early 1970s, technological changes saw the expansion of FM radio because the new technology of FM radio was able to provide a better listening experience than AM stations. Moreover, the increased availability of satellites for broadcast allowed FM stations to extend their markets and provide services to rural as well as urban listeners (Vipond, 2000). This meant that FM radio stations in both Canada and the United States began to enjoy commercial success and greater expansion—but this expansion came at the expense of AM radio (Ellis & Shane, 2004). Many AM stations faced extinction as "music listeners gravitated to better audio reception on the FM dial" (Riley, 2006). To compensate, many of these AM stations changed their format from all-music to talk radio. Other technological innovations also changed radio. Satellite technology allowed stations to maximize profits by distributing their shows nationally. In comparison to the old method of relaying shows from one station to another using telephone lines, satellite technology provided a much cheaper and technically superior method of transmitting a local broadcast nationally. (Douglas, 2002, p. 486)

This opened the door for radio hosts to take their shows to the national level, thereby creating media celebrities and ultimately paving the way for the rise of ultra-conservative talk-show stars like Rush Limbaugh and for shock jocks like Howard Stern, who now had a national rather than a smaller regional audience (Douglas, 2002, p. 486).

KEEPING RADIO LUCRATIVE

While much has been written about convergence and the creation of multi-platform media companies, little has been said about the effect it has had on radio. Convergence of corporations has been aided by deregulation throughout the Western world and has created economies of scale that eliminate competition and pool resources (Taras, 2001). According to the CRTC's annual broadcast monitoring report for 2006, the outcome of the consolidation has meant that "the tuning share by the largest radio groups has risen considerably from 54% in 1997 to 63% in 2005" (CRTC, 2006, p. 12). In 2006, over 50 percent of Canadians listened to radio stations owned by one of five private commercial radio companies: Corus Entertainment Inc., Standard Broadcasting Corporation Limited, Rogers Communications Inc., Astral Media Radio Inc., and CHUM Limited. Moreover, Corus, Rogers, Astral, and CHUM are all considered multi-media platform groups, with ownership of not only radio, but also television stations, television cable companies, specialty cable stations, and, in the case of Rogers, magazine publication, cellular phone systems, and video rentals.

Corus Entertainment held 17 percent of the national audience and 17 percent of the English-language radio listeners in 2006 (CRTC, 2007). According to the company website, Corus radio stations reach 8.4 million Canadians each week, with 50 radio stations in B.C., Alberta, Manitoba, Ontario, and Quebec (Corus Entertainment Radio, 2007). Corus Entertainment began as Shaw Communications Inc., and in 1999 became a publicly traded company. In addition to its radio stations, Corus also provides television service, including CMT—the Country Music Video Station, the W Network, YTV, and a pay-TV movie service. Animated-programming producer and distributor and children's publishing company Nelvana is owned by Corus as well. Standard Broadcasting Corporation Limited held 12 percent of the national tuning audience and 16 percent of the English-language radio listeners in 2006 (CRTC, 2007). In 2007, Standard owned 51 radio stations in 29 Canadian markets across the country. Rogers Communications Inc. is Canada's third-largest radio operator, holding 12 percent of the national-tuning share and 12 percent of English-language radio listeners in 2006 (CRTC, 2007). Rogers is also a multi-media-platform company, owning magazines such as *Chatelaine*, *Macleans*, and *Canadian Business*, as well as television stations including the Omni stations and Sportsnet Channel (Rogers Communications, 2007).

Finally, CHUM Limited held 6 percent of the national-tuning audience and 9 percent of English listeners in 2006 (CRTC, 2007). CHUM is owned by CTVglobemedia, a multi-media company that operates 35 radio stations, along with the CTV television network, the *Globe and Mail*, and several specialty channels, including TSN, the cable sports channel (CTVglobemedia, 2008).

In the French-language market, Astral Media is the big player, with 34 percent of the hours tuned to French-language radio in 2006. Corus follows with 22 percent of the hours tuned, and Cogeco Inc. is third with 10 percent (CRTC, 2007, p. 13). Astral Media has 21 FM radio stations in Quebec, one AM and seven FM radio stations in the Maritimes, and one television station (TATV) in Quebec. According to the company website, Astral Media Radio operates "Énergie, RockDétente and Boom FM networks, which represent a total of 21 FM stations across the province of Québec. Each week, more than three million listeners—an impressive one out of every two Québecers [*sic*]!" (Astral Media Radio, 2007). Cogeco Radio-Television Inc. owns and operates RYTHME FM radio stations in Montreal, in Quebec City, and in the Mauricie and Eastern Townships regions, as well as radio-station 93.3 in Quebec City. In addition, it operates nine television stations, including three Société Radio-Canada affiliated television stations (Cogeco Radio, 2007).

Consolidation in Canada's radio market is a relatively new phenomenon. In 1998, the Canadian Radio-television and Telecommunications Commission (CRTC) changed its Commercial Radio Policy to allow increased consolidation of ownership within the radio industry. Prior to 1998, the CRTC restricted ownership so that a company could only operate "one AM and one FM undertaking . . . in the same language and in the same market" (CRTC, 1998b). The new policy allowed companies to operate more than one AM and FM station in a market. These changes were the result of lobbying by the Canadian Association of Broadcasters (CAB), who attended CRTC hearings and argued that

> ownership restrictions make it difficult for radio to compete effectively with other forms of media for advertising revenue, and harm the industry's financial performance. The industry representatives argued that increased consolidation of ownership would allow the radio industry to become more competitive with other forms of media, strengthen its overall performance, and help attract new investment. Other benefits identified by the CAB included increased diversity among formats and increased resources for programming. (CRTC, 1998c, at 26)

Music industry representatives did not support this move, suggesting that diversity would be affected by increasing consolidation. Others "expressed concern that increased common ownership could lead to a reduction in the diversity of news voices in a market and could have a negative impact on smaller, independent radio stations, as well as on community radio stations" (CRTC, 1998c, at 25). Clearly, the decision was made by the CRTC as a way of ensuring the economic viability of the Canadian radio market and of keeping it competitive.

The impact of consolidation has been felt in many ways. For one thing, it has influenced the way radio stations staff their newsrooms. With the creation of multi-station companies in both AM and FM, these stations can further cut costs by operating out of one centralized newsroom. For example, in Edmonton, Corus owns four radio stations. All four rely on 630 CHED, the AM talk-radio station, for their news. The announcer identifies her/himself as providing the news from the 630 CHED central newsroom. The same thing happens in Winnipeg, with the CJOB AM newsroom offering centralized news for its sister FM stations. This has a number of effects. Most notably, the number of news voices and news offerings available from these stations has been significantly cut, diminishing the variety of news perspectives available. There has, however, been a second significant consequence, which has shown up on the reporting side of the news. Previously, each of these newsrooms would have had at least one reporter to cover the major news happenings of the day. CHED now handles all of the reporting for all four stations and does so with only two reporters. The same situation has occurred in Winnipeg at CJOB: the fewer reporters available to ask questions in a media-news scrum, the fewer opportunities to critically interrogate the political terrain. Think of it this way: it is easier for political spin doctors to control four reporters than eight.

And yet a third consequence of the pressure on the industry to ensure its economic viability has been a blurring of the distinction between news and entertainment. When I returned to radio in the late 1980s after a five-year hiatus, I was amazed by how much the business had changed. Gone is the formality of the old newsroom, with its clear distinction between entertainment (read: "fun") and news (read: "serious"). The 5-minute newscasts (or, in the morning or drive times, 10-minute newscasts offered every half-hour) have been replaced with shorter updates or eradicated altogether. Indeed, most commercial music-format radio stations appear to have significantly cut back on the news-gathering functions of their newsrooms and instead rely on what we used to call the "rip and read" method. That is, they rely solely on the radio wire service and newspapers for news copy instead of producing their own news stories. As well, the breakfast-show programs on most radio stations now consist of a team of announcers, and the news announcer is part of that team, expected to kibbutz and laugh while providing social commentary where necessary. This was simply not done when I was working in the 1980s. Then, the news man (and it was a field dominated by men, with women marginalized because their voices were not viewed as being authoritative enough to be the morning news-radio voice) sat behind glass in his news booth, delivering the news in a supposedly neutral and objective manner.

This does not mean that radio audiences are not provided with information. They clearly are, as radio hosts talk about the important news topics of the day, particularly the stories that made the front page of the local newspaper. However, the information comes across in a highly informal way and is usually replete with personal opinions and subjective and limited analysis. This new reality in the newsroom points to another type of convergence—documented by Taras—the convergence of news and entertainment (Taras, 2001). The move toward "infotainment" was an idea first discussed by Neil

Postman is his lament entitled *Amusing Ourselves to Death*. When stories about celebrities dominate the news, other stories about issues like public policy are ignored. Postman argues that the rise of successful magazines like *People* and *Us* changed how television viewed news, and also had an effect on radio:

> we appear to be left with the chilling fact that such language as radio allows us to hear is increasingly primitive, fragmented, and largely aimed at invoking visceral response; which is to say, it is the linguistic analogue to the ubiquitous rock music that is radio's principal source of income. (Postman, 1985, p. 112)

Thus, Canadian radio is also facing the dilemma of its television counterparts: Is it a business, or does it perform a public service function of informing the listener? Increasingly, the trend in both media is to view their role as that of a business, with an interest in preserving the corporate bottom line.

Canada's public broadcasting system is also feeling apprehension about its corporate bottom line. The CBC captured 12.5 percent of the Canadian radio audience, with CBC Radio One holding 8.9 percent of the audience share in the spring of 2006 and CBC Radio Two holding 3.6 percent (CBC/Radio-Canada, 2006). CBC Radio One has an information-radio format, while CBC Radio Two is committed to broadcasting Canadian music, including classical music.[1] CBC is Canada's truly national radio system, available in even the smallest communities in Canada, including the Canadian north. A non-commercial radio station, CBC has struggled with diminished government funding over the years.

In CBC's 2005–06 annual report, president and CEO of CBC/Radio-Canada Robert Rabinovitch wrote of the financial challenges the Crown Corporation faces:

> Securing stable, multi-year funding for CBC/Radio-Canada remains one of our greatest challenges. Unfortunately, this comes at a time when the corporation is faced with uncertainty around a number of key revenue sources. In 2005–2006, we continued to do our part to find funding internally through operating efficiencies and new revenues. But it is not enough. (CBC/Radio-Canada, 2006, p. 2)

Unfortunately, under the current political regime in Ottawa, the future remains uncertain. While the Conservative minority government may have bought some time for Rabinovitch, there are concerns that, if the Conservatives were to win a majority, that could drastically change. Current prime minister Stephen Harper, while campaigning in 2004, stated,

> I've suggested that government subsidies in support of CBC's services should be to those things that . . . do not have commercial alternatives . . . And I think when you look at things like main English-language television and probably to a lesser degree Radio Two, you could look there at putting those on a commercial basis. (Martin, 2006)

Overall in 2005–06, the CBC lost revenue as a result of the NHL lockout and a bitter labour dispute of its own that lasted until the fall of 2005. Those losses were offset somewhat by revenues from the coverage of the Torino Winter Olympics. Its Parliamentary appropriations increased to $946 million. However, the Annual Report makes it clear that "there is no question that the Corporation ultimately requires stable, multi-year government funding to surmount the many challenges it faces and to truly fulfil its mandate. We will continue to voice this need on behalf of Canadians" (CBC/Radio-Canada, 2006, p. 61).

There are other pressures now being felt by both commercial and public broadcasters from another commercial enterprise: subscription satellite radio. Satellite radio entered the Canadian market with two subscription services available in 2006—Canadian Satellite Radio Inc. (CSR) and SIRIUS Canada Inc. In August 2006, CSR reported that it had 120,000 subscribers and SIRIUS reported in November 2006 that it had over 200,000 subscribers (CRTC, 2006a). What this has meant is that while the Canadian radio-station market is highly concentrated, diversity may still be available for those willing to pay the price. However, it is still not clear what this new technology will mean for private and public radio in Canada. More recently, the rise of the iPod has caused some concerns in the United States for the profitability of SIRIUS and of XM, another satellite company. A radio market survey showed that both companies combined have less than 5 percent of the market share in large markets like New York and Los Angeles. This means that both companies have a subscription base of about 14 million in the United States. Compare this to sales of iPods, which have already passed the 88-million mark. iPods offer essentially the same type of service that satellite subscription radio does: portable music that is commercial free. Industry insiders suggest that "over the past six years, the widely popular device has eaten into the potential market for satellite radio, simply because the Apple player has become so ubiquitous" (Ingram, 2007). While satellite radio may not be overwhelmingly popular in Canada, its presence still allows non-Canadian celebrity jocks the opportunity to find listeners in this country, and further forces radio stations to be cognizant of their commercial appeal.

REGULATION OF RADIO: IS IT WORKING?

In Canada, the CRTC and the Canadian Broadcast Standards Council (CBSC) still play a major role in regulating what can (and cannot) be said on air. The CRTC can suspend broadcast licences, refuse to renew licences, or levy fines against radio and television stations based on complaints for violations of the Government of Canada Broadcasting Act (1991). There are two fundamental ways to control what can be broadcast. The first promotes diverse and balanced coverage, while the second polices harmful or defamatory content. While there is no "fairness doctrine" per se,[2] the CRTC does require balance. For example, "during an election period, a licensee shall allocate time for the broadcasting of programs, advertisements or announcements of a partisan political character on an equitable basis to all accredited political parties and rival candidates represented in the election or referendum" (Government of Canada Radio Regulations 1986, s.3). Moreover, the Broadcasting Act requires that "the programming originated by broadcasting undertakings should be of high standard" (Broadcasting Act, 1991, 3.1 [g]). Second, broadcasting regulations for radio state that the licensee shall not broadcast "any abusive comments" (Radio Regulations, 1986, s.6).

The CBSC also plays a role in determining broadcasters' codes of ethics; however, it is a self-regulatory board. The Code of Ethics in part outlines that "full, fair and proper presentation of news, opinion, comment and editorial is the prime and fundamental responsibility of each broadcaster" (CBSC, 2002, c.6). It goes further to suggest that controversial subjects should be treated fairly with all sides of a public issue presented (CBSC, 2002, c.7).

The standards in Canadian radio differ from American standards. As Ronald Cohen, the national chair of the CBSC points out,

> In Canada, we of course benefit from a combination of regulatory and self-regulatory measures to respond to public complaints about broadcast content. In the United States, the self-regulatory option does not exist. It would also be fair to observe that Canadian and American values regarding broadcast content issues are not identical. Here, avoiding discriminatory and sexist comments on air appears to be a greater concern than it is there. (CBSB 2004, p. 1)

Cohen says that, in Canada, the industry itself has worked at ensuring that broadcast content is controlled largely voluntarily without having to levy high fines or, as he suggests, with "No heavy bludgeons. No heavy artillery. No Canadian governmental regulation or intervention required" (CBSC, 2004, p. 1). It is clear, however, that this relative calm in the regulation of radio (and television) broadcast content works only because broadcasters "buy into the process." Cohen suggests that broadcasters "support the work of the Council because they know that, although its decisions cannot possibly provide the results they might hope for on every occasion, they will be thoughtful and balanced and will consider issues large and small before concluding" (CBSC, 2004, p. 4).

While privately owned commercial radio stations report to the CRTC and belong voluntarily to the CBSC, the CBC has additional regulatory requirements. The CRTC requires CBC programming to "reflect the multicultural and multiracial nature of Canada" (CRTC, 2000, at 6). This means that CBC Radio must attract hosts and guests who are demographically diverse. This also includes ensuring that women's voices are heard and are part of the broadcasting fabric. The same onus has not been placed on commercial radio broadcasters, who are only *encouraged* "to reflect the cultural diversity of Canada in their programming and employment practices, especially with respect to news, music and promotion of Canadian artists" (CRTC, 1998c, p. 213).

Moreover, the CBC is committed to ensuring journalistic fairness in its programming overall. It is mandated to have an ombudsman in place to investigate complaints regarding its programming. The English Services and French Services ombudsmen compile annual reports regarding their investigations, and these annual reports are provided to CBC/Radio-Canada's president and to the corporation's board of directors. The ombudsmen evaluate the performance of the CBC on three fundamental principles: "accuracy, integrity and fairness" (CBC Ombudsman). Their jurisdictional areas are information programs on radio, television, and the internet, and include "News and all aspects of Public Affairs (political, economic and social) as well as journalistic activities in agriculture, arts, music, religion, science, sports and variety." Complaints about entertainment are considered outside of the ombudsmen's mandate (CBC Ombudsman). In 2005–06, English Services Ombudsman Vince Carlin received 1,868 complaints, of which he reviewed 40 (Carlin, 2006). French Services Ombudsman Renaud Gilbert received 1,019 complaints in 2005–06, an increase of 10 percent over the previous year. Of the complaints received by the French Services ombudsman, 169 were regarding public-affairs programming and another 117 involved concerns about accuracy (Gilbert, 2006). This clearly indicates that CBC/Radio-Canada's commitment to fairness in its programming, including its talk-radio programming, is more than just lip service. The ombudsmen in both languages investigate complaints and then must report back to the board on the status of those complaints. There is no equivalent requirement of private broadcasters to ensure the same standards, and there is certainly no expectation that they do so.

Does industry self-regulation backed by the CRTC influence what commercial radio can air? Two case studies illustrate that market forces are more effective in controlling content than any attempts to regulate through government sanction or through self-regulation. The first case involves legendary American shock jock Howard Stern, who had a brief sojourn in Canadian radio in the late 1990s and early 2000s, with his syndicated program appearing on Toronto and Montreal radio stations. In September 1997, Stern's show was syndicated in Canada for the first time, and aired on CHOM-FM Montreal and CILQ-FM Toronto. The CRTC noted that in the 1997–98 fiscal year, it dealt with over 37,000 broadcasting complaints, with "a large proportion relating to the Howard Stern program" (CRTC, 1998a, p. 44). During the first two weeks that the Stern show was on the air, the CBSC received over 1,000 complaints, the bulk of which were in reaction to what were perceived as anti-French comments made by Stern. In his September 2, 1997 broadcast, Stern suggested that "there is something about the French language that turns you into a pussy-assed jack-off" (CBSC, 1997a). He also said,

> Anybody who speaks French is a scumbag. It turns you into a coward, just like in World War Two the French would not stick up for us. The French were the first ones to cave in to the Nazis, and certainly, certainly were over-productive for the Nazis, when they became their puppets. (CBSC, 1997a)

The CBSC further determined that Stern made other abusive comments aimed at identifiable groups, including Japanese, gays, Poles, Sikhs, blacks, and Arabs, among others. Moreover, his show was seen to regularly demean women by using terms like "'pieces of ass,' 'horny cow,' 'dumb broads,' 'dikes' (referring to women with even moderately feminist views) and 'sluts.'" Both regional panels in a joint decision ruled that the radio stations broadcasting the Stern program had contravened CBSC codes of behaviour (CBSC, 1997b & c). Meanwhile, Stern imitators began to appear in an attempt to recapture audiences lost to the shock jock. Toronto's *Humble and Fred* show on the Edge recouped their listeners from Stern by airing pranks such as a Good Friday promotion that suggested their show's producer would be crucified. As Tammy Silny, the radio manager of a media group in Toronto, put it, "Humble and Fred have become a little edgier since Stern came into the market, but they are certainly nowhere near him . . . But that's a good thing. We have clients who don't want to be on Stern. So Humble and Fred become that much more attractive" (Menon, 1998).

Ultimately, however, the Howard Stern show was yanked off the air more because of ratings than any type of regulatory manifest. In Montreal, he failed to live up to his reputation to deliver strong ratings and CHOM dropped the show in August 1998 (Fine, 1998; Bray, 1998). Toronto's Q107 cancelled Stern's program in November 2001 (Canadian Press, 2001) after his ratings had declined substantially. Stern's show dropped from being number one in his time slot to number six (Goddard, 1998). In other words, regulations did not stop Stern, poor ratings did.

In a more recent example, the CRTC took the unusual step of removing a radio broadcast licence because of persistent shocking and offensive content; however, writing this in 2008, radio station CHOI-FM in Quebec City remains on the air, with the ruling having little effect. In 1995, Jeff Fillion began as a morning host at CHOI-FM in Quebec City. Through the years, he and his co-host André Arthur[3] made names for themselves by providing a raunchy morning-radio program that, among other things, suggested that disabled people should be gassed and that foreign students at Laval University are children of cannibals because they come from the families of disgusting political leaders (Dixon, 2007).

In 2004, the CRTC refused to renew the licence for CHOI based on complaints it had received from listeners. In its July 13, 2004 broadcasting decision, the CRTC wrote that it was basing its decision on 47 complaints "it had received since CHOI-FM was acquired by Genex in February 1997. These complaints concerned the broadcast of abusive comment, offensive on-air contests, personal attacks and harassment" (CRTC, 2004, p. 271 at 4). This was an unprecedented move for the quasi-judicial agency, and the decision was met with complaints of censorship from the radio station's avid listeners. In a show of support, thousands marched on Parliament Hill in protest on August 10, 2004, as the station's owner tried to press the federal government into overturning the decision (Paraskevas, 2004). Anne-Marie Gingras argues that CHOI-FM, Fillion, and their lawyers throughout the 2004–05 hearings and procedures before the CRTC and the Quebec Cour Supérieure instrumentalized the issue of freedom of expression. She suggests that the idea of freedom of expression was used in an attempt to lend respectability to the station's actions (Gingras, 2007).

The CRTC decision culminated with a number of sanctions being imposed upon CHOI. The CRTC only provided the station with a short-term licence renewal in 2002 because of the complaints they had received about its morning programming. In its decision, the CRTC noted that the

> licensee's numerous failures to comply with the *Radio Regulations*, 1986 . . . and the condition of its licence related to sex-role portrayals. The Commission also notes the licensee's failures to meet the objectives of the Broadcasting Act that the programming originated by broadcasting undertakings should be of high standard. (CRTC, 2002, p. 189 at 13)

The complaints about CHOI included concerns that the morning show's host Jeff Fillon was disrespectful and vulgar and that "women are reduced to sex objects." Moreover, the "entire morning show regularly swears on the air" and the programming is "sexually explicit" (CRTC, 2002, p. 189 at 13).

The Quebec Regional Panel of the Canadian Broadcast Standards Council also had to respond to complaints about CHOI's programming. In a July 17, 2003 decision, the CBSC ruled that the radio station had breached two clauses in the CAB Code of Ethics. The first was the clause that pertains to "full, fair, and proper presentation" and the second was the clause that limits radio broadcasting that is "unduly sexually explicit" or that uses "coarse and offensive language" (CBSC, 2002). The CBSC was asked to make the ruling after Fillion and his co-host called rival radio host Jacques Tétrault a

> "conceited asshole," "that worthless piece of trash," "a loser," a "piece of vomit," "shit disturber" and a "tree with rotten roots" . . . Fillion also claimed that Tétrault had only achieved success on the coattails of others, was only interested in young women and was known to leave important business meetings for frivolous personal reasons. (CBSC, 2003)

The Quebec Regional Panel concluded that Fillion "was crude and offensive. He spouted ugly and generalized epithets, comprehensible only in their flailing nastiness and not because a serious listener might have actually understood what his competitor did, if anything, to merit criticism" (CBSC, 2003).

The radio station had suggested that if people did not like what they heard on the air they could sue the station, and Montreal weather reporter Sophie Chiasson did just that after Fillion called her "cruche vide" or "empty-headed." He said that she had "slept with men twice her age" and that the "size of her brain is not directly proportionate to the size of the bra." Chiasson's father testified during the hearing in Quebec's Superior Court and trembled with anger when he detailed what he had heard:

> "When he spoke about my daughter as a 'vacuum on four legs,' my mother, her grandmother, who is 79, wanted to know what it meant," Mr. Chiasson testified last week. "Hearing what was said on the air, that she performed fellatio to get a job, I was angry . . . That's when we said this had to stop." (Séguin, 2005)

Chiasson was awarded $300,000 in damages and another $40,000 to cover her court fees (Canadian Press, 2005). As a consequence of the civil suit, Fillion resigned as morning host at the radio station in March 2006, and in August 2006, he signed on with the

XM Satellite Radio Service's French language radio station (Canadian Press, 2006). In September 2006, CHOI was sold to Radio Nord for $12 million and continues to operate on the air in Quebec City (Dougherty, 2006). Again, it would appear that the regulatory functions of the CRTC were relatively toothless. CHOI has never been taken off the air, despite the sanctions imposed on it. Moreover, Fillion himself continues to push the envelope in radio programming without censorship on satellite radio.

TALK RADIO

As I indicated earlier in this chapter, information and talk-radio formats sprang up in Canada on AM radio because of technological advances that improved the reception of FM stations. Again, commercial considerations and not public altruism were behind the increased number of talk and information stations that began to appear across the country on the AM dial. These stations continue to be successful for their corporate owners. According to the Spring 2007 Bureau of Broadcast Measurements, talk-radio programs placed first in Winnipeg, Vancouver, and Edmonton. In 2006 in Winnipeg, talk radio CJOB was the most listened-to station (*Winnipeg Free Press*, 2007). In Vancouver, CKNW topped the daily-listening survey (Constantineau, 2007), and in Edmonton, all-talk CHED was number one (Sperounes, 2007).

There are claims that talk radio originated in the United States in the 1950s with a program called *What's On Your Mind?*, which ran out of Camden, New Jersey (Ellis & Shane, 2004). In Canada, the CBC began the first coast-to-coast open-line talk show, called *Cross Country Checkup*, in 1965 (Bergeron, 2004, p. 292). Political talk radio can be defined as "radio programs (usually sporting a call-in format) that emphasize the discussion of elections, policy issues and other public affairs" (Barker, 2002, p. 15). This compares with other types of talk radio, which can involve discussions of sports or conversations about music, parenting, or other issues. In Canada, the major talk-radio stations dedicate a good percentage of their broadcast hours to political talk; however, other talk categories are present, particularly sports call-in programs. The CBC, Canada's public broadcaster, offers talk radio that is quite political and offers not only a local and national perspective, but also an international focus, relying on news programming from international news outlets such as the BBC.

When the U.S. government dropped the Fairness Doctrine requirement for radio stations across the United States in the 1980s, it "paved the way for talk radio as we know it today. Neither hosts nor stations currently have an obligation to provide balance or voice to competing views" (Cappella et al., 1996, p. 7). This has resulted in a preponderance of conservative viewpoints. Talk-show host Blanquita Cullum contends, however, that the conservative viewpoints of talk radio counter the liberal media bias found in the evening news and in late night television talk (Cappella et al., 1996). According to *Talkers*, a magazine dedicated to talk media, the top five most popular radio hosts in the United States are all conservative: Rush Limbaugh, Sean Hannity, Michael Savage, Dr. Laura Schlessinger, and Laura Ingraham (*Talkers*, 2007).

Canadian talk-radio mirrors that of the United States in that it is also quite conservative. However, those conservative points of view are buttressed to a large degree by the more left-leaning CBC. Again, the commercial aspect of radio prevents talk-radio hosts from finding the same degree of celebrity as do hosts like Limbaugh, Savage, or Hannity. Simply put, Canada's population is not large enough to allow for the creation of these types of radio giants. Indeed, in Canada there is only one truly national talk radio host: Corus Radio's Charles Adler.

Adler broadcasts out of CJOB AM radio in Winnipeg, but he is heard across the country on Corus stations. Like his American counterparts, Adler is clearly conservative-leaning. A look at his website and blog at CJOB makes it clear that Adler is against increased taxes, for Canadian involvement in Afghanistan, and skeptical about global warming. In May and June of 2007, his guests on his program included Green Party leader Elizabeth May, Saskatchewan premier Lorne Calvert, and Liberal MP Gerard Kennedy. It is also clear that he is less than patient with some of his guests. For example, he runs excerpts of his program online that have been edited to play up their entertainment value. In one of his interviews he labelled NDP Defence Critic Dawn Black a "smackdown." Black had expressed her concerns about the guns used by the military, calling the guns "huge." In what can only be called a rant, Adler mocked Black, suggesting that he did not know why the NDP have a Defence Critic, because "they don't believe in defence, seriously." He went on to say that he would call the type of guns the NDP want "dwarf guns," but then he would have the "dwarf interest groups down my pie hole" (Adler, 2007).

Local radio hosts throughout Canada continue the conservative talk-show tradition. In Calgary and Edmonton, Dave Rutherford rules the talk-show airwaves on CHQR and CHED for Corus, while Corus radio's Richard Cloutier hosts the mid-morning show on CJOB in Winnipeg and Tommy Schnurmacher hosts the nine-to-noon show on CJAD in Montreal for Standard. In Montreal, Gilles Proulx brings his own brand of talk radio to francophone listeners. All provide the iconic talk show with a clearly articulated conservative perspective. The drive for private talk-show hosts to speak from a perspective may be seen as a continuation of the need to seek entertainment values in political discourse and is, as indicated, an obvious ratings winner. Ian Hutchby suggests that talk-show hosts have the requirement to take up counter-positions to respond to callers' points of view. He argues that

> Hosts then might be said to engage routinely in the activity of constructing the caller's talk as "controversial," of finding in whatever the caller says resources for presenting a controversially contentious counter-position. This construction of controversy is one of the central, demonstrably oriented, top features of talk radio. (Hutchby, 1992, p. 674)

Good talk-show hosts, according to Hutchby, closely monitor what callers say in search of "potential arguables" (Hutchby, 1992, p. 684). Susan O'Sullivan's analysis from the U.K. further indicates that successful guests to private radio call-in programs "display an understanding of the style, tone and what constitutes appropriate content for the show"

(O'Sullivan, 2004, p. 736). Thus, the format and the roles of the hosts and callers become formulaic in the production of a daily talk show.

The landscape of commercial talk radio in Canada is not only conservative; it is also overwhelmingly male. This follows the American experience of talk radio, which is dominated by male voices. As Douglas outlines, talk-radio hosts like Limbaugh and Stern are all "about challenging buttoned-down, upper-middle-class, corporate versions of masculinity that excluded many men from access to power" (Douglas, 2002, p. 485). Within the imagined talk-show community, beginning in the 1980s, it became very clear "who was included and who was excluded" (Douglas, 2002, p. 488). It became normalized practice for hosts to insult and yell at listeners "like abusive fathers and tough callers knew how to take it. In fact, talk radio proved to be a decidedly white male preserve in a decade when it became much more permissible to lash out at women, minorities, gays, lesbians and the poor" (Douglas, 2002, p. 488). Given Adler's comments about the fear of having the "dwarf interest groups" down his "pie hole" (Adler, 2007), it would appear that this masculinist style of discourse remains prevalent 20 years later.

CONCLUSION

Canadians can still rely on their radio stations to provide them with a Canadian perspective, particularly with the continued strength of the CBC in providing radio programming across the country. However, it is becoming clear that convergence, combined with the influence of infotainment and American-style talk radio, has had an impact on the type of information available. Overall, the number of companies offering radio-broadcast services has decreased and we have seen a rise of multi-media-platform groups that offer economies of scale (Taras, 2001). This has created concerns that the few powerful companies will strangle creativity and the transmission of new ideas, as well as public debate, as they scramble to make a profit and keep their shareholders happy (Taras, 2001). The move that started in the early 1990s to deregulate Canadian radio and allow increased concentration has, to a large degree, mirrored similar moves in the United States and Australia. In the United States, the decision to relax ownership limits was a way of allowing increased competitiveness that would in turn allow the ownership of "more stations to boost efficiency and save money due to program sharing, computerized station operations and the ability to access ever larger audiences" (Fairchild, 1999, p. 554). Fairchild argues that, in the United States, this has fundamentally reduced the "number of voices available on radio . . . and stifled almost all serious attempts to fostering diversity of ownership and information" (Fairchild, 1999, p. 557), and the same case can be made in Canada.

At the same time, we see a "dumbing down" of the information we receive. Increasingly, music-format commercial radio stations provide less solid news information, instead relying on shorter newscasts or consolidated newscasts from central newsrooms, combined with an increased emphasis on entertainment. News and information–format stations, on the other hand, also rely on ratings and vitriol to keep listeners entertained and engaged. This is backstopped to some degree by the CBC, which works as an alternative to the commercialization of the radio market. However, the bottom line is that for the 30 percent of Canadians who rely on radio as their source of information, that information is being packaged as entertainment.

Finally, perhaps more frightening is the relatively tenuous hold both the CRTC and the CBSC have on controlling the type of discourse that is being heard on our Canadian airwaves. Canada does have requirements with regard to what can and cannot be said on the radio, but the CRTC and CBSC have not been effective in implementing that type of control. Instead, when you look at the CHOI controversy in Quebec City, along with the earlier problems with Howard Stern in both Montreal and Toronto, market concerns were what drove the decision to change programming, and not an overarching concern about broadcast ethics. Radio in Canada, like other media, is clearly in flux, with market forces controlling what information is provided and how it is provided. The economic conditions under which both private and public radio operate will continue to dictate the level of political discourse their listeners receive.

Media Journal Assignment

1. Utilizing the Canadian Radio-television and Telecommunications Commission website, look up the latest Broadcast Policy Performance Report. Have the average number of hours that Canadians spend listening to radio changed since this chapter was published? If so, how? As Sampert indicates, in 2007, five multi-media companies owned the majority of the radio stations to which Canadians listened. Is that still the case or has this changed? If you find any changes, discuss what they indicate for the future of radio in Canada.

2. Monitor the drive-home program (usually from about 4 until 6 p.m.) of your local commercial talk-radio station over a two-day period, then listen to the drive-home program on your local CBC Radio One. How do the programs differ? Based on what you hear, can you determine the ideological leanings of either host, or were they relatively neutral? Provide examples.

Endnotes

1. In 2008, the CBC announced that it is broadening the type of music offered on CBC Radio Two, which has resulted in protests across Canada.

2. The United States was so concerned about commercial radio stations being used to promote only one viewpoint that it implemented a Fairness Doctrine that regulated the requirement for alternative viewpoints to be given access.

3. Arthur ran and won a seat as an independent in a federal Quebec City area riding in the 2006 election (Montreal *Gazette*, December 31, 2005, p. A12)

References

Adler, Charles. 2007. Adler Online. Entry post, June 12. At www.cjob.com (downloaded June 12, 2007).

Astral Media Radio. 2007. Available at www.astralmedia.com/en/radio/default/idigit (accessed June 11, 2007).

Barker, David C. 2002. *Rushed to Judgment: Talk Radio, Persuasion, and American Political Behavior*. New York: Columbia University Press.

Berdahl, Loleen. 2006. Democracy in Western Canada: An Analysis of the Looking West 2006 Survey. Canada West Foundation, July 2006.

Bergeron, Rosemary. 2004. "Canadian Talk Radio." In *Museum of Broadcast Communications Encyclopedia of Radio*, ed. Christopher H. Sterling and Michael Keith, 1:292. Chicago: Fitzroy Dearborn.

Berland, Jody. 1990. "Radio Space and Industrial Time: Music Formats, Local Narratives and Technological Mediation." *Popular Music* 9 (2): 179–92.

Bray, David. 1998. "Airwaves heat up with radio's fall ratings battle." *Kitchener Waterloo Record*, October 14, D9.

Canadian Press. 2001. "Howard Stern bumped from Canadian airwaves." *Cambridge Reporter*, November 24, C8.

———. 2005. "'Vicious, sexist' comments on radio net $300,000 fine." *Kitchener-Waterloo Record*, April 12, A3.

———. 2006. "Quebec radio school jock signs XM satellite deal." *Ottawa Citizen*, August 12, F7.

Cappella, Joseph N., Joseph Turow, & Kathleen Hall Jamieson. 1996. *Call-in Political Talk Radio: Background, Content, Audiences, Portrayal in Mainstream Media*. Philadelphia: Annenberg Public Policy Centre, University of Pennsylvania.

Carlin, Vince. 2006. "Office of the Ombudsman: English Services Annual Report 2005–2006." Available at www.cbc.ca/ombudsman/page/annual.html (accessed June 12, 2007).

CBC. 2007. "Office of the Ombudsman: Mandate." Available at www.cbc.ca/ombudsman/page/mandate.html (accessed June 12, 2007).

CBC/Radio-Canada. 2006. *Striking the Right Balance: CBC/Radio-Canada Annual Report 2005–2006*. Ottawa: CBC/Radio-Canada.

CBSC. 1997a. Canadian Broadcast Standards Council. "1996/1997 Annual Report: Summary of Complaints." Available at www.cbsc.ca (accessed June 17, 2007).

———. 1997b. Canadian Broadcast Standards Council Quebec Regional Panel. "CBSC Decision 97/98-0001." October 17. Available at www.cbsc.ca (accessed June 7, 2007).

———. 1997c. Canadian Broadcast Standards Council Ontario Regional Panel. "CBSC Decision 97/98-0015." October 18. Available at www.cbsc.ca (accessed June 7, 2007).

———. 2002. Canadian Broadcast Standards Council. *CAB Code of Ethics*. June 2002. Available at www.cbsc.ca (accessed May 27, 2007).

———. 2003. Canadian Broadcast Standards Council Quebec Regional Panel. "CBSC Decision 02/03-0115." July 17. Available at www.cbsc.ca (accessed June 7, 2007).

———. 2004. Canadian Broadcast Standards Council. *2003/2004 Annual Report*. Ottawa: Canadian Broadcast Standards Council, August 2004.

Cogeco Radio. Available at www.cogeco.ca/en/corporate_profile_o.html#television (accessed June 11, 2007).

Constantineau, Bruce. 2007. "Perennial top radio station hurt by loss of Canucks: CKNW's market share drops below 10 percent." *Vancouver Sun*, April 11, E1.

Corus Entertainment Radio. 2007. Available at www.corusent.com/radio/vritish_columbia/index/asp (accessed April 2, 2007).

CRTC. 1997. Canadian Radio-television and Telecommunications Commission. News Release. "CRTC approves applications by the CBC to convert its Toronto AM service to the FM band and to make other related changes." Ottawa, July 29.

———. 1998a. Canadian Radio-television and Telecommunications Commission. Performance Report. Ottawa, March 31.

———. 1998b. Canadian Radio-television and Telecommunications Commission. Commercial Radio Policy 1998. Public Notice CRTC 1998-41. Ottawa, April 30.

———. 1998c. Canadian Radio-television and Telecommunications Commission. Public Notice CRTC 1998-41. Ottawa, April 30.

———. 2000. Canadian Radio-television and Telecommunications Commission. Public Notice CRTC 2000-1. Ottawa, January 6.

———. 2002. Canadian Radio-television and Telecommunications Commission. Broadcasting Decision CRTC 2002-189. Ottawa, July 16.

———. 2004. Canadian Radio-television and Telecommunications Commission. Broadcasting Decision CRTC 2004-271. Ottawa, July 13.

———. 2006a. Canadian Radio-television and Telecommunications Commission. "Broadcasting Policy Monitoring Report 2006." Quebec: Government of Canada.

———. 2006b. Canadian Radio-television and Telecommunications Commission. *The Future Environment Facing the Canadian Broadcasting System*. Gatineau, Quebec.

———. 2007. Canadian Radio-television and Telecommunications Commission. Broadcasting Policy Monitoring Report 2007. Quebec: Government of Canada.

CTVglobemedia. 2008. Available at www.ctvglobemedia.com/en (accessed June 23, 2008).

Dixon, Guy. 2007. "Bumper crop of listeners for CBC Radio One." *Globe and Mail*, April 13, R3.

Dougherty, Kevin. 2006. "Unique hearing held on CHOI sale: Outlaw radio station on air without licence." *Gazette*, September 12, A7.

Douglas, Susan. 2002. "Letting the Boys Be Boys: Talk Radio, Male Hysteria, and Political Discourse in the 1980s." In *Radio Reader: Essays in the Cultural History of Radio*, ed. Michele Hilmes and Jason Loviglio, 485–503. New York: Routledge.

Ellis, Sandra & Ed Shane. 2004. "Talk Radio." In *Museum of Broadcast Communications Encyclopedia of Radio*, ed. Christopher H. Sterling and Michael Keith, 3:1371. Chicago: Fitzroy Dearborn.

Fairchild, Charles. 1999. "Deterritorializing Radio: Deregulation and the Continuing Triumph of the Corporatist Perspective in the USA." *Media, Culture and Society* 21 (4): 549–61.

Fine, Philip. 1998. "Stern mocks Quebec's French: Cheers and jeers greet shock jock's demise." *Globe and Mail*, August 28, D2.

Gilbert, Renaud. 2006. "Bureau de L'ombudsman Services Français Rapport Annuel 2005–2006." Available at www.radio-canada.ca/ombudsman/index/shtml (accessed June 12, 2007).

Gingras, Anne-Marie. 2007. "La question de la liberté d'expression dans les démêlés judiciaires et les revers administratifs de CHOI-FM." *Canadian Journal of Political Science* 40 (1): 79–100.

Goddard, Peter. 1998. "CHUM tops radio ratings." *Toronto Star*, December 15, F5.

Government of Canada *Broadcasting Act*, C. 1991.

Government of Canada *Radio Regulations*, S.O.R./1986-982.

Hilmes, Michele. 2002. "Rethinking Radio." In *Radio Reader: Essays in the Cultural History of Radio*, ed. Michele Hilmes and Jason Loviglio, 1–19. New York: Routledge.

Hutchby, Ian. 1992. "The Pursuit of Controversy: Routine Scepticism in Talk on 'Talk Radio.'" *Sociology* 26 (4): 673–94.

Ingram, Mathew. 2007. "i-Pod revolution turns satellite radio on its ear." *Globe and Mail*, February 22, TQ Front.

Martin, Don. 2006. "CBC drifts into PM's agenda." *National Post*, June 22, A5.

Menon, Vinay. 1998. "Morning has broken. They lost 30 percent of their audience to Stern. Now, a frantic year later, they're a way of life to their fans." *Toronto Star*, November 1, D16.

O'Sullivan, Susan. 2004. "'The whole nation is listening to you': The Presentation of the Self on a Tabloid Talk Radio Show." *Media, Culture and Society* 25 (5): 719–38.

Paraskevas, Joe. 2004. "5,000 rally to save radio station: Parliament Hill protesters demand 'liberty' for Quebec City broadcaster." *National Post*, August 11, A1.

Postman, Neil. 1985. *Amusing Ourselves to Death: Public Discourse in the Age of Show Business.* New York: Viking Press.

Radio Marketing Bureau. 2007. "Foundation Research Study 2007." Available at www.rmb.ca/public/file/rmbfoundation2007final.ppt#324,2,Objective (accessed June 11, 2007).

Riley, Michael. 2006. "Mic Check." *Ryerson Review of Journalism*, June 2006. Available at www.rrj.ca/issue/ 2006/summer/636/ (accessed August 11, 2008).

Rogers Communications. 2007. Available at www.rogers.com/english/aboutrogers/television/index.html (accessed April 10, 2007).

Séguin, Rhéal. 2005. "Quebec station sued over vulgar remarks." *Globe and Mail*, March 8, A8.

Sperounes, Sandra. 2007. "CHED keeps its grip on top spot." *Edmonton Journal*, April 11, D3.

Talkers Magazine Online. 2007. "The Top Talk Radio Audiences." Available at www.talkers.com (accessed May 27, 2007).

Taras, David. 2001. *Power and Betrayal in the Canadian Media*. Peterborough: Broadview.

Vipond, Mary. 2000. *The Mass Media in Canada*. 3rd ed. Toronto: James Lorimer.

Winnipeg Free Press. 2007. "Rock radio roars back to life, latest ratings suggest." April 11, D2.

Chapter 4

Belinda Stronach and the Gender Politics of Celebrity

Linda Trimble and Joanna Everitt[1]

INTRODUCTION

> She was a person of considerable public interest, the perfect storm of great wealth, good looks, lofty ambition and high profile love interests. More than any woman in the Commons today, Belinda Stronach brought sex, soap operas and high-fashion analysis to a staid, pin-striped Parliament Hill.[2]

Belinda Stronach retired from political life barely three years after her dramatic entry onto its stage in the spring of 2004. She began as a little-known corporate executive who sought the top job in the newly (re)formed Conservative Party of Canada. She was a minor political player at best, a failed leadership candidate who languished in the opposition benches until her government-saving political defection in 2005 was rewarded with a post in Paul Martin's cabinet. Yet Belinda Stronach attracted the media spotlight at all stages of her brief political career, outshining the other candidates (even the winner) during her leadership bid, garnering more headlines than a similarly high-profile floor-crosser, and certainly inviting more media attention than any other member of parliament who has made an equally abrupt exit from the House of Commons. Stronach illustrates the key features of celebrity politics, *popularization* and *personalization* (van Zoonen, 2006), and provides an excellent example of the phenomenon of the political celebrity. In many respects she was an unlikely candidate for this role, a virtual nobody on the political scene whose talents and achievements were dwarfed by the media attention she received. Somehow her actions and persona continued to fascinate the media. How is it that Belinda Stronach got caught in the eye of a media storm and what does this tell us about media, politics, gender, and celebrity?

This chapter explores the phenomenon of the political celebrity through the lens of the news coverage of Belinda Stronach at the two most highly reported stages of her political career: her bid for the leadership of the Conservative party (January to March 2004), and her defection to the Liberals just over a year later, on May 18, 2005. The chapter begins by examining the phenomenon of celebrity and the features of the celebrity politician, demonstrating how this image can be profoundly gendered. Drawing on the literature about political celebrity, media, and popular culture, we construct a conceptual framework for understanding Stronach's unique celebrity status in Canada that can be used to account for the nature of her media coverage. The final section draws from case studies of media coverage of her leadership bid and defection to reflect on the gender politics of mediated celebrity. We conclude that, while their celebrity status may result in politicians developing a higher-than-normal public profile, in the case of female politicians the nature of this profile can be particularly problematic and politically limiting. Female celebrities have typically come from the fashion or entertainment industries, and the coverage that journalists use to report on female political celebrities reflects this tradition. As a result, coverage of female political celebrities focuses on their physical appearance, sexuality, and personal relationships, as is the case for actresses or pop stars. This sexualization leaves an impression of superficiality and lack of intellectual substance, and serves to delegitimize their status as genuine politicians.

NEWS AS ENTERTAINMENT: MEDIA, POLITICS, AND CELEBRITY

> Her departure robs the federal scene of one of the few bona fide celebrities in the Commons—an heiress who mixed and mingled with the likes of former U.S. president Bill Clinton, had well-publicized romantic liaisons with a politician and a hockey star and who could stir a buzz in the political and gossip sections of the newspapers. (Delacourt 2007)

The concept of celebrity is intensely familiar to North Americans, who for decades have been bombarded daily with the trials and tribulations of celebrities such as Elizabeth Taylor, Elvis Presley, and Jacqueline Onassis, or the more modern examples of Lindsay Lohan and Britney Spears. A *celebrity* is a person who commands a high degree of public and media attention (see Turner 2004, p. 5; van Zoonen, 2006, pp. 290–91). We argue that, while most modern-day celebrities are in the entertainment industry (musicians, models, actors, or sports stars), they may also come from the fields of business (Bill Gates, Donald Trump, or Conrad Black) or politics (J.F. Kennedy, Pierre Trudeau, or Bill Clinton). It seems that every move celebrities make is the subject of news coverage, and the attention they receive has increased dramatically in the era of YouTube videos, gossip columns, blogs, and television talk shows. Why is the public so interested?

Celebrities are a product of contemporary **popular culture**, defined by Street (1997, p. 7) as "a form of entertainment that is mass-produced or made available to large numbers of people." Popular culture is, quite literally, popular—it is widely circulated and consumed—and it features a disproportionate interest in celebrities, particularly in their private lives (Turner, 2004, p. 8). The public finds "celebrities' success, fame and glamour so seductive that it seeks personal knowledge about them" (Berlanstein, 2004, p. 66). In other words, the mass media produce celebrities for public consumption because celebrities interest, entertain, and distract. They are a commodity for the media. As Turner (2004, p. 3) argues, "the modern celebrity may claim no special achievements other than the attraction of public attention." For the most part, a celebrity can be famous simply for being famous: consider Paris Hilton. This is possible because celebrity is not a property that individuals exhibit or a set of characteristics they embody; rather, it is a status that is discursively constructed (Turner, 2004).

Because of this, celebrities help to define cultural norms and values. They provide a text that is read by the public—"an embodiment of a discursive battleground on the norms of individuality and personality within a culture" (Turner, 2004, p. 25). As Turner explains in *Understanding Celebrity*, celebrities play a key social and cultural function in modern society by "elaborating the definition of the individual" and by "maintaining the discursive linkages between consumer capitalism, democracy and individualism" (2004, p. 24). Celebrities perform the narratives of contemporary culture and symbolize dominant myths, values, and aspirations (Berlanstein, 2004). By understanding celebrity—how it is constructed and consumed—we can understand elements of the culture that is producing and consuming it.

If the generic celebrity is a commodity of a celebrity-obsessed media, so too must be the *celebrity politician* (Street, 2004, p. 442). Street (2001, p. 273) gives the example of extensive (and breathless) media coverage of the birth of former British prime minister Tony Blair's fourth child, with one newspaper devoting seven pages to the story. This highly mediated representation of what is for ordinary families an intensely private event boosted Blair's popularity considerably. "Politics, it seems, had been truly 'personalized,' and politicians had become part of a nation's soap opera" (Street, 2001, p. 273).

Celebrity politics is a manifestation of the progressively more important role of entertainment in politics. *Entertainment* is the production of products and genres that are experienced as gratifying and enjoyable by the public (van Zoonen, 2005, pp. 9–10). Over time, competition within and between media sources, and the increasing dominance of television and other visual electronic media, have driven news media to adopt more of an "entertainment" approach to news coverage of politics than in the past. Through "sensationalized headlines, personalized stories, a focus on celebrity, increased attention to the private lives of public figures, and increased focus on the visual" (Muir, 2005, p. 56), political events are being represented as soap operas complete with story lines and personality clashes (van Zoonen, 2005, p. 7). Entertainment and politics intersect when the politician, rather than the issue, takes centre stage, and politicians often play along with the demand for personalized performances because they want—and need—such media exposure to enhance their public image (Street, 2001). For this reason, Stephen Harper allows journalists to photograph him taking his children to school and Stéphane Dion is pictured with his Husky, Kyoto. But how do politicians become celebrities? After all, not every politician has celebrity status; in fact, few do, even when they try to obtain it. Given the "dramaturgical rules of television," the traditional politician, who "studies administrative documents about which he then talks, negotiates and decides," is boring, and indeed the entire field of political ideas, institutions, and processes lacks entertainment value (van Zoonen, 2005, p. 71). So what are the determinants of political celebrity?

West and Orman (2002) identify five pathways to celebrity for politicians. First, one can become a celebrity by birth, as illustrated by celebrity families, such as the Kennedy clan in the United States. In Canada, Justin Trudeau's pursuit of a political career is enhanced by his father's legacy. Second is the celebrity politician who becomes famous by virtue of scandal. Britain's Jeffrey Archer, who was convicted of perjury in 2001, is a good example (see Corner, 2000). Third, there is the politician who achieves celebrity status by putting in a charismatic public performance; Bill Clinton and Margaret Thatcher come to mind. The fourth category, increasingly prevalent, is the celebrity who becomes a politician. There are several examples of sports stars and actors who have used their fame to help leverage political victories, notably bodybuilder-turned-actor-turned-California governor Arnold Schwarzenegger, or former NHL goalie Ken Dryden, who ran for the leadership of the Liberal Party.

West and Orman's fifth method of gaining celebrity status is to borrow the trappings and mechanisms of celebrity to win popularity. Techniques include association with "real" celebrities, through endorsements from, or photo ops with, entertainment or sports stars. Politicians can also try to emulate entertainment figures, "giving the voters a song and dance" by appearing on talk shows or performing as musicians (Street, 2001, p. 191). Finally, politicians increasingly harness the expertise of those who market celebrities (Street, 2004, p. 437; 2001, p. 192). Hollywood directors are hired to make political campaign advertisements, comedians to supply jokes for campaign speeches, and spin doctors to sell the "product" (the celebrity) to the media (and public). As van Zoonen (2006) argues, popularization and personalization have become the hallmarks of celebrity politics.

Belinda Stronach fits none of the categories outlined by West and Orman. Her father, Frank Stronach, though accorded some media attention as the founder of Magna International, is not a celebrity, so she was not born into the role, though she did enjoy name recognition as "daughter of." Stronach did not enter the media spotlight due to scandal, and she attracted only moderate media attention before she stepped into the political arena.[3]

She did not win acclaim through her performance as a politician; indeed, her very ability to enact the role of political leader was treated with derision by the press. She also does not fit with West and Orman's fifth category of celebrity politician, the politician who uses the tricks and trappings of celebrity to construct a popular and sellable image. Though Stronach had links with other political celebrities such as Bill Clinton, she did not actively deploy these during her leadership campaign, and the media had already turned its attention to her before her handlers could launch her website or land her a guest spot on the *Rick Mercer Report*. In other words, she did not fit the profile of a "typical" celebrity politician. As none of these explanations help us understand the attention paid to Stronach, we need to look elsewhere to account for her celebrity status.

In *Entertaining the Citizen*, van Zoonen (2005, pp. 82–85) offers another typology that may help in part to account for the experience of Belinda Stronach. This schema is based on the political context and the performance of the political celebrity within that context. It features two axes; first, a politician's political stance (as an insider or outsider), and second, the politician's persona (as ordinary or special). A political insider builds his or her career within political institutions such as political parties. Outsiders enter politics without this political experience. Politicians can also be perceived as ordinary ("regular guys" who are "just like us"), or they can be presented as special ("more special and capable than we") (van Zoonen, 2005, p. 82). Belinda Stronach was clearly an outsider as she entered politics via the Conservative leadership race, with no political experience, and she was also considered special, but not because she was seen as especially capable. Indeed, after the first blush of media attention faded, she was treated as incapable, even inept. To understand what made Belinda Stronach singular enough to be constructed as a celebrity politician we need to understand the gender dynamics underlying and shaping the phenomenon of celebrity politics.

THE GENDER POLITICS OF CELEBRITY

The practice of celebrity is by no means gender neutral and, as van Zoonen (2006) argues, the politics of gender shape the manufacture and consumption of political celebrities in a number of important ways. Think of the top female celebrities in North America. What do they do? More importantly, when are they talked about in popular media? How are they presented and evaluated? For women, much of current celebrity culture exhibits "hyper-femininity," with "fashion, sexuality, glamour and consumption as key ingredients" (van Zoonen, 2006, p. 298). Most images of female celebrity stem from Hollywood movies, television, pop music, and product advertising, often providing "visual pleasure for an apparently masculine spectator, the epitome of the male fetish" (van Zoonen, 2006, p. 291). Tropes of femininity are therefore situated in the body, and feature youth, glamour, and sexuality. Icons of glamour "seduce by association with one or more of the following qualities (the more the better): beauty, sexuality, theatricality, wealth, dynamism, notoriety, leisure" (Gundle & Castelli, 2006, p. 8). Female celebrity is, therefore, a celebration of femininity and female sexuality. This is not a recent phenomenon, and the results of Berlanstein's (2004) analysis of media coverage of nineteenth-century French female celebrities, writers, and actresses hold true today. He found that these women were portrayed in a way that "confirmed the widespread belief that public women would inevitably be unruly women. Illicit sensuality was part and parcel of the fame that the public expected famous women to perform for most of the nineteenth century" (Berlanstein, 2004, p. 72). In other words, women of renown have traditionally been considered as disturbing entities because of their sexuality.

Clearly, both long-standing and modern conceptions of female celebrity do not transpose themselves easily onto the political field (van Zoonen, 2006, p. 292). The political sphere continues to exhibit a sex-based division of labour determined by underlying assumptions about gender roles and the performance of political leadership. Because masculine identity is linked with public life (business, politics, the military . . .), it is infinitely easier for men to achieve celebrity status in politics based on their insider status than it is for women. Women's historical exclusion from the public sphere (with the exception of the entertainment business) makes them outsiders to politics, even when there are no longer any formal, legal barriers to admission.

As outsiders, it has always been difficult for women to achieve the same profile in politics as men. In the past they received less coverage than male politicians (Gingras, 1995; Kahn, 1994), and what coverage they did receive tended to present them as less viable candidates (Kahn, 1994; Kahn & Goldenberg, 1991; Ross, 1995). In their efforts to find an engaging hook upon which to hang their stories about female politicians, journalists frequently turned to the familiar frame of the female celebrity. It is perhaps for this reason that scholars examining female politicians' media coverage regularly reported the media's reliance on traditional gender-based stereotypes, their focus on personal characteristics such as clothing or hair rather than on the issues they are championing, and their tendency to impose a higher moral standard on women's sexuality than they do on men's (Robinson & Saint-Jean, 1995). Political women were regularly presented as outsiders, as disruptive (often sexual) forces in a male-dominated realm.

There is little evidence that this gender-differentiated coverage has diminished with the increase in the number of women entering political office. In fact, as women begin to pursue more high-profile political positions such as party leaders, which draws the media's attention, they continue to confront a very narrow and restrictive version of the celebrity identity, one that has more to do with glamour and sexuality than with power and charismatic public performance. As Schwartzenberg (1977) observed, political women face being accused of frivolity, coquetry, and having loose morals if they do not take care to downplay their femininity.

While downplaying their femininity may be wise for female politicians, this option is not always available. A woman who is older and childless, or whose children are grown, may be able to emulate a masculine persona. But for younger women, and especially attractive women like Belinda Stronach, who develop celebrity status because the media are intrigued by their youth or glamour, the sexual connotations may not be avoidable. In an era of celebrity politics, with its increasing focus on the personalities and private lives of politicians, women's sex, sexuality, and private personas are a natural site of media interest. The double bind for women in this position is clear; their sex gains them attention, but the attention is centred on their sex. Muir's (2005, pp. 60–67) analysis of the rise and fall of Australian Democrat leader Natasha Stott Despoja shows that political celebrity is a dangerous business for women because of its trivializing and sexualizing tendencies. The Australian media were fascinated with Stott Despoja's image. She was "young, single, blonde, petite and attractive," a "powerful contrast to politics-as-usual," but ultimately she was dismissed and derided as an example of style over substance; "celebrity style and politics were opposed as mutually exclusive categories in a way that signals danger for other young, and particularly, *female* politicians" (Muir, 2005, p. 67). Belinda Stronach provides an excellent example of this danger zone for women politicians.

METHODOLOGY

In order to better understand the gendered nature of political celebrity, we focus on the most reported and mediated events in Belinda Stronach's political career—her Conservative party leadership bid and her defection from the Conservatives to the (then) governing Liberals. While other stories, such as Belinda Stronach's imputed relationship with hockey star Tie Domi and her treatment for breast cancer, reached prominence, we chose to focus on her political career rather than her personal life, as these best illustrate the degree to which popularization and personalization of a celebrity politician have intruded upon their political roles. The quantitative and qualitative data for this chapter were gathered from analysis of coverage of these events in Canada's national newspapers, the *Globe and Mail* and the *National Post*. These two English-language national newspapers were chosen because of their large, nationwide readerships and their agenda-setting roles among the Canadian media (Taras, 1999, p. 18), and, in particular, because they devoted considerable resources to the news events analyzed in our study. Finally, we would argue that, because of the reputation of these two newspapers as primarily "news"-focused media sources, any tendency toward celebrity coverage will only be magnified in other less reputable news sources.

We analyzed a census of *Globe and Mail* and *National Post* stories about each of the news events, including all news stories, opinion pieces, editorials, and columns. Reportage of the Conservative Party of Canada leadership race was collected from the date the first candidate, Stephen Harper, entered the race (January 13, 2004) to two days after the vote (March 22, 2004), a search strategy that garnered 268 stories about the contest and its three candidates: Stephen Harper, Belinda Stronach, and Tony Clement. For Belinda Stronach's decision to cross the floor of the House of Commons, we examined all coverage of the defection in the four days immediately following the news event. There were 91 news articles printed in the two national papers from May 18, 2005, to May 21, 2005. These were compared to the 38 articles referring to David Emerson in the four days (February 7 to February 10, 2006) following his floor-crossing after the 2006 election.

This study employs both content analysis and discourse analysis. Content analysis is a methodology that uses "objective and systematic counting and recording procedures to produce a quantitative description of the symbolic content in a text" (Neuman, 2000, p. 293). This allows us to make explicit comparisons between the amount and nature of the coverage received by Belinda Stronach and her male counterparts. Discourse analysis, on the other hand, is a qualitative methodology that acknowledges that language is a form of social interaction and focuses on its meaning based on the cultural and social contexts in which it is used. This approach enables us to explore in more depth the gendered nature of the language that was employed to describe Stronach and the implications of this type of coverage for women who achieve political celebrity status.

As our interest is in the degree to which Belinda Stronach's coverage matched that of a celebrity politician, we focus specifically on the issues of popularization and personalization, the two defining characteristics of celebrity coverage. *Popularization* is defined as a high degree of media visibility and prominence in a news story. In the content analysis, this visibility is measured in five ways: whether or not each candidate was named in the story, named first in the story, named four or more times in the story, named in the headline, and named first in the headline. *Personalization* is assessed by the extent to which a politician's coverage focuses on them as an individual, on their private lives, or on their intimate selves. This type of coverage foregrounds issues of performance, style, and aesthetics, and does so by drawing attention to a politician's looks, dress, and sexuality. To determine the degree to which this highly personalized coverage was applied to the politicians under study, our content analysis is based on an assessment of whether or not the stories mentioned their looks or family life and how they were named or referred to in their coverage.[4] The discourse analysis complements the content analysis by providing examples from the news stories that illustrate the popularized and personalized nature of this coverage in more detail.

THE "CELEBRITIZATION" OF BELINDA STRONACH
Act One: The Leadership Race

The first marker of celebrity is popularization. That Belinda Stronach was marked as a celebrity before she stepped foot on the political stage is indicated by the fact that her candidacy for the leadership of the Conservative party was the focus of considerable news coverage in the week *before* her official announcement on January 21, 2004, garnering eight stories in the *National Post* and seven in the *Globe and Mail*, including several in-depth profile pieces. Stronach surprised press and public alike when rumours of her intention to contest the leadership of the newly (re)formed Conservative Party of Canada were leaked to the print media in early January, 2004. Apart from playing a modest role in brokering the deal that created the Conservative party by effecting a merger between the Progressive Conservative and the Canadian Alliance parties, Stronach had no political training or background. However, she was the daughter of a successful auto-parts manufacturer and had recently taken over as CEO of Magna International from her father. She was a young (37-year-old), glamorous, jet-setting multi-millionaire with connections to international notables and world leaders, including former U.S. president Bill Clinton—all factors that catapulted her into the position of a celebrity in the media's eyes.

Stronach lost the contest to Stephen Harper on the first ballot, but she ran a well-financed, -staffed, and -organized campaign, enjoyed considerable backing from party insiders, and placed a respectable second, winning 35 percent of the vote.[5] Right from the start her lack of political experience and history in either the Progressive Conservative or Canadian Alliance parties made her a long-shot candidate. Such candidates typically receive limited media attention, often being included at the end of stories about other candidates. However, this was not the case for Belinda Stronach. Despite her second-place standing in the leadership race, Stronach garnered considerably *more* attention from the national newspapers than did either of her male competitors. While all three candidates were named in most of the news stories, Stronach was named first in 47 percent of the stories, and referred to four or more times in 60 percent of the stories. In contrast, the front-runner and eventual victor, Stephen Harper, was the first candidate named 43 percent of the time, and was named four times or more in 47 percent of the stories. Only 10 percent of the news stories named Tony Clement first, and just over a quarter (26 percent) named him four or more times.

Another way to measure visibility is through the analysis of headlines. Headlines are arguably the pinnacle of news visibility as they signal what the story is about and shape interpretations by readers (van Dijk, 1991, p. 50). Headlines are often the only part of the story that is read or recalled (van Dijk, 1991, p. 69). High levels of visibility are conferred when a candidate is named, and ideally named first, in a headline. Many of the national newspaper headlines accompanying the stories on the leadership contest did not name any of the candidates, but Stronach was the most likely of the three contenders to see her name in the headlines and to be named first. Of the headlines that did name names, Stronach's appeared first over half of the time (52 percent), while Stephen Harper was named first far less often, in 34 percent of the headlines naming one or more of the candidates. Tony Clement's name appeared first in only 14 percent of these headlines.

Since only eight stories (6 percent) mentioning Stronach evaluated her as a viable candidate, and none of these indicated she would beat Stephen Harper, Stronach's visibility did not result from a perception that she posed a serious challenge to the eventual winner. Furthermore, Stronach's prominence was maintained throughout the campaign. We created a prominence index in which each of the measures of visibility listed above was granted a value of one, with a maximum score on the index of five.

As Figure 4.1 confirms, Stronach's prominence in the news stories was indeed highest in the entry phase of the campaign, and it remained high. During the first two weeks of the campaign, a period in which the media concentrated on the candidates and their campaign launches, Stronach scored 3.18 out of 5 on the prominence index, with Harper at only 1.51.

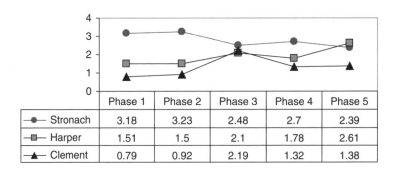

	Phase 1	Phase 2	Phase 3	Phase 4	Phase 5
Stronach	3.18	3.23	2.48	2.7	2.39
Harper	1.51	1.5	2.1	1.78	2.61
Clement	0.79	0.92	2.19	1.32	1.38

Figure 4.1 Mean Scores on Prominence Index by Candidate, Two-Week Campaign Phases

The three candidates converged at the mid phase of the leadership campaign, when coverage shifted to candidates' activities, especially televised debates, changes in levels of support from elites and rank-and-file members of the party, and policy pronouncements. Stronach's drop may have reflected her decision not to participate in a televised debate. But she took the lead for the fourth phase of the campaign (2.7 to Harper's 1.78). It was only in the last two weeks of the campaign, with Harper's win a foregone conclusion, that his news prominence marginally exceeded Stronach's. However, it is remarkable that, during the final two weeks of the campaign, with polls showing a first-place victory for Harper, the media continued to focus on Belinda Stronach. The finding that the media's interest in Stronach was sustained throughout the campaign begs explanation because even high-profile female candidates such as Elizabeth Dole struggle for media visibility when seeking party leadership positions.

The discourse analysis demonstrates that the most obvious explanation is Stronach's celebrity persona. As one reporter commented, "There is, undoubtedly, a 'glitz' factor in Ms. Stronach's candidacy that contrasts sharply with the grey and dull image of the new Conservative Party . . ." Labelled the "It Girl of the political right,"[6] Stronach had news value[7] because of her unanticipated entry into the contest and her strong second-place position. But, more importantly, she was news because of her (gender-based) political celebrity status. A writer for the *Globe and Mail* said the leadership contest was not much of a story without Stronach's candidacy: Roy MacGregor wrote, "In a party whose popular, if somewhat unfair image is of high collars and muttonchops, no one would say an attractive, successful young woman is anything but a bonus to a race the country would otherwise have ignored."[8] *Globe and Mail* pundit Margaret Wente put it quite directly: "The media are kissing the ground in front of her because she adds some spice and sex appeal to an otherwise terminally dull event."[9] These comments suggest that the novelty value of Stronach's gender, physical attractiveness, and glamorous image explain her high level of visibility and prominence throughout the campaign, and particularly in the entry and end-game phases. In other words, the media quickly transformed Stronach into a political celebrity during the leadership campaign as a way to add interest and "entertainment value" to an otherwise uninspiring political event.

Personalization is the second marker of celebrity status. It establishes a personal rapport between the public and the celebrity by allowing a media audience to become intimately familiar with the celebrity through stories about family, love life, and personal appearance. Such coverage is particularly problematic for women because it reinforces traditional public/private divisions within society that have limited women's opportunities to the domestic sphere of the home and family. Women have struggled against these gendered divisions in their efforts to win elected office and the right to be seen as legitimate participants in the public world of politics. Yet again and again evidence demonstrates that their coverage has focused on the personal and domestic (Kahn, 1996; Heldman et al., 2005; Devitt, 1999).

Our content analysis identifies the degree to which Stronach's coverage was more personalized than Harper's or Clement's. The findings on appearance were most striking.

If any reference was made to the candidate's looks, clothing, sexual allure, or body, it was coded as an allusion to appearance. Stephen Harper's appearance was discussed in only two stories[10]—that is, in 1 percent of the stories that mentioned him. Tony Clement's appearance won marginally more notice, as his "earnest nerd" persona was mentioned in 3 percent of stories (five of the stories that discussed Clement). In contrast, Belinda Stronach's appearance was discussed in 77 stories—33 percent of the news stories that mentioned her. Her hair, wardrobe, body, and sexual attractiveness were scrutinized and analyzed, often using explicitly gendered references. Stronach was called "young," "attractive," "beautiful," and a "hot babe" with "bodacious good looks." She was cited as the candidate with "sex appeal," called "sexy" outright and, most outrageously, labelled "better than Viagra."[11] In 30 of the stories mentioning her looks (40 percent), Stronach's appearance was the *first* topic of discussion.

There was also a difference in the levels of media attention to the marital status and family life of the male and female contenders. The two male candidates offered the quintessential family model, with wives and young children. That this was not of much interest to the press is indicated by the findings. Stephen Harper's marriage and/or family were discussed in only seven of the stories that mentioned him (3 percent), and Clement's in a mere four stories (2 percent). Like her competitors, Stronach had young children, but the fact that she was twice divorced not only set her apart; it was discussed frequently in the coverage. Stronach's marital and/or parental status was raised in fully 28 (12 percent) of the stories that mentioned her. Belinda Stronach was called a "single mom millionaire," the "young mother who would be prime minister," and, less flatteringly, a woman with two failed marriages.[12] The media's interest in Stronach's personal life was illustrated by the interview questions *National Post* columnist Don Martin posed to her during the campaign. "Is it hard to be a single mom on the road? Is your being beautiful an asset or a liability? Are you dating anyone?" he asked.[13] Media coverage of Elizabeth Dole's presidential campaign shows that attention of this sort tends to override discussion of the candidate's political experience and issue positions (Aday & Devitt, 2001; Heldman et al., 2005; Gilmartin, 2001). The end result is that the focus on a woman's looks or sexual availability detracts from substantive coverage of her campaign and issue positions.

Act Two: The Defection

Belinda Stronach's celebrity status was further illustrated by the media-feeding frenzy that occurred in response to her defection from the Conservative to the Liberal party. Unlike the coverage of the leadership campaign, which occurred over several weeks, Stronach's floor-crossing resulted in a short but intense period of news. Television news stations interrupted their programming to go live to the May 17, 2005 news conference featuring Stronach and Prime Minister Paul Martin, and the event was the lead story that evening on the national television news (Martin, 2006, p. 20). Print coverage began the day after the event, May 18, and newspapers devoted considerable column inches to the defection. During the four-day search frame for our study, May 18–21, 2005, Stronach's floor-crossing was discussed in 91 articles in the two national newspapers: 42 stories in the *Globe and Mail*, and 49 stories in the *National Post*. On the first day of reportage, May 18, both newspapers devoted their front page to the story, with banner headlines. The *Globe and Mail* ran 17 articles about the defection on its first day of coverage, three of them on the front page, and all under the standing head "Stronach Crosses the Floor." The *National Post*'s "day after" coverage featured 20 articles, two of which were on the front page. The event was discussed at length and in detail in the news and opinion sections of both papers and even made it to the business pages, where the impact of the defection for the markets and the dollar was assessed. This highly analyzed event can be contrasted with the coverage received by David Emerson when he switched from the Liberals to the Conservatives immediately after the 2006 election. Emerson's defection was mentioned in less than half as many (38) articles published by the national newspapers in an equivalent four-day time frame (February 7–10, 2006).

Both Stronach and Emerson won cabinet posts as a result of their partisan switching, so the "prize" was equally newsworthy. The key difference in these defections is that Stronach's helped save the government of the day, albeit temporarily, from defeat in a confidence motion, while Emerson's simply helped to save Stephen Harper from the criticism that he did not have cabinet representation from Canada's major cities. Belinda Stronach crossed the floor at a crucial moment for the minority Liberal government, as her vote plus those of two independents ensured the government's survival. That this was a significant aspect of the story was illustrated by lead top of fold stories in both national newspapers on May 18. The *Globe*'s was titled "Martin's White Knight: Stronach's switch may be enough to save the Liberal government."[14] "Blonde bombshell: Defection gives Grits vote edge," said the *Post*.[15] David Emerson crossed the floor immediately after the 2006 election, when the fate of the newly elected Conservative minority government was not in doubt. Re-elected as a Liberal in Vancouver-Kingsway, Emerson was convinced to change sides when Prime Minister Steven Harper asked him to join the Conservative minority government as Minister of International Trade. While stories about Stronach's defection focused on the reasons for Stronach's decision and its implications for the government and the Conservative party, articles about Emerson's defection mentioned it in the context of Harper's crafty cabinet-building. In short, Stronach herself was "the" story, the star player, while Emerson was positioned as a minor character in a larger drama.

This conclusion is supported by our content analysis of the first day of coverage. As Figure 4.2 shows, the two defectors had remarkably different levels of news coverage in the *Globe and Mail* and *National Post*. Stronach was far more likely to be named in the headlines and to be named first in the stories. As well, her defection was the main topic of a majority of the headlines and stories, while Emerson's was not. Instead, in Emerson's case the focus was on Stephen Harper and his new minority government. Harper was named first in 71 percent of the headlines and 65 percent of the stories about Emerson's defection.

Undoubtedly, part of the explanation for the Stronach defection's prominence was the news value of a defector helping to save the day for the Martin government. But we argue

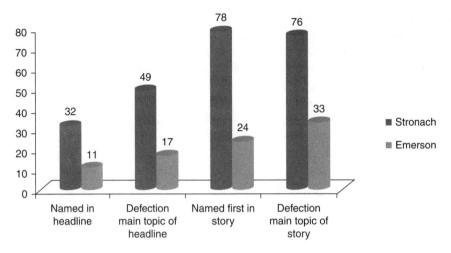

Figure 4.2 News Visibility of Defector and Defection, on First Day of Coverage

(reported as a percentage of total stories printed on the first day of coverage)

that this is only part of the explanation and it does not account for the highly gender-specific language used in her coverage. The "celebritization" of Belinda Stronach, set in motion during her campaign for the Conservative leadership, had been firmly established by the time she crossed the floor. In fact, her celebrity status and the personalized coverage that comes along with it—focusing on glamour, sexuality, and impropriety—helps to explain the amount, tone, and substance of the national newspaper coverage of her defection. It also helps explain why the media's response to her floor-crossing was so different from its reaction to that of David Emerson.

The popularization of Belinda Stronach is evident in the sheer volume of coverage, but it is also evident in the substantive elements of the reportage. The enormous news value of the event was illustrated by the positioning and emphasis of the coverage. Stronach's defection was a front-page story for three days, May 18–20, with the *Globe* printing three articles per day on the front page and the *Post* offering two stories per day at the front of the paper. The hyperbolic language used was such that it was hard for anyone to be unaware of Stronach's decision to change parties; the event was called "surprising," "stunning," a "bombshell," "spectacular," "dramatic," "sensational," "shocking," and "mind-boggling." It caused such a buzz that, in the words of Senator Marjory Le Breton, "even the people that wash your hair were talking about it."[16] Indeed, CNN deemed Stronach's defection the "political play of the week."[17] The saga was presented in salacious, intimate detail. Both newspapers featured hour-by-hour accounts of Stronach's final hours as a Conservative, describing everything from the menu for her pre-defection dinner with Prime Minister Paul Martin to the strategy for keeping the move secret. The *Globe and Mail* further signalled its assessment of the importance of the story by immediately commissioning what must have been a very expensive overnight poll to assess voter reactions to Stronach's move.[18] Moreover, business writers gave Stronach credit for a rise in the value of the Canadian dollar, calling it the "now famous 'Belinda bounce'"[19] and the "Belinda bump."[20] Columnists said Stronach's defection would go down in history. Stronach "is unassailably a piece of Canadian folklore" said a writer from the *Globe*,[21] and "Ms. Stronach's exit promises to take its place alongside some enduring moments of Canadian political skulduggery" opined a *Post* columnist.[22]

Personalization, the second pillar of celebrity status, was obvious in the newspaper treatment of Belinda Stronach's floor-crossing. Unlike the situation for David Emerson, who was only ever referred to in headlines using his last name, only 58 percent of the headlines referred to Stronach in this more impersonal manner. Instead, her coverage was much more intimate, with 19 percent of the headline references using both her first and last names and 23 percent referring to her simply as "Belinda."

The defection itself was described in highly personalized—and feminized—language, which referred to it as "nuptials," a "match," and a "political marriage."[23] The "Blonde bombshell" headline[24] played on Stronach's sexuality and celebrity status, as the term "blonde bombshell," used first in reference to screen star Jean Harlow in the 1930s, is widely used to refer to sex symbols or pin-up girls. However, the most significant indicators of personalization are the tabloid-like quality of media attention to Belinda Stronach's relationship with Deputy Conservative Leader Peter MacKay and the sexualization of her defection.

Belinda Stronach and Peter MacKay had been labelled the "hot, hot Tories,"[25] their months-old relationship called the "ultimate political glamour item."[26] It was, according to the national press, a "glitzy affair that livened up the stodgy image of the Conservative party" and "made them the Brad and Angelina of Parliament Hill."[27] Stronach's decision to leave the Conservative party meant the love affair with Mackay was over, and reporters and columnists delighted in telling the story, pointing out its soap-opera sensibility and Shakespearian qualities.[28] Indeed, almost half of the articles about the defection made reference to the failed romance; 20 of the *Globe*'s articles (48 percent) and 21 of the *Post*'s (43 percent) talked about the relationship. The breakup was the exclusive focus of several high-profile stories, four printed in the *Globe and Mail* and seven in the *National Post*. Both newspapers highlighted the doomed romance on the first day of coverage. Margaret Wente, who devoted two columns to the Stronach–MacKay angle, told the story this way:

> You've got to feel for Peter MacKay . . . He must feel as though she'd stabbed one of her four-inch stilettos straight through his heart.[29]

The narrative was one of a devastating betrayal by a woman who had chosen her career over her lover. Headlines portrayed MacKay as the victim, Stronach as the cruel and heartless femme fatale. The *Globe and Mail* and the *National Post* ran front-page headlines that rivalled those found in more salacious media sources such as the *National Enquirer* or *Star Magazine*. A *Globe and Mail* headline in the national news section on

May 18 declared: "Mackay 'terribly badly' hurt, Harper says: Stronach wined, dined by the PM while boyfriend attended fundraiser."[30] The second day of coverage featured a front-page *Globe and Mail* story whose headline informed readers that "Mackay pleaded with his lover into wee hours"; the body of the story said MacKay was "devastated" by a "confession that ripped out his heart."[31] The *National Post* did not put the relationship story on page one, but gave it two front section articles on May 18. "'Peter taking it pretty hard,' Harper says; Goes underground" declared one headline.[32] Moreover, the *National Post* treated Mackay's retreat to Nova Scotia as national news on May 19: "'The heart's got to heal,' MacKay says: Had no idea: Tory MP goes home to the farm to lick his wounds."[33] And the *Post* kept the drama alive with a discussion of Stronach's and Mackay's reactions to each other in the House of Commons on the day of the vote: "The eyes have it as former lovers face off: Awkward glances and jeers in a tense day in the House" said the headline.[34] Both national newspapers reported Peter MacKay's angst-ridden comment in the aftermath of the Liberal government's victory in the House: "I'm going to go home and maybe walk my dog. Dogs are loyal."[35] The moral of the story was summed up by a story in the *National Post*, opining that Peter Mackay was "a decent, trusting guy who'd just been given a royal shafting by one hard-hearted bimbo."[36]

The most vitriolic of the coverage included "sexually charged insults," said *Globe and Mail* opinion writer Judith Timpson:

> A woman can get naked in public almost any old way she wants these days. . . . But if some of the highly vituperative and sexually tinged reaction . . . to Belinda Stronach's leap into the Liberal Cabinet is any indication, she should not, under any circumstances, go naked with her ambition. Unless of course she does not mind being called a whore . . .[37]

Timpson refers to the highly sexualized taunts levelled at Stronach in the aftermath of the defection. Belinda Stronach was called a "political whore" or "political harlot," who demonstrated "politically slatternly behaviour" by "whoring herself for power" and "prostituting herself for a price."[38] "Would all of this outrage have been pitched at the same decibel level and carried the same sexually charged insults if Belinda Stronach were a man?" Timpson wondered. "Or is she getting slammed harder because she is a woman, and not just any woman but a beautiful woman; furthermore, not just a beautiful woman, but a beautiful blond woman who has inherited her father's money and corporate empire?"[39]

It is hard not to conclude that Stronach's sex had a significant impact on the nature of the coverage her floor-crossing received. In none of the reports awarded to Emerson's switch to the Conservatives was he ever referred to as a "whore" displaying inappropriate political ambition. Instead, his defection was "simply business" as he was compared to "a top level chief executive about to defect to his company's closest rival."[40] Moreover, Emerson's floor-crossing was a good deal that was "brokered" by Conservative party insiders in an effort to capture a politician who was pragmatically "rejecting partisanship"[41] so that he could better look after the good of his city, province, and country.

Discussion

> She has dumped two husbands, a future prime minister and at least one boyfriend . . .
> She samples the opposite sex like canapés. . . . When she tires of them (or a political
> party, for that matter) she sheds them with a steely resolve.[42]

Belinda Stronach had political-celebrity status that was uncommon among Canadian
politicians: she was a young, glamorous socialite in a world of unexciting, middle-aged
men. Her newsworthiness is easily demonstrated by the nature of the coverage that she
received during both her leadership campaign and the floor-crossing episode. The amount
of coverage, her prominence in headlines, the frequency with which she was named first in
the stories, references to her entertainment value during the leadership campaign, and the
detail that the media employed in describing her defection all marked her as a celebrity,
despite her limited political experience or power.

Furthermore, Belinda Stronach's celebrity status was made explicit in many of the
articles written about her. During her leadership campaign, *Globe and Mail* columnist
Lysiane Gagnon attributed the excitement surrounding Stronach among the press corps
to the fact that "the media can't resist the 'star quality' of a young, blond, attractive
figure."[43] After her defection, a *Globe and Mail* article labelled Stronach "one of the
[Conservative] party's few celebrities."[44] Similarly, a *National Post* editorial called her
"a glamorous businesswoman who brought a touch of celebrity to the party."[45] Stronach's
popularity and profile were confirmed with references to her as a "high profile MP," a
"star," or a "media star" who enjoyed "fame."

Attention was drawn to Stronach's fame and celebrity in several additional ways. Her
glamorous image was highlighted, with attention to her appearance, wealth, and
wardrobe. References were made to her hair colour—including "great blond hope," "dishy
blond," "Bubba's blond pal," "young blond looker," and "Parliament Hill Barbie"—and
she was described as a "glamorous Toronto Tory."[46] and a "glamorous businesswoman"[47]
who "dressed in Prada and Gucci."[48] Given this, it is not surprising that reporters offered
delicious details about her associations with the rich and famous. "She dined with movie
stars" announced one article,[49] and several others discussed a dinner with former U.S.
president Bill Clinton that "provided fodder for the U.S. supermarket tabloids."[50]
A *National Post* editorial titled "The Belinda, and the damage done" implied Stronach had
the same kind of media draw as "The Donald," famous American tycoon Donald Trump.[51]
A *Globe and Mail* story called her "Material Girl" in a headline, an obvious reference to
American pop icon Madonna.[52]

However, despite the fact that media coverage is the lifeblood of political careers, it
is a truism to say that not all press is good press. While Belinda Stronach received a lot of
news coverage, the high degree of personalization in these stories meant that it was not
necessarily the type of coverage that enhanced her profile as a serious politician. Over the
course of the Conservative leadership race and in the aftermath of her defection, Belinda
Stronach endured constant press inspection of her physical, personal, and private life. As
might be expected in the case of a female celebrity, the national newspaper coverage of

these two events drew attention to her physical attractiveness, her sexuality, and, in particular, her relationships to high-profile men. While enhancing Stronach's visibility, this coverage had the impact of casting her as an "untraditional" and potentially superficial, and less convincing, leadership contender or politician.

No one would seriously expect Madonna or Jennifer Aniston to be considered credible political candidates, and the media's framing of Belinda Stronach as a celebrity politician made it more difficult for her to be taken seriously. Indeed, journalists themselves viewed her political skills with skepticism. During her leadership bid she was called humble and unpretentious, decent, smart, a fast learner, calm, competent, tough, disciplined, and focused. However, despite these assessments, journalists, columnists, and party pundits alike seemed to compete for innovative ways of labelling what they perceived to be her many inadequacies. Stronach was called a "blank slate" and judged as unqualified, uninspired, unconvincing, and unimpressive. Both newspapers frequently used the phrase "highly scripted political neophyte" to emphasize that Stronach was new to the political game (despite the fact that she had previously attended party conventions and had connections to many prominent politicians). Some columnists suggested Stronach was a "little more than a cardboard cut-out fronting the ambitions of her backroom campaigners,"[53] who, by implication, were the experienced and knowledgeable male party elites. Similarly, throughout the coverage of her floor-crossing the media emphasized this image of dependency by focusing on the advice she received from former Ontario Liberal premier David Peterson and her late-night secret dinner meeting with Paul Martin. Perhaps most illustrative of the consensus among journalists that Stronach had little political independence was their focus on what her boyfriend, Conservative MP Peter McKay, thought about her defection, rather than on the explanations she herself gave for her actions.

The suggestion that during her political career Belinda Stronach was being manipulated by powerful backroom boys to serve as a front or as an advertising gimmick for their political parties is not at odds with other messages that are implicitly conveyed with celebrity coverage. It is the political equivalent of using Madonna to sell shampoo or Celine Dion to sell cars. Such celebrities are employed for their star quality, not for their ability to substantively assess the product they are endorsing. This type of coverage enabled columnists to concur with the Toronto street performer whose song deemed Belinda Stronach to be "better than Viagra" for a party in need of a lift while at the same time allowing a *National Post* columnist to express the opinion that he could "think of few examples of a candidate so signally lacking in . . . [the] political, professional or intellectual qualifications . . . to be Prime Minister."[54] In essence, the national newspapers were advancing an intensely essentialist proposition: while a young, attractive woman could use her sex appeal to sell the party to voters, she was by nature unqualified for political life or leadership.

Of particular concern was the fact that her celebrity status allowed the press to employ a tabloid-like approach to their coverage of her defection to the Liberals; they focused on Stronach the woman, rather than on Stronach the politician. This celebrity focus gave journalists the freedom to frame her decision to leave the Conservatives in terms of personal goals and ambition rather than political ideas and values. Stronach was presented as an attractive, glamorous woman who "chose power over love," as a *Globe* editorial put it.[55] She demonstrated "an uncommon interest in power," and acted like an "ambitious little rich girl who didn't get her own way for once and flounced out of the party in a fit of pique."[56] *Post* columnist Don Martin, who literally wrote the book about Belinda Stronach (Martin, 2006), expressed outrage at Stronach's behaviour: "The personal cost of her high-fashion turncoating was so high, in terms of losing a party and boyfriend, you want to believe she was driven by altruistic national concerns instead of merely a raw personal ambition clogging the empty space where her cold heart used to beat."[57] This allegedly shocking display of "naked ambition"[58] was unseemly for a woman to possess, yet it fit with the dangerous and not-to-be-trusted femme fatale image that the media were creating for her.

All in all, the popularization and personalization of Belinda Stronach by the media served to create an image of her as either a silver-screen starlet who showed her party to advantage but lacked the substance to be able to contribute to its debates, or as a modern Mata Hari who was prepared to betray her colleagues for her own personal gain. Neither characterization was true, and neither aided in her efforts to be viewed as a legitimate politician.

CONCLUSION

As Duerst-Lahti and Kelly (1995, p. 24) observe, politics "has historically borne an explicitly masculine identity." Because male leadership is normalized and unquestioned, females who aspire to political leadership uproot entrenched gendered assumptions. As a result, "women who are considered feminine will be judged incompetent" (Jamieson, 1995, p. 16). National newspaper coverage of Belinda Stronach illustrates the sexist double-bind confronting politically ambitious young women. While Stronach's political career received a plethora of media attention, a considerable amount of it scrutinized her looks, wardrobe, sexual attractiveness, and personal life while mocking her leadership aspirations and deriding her qualifications for political office. Press coverage of her leadership race and her defection to the Liberal party confirms both the intensely performative nature of gender in political spaces and the tendency of the media to normalize male leadership. It also demonstrates the media's willingness to resolve the cognitive dissonance produced by a female interloper in a "man's world" by playing up her femininity and framing her in a way that fits with traditional female roles in society (Robinson & Saint-Jean, 1991). In doing so, the press uses a variety of discursive techniques to remind readers that the female politician is, first and foremost, female (Trimble & Arscott, 2003, p. 93), subtly and sometimes not so subtly implying that these women would be more appropriately found in the private world of the home and family than in the public world of politics.

This tendency is accentuated by the overlay of a celebrity frame to female politicians. Such a frame disrupts the distinction between popular culture and entertainment and the more serious business of politics, making it possible for coverage to focus on a politician's personal life and public appearance and to downplay their substantive policy positions. Through the combination of personalizing discourses that act as de-qualification devices by situating the politician firmly in the domestic realm and a popularizing focus that presumes that this private experience is of interest to an expectant audience, the news media highlight the incongruity of a celebrity woman in the political world.

Media Journal Assignments

1. Examine your local paper's entertainment page over a three-day period. How are female "celebrities" portrayed? How does this portrayal compare to the coverage of male celebrities? Discuss and provide examples where possible.

2. Analyze your local paper's treatment of female candidates during the last municipal, provincial, or federal election campaign. How much attention are they given? Are they visible only because they are viewed as novelties? Are they treated in the same manner as men? If not, what are the differences? (You may have to use microfiche or databases like Factiva to access these articles.) Discuss and provide examples.

Endnotes

1. We wish to thank University of Alberta Ph.D. students Laura Way and Amee Barber for their expert and conscientious research assistance on this project.

2. Don Martin, "Always the Possibility of a Comeback," *National Post*, April 12, 2007, p. A5.

3. Prior to her entering the Conservative leadership race Stronach had been mentioned in various news stories about her role as a patron for fashion designer Joeffer Caoc in the late 1990s, her society marriage to Norwegian Olympic speedskater Johann Olav Koss on New Year's Eve 1999, or her role as one of Canada's up-and-coming businesswomen. None of these activities, however, made her a commonly recognized household name.

4. Coding of all news stories about the leadership race was completed by one of the authors based on a detailed coding instrument. To test for inter-coder reliability, 20 percent of the news stories from each newspaper were selected randomly for coding by an independent researcher. Inter-coder reliability averaged 93 percent for the *Globe and Mail* and 91 percent for the *National Post*, thus indicating a more than acceptable level of agreement across all coding categories. Coding of news stories about the defections was completed by a research assistant, with one of the authors completing the cross-coding, determining that reliability averaged 97 percent for the *Globe and Mail* and 94 percent for the *National Post*.

5. Clement won 10 percent of the votes. Stephen Harper won the race on the first ballot with 55 percent of the votes.

6. Roy MacGregor, "Canada waits to hear from the new 'It Girl' of the political right, Belinda Stronach," *Globe and Mail*, January 17, 2004, p. A4.

7. The news value of an event or issue is assessed by editors based on its prominence, proximity, timeliness, conflict, or unusualness (Scharrer, 2002, p. 395).

8. Roy MacGregor, "An uneven but compelling performance," *Globe and Mail*, January 21, 2004, p. A1.

9. Margaret Wente, "Belinda lives and works in a world that Daddy built," *Globe and Mail*, January 20, 2004, p. A17.

10. One news story referred to Harper's suit, and, in another story, the columnist pronounced Harper "handsome."

11. See Allana Mitchell, "'Magna spice' plays gender card," *Globe and Mail*, March 17, 2005, p. A5.

12. Don Martin, "I don't think we should attack wealth, success," *National Post*, January 28, 2004, p. A7; Roy MacGregor, "Canada waits to hear from the new 'It Girl' of the political right," *Globe and Mail*, January 17, 2004, p. A4.

13. Don Martin, "I don't think we should attack wealth, success," *National Post*, January 28, 2004, p. A7.

14. Campbell Clark and Brian Laghi, "Martin's white knight: Stronach's switch may be enough to save the Liberal government," *Globe and Mail*, May 18, 2005, p. A1.

15. Anne Dawson, "Blonde bombshell: Defection gives Grits vote edge," *National Post*, May 18, 2005, p. A1.

16. Siri Agrell, "Just as good as hockey for pub crowd: Fans split on result," *National Post*, May 20, 2005, p. A4.

17. Sheldon Alberts, "Stronach's defection 'political play of the week,' CNN commentator says," *National Post*, May 21, 2005, p. A8.

18. Campbell Clark, "Defection reinforces public's views; Stronach fails to win converts with move, Strategic Counsel/Globe/CTV poll finds," *Globe and Mail*, May 19, 2005, p. A4.

19. Simon Beck, "Foreign currency traders ask: Who is Belinda?" *Globe and Mail*, May 21, 2005, p. B2.

20. Terence Corcoran, "Bump and grind," *National Post*, May 18, 2005, p. FP23; Eric Reguly, "Stronach's competition credo," *Globe and Mail*, May 19, 2005, p. B2.

21. Rex Murphy, "Harper may be the real winner," *Globe and Mail*, May 21, 2005, p. A19.

22. Andrew Duffy, "She's not the first political turncoat," *National Post*, May 18, 2005, p. A4.

23. John Ivison, "Spring nuptials in a heartless machine," *National Post*, May 18, 2005, p. A2; Melissa Loeng and Mark Kennedy, "The 'old friend' who made the match: David Peterson: A chance meeting at Toronto gala culminated in dinner at 24 Sussex," *National Post*, May 18, 2005, p. A3.

24. See n. 15, above.

25. Simon Doyle, "'The heart's got to heal,' MacKay says: Had no idea: Tory MP goes home to the farm to lick his wounds," *National Post*, May 19, 2005, p. A6; "The eyes have it as former lovers face off: Awkward glances and jeers in a tense day in the House," *National Post*, May 20, 2005, p. A8.

26. Bruce Garvey, "A wannabe's latest ego trip," *National Post*, May 18, 2005, p. A22.

27. Anne Kingston, "MacKay has served his purpose: In last boyfriend duty, he informed leader of decision," *National Post*, May 18, 2005, p. A5.

28. Margaret Wente, "Sex, lies and audiotape; Before we leave this week's national soap opera to return to our regularly scheduled programming, test your knowledge with this current-affairs quiz," *Globe and Mail*, May 21, 2005, p. A10; John Ivison, "You're Bard—the lot of you: Tragi-comedy on the Hill worthy of Shakespeare," *National Post*, May 19, 2005, p. A7.

29. Margaret Wente, "Martin's white knight; Between love, business and ambition, love generally winds up third," *Globe and Mail*, May 18, 2005, p. A1.

30. Jane Taber, "MacKay 'terribly badly' hurt, Harper says; Stronach wined, dined by the PM while boyfriend attended fundraiser," *Globe and Mail*, May 18, 2005, p. A7.

31. Shawna Richer, "Belinda Stronach's full 48 hours; MacKay pleaded with his lover into wee hours," *Globe and Mail*, May 19, 2005, p. A1.

32. Grant Robertson, "'Peter taking it pretty hard,' Harper says: Goes Underground," *National Post*, May 18, 2005, p. A5.

33. Simon Doyle, "'The heart's got to heal," MacKay says: Had no idea: Tory MP goes home to the farm to lick his wounds," *National Post*, May 19, 2005, p. A6.

34. Simon Doyle, "The eyes have it as former lovers face off: Awkward glances and jeers in a tense day in the House," *National Post*, May 20, 2005, p. A8.

35. Jane Taber, "'Material Girl' latest to do capital dance," *Globe and Mail*, May 21, 2005, p. A6; Anne Trueman, "After campaigning in Labrador today, MacKay will return to his 'loyal' dog," *National Post*, May 21, 2005, p. A6.

36. "*National Post* team offers Mr. MacKay a little over-the-top feedback," *National Post*, May 19, 2005, p. A6.

37. Judith Timson, "Naked Ambition may be taboo for women, but guts count," *Globe and Mail*, May 19, 2005, p. A7.

38. Christie Blatchford, "Even for Liberals, 'gutsy' is a bit too much," *Globe and Mail,* May 18, 2005, p. A8; Katherine Harding, "Stronach a traitor, westerners say," *Globe and Mail*, May 18, 2005, p. A9; Tim Naumetz, "Female Grit MPs Condemn Insults," *National Post*, May 19, 2005, p. A6; Ruby Dhalla, "Criticism is acceptable. Sexism is not," *National Post*, May 19, 2005, p. A20.

39. Judith Timson, "Naked Ambition may be taboo for women, but guts count." *Globe and Mail*, May 19, 2005, p. A7.

40. John Ivison, "Defection of a 'small c Liberal,'" *National Post*, February 7, 2006, p. A6.

41. Jane Taber and Steven Chase, "Reynolds brokered Emerson's right turn," *Globe and Mail*, February 7, 2006, p. A1.

42. Sarah Hampton, "Life with Father," *Globe and Mail*, April 23, 2007, p. L3.

43. Lysiane Gagnon, "What was Mulroney thinking?" *Globe and Mail*, February 9, 2004, p. A11.

44. Campbell Clark and Brian Laghi, "Martin's White Knight: Stronach's switch may be enough to save the Liberal government," *Globe and Mail*, May 18, 2004, p. A1.

45. *National Post*, "The Belinda, and the damage done," May 18, 2005, p. A20.

46. Campbell Clark and Brian Laghi, "Martin's White Knight: Stronach's switch may be enough to save the Liberal government," *Globe and Mail*, May 18, 2004, p. A1.

47. *National Post*, "The Belinda, and the damage done," May 18, 2005, p. A20.

48. Margaret Wente, "Martin's white knight: Between love, business and ambition, love generally winds up third," *Globe and Mail*, May 18, 2005, p. A1.

49. Ibid.

50. Jane Taber, "MacKay 'terribly badly' hurt, Harper says; Stronach wined, dined by the PM while boyfriend attended fundraiser," *Globe and Mail*, May 18, 2005, p. A7; Simon Doyle, "'The heart's got to heal," MacKay says: Had no idea: Tory MP goes home to the farm to lick his wounds," *National Post*, May 19, 2005, p. A6.

51. *National Post*, "The Belinda, and the damage done," May 18, 2005, p. A20.

52. Jane Taber, "'Material Girl' latest to do capital dance," *Globe and Mail*, May 21, 2005, p. A6.

53. Brian Laghi, "Stronach strives to dismiss argument she lacks substance," *Globe and Mail*, March 6, 2004, p. A10.

54. Andrew Coyne, "Stronach is not remotely qualified to be PM," *National Post*, March 6, 2004, p. A18.

55. *Globe and Mail*, "Friend or foe? Both," May 19, 2005, p. A18.

56. John Ivison, "Spring nuptials in a heartless machine," *National Post*, May 18, 2005, p. A2.

57. Don Martin, "All up to crusader and quitter," *National Post*, May 19, 2005, p. A1.

58. Judith Timson, "Naked Ambition may be taboo for women, but guts count." *Globe and Mail*, May 19, 2005, p. A7; Tom Blackwell and Siri Agrell, "Stronach stuns prominent Tory friends: 'It's obviously about naked ambition rather than public policy or principle," *National Post*, May 18, 2005, p. A4.

References

Aday, Sean & James Devitt. 2001. "Style over Substance: Newspaper Coverage of Elizabeth Dole's Presidential Bid." *Harvard International Journal of Press/Politics* 6 (2): 52–73.

Berlanstein, Lenard. 2004. "Historicizing and Gendering Celebrity Culture: Famous Women in Nineteenth-Century France." *Journal of Women's History* 16 (4): 65–91.

Corner, John R. 2000. "Mediated Persona and Political Culture: Dimensions of Structure and Process." *European Journal of Cultural Studies* 3 (3): 386–402.

Delacourt, Susan. 2007. "Heiress found life as MP 'tough.'" *Toronto Star*, April 12, A1.

Devitt, James. 1999. *Framing Gender on the Campaign Trail: Women's Executive Leadership and the Press.* Washington, D.C.: A Report for the Women's Leadership Fund.

Duerst-Lahti, Georgina & Rita Mae Kelly. 1995. "On Governance, Leadership and Gender." In *Gender Power, Leadership and Governance*, ed. Georgina Duerst-Lahti and Rita Mae Kelly, 11–37. Ann Arbor: University of Michigan Press.

Gilmartin, Patricia. 2001. "Still the Angel in the Household: Political Cartoons of Elizabeth Dole's Presidential Campaign." *Women & Politics* 22 (4): 51–67.

Gingras, François-Pierre. 1995. "Daily Male Delivery: Women and Politics in the Daily Newspapers." In *Gender and Politics in Contemporary Canada*, ed. François-Pierre Gingras, 191–207. Toronto: Oxford University Press.

Gundle, Stephen & Clino T. Castelli. 2006. *The Glamour System.* New York: Palgrave Macmillan.

Hampton, Sarah. 2007. "Life with father." *Globe and Mail*, April 23, L3.

Heldman, Caroline, Susan J. Carroll, & Stephanie Olson. 2005. "'She Brought Only a Skirt': Print Media Coverage of Elizabeth Dole's Bid for the Republican Presidential Nomination." *Political Communication* 22 (3): 315–35.

Jamieson, Kathleen Hall. 1995. *Beyond the Double Bind: Women and Leadership.* New York: Oxford University Press.

Kahn, Kim Fridkin. 1994. "The Distorted Mirror: Press Coverage of Women Candidates for Statewide Office." *Journal of Politics* 56 (1): 154–73.

Kahn, Kim Fridkin & Edie N. Goldenberg. 1991. "Women Candidates in the News: An Examination of Gender Differences in U.S. Senate Campaign Coverage." *Public Opinion Quarterly* 55 (2): 180–99.

Martin, Don. 2006. *Belinda: The Political and Private Life of Belinda Stronach.* Toronto: Key Porter Books.

———. 2007. "Always the possibility of a comeback." *National Post*, April 12, A5.

Muir, Kathie. 2005. "Media Darlings and Falling Stars: Celebrity and the Reporting of Political Leaders." *Westminster Papers in Communication and Culture* 2 (2): 54–71.

Neuman, W. Lawrence. 2000. *Social Research Methods: Qualitative and Quantitative Approaches.* 4th ed. Toronto: Allyn and Bacon.

Robinson, Gertrude & Armande Saint-Jean. 1991. "Women Politicians and Their Media Coverage: A Generational Analysis." In *Women in Canadian Politics: Toward Equity in Representation*, ed. Kathy Megyery, 127–69. Vol. 6 of *Research Studies for the Royal Commission on Electoral Reform and Party Financing.* Toronto: Dundurn Press.

Robinson, Gertrude & Armande Saint-Jean. 1995. "The Portrayal of Women Politicians in the Media: Political Implications." In *Gender and Politics in Contemporary Canada*, ed. François-Pierre Gingras, 176–90. Toronto: Oxford University Press.

Ross, Karen. 1995. "Gender and Party Politics: How the Press Reported the Labour Leadership Campaign." *Media, Culture & Society* 17: 499–509.

———. 2002. *Women, Politics, Media: Uneasy Relations in Comparative Perspective.* Cresskill, N.J.: Hampton Press.

Scharrer, Erica. 2002. "An 'Improbable Leap': A Content Analysis of Newspaper Coverage of Hillary Clinton's Transition from First Lady to Senate Candidate." *Journalism Studies* 3 (3): 393–406.

Schwartzenberg, R.G. 1977. *L'état spectacle: essai sur et contre le star system en politique*. Paris: Flammarion.

Street, John. 1997. *Politics & Popular Culture*. Cambridge: Polity Press.

————. 2001. *Mass Media, Politics, Democracy*. New York: Palgrave.

————. 2004. "Celebrity Politicians: Popular Culture and Political Representation." *British Journal of Politics and International Relations* 6 (4): 435–52.

Taras, David. 1999. *Power and Betrayal in the Canadian Media*. Peterborough: Broadview Press.

Trimble, Linda & Jane Arscott. 2003. *Still Counting: Women in Politics across Canada*. Peterborough: Broadview Press.

Turner, Graeme. 2004. *Understanding Celebrity*. London: Sage.

van Acker, Elizabeth. 2003. "Portrayals of Politicians and Women's Interests: Saviours, 'Sinners,' and 'Stars.'" Paper presented to the Australasian Political Studies Association Conference, University of Tasmania, Hobart.

van Dijk, Teun A. 1991. *Racism and the Press*. London: Routledge.

van Zoonen, Liesbet. 2005. *Entertaining the Citizen: When Politics and Popular Culture Converge*. New York: Rowman & Littlefield.

————. 2006. "The Personal, the Political and the Popular: A Woman's Guide to Celebrity Politics." *European Journal of Cultural Studies* 9 (3): 287–301.

West, Darrell & John Orman. 2002. *Celebrity Politics*. New Jersey: Prentice Hall.

Newspaper Articles Cited as Primary Sources

Note: Articles cited in this study are listed here in chronological order of appearance by newspaper, date, and page number. Where more than one article appears on a given date and page, the articles are cited in alphabetical order by author.

Globe and Mail

MacGregor, Roy. 2004. "Canada waits to hear from the new 'It Girl' of the political right, Belinda Stronach." January 17, A4.

Wente, Margaret. 2004. "Belinda lives and works in a world that Daddy built." January 20, A17.

MacGregor, Roy. 2004. "An uneven but compelling performance." January 21, A1.

Gagnon, Lysiane. 2004. "What was Mulroney thinking?" February 9, A11.

Laghi, Brian. 2004. "Stronach strives to dismiss argument she lacks substance." March 6, A10.

Mitchell, Allana. 2005. "'Magna spice' plays gender card." March 17, A5.

Clark, Campbell, and Brian Laghi. 2005. "Martin's white knight: Stronach's switch may be enough to save the Liberal government." May 18, A1.

Taber, Jane & Karen Howlett. 2005. "How it happened: Seeds may have been planted by summons to see Harper over controversial remarks." May 18, A1.

Wente, Margaret. 2005. "Martin's white knight; Between love, business and ambition, love generally winds up third." May 18, A1.

Taber, Jane. 2005. "MacKay 'terribly badly' hurt, Harper says; Stronach wined, dined by the PM while boyfriend attended fundraiser." May 18, A7.

Blatchford, Christie. 2005. "Even for Liberals, 'gutsy' is a bit too much." May 18, A8.

Harding, Katherine. 2005. "Stronach a traitor, westerners say; Defection adding to the feelings of alienation, professor says." May 18, A9.

Globe and Mail. 2005. "Friend or foe? Both." May 19, A1.

Richer, Shawna. 2005. "Belinda Stronach's full 48 hours; MacKay pleaded with his lover into wee hours." May 19, A1.

Clark, Campbell. 2005. "Defection reinforces public's views; Stronach fails to win converts with move, Strategic Counsel/Globe/CTV poll finds." May 19, A4.

Galloway, Gloria. 2005. "Harper drove Stronach from Tories, friend says." May 19, A6.

Timson, Judith. 2005. "Naked Ambition may be taboo for women, but guts count." May 19, A7.

Reguly, Eric. 2005. "Stronach's competition credo." May 19, B2.

Immen, Wallace. 2005. "Lessons learned from Belinda's flip; Belinda Stronach's defection offers insights on the right and wrong ways to make a career move." May 20, C1.

Taber, Jane. 2005. "'Material Girl' latest to do capital dance." May 21, A6.

Wente, Margaret. 2005. "Sex, lies and audiotape; Before we leave this week's national soap opera to return to our regularly scheduled programming, test your knowledge with this current-affairs quiz." May 21, A10.

Murphy, Rex. 2005. "Harper may be the real winner." May 21, A19.

Beck, Simon. 2005. "Foreign currency traders ask: Who is Belinda?" May 21, B2.

Taber, Jane & Steven Chase. 2006. "Reynolds brokered Emerson's right turn." February 7, A1.

National Post

Martin, Don. 2004. "I don't think we should attack wealth, success." January 28, A7.

Coyne, Andrew. 2004. "Stronach is not remotely qualified to be PM." March 6, A18.

Dawson, Anne. 2005. "Blonde bombshell: Defection gives Grits vote edge." May 18, A1.

Ivison, John. 2005. "Spring nuptials in a heartless machine." May 18, A2.

Loeng, Melissa & Mark Kennedy. 2005. "The 'old friend' who made the match: David Peterson: A chance meeting at Toronto gala culminated in dinner at 24 Sussex." May 18, A3.

Blackwell, Tom & Siri Agrell. 2005. "Stronach stuns prominent Tory friends: 'It's obviously about naked ambition rather than public policy or principle." May 18, A4.

Duffy, Andrew. 2005. "She's not the first political turncoat." May 18, A4.

Kingston, Anne. 2005. "MacKay has served his purpose: In last boyfriend duty, he informed leader of decision." May 18, A5.

Robertson, Grant. 2005. "'Peter taking it pretty hard,' Harper says: Goes Underground." May 18, A5.

National Post. 2005. "The Belinda, and the damage done." May 18, A20.

Garvey, Bruce. 2005. "A wannabe's latest ego trip." May 18, A22.

Shecter, Barbara. 2005. "Stronach's move gives banks hope: Merger guidelines could pass." May 18, FP7.

Corcoran, Terence. 2005. "Bump and grind." May 18, FP23.

Dawson, Anne & Allan Woods. 2005. "Drama on the hill: Day of political life & death." May 19, A1.

Martin, Don. 2005. "All up to crusader and quitter." May 19, A1.

Doyle, Simon. 2005. "'The heart's got to heal,' MacKay says: Had no idea: Tory MP goes home to the farm to lick his wounds." May 19, A6.

National Post. 2005. "*National Post* team offers Mr. MacKay a little over-the-top feedback." May 19, A6.

Naumetz, Tim. 2005. "Female Grit MPs Condemn Insults." May 19, A6.

Ivison, John. 2005. "You're Bard—the lot of you: Tragi-comedy on the Hill worthy of Shakespeare." May 19, A7.

Dhalla, Ruby. 2005. "Criticism is acceptable. Sexism is not." May 19, A20.

Agrell, Siri. 2005. "Just as good as hockey for pub crowd: Fans split on result." May 20, A4.

Doyle, Simon. 2005. "The eyes have it as former lovers face off: Awkward glances and jeers in a tense day in the House." May 20, A8.

Martin, Don. 2005. "Martin's reign of error." May 21, A1.

Trueman, Anne. 2005. "After campaigning in Labrador today, MacKay will return to his 'loyal' dog." May 21, A6.

Alberts, Sheldon. 2005. "Stronach's defection 'political play of the week,' CNN commentator says." May 21, A8.

Ivison, John. 2006. "Defection of a 'small c Liberal.'" February 7, A6.

Chapter 5

When the Message is the Meaning: Government Advertising and the Branding of States

Jonathan Rose and Hugh Mellon

INTRODUCTION

Communication is essential to government. Karl Deutsch described it as the nerves of government—the way in which governments sense and feel the outside world. As the pace of life quickens and citizens feel less directly engaged by politics, there is a growing trend for governments to reach out through organized advertising campaigns. Exercise more, join the military, show up to vote, consider the government's definition of this or that issue—all of these and more involve government advertising. Advertising is purposive communication in that it aims to educate, persuade, redefine a problem, and/or encourage a citizen response. With modern polling and communications specialists advising governments, advertising is becoming a major tool of government communication, and perhaps its most ubiquitous form. While the Gomery Commission (discussed in Chapter 16) spotlights the relationship between advertising agencies and government, it is worth remembering that, as a vehicle of communication, government advertising has been around for a very long time.

In answer to the question "Why advertise?" the federal government responds that it "has a duty to tell its citizens about its initiatives, decisions, and priorities. Government organizations advertise to inform Canadians and non-Canadians about their rights and responsibilities, government policies, programs, services, and initiatives, or about dangers and risks to public health, safety or the environment, such as tobacco cessation or climate change" (Canada, 2003, p. 9). In other words, advertising is an important part of creating legitimacy for government policies. If the government wants compliance with a policy (such as filing taxes) or to change behaviour (such as reducing our carbon footprint), advertising ensures an unmediated message to citizens.

In the past, parliamentary traditions saw members of Parliament, speeches by leaders, and political-party membership as the primary conduits of information between governments and citizens. Yet communication demands have grown and the complexity of issues like tax reform, the environment, and costly health-care choices challenges the time and knowledge of even the most diligent elected legislator. Political-party membership is now limited to a small minority and leaders' speeches often go unread and unwatched. Meanwhile, governments have access to modern polling techniques and communication strategists. Access to these professionals, either within government or through contractual arrangements with private-sector firms, allows the careful organization of coordinated advertising plans. Hence advertising may serve to a) educate; b) redefine a problem; c) shift public opinion; d) supplement the work of elected members; e) solicit public input; and/or f) shape external perceptions of Canada and its government. It may also be argued that advertising serves the purpose of contributing to partisan attacks by a prime minister or premier's political party.

In their portrait of the workings of the Chrétien government, Greenspon and Wilson-Smith emphasize the importance attached to communication planning in the development of the annual government budget. As Finance minister, Paul Martin was noted for his heavy reliance on pollsters and communications advisors. "In the old days, communications had been viewed internally as a necessary evil, peripheral to the main functions of the department . . . Now the communications function began at the front end of the policy process. If it couldn't be communicated, if it didn't fit into a communications plan, it never got near the door" (Greenspon & Wilson-Smith, 1996, p. 271). Communications planning also figured prominently in the Chrétien government's handling of the national-unity file, but with disastrous results, as the Auditor General's Office subsequently uncovered extensive waste, lack of proper controls, and confusion over political-bureaucratic responsibilities.

The government's frequency of reliance on advertising bears emphasizing, for it has been around for a long time. In fact, advertising has been an important arsenal in the apparatus of the state for the past 100 years. In the late nineteenth and early twentieth centuries, the federal government used advertising to lure new immigrants to Canada (see Rose, 2003, p. 156). "Free land clubs" was the slogan used to entice would-be immigrants to a country whose winters were described as "bracing" and "invigorating." Early settlers facing Canadian winters in a time before modern advances in clothing and building materials may be forgiven for questioning the enthusiastic descriptions of Canadian winters. (Clearly government hyperbole in advertising is not limited to the twentieth century.)

This chapter is designed to lead students and readers to reflect on the range of government advertising, its capabilities and potential dangers, and the possible regulation of its use. Since it is such a major means of government communication, we should have a greater understanding of its dimensions. The chapter pays special attention to particular sets of debates within the field of government advertising. One of these involves the issue of branding, which marries advertising to the development of a brand image for the advertising jurisdiction, whether it is a city, a province, or a country. A second is concerned with the effectiveness of government advertising, although in practice these effects are often difficult to measure. A third focuses attention on the contribution of logos and brands to brand formation and differentiation. A fourth topic deals with the recognition of emerging government-advertising trends in the world's largest media market, namely the United States, which at present is engaged in huge advertising strategies. Finally, there is a discussion of the parameters necessary for the regulation of government advertising. Here, for reasons of space and time, attention will be directed to two widely discussed cases, namely the Gomery Inquiry into the advertising excesses of the Chrétien government and the emerging regulatory set-up in Ontario, which is an innovator in attempting to set ground rules for regulating government advertising.

RECENT TRENDS IN GOVERNMENT ADVERTISING: THE STATE AS BRAND

We are probably all aware that advertising involves efforts at persuasion and the provision of information, but these objectives are only part of the story. Also of great importance is the manner of shaping and presenting the object whose promotion is desired. In commercial advertising, this can be many things—a car, a type of perfume or alcohol, or frozen pasta. With governments there are similar pressures at work. Something is being promoted, but what is it? How can it be made more appealing? More attractive, stylish, cool, or engaging? This brings us to the concepts of government and state branding. Here, advertisers, pollsters, wordsmiths, and communications gurus work to refine a brand for the jurisdiction they represent. Branding thus involves several key elements. First is the preparatory gathering of intelligence on how people perceive the government, country, or jurisdiction in question. What would make the jurisdiction more appealing to investors, citizens, tourists, etc.? Who is it that the jurisdiction wishes to win over? All of these factors are added to the mix in the search for an appealing brand. This process then brings together the research on current attitudes, desired market sectors and audiences, and communications objectives, in hopes of crafting a brand image with presence and appeal.

Politicians are clearly aware that the nation-state needs to create an image that has favourable connotations. Valéry Giscard d'Estaing, former president of France, has suggested that Europe needs to rebrand itself, perhaps even changing its name to the United States of Europe. "We need a name which gets across our brand," he said (Rotzoll & Haefner, 1996, p. 2). Nelson Mandela's branding of South Africa as a "rainbow nation" also speaks to the effort of leaders to change perceptions. A rainbow, with its mixture of different colours, is a perfect metaphor for post-apartheid South Africa, and was embraced by opposition leaders and the media as an appropriate symbol for the new nation. Canada has a national tourism agency that works to shape perceptions of Canada and to foster a sense that Canada is an attractive destination. Even small nations have felt the need to market themselves. The kingdom of Jordan has embarked on a path of state marketing. King Abdullah himself chairs an organization called "Jordan First," which is the slogan of the new Jordan. Belgium, too, has joined the fray. Prime Minister Guy Verhofstadt has hired a company to change its public reputation after scandals involving child pornography, corruption, and tainted chicken. Peter van Ham writes that "in an attempt to clear the air, Belgium has decided to introduce a new logo and hip colors and will sport the cool Internet suffix '.be' as its international symbol" (van Ham, 2003, p. 2). Additionally, the country has used Virgin as its model, presenting it as an example of a small company that "isn't big but you see it everywhere you look" (ibid.). Elsewhere, tiny Estonia has changed its label to "pre-EU" or even "Scandinavian" instead of identifying as a "Baltic" state or a "Post-Soviet" state. Just how did such a situation arise and what are the implications of national governments marketing themselves in the same way that companies market soap or hamburgers?

Marketing and brand development may on occasion involve challenges to, or critiques of, rivals. States have used marketing to create positive impressions, but the roots of marketing to create negative impressions also run deep. Ying Fan argues that the tendency to portray other nations less favourably is a much more common technique than positive marketing:

> In political marketing, manipulating the images of one's own country against those of enemy countries has long been used as a powerful weapon in propaganda, from the evil Soviet Empire in the Cold War to the recent labelling of three countries as the "axis of evil." A name could also be coined to brand a region: for example, Hong Kong, Taiwan, Korea and Singapore were widely referred to as the Four Dragons in the 1980s. (Fan, 2006, p. 7)

The roots of state branding can be found in the early twentieth century. It was then that the historical and deep connections between governments, political parties, and advertising firms were formed. In Canada, Reg Whitaker asserts that links between ad agencies and the Liberal Party were forged after World War I. Whitaker writes that if "experts could package and sell a war, presumably they could package and sell the Liberal party" (1977, p. 222), and, in a foreshadowing of the examination by the Gomery Inquiry in 2005 of connections between the governing Liberal Party and advertising agencies, Whitaker goes on to claim that "in Canada, government and political advertising are inextricably linked" (p. 219). As is the case with most developments in modern political communications, the United States was one of the early proponents of using public relations and spin to change public opinion about private as well as public goods. In the 1930s and 1940s George Gallup urged the government to extol the power of opinion polling to counter the effect of entrenched interests and provide itself with guidance. Gallup presented polling as a democratizing influence and a tool of accountability (see Robinson, 1999, pp. 40–41), and, in doing so, established the dependency of modern governments on private polling firms. In addition to establishing the link between public-relations officials and government, the United States was also one of the first countries to eagerly embrace the connection between political parties and advertising. This shouldn't be a surprise. At present, the United States spends more money on advertising than 66 other nations combined, including all of the other members of the G7 (Rotzoll & Haefner, 1996, p. 2). In the political realm, advertising is almost the sole currency. For example, the cost of mounting a Senatorial campaign, much of which is spent on advertising, can average over $5 million (Newman, 1999, p. 14). In the 2008 presidential election, Democratic Party candidate Hilary Clinton was expected to spend $50 million on advertising for the nomination and election (Schouten, 2007).

The advertising of government plans may invite questions as to the boundaries between advertising for the public good and advertising for the partisan advantage of the governing party. Determining how and where this line should be drawn is one of the most challenging tasks in the field of public-sector advertising. Once in power, political parties have an added advertising arsenal at their disposal. The intersection between political-party marketing and communication planning/state branding suggests at least two things about the discourse of politics. First, that a study of modern politics cannot be divorced from an understanding of the role of the use of symbols, icons, and logos in the organization and management of the communications of political actors. Second, that there are legitimate fears about the possibility of partisan advantage, necessitating regulation to ensure fairness and equality of opportunity for all political players.

Another issue of concern is the relationship between advertised messages and the behaviour of political leaders. When there is dissonance, cynicism erupts. The public grows weary of seeing politicians as empty vessels for prepackaged messages. A infamously leaked memo from Philip Gould, Tony Blair's strategy and polling advisor, admits that the public saw the Labour Party as "spin, no substance" (Scammell, 2003, p. 133). Ronald Reagan's speech writer Peggy Noonan argues that cynicism is a result of speech writers who are paid to write sound bites and wrap speeches around them (Noonan, 1990, p. 73). Skilled wordsmiths and media gurus may lose touch with the complexity of reality, and politicians rely heavily on the phrases of others. Roderick Hart (1987) argues that the tremendous increase in the number of speeches that leaders must give necessarily means that we know less about the leaders than we did before the advent of electronic media. According to Bruce Newman (1999), all of this creates not only a devaluation of politics, but also, in fact, an abdication of governing.

While there is a well-developed literature on political-party advertising, scholars who study state branding remind us that the advertising of states' behaviour between elections is as noteworthy as party advertising during elections. Unfortunately, the advertising by governments between elections is much less studied. This has tragic consequences, for we need to assess the relation between state advertising and state legitimacy. State legitimacy speaks to public belief and acceptance of the state's right to govern and its work in the common interest of the political community. In cases of both party advertising and government advertising, there is the danger of advertising overwhelming discernment. Kathleen Hall Jamieson argues forcefully that the visual grammar of television is associative and that "a person adept at visualizing claims in dramatic capsules will be able to use television to short-circuit the audience's demand that those claims be dignified with evidence" (Jamieson, 1988, p. 13). Her argument that visual claims are more effective than verbal claims at making weak arguments seem powerful should concern us all.

When applied to the marketing of states, the effect of advertising may be harder to discern, but more invidious than the marketing of consumer products. It is harder to discern because there is no "product" to purchase, no easy way of determining the effectiveness of an advertisement. Our preconceptions of a particular nation-state also influence our encounters with any marketing of that nation-state, compounding the difficulty of measuring the effect of the advertising. Indeed, one of the fundamental problems of the literature concerning advertising's effects is that it is difficult to sepa-rate one's perception of the product from one's own preconceptions. Do we think more positively of the British image because of the marketing of "Cool Britannia," or as result of the media coverage of British subjects, or perhaps as a result of ideas that we already had about the U.K.? Did early settlers to Canada feel better about heavy snow and cold winds in light of the government's promotion of "bracing" and "invigorating" conditions?

Although it is beyond the bounds of this chapter, there is reason to study press reac-tion to government promotional and branding campaigns as well. Are catch-phrases picked up? Are the definitions of problems adopted? These and other questions merit exploration for Kunczik (2003, p. 121), who argues that "as a rule, no precise linkage between commissioned PR activities and what appears in the mass media can be traced. Typically, one can do little more than guess at what suggestions were made, which were expected and how they were implemented. The precise nature of the intervention remains somewhat of a mystery."

One of the most intractable problems in the marketing and advertising literature is whether we can assess the effectiveness of marketing and advertising campaigns. As a form of communication, advertising shapes our sense of values—even if it does not change or affect our buying habits. As Stephen Kline writes, we should see "advertising not as manipulation but as a vehicle for situating . . . brands within established cultural patterns and ideas" (1993, p. 27). In addition, the grammar of advertising invites a certain way of interacting with the world. It does not encourage reflection or deliberation, but rather encourages the application of marketing principles, such as the famous four Ps: product, pricing, promotion, and placement. Paul Rutherford argues that it shouldn't be a surprise, then, "that a writer in *Advertising Age* (28 November 1988) would describe the launch of George Bush as a 'line extension' of the presidency of the renowned Ronald Reagan" (2000, p. 6). Moreover, his son, George W. Bush, has taken the crafting of media events to new heights—or depressing depths. Bush Jr.'s landing on the deck of the aircraft carrier *Abraham Lincoln* and declaring the Iraq War over was not just political theatre. It repre-sented the placement of political leaders among stage props. After September 11, 2001, Bush spoke on Ellis Island in New York, with the Statue of Liberty lit up by three barges of giant Musco lights—the kind used to illuminate sports stadiums. While it was he who was speaking, the real subject was the Statue of Liberty and the values that it has come to symbolize.

One may ask whether these staged events worked. The Iraq War drags tragically onward and the United States has faced international and judicial challenges to its treatment of political prisoners and the alleged excesses of security-force tactics. Meanwhile, media polls suggest voter fatigue and distrust of President Bush's leadership and vision. There is no obvious or well-established means to evaluate the success of such staged events and communications, but there are grounds to critique their relation to serious public debate.

A primary hurdle in the measurement debate is that advertising and branding are not launched into a vacuum where everything that subsequently happens may be charted. Rather, they are propelled into an environment where people meet them with preconceptions and prejudices, and on the basis of their own personal experiences. The impact of years of socialization and the reinforcement of a dominant frame will profoundly affect the symbol that is called to mind when thinking about a state. Repositioning something as complex and, often, contradictory as the image of a nation-state is made even more difficult because of the resistance individuals have to changing long-held perceptions amid the cacophony of messages of persuasion coming at them in today's media environment. Kunczik contends that we select those events that reinforce our preconceptions. He provides as an example the story of how "in September 1947, a six-month propaganda campaign to promote the United Nations was begun in Cincinnati (its slogan was 'Peace begins with the United Nations—the United Nations begins with you'). It was largely unsuccessful because those who paid attention to the message were primarily individuals already interested in and informed about the United Nations" (2003, p. 119).

Another observer, Fan, also expresses concern that political leaders are placing greater emphasis on the value of branding their nations than is warranted by the evidence of its success. He states,

> Nation branding has been vaunted as a panacea—something equivalent to a grand national economic development strategy—desperately needed by developing countries . . . Nation branding is believed to be able to work miracles and solve many of the world's problems, for example the poverty gap between the North and the South. It is undeniable that branding is an extremely powerful tool, but it is equally important to realize that branding is only one part of a marketing strategy which itself is a part of the whole business strategy. Branding will not work if other components of the strategy (finance, R&D, production, distribution) fail to deliver what the customers want. Nation branding is no exception. (Fan, 2006, p. 11)

Nation-states have recently realized this truth. It is easier to try and change perceptions than the material conditions of citizens. In Canada, recent efforts at rebranding the Canadian Forces were met by resistance from focus groups who could not reconcile the past scandals of the Canadian Forces with their apparently new inclusivity (Aubry, 2003, p. 1). Governments persist in believing that if they are successful in changing public opinion based on a revamped logo, they need not change behaviour. A Hollywood film called *The Big Dance*, produced in association with the White House in 2003, is an attempt to show President Bush as a determined and principled leader. Using a medium that has such strong currency among Americans represents the formal merger of Washington's ambitions with the Hollywood entertainment industry (Saunders, 2003). While it is now formalized, the link has existed for years. Arnold Schwarzenegger's candidacy for governor of California blurred the line between politics and entertainment. Ronald Reagan's governorship and presidency did the same. Both make politics and show business inseparable by trading on-screen characters to advance political aspirations.

THE POWER OF LOGOS AND SLOGANS IN BRAND BUILDING

One of the central features of branding campaigns is to identify the product with a logo. Logos are a pivotal way of reinforcing the values of the advertising campaign in one discrete sign. Much of advertising and promotion are attempts to link a symbol to a core value: the Statue of Liberty to freedom, the Mounties to a Canadian approach to nationalism and order, the demise of the Berlin Wall to liberation and the decline of Communism—all are examples of iconic symbols standing for political values. The logo then becomes an essential way of tying that value to the symbol. Moreover, in a landscape cluttered with the debris of advertising signs, logos are an important cultural artifact, providing differentiation from other competing modes of identification.

The logos and slogans of nation-states serve the dual purpose of acting as promotional vehicles with which to compete in the marketplace of nation-states and also as cultural touchstones that function as condensed yet powerful symbols for the nation-states. As such, logos present themselves as a tool for product differentiation as well as an agent of political socialization. Note, for example, the $2.4-million advertising campaign implemented to respond to out-migration and disinterest in Canada. The Manitoba government developed the slogan "Spirited Energy" and coupled it with "advertising that aims to move beyond mosquitoes and cold weather" (Friesen, 2006, p. A5).

As a vehicle of product differentiation, logos of nation-states or political communities are a frequent element of the state's presentation of its character and strategic advantages in a manner designed to be memorable and striking. As this chapter goes to submission, the organizers of the upcoming Vancouver Olympics have unveiled their mascots and slogans in a brightly themed media event. Symbols and slogans are jealously guarded and frequently resorted to. An obvious example of this is the French government's strong protection of the champagne trademark. This is not just confined to nation-states. The city of Toronto developed a $4-million branding strategy designed to "trumpet Toronto's ethnic diversity, imminent expansion of cultural institutions and trendy new entertainment areas." The rebranding exercise was seen an important means of differentiating Toronto from Vancouver's "spectacular urban setting" and Montreal's "European flavour and year round festivals" (Lewington, 2004, p. A13). After the return of Hong Kong to Chinese control, a major campaign was undertaken to retain its market orientation. Hong Kong was dubbed "Asia's World City," and a striking dragon logo was developed (Vines, 2001).

Perhaps the most contemporary example is the aesthetic and political controversy that attended the logo and ad design for the London 2012 Olympics, when the winning logo, selected out of over 1,000 possible designs submitted, was met with a rain of scorn. Tessa Jowell, the Minister for the Olympics, upheld the choice at the ceremony at which the logo was unveiled. "This is not just a marketing logo," she proclaimed, "but a symbol that will become familiar, and instantly recognizable and associated with our Games in so many ways during the next five years" (BBC, 2007).

When logos serve to evoke a culture by acting as a condensed symbol for a nation, city, or state, it should give us reason to pause. Writing of the branding of cities in the Netherlands, Hans Mommaas argues that logos provide "identification, recognition, continuity and collectivity" (Mommaas, 2002, p. 34). The marketplace for automobiles or fast food is crowded, so the Mercedes logo or golden arches are an attempt to sear the brand in the minds of consumers. This is also true of the logos of nation-states. It is almost a cliché to say that globalization has two conflicting tensions, one toward homogenization and the other toward tribalism. Branding expands in significance in an era of globalization where identity and community are up for debate and redefinition.

Students of communication reflect on the contribution of logos and images to the shaping of perceptions and expectations. Government ads encouraging patriotism and military service, for example, lend stature to the men and women of the military and encourage us to think of the ads when military issues are raised. This ignites a further set of speculations. Do we recall ads as shorthand for the values of their messages, and does this make them an incredibly powerful tool? Do advertising images possibly become construed as reality, given their power to burrow their way into people's minds and memories? Why, for example, is it still important to successive Quebec governments that their car licence plates carry a call to remember? For a province that has long argued its historic and social distinctiveness, this reminder serves as a stand-in for the actual act of remembering.

BRANDING AND GOVERNMENT ADVERTISING IN THE UNITED STATES: THE NEW FACE OF PROPAGANDA?

The gap between public attitudes toward the state and a manufactured image of the state can often be too large to be closed by any state-rebranding exercise. Perhaps nowhere was this more clear than in the experience of the United States, where a Sisyphean marketing challenge was given to Charlotte Beers, the first U.S. Undersecretary of State for Public Diplomacy, whose job was to "shape effective messages explaining U.S. policies in new and ongoing issues" (State Department website, 2003). She was hired just days after the U.S. invasion of Afghanistan in October 2001 and given an unprecedented amount of money—over half a billion dollars in 2002—for selling America and its values to the Muslim world in particular (Beers, 2002). She has described the United States as a "beautiful brand" and television as a "fast delivery system" for the American government's message (McKenna, 2003, p. 2). Examining the failure of her efforts might provide some insight into why success of state branding is uncertain.

Many of the techniques used were no more evolved than the propaganda attempts of 60 years earlier. Efforts in Afghanistan such as dropping pamphlets that showed women being beaten by the Taliban or distributing radios that were only able to receive Voice of America failed miserably (see Leonard, 2002, p. 48). Crude tag lines on the pamphlets, such as "Is this the future you want for your women and your children?" did not resonate with an audience whose primary concerns lay elsewhere. Other endeavours, such as the $15-million Shared Values campaign that featured Muslims talking in glowing terms about their life in the United States, were quietly and quickly scrapped by the State Department (McKenna, 2003, p. 2). The goal of the Shared Values campaign was to use advertising to make the argument that the United States was a misunderstood place. The radio, print, and television ads showed Muslims of all ages extolling the virtues of living in the United States. One ad showed a young Lebanese-born woman with her three smiling children at a school softball game saying, "I didn't see any prejudice anywhere in my neighborhood after Sept. 11" (Perlez, 2002). Designed to be broadcast in a number of Islamic countries, the U.S. government found them rejected by nations who would not accept paid programming from a foreign country. The campaign was decried as being "Muslim as apple pie" (Perlez, 2002) by some who thought it did not respond to the perceived problems in U.S. policies, but merely papered them over with ads. In Indonesia, an ally in the "war on terror" and one of the few Islamic nations that has shown support of U.S. policies, the ads were seen as not "relevant to Muslims' concerns" (Murphy, 2003). While perhaps not directly attributable to the ad campaign, according to a U.S. Department of State/Pew Research Center Poll, the percentage of Muslims who viewed the United States favourably had fallen from 75 percent in 1999 to 61 percent in 2002 (Murphy, 2003).

One cannot radically transform impressions of nation-states through branding exercises alone. In the case of the U.S. branding exercise, the target audience was "non-elite" 15-to-59-year-olds (Perlez, 2002) rather than elite opinion leaders, and the vehicle was advertisements—something with which Charlotte Beers, a former ad executive, had some familiarity. The range of opinion among this group, it is fair to say, must be quite broad, and no advertisement will resonate with the entire cohort, especially during a time of upheaval, when opportunity to rethink reality is at a premium. The diversity of beliefs among target audiences is captured by John and Nicholas O'Shaughnessy, who write that "it is not easy for a nation, as opposed to a brand of product, to have a consistent persona because a nation is such a constellation of different images" (2000, p. 60). There are few comparisons in commercial marketing, where the audience is as amorphous and heterogeneous as the one for state branding. Advertising requires knowledge of the target demographic group, as well as repetition of a plausible message. The early efforts from the Office of Public Diplomacy did not seem to pay heed to either of these basic rules.

A further explanation for the failure of U.S. efforts might be found in the difficulty of generating new ideas rather than managing existing ones. Peter van Ham writes,

> Brand management involves the process of cautious, often measured supervision of existing perceptions. In this sense the U.S.A. is considered a "corporate brand" since the U.S.A. (or "America") is not *itself* the primary brand, but the manager of a series of related sub-brands (its art, sports, media and technology, as well as its foreign policy). (2003, p. 433; emphasis in original)

What this suggests is that the branding campaign of the U.S. government failed because it did not manage existing perceptions; rather, it attempted to alter the perceptions of the state.

As van Ham notes, one's perception of "Brand U.S.A." is inextricably linked to what he calls the "sub-brands"—the things around which we form our opinions. Nation-states wish to change the corporate brand, but our affective orientation to nation-states is linked to the substantive manifestations of that brand—its cultural products, such as film, media, art, and sport. To put it in the marketing parlance of John and Nicholas O'Shaughnessy, "It is too difficult to put across a positive image of a nation that emotionally resonates with the consumer sufficiently to affect behavior over the whole range of a nation's products" (2000, p. 63). In Australia, a branding campaign failed because of the inability of any one marketing exercise to reconcile the diverse and competing images of that country. One study of this campaign found that for it "to make sense, there must be some agreement among the people of Australia as to an Australian identity. One can question whether such an agreement exists" (Fischer & Byron, 1997, p. 95).

While governments around the world are engaging in state-branding exercises, there have also been efforts to limit government advertising. The last section of this chapter explores some recent changes to how governments advertise in Canada. As with other aspects of public policy, what we find is that innovation follows allegations of improprieties. The two cases examined below are the changes brought about by the Gomery Inquiry and by reforms enacted at the provincial level in Ontario.

Governments regulate for a variety of reasons. Among them are promotion of desirable behaviour, protection of public safety, rationing of scarce goods, enforcement of rules where something less than the force of criminal sanctions is considered necessary, and cultivation of expertise in vitally important fields such as bank practices or energy supplies. One of the areas marked by increased regulatory attention is the conduct and character of government advertising. The scandalous excesses that provoked the Gomery Inquiry are dealt with elsewhere in this volume (see Chapter 16), but merit attention here as well for the fallout from the Inquiry, which has had a major impact on advertising and its regulation throughout both the federal and the provincial governments. Two major innovations in regulating government advertising have been implemented, at the federal level and in the province of Ontario, as a result of the Gomery Inquiry. Both of these will be examined below.

There are two main issues to consider in the following discussion of public-sector advertising and its regulation. First, what to regulate. Reference to the federal and Ontario examples suggests emphasis on financial propriety and the distinction between public service and partisanship. The second is how to regulate. One of the consequences of the excesses that led to Gomery was the review mandate exercised by the Auditor General to assess the value obtained for public expenditures. Federal and provincial government auditors seem likely to remain central to regulatory surveillance. Let us now turn to elaboration on the character and agents of the actual regulation.

GOMERY AND ADVERTISING CHILL

The Auditor General of Canada in 2003 examined federal-government advertising, its sponsorship program, and public-opinion activities. Finding massive improprieties in its advertising and sponsorship policies, the government responded by calling for a Commission of Inquiry led by Justice John Gomery. The Gomery Inquiry represents the most important contemporary review of government advertising and contributed to increased attentiveness to the entire government-advertising regime in Canada. Its findings chronicled "a depressing story of multiple failures to plan a government program appropriately and to control waste . . . which contributed to the loss and misuse of huge amounts of money at the expense of Canadian taxpayers" (Canada, 2005, p. xix). Among its recommendations were an increase in the number of suppliers for advertising, thereby ensuring a greater number of firms bidding on advertising contracts; payment for advertising based on hourly remuneration rather than on commission, which encouraged large media expenditures; precautions to ensure that firms bidding on government contracts are at least 80 percent Canadian owned; and an Annual Report from the government on its advertising activities (Canada, 2006, p. 159).

The effect of Gomery has been immediately evident on the advertising efforts of the government. Immediately following the Auditor General's report, there was a planned reduction of 15 percent in the advertising expenditures of the government. The government's Annual Report shows a significant decrease from 2002 to 2003, when total advertising expenditures were $111 million. In 2005–06, total expenditures by the federal government were at an all-time low of $41.3 million (Canada, 2007, p. 6). Another effect of the Gomery Inquiry has been greater transparency around which departments spend the most. Prior to the annual report, the data were published only in marketing-trade magazines, making it difficult for citizens to have access to this information. The annual report for 2005–06 indicates that the largest advertiser within the federal government was the Department of National Defence, which accounted for over one-third of all expenditures. In the previous three years, the top spender had been the Department of Health, and Defence was either third or fourth. Its ascension to number one provides us with an important indicator of the communication goals of the government.

THE ONTARIO GOVERNMENT'S EFFORTS

Canada's position at the forefront of advertising regulation is not only a result of the federal Auditor General's audit in 2003 and the Gomery Report in 2006. A further development can be seen at the provincial level in Ontario. That government's Government Advertising Act, 2004 is the first piece of legislation anywhere in the world that attempts to regulate government advertising. The main thrust of this legislation is to prohibit partisan advertising by government.

Partisan advertising occurs when governments use tax dollars to promote a policy that is closely related to the governing party. Making distinctions between the governing party and the government can be difficult, but there have been several notable examples where the line is quite clear. For example, the federal Conservative government under Brian Mulroney advertised the GST when it was still a policy before Parliament. Since its ads mentioned "the proposed GST," it was clear that, because it had not yet become law, any advertisements could be reasonably interpreted as partisan advertising for the governing party, which sponsored the legislation. A clearer example can be found in the advertising in the run-up to the 1981 provincial election in Ontario. Tourism ads that touted the allure of Ontario with the slogan "Life is good, Ontario. Preserve it. Conserve it" were seen to be a thinly veiled ad for the governing Progressive Conservatives. However, it was more likely the period between 1996 and 2003, when the Mike Harris government relied heavily on advertising to sell its "Common Sense Revolution," that provided the main impetus for the Government Advertising Act, 2004. During that period, the Harris government enacted a wide-ranging educational-reform package that relied on many forms of communication, including significant advertising, to support it (Kozolanka, 2007). The ads were provocative and arguably incendiary. For example, the government ran a controversial ad that implored teachers to "spend a little more time with their students," for "education is far too important to be held hostage by the teachers' illegal action" (see Dougan, 2007; Kozolanka, 2007, p. 197).

Against this backdrop of advertising by a previous government, the McGuinty government enacted legislation that banned partisan advertising. This legislation demands that all provincial government ads be approved by the independent Office of the Auditor General of Ontario (OAGO), which assesses them against the criteria demanded by the Act. This means that ads

> must be a reasonable means of achieving one or more of the following purposes: 1) to inform the public of current or proposed government policies, programs or services available to them; 2) to inform the public of their rights and responsibilities under the law; 3) to encourage or discourage specific social behaviour in the public interest; 4) to promote Ontario or any part of Ontario as a good place to live, work, invest, study or visit or to promote any economic activity or sector of Ontario's economy. (Ontario, 2004, Section 6.1)

The Act also says that all ads must say "Paid for by the Government of Ontario" and cannot include the name or voice of any member of the legislature. The broadest category to which all ads must adhere is that ads "must not be partisan" (Section 6.2); however, the Act is silent on what that means. Auditors General have not traditionally been charged with these sorts of tasks. Their work has been associated with ensuring that after-the-fact spending has met some predetermined goals, such as financial propriety or value for money. Deciding a priori whether a policy is appropriate is new for the OAGO. Moreover, the criteria to be met are very broad, leaving significant latitude to the OAGO. Perhaps because of this, the Office created an Advertising Working Group comprised of a lawyer with a practice in advertising and a political scientist who writes about government advertising, as well as regular staff members. This working group adds an extra layer of independence to the process, while ensuring that the final decision lies with OAGO. Since the Act's inception, all ads have either been acceptable on the first review by the Auditor General or have subsequently been modified to ensure that they meet the Act's requirements. At the time, this was the first piece of legislation in the world that regulated the content of government advertisements.

CONCLUSION

Ultimately, social science research often generates more questions than answers. This is certainly true with regard to government advertising. We know that it remains an important part of governing and that the amount of resources allocated to the task is huge. Governments advertise for a variety of reasons and in the course of their efforts hope to maintain and enhance government legitimacy.

This chapter has introduced students to an active set of contemporary debates. Conclusive answers to questions posed within this debate are elusive, but this should not lead us to overlook the important scholarship that has been done. Likewise, it should prod future scholars and students to engage these issues. Consider why and how governments communicate with their citizens and with the world as a whole. Imagine what constitutes true or genuine discussion and assess the political dynamics involved. In a rapidly changing and complex world, governments rely upon advertising to communicate important messages. It is critical that all of us reflect on how this can best be done.

In light of this, let us close by emphasizing six key observations: 1) government advertising is a long-standing yet under-studied element of the political environment; 2) while governments have legitimate reasons to advertise (public education, public safety, policy awareness and promotion, political socialization, etc.), there are reasons to remain vigilant, for advertising can also be used for partisan advantage, for downgrading opponents or other countries, or as an alternative to open debate and citizen–government engagement; 3) government advertising is a complex area of communication study for reasons such as the fact that advertising often utilizes historic national symbols and values, public money is involved, and, ultimately, the impact of advertising campaigns on citizen trust and government legitimacy is uncertain; 4) there is active national debate over the controls and regulations needed to monitor government advertising and the associated expenditures; 5) there is an escalating trend toward state branding that may raise the profile and appeal of a country while at the same time facilitating manipulation of events and images to serve self-interested political goals; and, finally, 6) political scientists and their students need to reflect on the nature and power of advertising, as, judging by U.S. and world trends, the extent and cost of these activities will continue to rise.

Media Journal Assignments

1. Go to your province's website. What evidence is there of "branding" of your province? Is it effective?

2. Look through your local daily newspaper and try to find examples of government advertising. How many ads did you find? What products or services are they attempting to sell? How effective do you think they are?

3. Go to www.youtube.com and type in "negative ads Canada" in the search engine. What type of ads do you see? Now type in "negative ads" in the search engine. What kinds of ads are available using these search terms? How do they compare to the ads found in your first search? Which do you think are more effective? Why?

References

Aubry, Jack. 2003. "Forces reject logo for 'sissies.'" *Ottawa Citizen*, May 26.

BBC Website. 2007. "London Unveils Logo of 2012 Games." June 4. Available at news.bbc.co.uk/sport2/hi/other_sports/olympics_2012/6718243.stm (accessed September 2008).

Beers, Charlotte. 2002. "Funding for Public Diplomacy: Statement before the Subcommittee on Commerce, Justice, and State of the House Appropriations Committee." U.S. State Department. Available at www.state.gov/r/us/9778.htm (accessed May 2007).

Canada. 2003. "A Year of Review: Annual Report on the Government of Canada's Advertising, 2002–2003." Ottawa: Communication Canada.

———. 2005. "Commission of Inquiry into the Sponsorship Program and Advertising Activities (Gomery Commission). Who is Responsible? Fact Finding Report." Ottawa: Public Works and Government Services Canada.

———. 2006. "Commission of Inquiry into the Sponsorship Program and Advertising Activities (Gomery Commission). Restoring Accountability: Recommendations." Ottawa: Public Works and Government Services Canada.

———. 2007. "Sustained Commitment: Annual Report on Government of Canada Advertising Activities, 2005–2006." Ottawa: Public Works and Government Services Canada.

Deutsch, Karl Wolfgang. 1963. *The Nerves of Government: Models of Political Communication and Control*. New York: Free Press.

Dougan, Laura. 2007. "What Does It Really Mean to be Partisan? An Analysis of Government Advertising in Ontario." Paper presented to the Canadian Political Science Association, Saskatoon, June 2007.

Fan, Ying. 2006. "Branding the Nation: What Is Being Branded?" *Journal of Vacation Marketing* 12 (1): 5–14.

Fischer, Wolfgang Chr. & Peter Byron. 1997. "Buy Australian Made." *Journal of Consumer Policy 20* (1): 89–97.

Friesen, Joe. 2006. "Friendly Manitoba rebrands." *Globe and Mail*, December 5, A5.

Greenspon, Edward & Anthony Wilson-Smith. 1996. *Double Vision: The Inside Story of the Liberals in Power.* Toronto: Doubleday.

Hart, Roderick. 1987. *The Sound of Leadership: Presidential Communication in the Modern Age.* Chicago: University of Chicago Press.

Jamieson, Kathleen Hall. 1988. *Eloquence in an Electronic Age.* New York: Oxford University Press.

Kline, Stephen. 1993. *Out of the Garden: Toys, TV and Children's Culture in the Age of Marketing.* Toronto: Garamond.

Kozolanka, Kirsten. 2007. *The Power of Persuasion: The Politics of the New Right in Ontario.* Montreal: Black Rose Books.

Kunczik, Michael. 2003. "States, International Organizations, and the News Media: Problems of Image Cultivation." In *Political Communication in a New Era: A Cross-National Perspective,* ed. Philippe J. Maarek and Gadi Wolfsfeld, 117–38. London and New York: Routledge.

Leonard, Mark. 2002. "Diplomacy by Other Means." *Foreign Policy 132* (September–October): 48–56.

Lewington, Jennifer. 2004. "Toronto selling itself to the world." *Globe and Mail*, April 8, A13.

McKenna, Barrie. 2003. "Chief pitchwoman for U.S. image resigns post, citing health reasons." *Globe and Mail*, March 4, A9.

Mommaas, Hans. 2002. "City Branding: The Necessity of Sociocultural Goals." In *City Branding: Image Building and Building Images,* ed. Veronique Patteeuw and Urban Affairs, 32–48. Rotterdam: Nai Uitgevers.

Murphy, Dan. 2003. "U.S. Ads Miss Mark, Muslims Say." *Christian Science Monitor,* January 7. Available at www.csmonitor.com/2003/0107/p06s01-woap.html (accessed May 2005).

Newman, Bruce. 1999. *The Mass Marketing of Politics: Democracy in An Age of Manufactured Images.* Thousand Oaks: Sage.

Noonan, Peggy. 1990. *What I Saw at the Revolution: A Political Life in the Reagan Era.* New York: Ballantine.

Ontario. *Government Advertising Act,* S.O. 2004, 20.

O'Shaughnessy, John, and Nicholas J. O'Shaughnessy. 2000. "Treating the Nation as Brand: Some Neglected Issues." *Journal of Macromarketing 20* (1): 56–64.

Patteeuw, Véronique & Urban Affairs, eds. 2002. *City Branding: Image Building and Building Images.* Rotterdam: Nai Uitgevers.

Perlez, Jane. 2002. "Muslim-as-apple-pie videos are greeted with skepticism." *New York Times,* October 30, A1.

Robinson, Daniel. 1999. *The Measure of Democracy: Polling, Marketing Research, and Public Life, 1930–1945.* Toronto: University of Toronto Press.

Rose, Jonathan. 2003. "Government Advertising and the Creation of National Myths: The Canadian Case." *International Journal of Non-profit and Voluntary Sector Marketing 8* (2): 153–65.

Rotzoll, Kim B. & James E. Haefner, with Stephen R. Hall. 1996. *Advertising in Contemporary Society: Perspectives Toward Understanding.* 3rd ed. Urbana: University of Illinois Press.

Rutherford, Paul. 2000. *Endless Propaganda: The Advertising of Public Goods.* Toronto: University of Toronto Press.

Saunders, Doug. 2003. "White House insider cleans up Bush's image on film." *Globe and Mail*, May 28, 1.

Scammell, Margaret. 1995. *Designer Politics: How Elections are Won.* St. Martin's Press: New York.

———. 2003. "Citizen Consumers: Towards A New Marketing of Politics." In *Media and the Restyling of Politics: Consumerism, Celebrity, and Consumerism*, ed. John Corner and Dick Pels, 117–36. London: Sage.

Scammell, Margaret & Holli A. Semetko. 1995. "Political Advertising on Television: The British Experience." In *Political Advertising in Western Democracies*, ed. Lynda Lee Kaid and Christina Holtz-Bacha, 19–43. Thousand Oaks, Ca.: Sage.

Schouten, Fredreka. 2007. "Democrats Hold Cash Edge over Republicans in '08 Bids." *USA Today* Website. Available at www.usatoday.com/news/politics/election2008/2007-10-15-q3-reports_N.htm (accessed November 2007).

van Ham, Peter. 2001. "The Rise of the Brand State: The Postmodern Politics of Image and Reputation." *Foreign Affairs* 80 (5): 2–6.

———. 2003. "War, Lies, and Videotape: Public Diplomacy and the USA's War on Terrorism." *Security Dialogue* 34 (4): 427–44.

Vines, Stephen. 2001. "Hong Kong Woos Business." BBC Online. Available at http://news.bbc.co.uk/2/hi/business/1348984.stm (accessed September 8, 2008).

U.S. Department of State. Available at www.state.gov/r/pa/osc/ (accessed January 2008).

Whitaker, Reginald. 1977. *The Government Party: Organizing and Financing the Liberal Party of Canada.* Toronto: University of Toronto Press.

10 largest media corporation: (2010)

1- Comcast/NBC Universal
2- the Walt Disney Company
3- News Corp Ltd.
4- Viacom Inc/CBS corp
5- Time Warner Inc.
6- Sony Entertainment
7- Bertelsmann AG
8- Vivendi SA
9- Cox Enterprises Inc.
10- Thomas Reuters Corporation

Parent corporation

1- CBC ⟶ Viacom — Sumner Redstone
2- NBC ⟶ GE/Comcast — Bob Wright
3- ABC ⟶ Walt Disney —
4- Fox ⟶ Newscorp — Rupert Murdoch's

---

4 major realms of convergence

1. the convergence of technology
2. the convergence of corporation
3. the convergence of culture
4. the convergence of information w/ technology

Propaganda Model

1. Sumership
2. Advertising
3. Source
4. Flack
5. Enemies

Part II
Contests, Conquests, and Coronations: Elections as Media Events

Elections are the Olympics of political reporting, the quintessential media spectacle (Taras, 1999, p. 51). Elections certainly meet Dayan and Katz's (1992) criteria for a television media event, as election-night coverage interrupts regular programming for live broadcasts featuring in-studio analysis and reporters on location. When the results start coming in, rival stations compete to provide up-to-the minute information about electoral turnout and early poll returns and each strives to be the first to declare the winner, usually with the latest computer technology and impressive graphics and sound effects. All forms of news media see elections as the gold standard of political news, and they devote considerable time, money, and strategic attention to election campaigns.

Coverage of elections features the scripts associated with each of the three dominant types of media events identified by Dayan and Katz: contests, conquests, and coronations. In the lead-up to voting day, election coverage is all about the **contest** between parties to win seats. Election outcomes are covered like **coronations**, with the spotlight on the winner. Elements of the **conquest** can also emerge in election reportage if a new party wins, or an established party wins in a landslide or consolidates its hold on power. Each of these scripts emphasizes the game, or "horse-race," element of election campaigns (Trimble & Sampert, 2004). During election campaigns, journalists focus on who is winning, who is losing, and why, and as a result they highlight personality and performance, gaffes and errors, strategic miscues, and confrontations. For the news media, the game frame is attractive because it makes for stories that are easy to grasp; we all know what it means to be winning or losing, but readers don't immediately see the relevance (or excitement) of fine differences between policy positions (Mendelsohn, 1993, p. 150). It is easier to invoke strategic elements of election campaigns than it is to communicate alternate ideological visions or subtle differences between party stances on policy issues.

This section of the book examines the implications of presenting elections as media events. Does construction of elections as the Olympics of politics spur interest in campaigns, capturing citizen attention with lively images, cynical exposés of leaders' mistakes and missteps, and narratives about "the thrill of victory, and the agony of defeat"? Or do such representations shut certain interests and actors out of the mediated campaign, deprive voters of crucial information, and cultivate cynicism, negativity, distrust, and even disengagement? In **Bob Cox**'s experience, the truth lies somewhere in between the ideal view and the deeply cynical interpretation of the media's role and impact. Bob has spent 25 years working in Canadian daily journalism, after starting as a summer student at the *Globe and Mail* in 1983. Since then he has held different jobs at several newspapers, including general reporter for the *Cobourg Star*, court reporter for the *Winnipeg Free Press*, city editor of the *Edmonton Journal*, and national editor of the *Globe and Mail*. Bob also spent 10 years at the Canadian Press news agency, including six on Parliament Hill in Ottawa covering national politics. In May 2005, Cox was appointed editor of the *Winnipeg Free Press*, a role he held until July 2007, when he became publisher of the newspaper. In Chapter 6, "Covering Political Campaigns: A Practitioner's View," Cox maintains that elections are far from free and open discussions about a wide range of issues and interests, as neither parties nor media want to relinquish control of the campaign agenda. Cox argues that this is a battle journalists often lose. Even though journalists want to reveal the tactics and obfuscations that underpin carefully crafted campaign agendas and attempt to dig out the stories parties don't want voters to hear, political parties go to great efforts to keep candidates and leaders on message, controlling the information released to the media, and funnelling communications through "war rooms" and the internet. Because the news media focus their campaign efforts on the party leader's tours, they insulate themselves from independent sources of information and insight. News media follow the leaders despite the limitations of this strategy because elections are a race to the finish line and news audiences want to know "how the racers are doing." Cox warns that the rising costs of election reporting restrict the ability of news organizations to get on the campaign trail to talk to voters, leaders, and candidates; increasingly the coverage comes from a select few centralized national sources, beyond the control of the local press.

Stuart Soroka and **Blake Andrew** also examine the pros and cons of horse-race coverage and argue that it is less problematic than many critics suggest. Chapter 7, "Media Coverage of Canadian Elections: Horse-Race Coverage and Negativity in Election Campaigns," analyzes reporting of the 2004 and 2006 national election campaigns by seven major Canadian daily newspapers. Soroka and Andrew's data reveal an overwhelming emphasis on the horse race, especially polls and campaign strategy, with less than half of the coverage focusing on campaign issues. Moreover, while most articles conveyed neutral impressions of parties and leaders, those which did offer evaluations were more likely to be negative than positive. These findings confirm trends observed by analysts for decades, but Soroka and Andrew depart from many commentators by emphasizing the value of negative evaluations and horse-race reporting. By focusing on the electoral contest and providing easily assimilated information on the viability of candidates and parties, the media are helping voters decide how to cast their ballots. Additionally, Soroka and Andrew argue that the prevalence of negativity in election coverage signals that the media are performing the monitoring function necessary for a healthy democracy. Negative evaluations of parties and leaders both capture the interest of audiences and hold governments accountable.

Chapter 8, "Covering Muslim-Canadians and Politics in Canada: The Print Media and the 2000, 2004, and 2006 Federal Elections," offers a more critical assessment of media performance in Canadian election reporting. **Yasmeen Abu-Laban** and **Linda Trimble** examine the quantity and nature of English-language newspaper coverage of Canadian Muslims during the three most recent Canadian national elections, and their findings illustrate the power of the news media to decide whose interests are interesting at election time. As Abu-Laban and Trimble expected, Muslim-Canadians, who were virtually invisible in election-news coverage during the 2000 Canadian election, became the subject of more coverage after the events of September 11, 2001, largely because they were identified as a voting bloc, and thus relevant to the horse-race aspects of the campaign. However, even post 9/11, with Muslims more likely to be recognized as Canadian citizens and interested voters, Muslim-Canadians were homogenized, stereotyped, and misrepresented as religious fundamentalists and extremists. As a result, the coverage did little to contest negative portrayals of a diverse and historically significant population in Canada. Abu-Laban and Trimble argue that, by relying on the game frame in the coverage of the election process, journalists are limited in their capacity to provide Canadian society with a broader understanding of the demographic characteristics and policy interests of Canadian Muslims.

In Chapter 9, **Christopher Adams**, who is both a pollster and an academic, explores the history of opinion polling and maps its emergence in Canadian politics as a critical element of political campaigning. "Polling in Canada: Calling Elections," argues that the political use of opinion polls should be understood as part and parcel of the market-research and advertising industries, which use opinion research to determine consumer preferences for anything from beer to internet service providers. As Adams points out, media organizations, politicians, and voters rely on polling research before and during an election campaign, with the result that the polling industry has grown in both its technology and its precision. Polling helps the media propel the election story forward with statistical analysis of who is ahead and who is losing. As do Soroka and Andrew, Adams argues that the use of polls by media helps rather than hinders electoral engagement, as by providing consistent information about the shifting fortunes of political parties, news media help voters decide how their votes can be effectively deployed.

Dayan and Katz argue that media events such as elections serve to personalize politics, open politics to investigation and inquiry, chronicle political change, provide insights into how the political system works, and "socialize citizens to the political structure of society" (1992, pp. 201–3). The chapters included in this section illustrate the crucial role of the news media in linking political campaigns to voters and providing the information necessary for democratic engagement and political decision-making. However, they also challenge Dayan and Katz's rather benign view of the role of news intermediaries during election campaigns, raising cautions about the limitations and dangers of dominant election narratives.

References

Dayan, David & Elihu Katz. 1992. *Media Events: The Live Broadcasting of History.* Cambridge: Harvard University Press.

Mendelsohn, Matthew. 1993. "Television's Frames in the 1988 Canadian Election." *Canadian Journal of Communication* 18: 149–71.

Taras, David. 1999. *Power and Betrayal in the Canadian Media*. Peterborough: Broadview Press.

Trimble, Linda & Shannon Sampert. 2004. "Who's in the Game? The Framing of the Canadian Election 2000 by the *Globe and Mail* and the *National Post*." *Canadian Journal of Political Science* 37 (1): 51–71.

Chapter 6

Covering Political Campaigns:
A Practitioner's View

Bob Cox

INTRODUCTION

In the 1993 federal election campaign, Liberal leader Jean Chrétien was steadily building a big advantage over Prime Minister Kim Campbell. Chrétien was burnishing his image as the little-guy outsider, which was effective, but totally at odds with the reality that he was a seasoned Liberal insider. He had three decades under his belt as an MP, many of those as a senior cabinet minister. He had personal and professional connections to the richest, most powerful people in the country.

As a Canadian Press reporter, I was on his campaign tour one day in and around Montreal—a typical day with a couple of speeches and exactly one opportunity for reporters to ask questions of the leader, in plenty of time to make the evening television newscasts. Then there was nothing on the schedule. A number of us went to dinner and retired to a bar. A television reporter for Radio-Canada walked in toward the end of the evening and showed us the script of an item of his that had just aired. He had caught Chrétien attending an exclusive private reception for well-heeled Liberal donors. The reception was not on Chrétien's public agenda. It was a pretty natural setting for Chrétien, but hardly the image he wanted—rich patrons buying access to a likely future prime minister at a Montreal mansion. I quickly made sure the Radio-Canada scoop got on the CP wire. It spread across the country in both languages.

It was one of the few missteps that Chrétien made on his march to a landslide victory that fall. And it never would have been made public if the well-oiled election machine around Chrétien had succeeded in keeping his whereabouts secret.

Covering election campaigns is all about trying to do this—get beyond the official and well-rehearsed lines of politicians running for office to find out what is really going on. It is a frustrating business for journalists. The most successful political parties organize to get out carefully crafted messages and control access to leaders and candidates in a way that minimizes chances of anyone getting off message—or showing how they really think. Journalists have to find a way through these barriers.

They also face their own problems. Their public-service function suggests they should focus on issues and policies to guide voters through a myriad of promises. Yet elections are horse races. The story of who is winning and who is losing often overshadows the issues. Journalists chafe against parties setting the agenda, but find it very difficult to get away from official campaigns. News organizations are also in the competitive business of winning audiences, so they have to tailor coverage to win and keep audiences—what's sexy can overshadow what's important, the scoop of the moment can overshadow the bigger picture. Then there is the question of money. It governs the coverage journalists can provide. Can they travel with leaders or must they rely on wire services? Can they do polls? Can they pursue stories away from the daily campaigns? Finally, there is changing technology. Virtually every campaign brings a new wave that swamps the old ways of covering elections.

The purpose of this chapter is to examine how journalists cover political campaigns, the challenges they face, and why they make the choices they do—as seen through the eyes of a journalist who has been reporting on politics and overseeing political coverage regularly since 1983.

THE OFFICIAL CAMPAIGN

In the 2004 federal election campaign, the Liberals under Paul Martin effectively raised doubts in many voters' minds about the possibility of a hidden agenda of the newly reunited Conservatives under Stephen Harper. As Paul Wells says in his book *Right Side Up*, this was fuelled in part by comments by a number of Conservative candidates. One questioned official bilingualism, another likened abortion to beheading, and an old video of another showed him heaping scorn on how the courts interpreted gay rights (Wells, 2006, p. 127). This was great fodder for news reporters—just the kind of stuff that had been landing candidates from the old Reform and Alliance parties in hot water for years. It was enough to allow Martin to reverse Harper's gain in the polls and win a minority government.

In the 2006 campaign, none of this happened for one simple reason—it was virtually impossible to find a Conservative candidate to say anything about anything. Harper's war room (the central coordinating office for his campaign) tightly controlled every public statement. Candidates were kept to approved scripts, common talking points, or not talking at all. The intent was to stay focused on the central messages being put out daily by Harper or one of his prominent candidates. The strategy worked, and Conservative candidates did not shoot themselves or their party in the foot. They left it to the Liberals to make mistakes. And mistakes happened. For example, top Liberal strategist Scott Reid was pulled from public appearances after he attacked a Conservative promise to provide direct child-care payments to parents. Reid suggested on a Sunday television program that people who got $25 a week for child care would blow it on popcorn and beer. The comments showed an attitude that many voters did not like. They saw what a top Liberal was really thinking—something that wasn't happening with most of the Conservatives.

Political parties want to win elections and they want to get out their message. They go to great lengths to get out messages unfiltered, unchallenged, and, preferably, spun in a positive light. Elections are not free and open discussions. Politicians do not discuss policy until they are ready to do so. They most often release positions gradually to get maximum news exposure. And they provide just the information that serves their purpose, not necessarily full information.

During the 2004 federal election, Harper proposed a massive decrease in federal income taxes—by about 25 percent. It was a central part of the Conservative election platform. Party officials should have been well versed on it. But on the day Harper announced the policy, it did not appear that the party wanted it studied particularly closely. They preferred news items about Harper the tax cutter, without telling people exactly what it might mean for them. As an editor at the *Globe and Mail*, I pressed the reporter with Harper to get specific examples of what the tax cuts would mean for people of different income levels—someone earning more than $100,000 a year, a family making $60,000, etc. Party officials could produce no one to provide such numbers, even though calculating the impact of tax changes is simple mathematics if you know the new and the old rules. So I looked up a current tax guide on the web and did the math myself. I gave my numbers back to the reporter to run by someone in the Conservative party. No one would confirm them. It became clear that these details were not what the party wanted released on that day. In the 2006 election, Harper went with a much simpler tax proposal to cut the federal goods and services tax by two percentage points. It was simple, did not require complicated calculations, and got out the message that the leader was a tax cutter.

There is a good reason why parties often do not want to get into details—they do not have an impact on most voters, who tend to remember only big events and major policies. During the 2007 Manitoba election, editors at the *Winnipeg Free Press* decided that coverage of one-a-day announcements was being lost on many readers. We started running Saturday summaries of what happened over the course of a full week in the campaign. Readers repeatedly mentioned the Saturday summaries as the best thing about the *Free Press*'s election coverage. On the final Saturday we simply ran a summary of party positions on all relevant issues so voters who might not have heard anything else about the campaign could make an informed choice. Other media also generally offer these summaries at election time—many of them online—so that policy information is readily available to any voter who is making detailed comparisons.

During elections, a party's messaging is funnelled almost exclusively through the leader's tour, which consists of the leader, political advisers, and journalists travelling around the country or province. The idea is to convey the impression that the politicians are out meeting voters, but the reality is that the tour is contained largely within a combination of buses, airplanes, and hotels. The messages are controlled by the parties. In some cases, the object of tours is to keep leaders away from people—and journalists— rather than meet them. During Ralph Klein's tenure as Alberta premier, his handlers employed what they called a "boy in the bubble" strategy, keeping Klein in carefully controlled appearances during campaigns to minimize the risk he would face difficult or embarrassing situations.

Politicians often complain that journalists just want to trip them up and practice "gotcha" journalism. But there is a simple reason why journalists probe how politicians think when they are off message. Governing presents all sorts of challenges not covered by a political platform. Leaders change their minds all the time based on circumstances. Brian Mulroney once opposed free trade—and then negotiated it with the United States when he came to believe it was the right thing to do for the future of Canada's economy. Jean Chrétien promised to kill the goods and services tax—and then did no such thing, after the federal Finance Department persuaded him that the government could not afford to do away with it. Ontario premier Dalton McGuinty signed a pledge not to raise taxes— and then imposed a huge increase in health-care premiums after taking power, saying that the government needed the revenues to preserve the health system. Stephen Harper promised not to change the rules governing tax-protected income trusts—and then changed the policy suddenly on Halloween night, 2006. Many large Canadian firms were planning conversions to income trusts that would have siphoned billions of dollars in taxes away from the federal treasury.

Since a leader's tour is not always the best place to find out what is going on, reporters look elsewhere for news. They talk to voters away from the campaigns, they do reality checks on announcements to determine their true implications, and they try to get inside knowledge of what is happening in a campaign. During the 2006 election, the Canadian Press news service did a very good job of getting inside the Liberal campaign, revealing a number of party platforms the day before they were supposed to be announced. Paul Wells describes a hilarious scene while the Liberal tour was on a refuelling stop in Calgary. Reporters learned that the party's next-day announcement on post-secondary education was already on the wire, that Paul Martin had apologized for the Chinese head tax on a Vancouver radio station, and that one of Martin's own MPs had boycotted the leader's health-care announcement earlier in Victoria. "Suddenly it seemed that the only place in Canada where you could be perfectly insulated from news about Paul Martin was on Paul Martin's campaign plane," Wells wrote (2006, p. 219).

A lot of what you get on a leader's tour is spin. Party officials tell you how great their campaign is and what is wrong with all the other parties. They try to colour your reporting and, especially if you are a columnist, win you over. The age of virtually universal communication has made it more difficult for parties to do this, since reporters have instant access to outside information to do their own research. But campaigns do not stop trying. It is sometimes amazing how friendly political advisers are during campaigns, as opposed to at other times. During the 2003 Ontario election, I received calls from two people on Liberal Dalton McGuinty's team while I ran the national desk at the *Globe*. I had attended university with one in the early 1980s and had known the other later in the 1980s. I had not spoken to either in more than a decade. The McGuinty team, it seems, was pulling out all the stops in their media offensive by exploiting every personal connection to journalists they could find.

For some time, news outlets have tried to get away from leaders' tours. Larger news outlets routinely assign many reporters to get election-related stories away from the tours. For example, in 2000, the *Globe and Mail* assigned veteran reporter John Gray to regularly visit Orangeville, Ontario, to find out what so-called ordinary folks were saying. In 2004, Global TV put its entire nightly newscast on a bus, becoming the first national television news broadcast to go to air each night from a different city. It was a gimmick, and you can rightly ask why it took an election campaign to get the national newscast out of the studio, but it was a real effort nonetheless to find out what Canadians were thinking.

News outlets try to come up with new ways of covering an election every time there is a new contest. Some have even tried to skip daily coverage of the party leaders to deploy journalists elsewhere. But these efforts have always been abandoned fairly quickly because, after all, it is a horse race. Journalists find the most excitement watching the horses run, and generally audiences agree.

ISSUES VERSUS CONTEST

Stories about political campaigns can be broken down into two main categories—issues, and who is winning. The issues—policies, economic conditions, social issues, government behaviour, etc.—are supposed to be at the core of any debate over choosing a government. News organizations cover this category as part of their public-service function. Who will win and how is the story of the polls—strategy, competition, and, sometimes, nastiness— at the centre of how political parties try to gain power. News organizations cover this category because everyone loves a horse race.

You can guess which coverage is more likely to gain an audience. Every newspaper that I have ever worked at has put a great deal of emphasis on stories that show who is ahead in an election. A story on an exclusive poll almost always grabs the flare or main headline position in papers and top spot on news broadcasts, regardless of what else is happening in a campaign. To begin with, the news outlet sponsoring the poll has probably spent a lot of money to get the information. And if there is a change in the mood of the electorate, all news outlets want to be first to report it, analyze it, and discover what impact it is having on various campaigns.

Some news outlets have moved away from polling, taking a public stance that too much of it is not good for the electoral process. The CBC has not done polling in recent elections, but has presented summaries of other media polls weekly. Some news media do not do polls because they do not want to spend the money. Yet others have wholeheartedly embraced polling—the *Globe* published a daily tracking poll each day of the 2005–06 federal campaign, giving readers the kind of rolling poll information that political parties see.

News organizations usually start campaigns by assessing both the issues and the horserace categories, and planning coverage based on those assessments. Editors will look at what is expected to be most important in a contest and who will legitimately vie for power, and allocate resources accordingly. In elections where the outcome is seemingly not in doubt, editors usually plan less coverage of both the issues and the horse race, since there will be less interest in the contest.

It is quite common to look at what issues are uppermost on the minds of voters and consider how those issues can be covered from the point of view of the political contest. Such issues as personal safety and crime, health care, tax levels, national unity, government accountability, and economic security (jobs and unemployment) have traditionally been at or near the top of what people say they are concerned about. Recently the environment has taken over the top spot. Other issues, such as the war in Afghanistan, pop up from time to time.

In national elections, virtually all media outlets poll at the start of a campaign to find out where the parties stand. The top journalists and most resources are assigned to campaigns with a legitimate shot at forming government. Lesser parties and their supporters constantly complain about this. In 2006, the New Democrats felt they got short shrift even as they gained seats in the Commons. As Christopher Waddell and Christopher Dornan point out in *The Canadian Federal Election of 2006*, the NDP was mentioned in only two front-page headlines in the *Globe and Mail* during the campaign. One reported the decision of Canadian Auto Workers Union president Buzz Hargrove to support Paul Martin and the Liberals instead of the New Democrats. And one reported on falling NDP fortunes in Ontario (Waddell & Dornan, 2006, p. 234).

As campaigns progress, news outlets tend to shift to a greater emphasis on who is leading and likely to win. In 2006, the CBC claimed to have broken this trend. An independent report done on CBC coverage of the federal election campaign concluded that the CBC presented an even balance of policy and strategy discussions through to the final two weeks of the campaign, when talk of shifting momentum and the final outcome prevailed. The report, *Balance in News Coverage of the 2006 Election Campaign*, was done by ERIN Research. It claimed that CTV shifted into horse-race mode after the first few weeks of the campaign, and paid a disproportionate amount of attention to the two main parties and their leaders. It is quite understandable that news outlets pay the most attention to the main parties—their policies and actions need the most scrutiny precisely because they may form government.

It is a constant complaint of political parties that the news media focus too much on who is likely to win an election and not enough on issues. This is a strange complaint, given that most political parties themselves focus almost exclusively on what they have to do to win and engage in a pitched battle to gain votes. Quite often such criticism is driven by nothing but the desire to keep bad news away from the public. Knowledge of who is winning and who is losing certainly affects voting. There can be a bandwagon effect, or people can change their votes strategically to ensure one party does not win a landslide, or they may feel free to vote for an alternative candidate, knowing that it will not change which party wins an election. Whatever use voters make of the information, they deserve to know it.

Parties themselves have access to constant polling during campaigns. They often do not want the public to know if they are slipping in support because the trend may get worse. Sometimes even leading parties do not want the true status of an election race known. Manitoba premier Gary Doer has complained a number of times about the publication of a poll in the final days of the 2003 provincial election that predicted he would win a landslide victory. The actual election result was somewhat less than a landslide, and Doer argues that the poll made NDP supporters complacent and less likely to vote. In other words, he wanted to keep his own troops motivated, and telling them what was really going on was not part of that strategy. But revealing what is really going on is precisely what journalists are trying to do as they discover and explain what is happening behind the scenes in campaigns. Did Manitoba voters not deserve to know that the NDP was headed to an overwhelming victory? Electorates usually do not feel they are well served by massive majorities, and people's choices can be affected by the knowledge that they may be headed toward such a government.

Journalists cover political races by watching how the racers are doing. You would not cover a leg of the Tour de France by talking only about the merits of different tires, how steep the hills are, and what the weather is like. Those are all issues, but what really interests people is how the riders are doing in the race. You focus on the leaders because, let's face it, they are doing the best and are the most interesting. That's where the excitement is.

Of course, there is a lot more at stake in an election than in a bike race. But the news values that determine how the Tour de France gets covered are not so different from the ones applied to an election. Excitement, action, conflict—these are all elements that journalists regularly look for in news stories. They are found in the heart of a contest—the race—and that is where journalists go for stories.

The democratic process also gets attention during campaigns. In the 2000 federal election, voter turnout was initially reported by Elections Canada to be the lowest ever in a national election, hovering just above 60 percent. The agency later adjusted the figure to 64 percent after realizing the voters' list was inflated by almost a million names. Nonetheless, only 25 percent of people aged 18 to 24 voted. Many news outlets took on the issue in the 2004 campaign, trying to find ways to encourage the youth vote. The *Globe and Mail* ran "Will Chandler Vote?" a series by reporter Michael Valpy, who followed around a university student named Chandler Powell, who was supposedly undecided on whether to vote. The fact that Powell agreed to Valpy's scrutiny suggested he was pretty interested in the political process to begin with, and he voted in the end. So what did all the attention to this issue accomplish? Voter turnout really did fall to a historic low in 2004—about 61 percent, according to Elections Canada.

ARE JOURNALISTS BIASED?

I received my usual envelopes of clippings after the 2007 Manitoba election. They were accompanied by the usual letters accusing the newspaper of bias, pointing out nice photos we had run of New Democrat leader Gary Doer and unflattering ones we had run of Conservative leader Hugh McFadyen. These were all signs of bias, the writers said. One batch that I received pointed to a front-page picture of Doer on the night of winning re-election as a sign of bias. What other picture would a newspaper run the day after an election but one of the winners? Another batch included a photo of Hugh McFadyen wearing a Winnipeg Jets jersey as a sign we were biased against him. The writer seemed to have missed the point that McFadyen put the jersey on himself and held a news conference.

Bias is in the eye of the beholder. If you are looking for it and you are persuaded that it exists, you are likely to find evidence to support your belief.

Political parties do a lot of looking for it. After winning the election in 2006, the Harper government divided all news outlets into friendly and unfriendly and treated them accordingly. Friendly outlets get access and interviews; unfriendly ones often do not even get phone calls returned. Of course, bias does exist in the news media. But when it does it is usually obvious—even part of a journalist's job. I have never experienced a mainstream news organization with a *hidden* agenda to be biased against any political party.

Journalists who are biased include columnists and other commentators whose whole purpose is to have informed opinions and argue their points of view. Then there are media outlets who pander to an audience with a particular political leaning—such as the *Sun* newspapers, which are unrelentingly conservative. Most media outlets, however, have a goal to be fair and balanced during election campaigns.

Make no mistake; good journalists are out to find flaws in politicians and their parties. They want to scratch and dig and, if they find out something embarrassing, get it on the web, on air, or in print as fast as they can. But that is not bias. It is simply part of the high level of scrutiny that politicians invite when they step into public life. Remember, many of the same journalists who dug up dirt on Brian Mulroney did the same for Jean Chrétien and are now closely looking at Stephen Harper.

There is also a very interesting thing about most complaints of bias from political parties—it is usually the losing parties that make the allegations. In part, this is because of the dynamic that usually develops at the end of a campaign. A leading party is seen as being a winner; everybody on the campaign is feeling good and getting along with the media. There is a halo effect, so that is what the media report. The losing party feels every news item and headline is slanted against them. A negative aura of defeat envelopes the campaign, so that is what the media report.

It is rarer when a winning party makes the complaint, but it still happens. The reason is that all political leaders need enemies, real or imagined, to rally the troops. Conservatives need Marxists to keep their troops motivated. Liberals need right-wingers with a hidden agenda for social conservatism. And they all need the media to punch at once in a while.

COMPETITIVE EDGE

In journalism, everybody wants to beat the competition, to be the best at covering politics, and do something that attracts and keeps an audience. Newspapers focus on their columnists and deeper analysis; television loves live debate and discussion of issues; websites and radio emphasize speed.

In every election, it seems, various news outlets come up with "new ways" to cover politics. Some of them border on the ridiculous. MuchMusic discovered politics in the 1990s and exposed politicians to interviews by veejays about their favourite music and popular culture. A visit to the station's Toronto studio became obligatory for political leaders. You have not seen uncomfortable until you have seen Jean Chrétien fumbling around trying to look at a piece of paper in his hand with his "favourite" song written on it—*Closing Time* by Leonard Cohen, no doubt carefully selected by a young Liberal staffer.

In the 2005–06 federal election, the CBC's new political coverage included matching up MPs and voters for short taxi rides, speed dating between undecided voters and political strategists, an online strategy game simulating the federal election, and the use of a secret strategist commenting on the campaign while not revealing his identity. It was certainly not your typical political coverage.

Of course, everybody wants a scoop. The best scoops in political campaigns are finding out what is coming next and revealing behind-the-scenes information that the parties do not really want public. As mentioned earlier, Paul Martin's 2005–06 campaign was bedevilled by leaks of upcoming announcements. The entire Liberal platform was obtained by Conservative publisher Ezra Levant and posted on the website of his magazine, *Western Standard*, the night before it was to be released.

Sometimes the desire for the big story elevates a relatively minor event into something much more. In late 2005, the Liberal government announced it would not change its rules for tax protection on income trusts. The NDP noticed a spike in trust trading the day of the announcement and complained to the RCMP. In the middle of the election campaign, the RCMP informed New Democrat Judy Wasylycia-Leis that they were conducting an investigation. Wasylycia-Leis called a news conference. Virtually all media jumped all over the story of the cops investigating the Liberals. The income-trust investigation became top news. The Conservatives used it to reinvigorate their claims of Liberal corruption. There were suggestions that all sorts of Liberals had benefited from advance knowledge of the income trust announcement. The investigation firmly turned the tide against Paul Martin's election hopes.

The only problem was that it was not much of a story, and certainly not evidence of Liberal wrongdoing. Thirteen months after the Conservatives won a minority government, a single charge of criminal breach of trust was laid against a bureaucrat in the Finance department who was in charge of tax policy. No politicians or Liberal staffers were charged. The desire for a big scandal had created stories that did not have all the facts. But the damage was already done.

MONEY DETERMINES EVERYTHING

In the 2005–06 federal election campaign, two journalists covering the contest rented a Hummer, equipped it with all the latest electronic gear, hired a driver, added a fridge, and paid for all the fuel needed by the gas guzzler. The reason the *Sun*'s Greg Weston and the *National Post*'s Don Martin did it was simple—to save money. Weston, writing in his *Sun* column during the campaign, calculated the duo would save $20,000 a week over what the Conservatives would have charged them to ride on the buses and airplanes of the official Harper campaign. Elections are expensive for media outlets to cover. The biggest determinant of what kind of election coverage you will get from any particular media outlet is how much the organization has to spend. Everything from how many pages a newspaper devotes to campaign coverage to how often you see a television reporter on the road is determined by money. The costs can add up very quickly. Weston and Martin noted that the Conservatives, Liberals, and NDP were all charging $9,500 per reporter to be on a leader's tour. Add things like hotel bills and some meals and the cost was $11,000 per week per leader. The eight-week campaign could have cost a media outlet more than $250,000 just to cover the leaders, Weston estimated.

That is beyond the reach of all but the largest news organizations, and can even affect big outlets' coverage decisions. Weston's calculations are interesting for what he did not include—coverage of Bloc Québécois leader Gilles Duceppe's campaign. Few English news organizations outside Quebec spend much time at all with Duceppe during federal campaigns, in part because of the cost involved for a part of the election story that is not as important to their audiences as the other leaders.

Most larger organizations—national newspapers, television networks, national wire services—still bite the bullet and pay the substantial cost of following major political leaders around the country. Regional media, however, have all but stopped covering national campaigns. Virtually all coverage of the leaders seen in regional media—city newspapers and local television and radio stations—comes from central national sources, beyond the control of regional news editors. The impact of this is largely unstudied. Most analyses of how media cover elections focus on major newspapers, including the *Globe and Mail*, the *National Post* and the *Toronto Star*, and national television networks, including the CBC, CTV, and Global. The majority of Canadians, however, get national news funnelled through a regional media outlet—local newspapers, television, and radio.

Local reporters hook up with a national campaign only when it swings through their area and there are no travel costs. This gives rise to a favourite trick of national leaders—granting local interviews that national reporters do not have access to, at least not right away. There are fewer tough questions—lots of regional journalists are pleased just to be talking to a national leader—and controversies are often put aside by reporters less versed in national politics and more interested in getting a local angle anyway. The resulting coverage often focuses on the simple fact that a news organization got the interview at all, rather than the substance of the campaign. A leader gets exposure without too much risk.

Current prime minister Stephen Harper certainly uses this tactic, but he is far from the first. Brian Mulroney tried it at times, as did Paul Martin. Remember the scene on the Liberal tour in the 2005–06 campaign discussed earlier in this chapter. Martin quietly visited a Chinese-language radio station in Vancouver, where he apologized for the racist head tax. National reporters—the ones whose employers were paying big bucks to have them on the national campaign tour—found out about the story while on a refuelling stop in Calgary (Wells, 2006, p. 129).

The rising cost of covering elections will also make it difficult for the new generation of web journalists to ever get on the leaders' planes, and could substantially change the way campaigns are covered. Web outlets generally do not have the resources to put reporters or bloggers on a campaign, with the exception of people already associated with traditional news organizations.

Money plays the key role in coverage decisions at every level of politics. In the 2007 Manitoba election campaign, only one Winnipeg media outlet—the *Winnipeg Free Press*—travelled with leaders outside of the city. The entire campaign took place in Winnipeg, according to the majority of news outlets that service the whole province. As well, only one poll was commissioned by media outlets. The *Winnipeg Free Press* and Global TV paid more than $20,000 for the single poll. The only other public poll was an internet survey released in the final days of the campaign. Both polls correctly predicted the New Democrats would hold on to power with a strong majority government. But the reluctance of media outlets to spend any money on travel or polling greatly limited the number of sources voters had for certain kinds of information. Money shaped the campaign coverage. It also gave political parties an advantage. Major political parties do nightly polling during campaigns and have daily updates on how they are doing. They tailor appearances, announcements, and public comments around what they know.

Voters have greater difficulty understanding what is going on when they do not know such information. In the Manitoba campaign, Conservative leader Hugh McFadyen made what appeared to be a rash promise that a Conservative government would get a National Hockey League team back to Winnipeg to replace the much-mourned Jets. The promise was almost immediately ridiculed. Some observers later blamed it for McFadyen's election loss. What voters did not know at the time—but the political parties did—was that the promise was an effort to inject some life into a faltering campaign. Falling support for the Conservatives was showing up in nightly polls. The polls explained everything, but voters knew nothing of the polls. Without that knowledge, many wondered what on earth McFadyen was doing.

Current trends suggest even less, rather than more, coverage of political campaigns. It is instructive to remember that newspapers, which have traditionally provided the most comprehensive coverage of campaigns, derive virtually no revenue from elections. Political parties spend most of their money on television advertising. Election coverage rarely improves circulation, except for the day after the vote when results are in. Despite the money television gets from elections, news directors look for content that draws audiences. Campaign coverage does not generally do that. The exception is election-night broadcasts, into which television stations and networks traditionally put a lot of resources. The purse strings are not about to get any looser for the coverage of political campaigns.

TECHNOLOGY

It is almost quaint now to remember the scene at the Ottawa Conference Centre in June of 1990 when the provincial premiers and Prime Minister Brian Mulroney got together to try to save the Meech Lake Constitutional Accord. Sure, the fate of the country was at stake—according to some—but what was really neat was the new generation of cellphones making their first appearance in national Canadian political affairs. The first mobile phones, which were roughly the size of bricks, were being replaced with highly portable models that could be held in the palm of your hand, even folded into a jacket pocket. All the top political aides and journalists were carrying them. At the time, few of the participants realized they were starting a revolution. The phones allowed people to talk when they wanted, without having to wait for a land line or a face-to-face encounter. The usual political gossip and rumours—and sometimes even real information—started to ricochet around at unheard-of speed. The talks at times took on a frenzied atmosphere that was instantly reflected to a national television audience live on CBC Newsworld. Barely noticed was how much impact a leap forward in technology had on the conference, or the sense of urgency felt by much of the country.

Technology has always seemed to sneak up on political campaigning, then plunge it into a whole new era, seemingly without warning. There is, however, usually lots of warning for anybody paying attention. Television was around for more than a decade before it made a major impact on a political campaign. Likewise, the internet existed for almost as long before it made a mark.

Until the 1950s, political campaigns were largely defined by newspaper coverage and, to a lesser extent, radio coverage. In his book *The Player: The Life and Times of Dalton Camp*, author Geoffrey Stevens recounts how in 1952 the New Brunswick Conservatives sent their entire platform to newspapers as a paid advertisement. "It was still the age of innocence," Stevens wrote. "Television was not a factor in 1952" (2003, p. 69). During the provincial campaign, Camp, a young political operative at the time, produced radio commercials and wrote daily columns for newspapers that ran under the byline L.C. House in space paid for by the Conservatives. These columns were closely followed by New Brunswick voters, and, with their help, the Conservatives upset a Liberal dynasty in the province. Such a campaign is inconceivable today.

The most successful political parties are usually one technological step ahead of their opponents. It is not so much that successful political parties master new technology—though they certainly do that—it is that they master how news outlets are using the new technology to reach audiences and designing campaigns to get maximum benefit from the changed media landscape. The advantage usually lasts only for one campaign, as other parties catch up and the media get used to the new techniques—and are jaded by them.

Television gradually started replacing print and radio as the main campaign medium in the 1960s. But it was Pierre Trudeau who mastered the medium and gained huge advantage in 1968 by doing so. After that, every national political campaign was a television campaign, with political parties designing their efforts to get maximum exposure on the nightly news. Many journalists, especially print journalists, grumbled that leaders' campaigns consisted of little more than travelling back and forth across Canada looking for attractive backdrops for television cameras. Political parties did not care much about the complaints, knowing that the majority of people got their news from television and that whatever was on television influenced all news coverage.

For most of the past 40 years, this has been a pretty good description of leaders' tours. Each day political leaders would have a schedule designed around getting on the evening television news. Major events and announcements would take place by early afternoon, giving television journalists plenty of time to process and edit film and video. Coverage generally consisted of what one leader was doing at a time, since leaders were moving separately around the country and journalists did not know instantly what was being said elsewhere. Campaign tours usually moved larger distances by air in the evenings after everybody had filed.

Campaigns and the journalists covering them could be out of reach for hours. There is a famous picture of Robert Stanfield, Conservative leader in the 1970s, fumbling a football during the 1974 federal election campaign. For many, the photo cemented an image of Stanfield as a bumbler versus the athletic, coordinated Pierre Trudeau. But the Stanfield campaign was unaware the photo existed until many hours after it was taken. Photographer Doug Ball snapped it during a stop in North Bay on the way to Vancouver. As Ball recounted to a CTV interviewer in 2005, he gave his film to a Canadian Press editor for processing and filing. Later he learned it was on the next day's front page of the *Globe and Mail*. The Stanfield campaign, and even Ball himself, did not learn until arriving in Vancouver what the picture looked like. The damage was already done.

Today a very different scenario would likely play out. The photo would be on the web within minutes of being taken. Political aides to whatever politician was photographed would begin protesting immediately that it was out of context, unfair, and irresponsible. They would produce their own photos of the leader catching a football flawlessly. (Stanfield actually caught the football on several throws, and fumbled once. A photo of him catching the ball appears in *Life on a Press Pass*, by Lynn and Doug Ball). Bloggers sympathetic to the political party in question would start a web campaign against the news outlet that produced the picture, claiming it was biased against the party leader. Other media and political pundits would get into a debate about whether the photo should be used. By 5 p.m., Newsworld's Don Newman would be featuring the debate on *Politics*, a must-view program for political junkies. Many newspapers would print it the next day. All would have stories on the controversy over the picture. Any impact of the photo itself would be blunted, if not erased.

Much has been written and said about the modern political war room—filled with party workers and strategists plotting the next campaign move. But little has been said about the technology that makes these offices effective. It's good to recall that the age of instant communications actually did not start with the World Wide Web, but with the cellphone and all-news television. By the 1990s, journalists wanted not just daily announcements, but same-day (or hour) reactions to what was happening elsewhere. All-news television created an instant forum for discussion of what was happening in a campaign.

It was the federal Liberals who took first and best advantage of this change. In the 1993 federal election, the party used a quick-response team using the new technology. In their book *Double Vision*, authors Edward Greenspon and Anthony Wilson-Smith describe a system in which an aide in Ottawa got information about the Kim Campbell campaign and quickly communicated with the travelling Chrétien team. Parties have always used central offices to coordinate campaigns, but previously did not have the communications technology to react so quickly. Prime Minister Campbell made a number of mistakes that the Liberal team processed and made into fodder for Jean Chrétien in minutes. On the day the election was announced, Campbell said she did not expect the unemployment rate to drop below 10 percent until the turn of the century. Liberal strategists phoned the Chrétien bus as it left Ottawa and at his first stop he was blasting the Conservative priority of jobs for 2000, versus the Liberal priority to create jobs right away (Greenspon & Wilson-Smith, 1996, p. 27).

By the next campaign in 1997, every party had heavily wired war rooms and quick-response teams. The teams were not just equipping their leaders for battle; they were also giving information to candidates and other party representatives with which to attack opponents. They have become such a part of how political parties operate that they now exist between elections as well. Prime Minister Stephen Harper unveiled his Conservative party's election war room to the news media in the spring of 2007. There was no campaign on at the time, just the possibility of one, since Harper had only a minority government. The room had been operating for months.

Cellphones, BlackBerries, instant messaging, and the internet are all indispensable for the modern political party and the modern political journalist. They have made campaign coverage instant as well. Live television has been able to do this for some time, but television is selective and has limited airtime, generally covering only big announcements and events. The internet makes every reporter and blogger able to instantly transmit information. A journalist can tap out an item on a BlackBerry and it is on a website before a politician stops speaking. The result is instant attention to what is going on.

Analysis of media coverage of the 2005–06 federal election has largely overlooked the most important development in the campaign—for the first time, mature, web-based news outlets reached an audience that was big enough to make a difference. Stephen Harper should be spoken about in a Trudeau-like way when it comes to mastering a new medium. His campaign was the first to use the reconfigured media world to full advantage. The internet had been around for a decade prior to the 2005–06 federal campaign. News websites and bloggers had also been growing in numbers and reach. But it took until the 2005–06 vote before the audience for this new medium was big enough to form a central part of campaign strategy.

Harper's team was the first to grasp that making news very early in the day was the best way to reach a largely web audience, and the web would influence other news coverage just as television once had. (Web traffic on most news sites is generally at the highest levels in the mornings, shortly after people arrive at work.) During the first few weeks of the campaign, Harper came out with short, simple announcements daily, usually early in the morning. I got used to seeing Harper at the top of the web news queue every morning when I arrived at my office around 8:30 a.m. Harper's tour travelled later in the day while everyone else reacted to what he had said. Harper set the agenda by changing both the timing and the form of his announcements to adapt to the new news technology. His announcements were perfect for quick web hits and could usually be found at the top of news websites for several hours, updated regularly with reaction from others.

Radio, and television to a lesser extent, has always been able to get out a message quickly. But the web puts a message out and leaves it there all day, any time anyone wants it. And in the modern media world, every reporter for television, radio, or newspapers is filing to a web service.

Harper's approach helped push the Conservatives from a position trailing the Liberals at the start of the campaign to a minority government by its end. A political party's mastery of the technology that was being used to send out news had helped win another election.

New technology can also hurt a political party. The web has allowed faster dissemination of embarrassing material about politicians, and allowed it to remain in the public domain when politicians do not want it there. In 2006 the Liberals produced a series of attack ads on Stephen Harper, including an ominous one saying he wanted to increase the military presence in cities. The Liberal party never aired the ad, and quickly took it down from its website. But CTV had already archived and posted the 30-second clip. It survived forever on the web.

Much has been made of the advent of bloggers on political campaigns. They have certainly increased the level of political chatter on the web. Highly partisan blogs put out party messages and attack opponents. Less partisan blogs—usually associated with news websites—provide daily, or even hourly, commentary on politics, sometimes serious, sometimes less so. Some, such as Paul Wells's blog for *Maclean's*, have become must reads on campaigns. Independent bloggers are certainly part of politics and political campaigns. They are likely to grow in importance, and some will achieve the influence currently enjoyed by better-known pundits, commentators, and columnists. But thus far, they have had only limited and sporadic impact on campaigns.

CONCLUSION

I became hooked on watching politics on a December night in Ottawa in 1979. As a student I went to the visitors' gallery in the House of Commons to watch the young Conservative government of Joe Clark go down to defeat. I've been watching, and conveying what happens to others, ever since. However, I can honestly say that the messages I have sent to audiences have always been incomplete. Journalists almost always present an imperfect picture of what is really going on, their efforts curtailed by the various factors discussed in this chapter. This does not mean that the news media are unreliable. But for voters it means that there is always more to report, more to learn, and more to understand than gets reported in any campaign. Finding out what is really happening requires constant effort.

References

Ball, Lynn & Doug Ball. 2005. *Life on a Press Pass*. Belleville, Ont.: Wallbridge House Publishing.

Burman, Tony 2006. "Voters' voices: How you helped shape our election coverage." CBC.ca, January 24. Available at www.cbc.ca/news/about/burman/20060124.html (accessed August 19, 2008).

ERIN Research. 2006. *Balance in News Coverage of the 2006 Election Campaign*. Final Report, November 29, 2005–January 6, 2006. Prepared for the CBC. Available at www.cbc.ca/news/about/burman/pdf/ERIN_report-2006.pdf (accessed August 18, 2008).

Greenspon, Edward & Anthony Wilson-Smith. 1996. *Double Vision: The Inside Story of the Liberals in Power*. Toronto: Doubleday Canada.

Stevens, Geoffrey. 2003. *The Player: The Life and Times of Dalton Camp*. Toronto: Key Porter Books.

Waddell, Christopher & Christopher Dornan. 2006. "The Media and the Campaign." In *The Canadian Federal Election of 2006*, ed. Christopher Dornan and Jon H. Pammett, 220–52. Toronto: Dundurn.

Wells, Paul. 2006. *Right Side Up: The Fall of Paul Martin and the Rise of Stephen Harper's New Conservatism*. Toronto: McClelland & Stewart.

Chapter 7

Media Coverage of Canadian Elections: Horse-Race Coverage and Negativity in Election Campaigns

Stuart Soroka and Blake Andrew

INTRODUCTION

The 2004 and 2006 Canadian federal elections seemed rather different. A common interpretation (indeed, our own interpretation elsewhere; see Andrew, Maioni, and Soroka, 2006) was as follows. The 2004 election campaign presented a very narrow set of issues to Canadian voters. Opposition parties hammered Canadians with the following message: Think about the sponsorship scandal, and punish this Liberal Party for it. The Liberals countered with a different reading of the scandal, of course, and warned Canadians what Conservatives might do with social policies (particularly same-sex marriage and abortion) and health care. With only a few fleeting exceptions, the parties' campaigns were made up entirely of these few issues, and this was clearly reflected in media coverage. News content focused on sponsorship, social policy, and health care, and—in the absence of any other policy content—the horse race.

The 2006 election was rather different again, and not only because it resulted in a change in government. The campaign itself was also a memorable one. It was regarded by many as a campaign of ideas and issues—policy platforms, above and beyond the government accountability issue, were not just on the table during the 2006 campaign; they actually took up much of the space there, particularly in the early weeks of the campaign. Indeed, from a news-media perspective, the anatomy of this Canadian election felt at the time quite different from the previous one. Canadians read more about issues, and they were exposed to a wider conversation about substantive policy options.

There were nonetheless two features common to both campaigns. First, even as the volume of horse-race coverage varied, for instance, it was ubiquitous in both. This was particularly striking in the final weeks of both campaigns. Second, just as prevalent was negative rather than positive news coverage. Regardless of party, leader, issue, or campaign, negative judgments outweighed positive ones in campaign coverage. In this chapter, we cover some of the features unique to the 2004 and 2006 elections; our focus, however, is on these two generalizable trends. We identify these two features of Canadian elections, drawing on an exhaustive content analysis of thousands of campaign-period election stories. We consider the critical importance of policy content, examine the issues most prominent in the 2004 and 2006 campaigns, and explore briefly the possibility that different newspapers covered the campaigns differently. But we also try to account for, and perhaps justify, the prevalence of both horse-race content and negativity in election coverage.

PRESS COVERAGE OF THE 2004 AND 2006 FEDERAL ELECTIONS

Data reported in this chapter are drawn from two separate content analyses of print-media coverage of the 2004 and 2006 federal election campaigns. Both are available online from the Media Observatory of the McGill Institute for the Study of Canada (http://media-observatory.mcgill.ca). The studies were conducted separately but are directly comparable, methodologically speaking. Each tracks all campaign content—news, editorials, and opinion pieces—published in seven major daily newspapers across Canada (five English-language, two French-language): the *Vancouver Sun*, the *Calgary Herald*, the *Toronto Star*, *Le Devoir*, *La Presse*, the *National Post*, and the *Globe and Mail*. Daily coding for the 2004 election began one week before the writ dropped, lasting six weeks until the day of the election, June 28, 2004. The 2006 campaign—among the longest in Canadian history—accounts for eight weeks of coding material before the election on January 23, 2006. In total, 6,694 articles are included in this data set: 4,280 news stories and 2,414 editorial and opinion pieces.

In both 2004 and 2006, starting at the official election campaign kick-offs, the Media Observatory's team of coders began to scrutinize the main news sections of the major Canadian dailies. There were about a dozen coders for each campaign, introduced to the study during formal training sessions that included a series of practice coding exercises and a guide for our online data-entry system. Coding took place daily as the campaign progressed. Coders were responsible for a different newspaper each week so that we could test for any coder effects or bias. Stories were also randomly selected for double-coding throughout the campaign to check "inter-coder reliability"—the consistency with which different coders came up with identical codes. All measures included in this analysis achieved an appropriate level of reliability. Detailed methodological information is available on the Media Observatory website.

Coders began each day by identifying articles about the campaign in their assigned newspaper. This content was then coded for mentions of issues, parties, and leaders, as well as positive, negative, or neutral tone. This method of coding indicated which parties or leaders received positive or negative treatment and which issues dominated the campaign. It also showed which parties were associated (positively or negatively) with leading issues, and suggested which parties were driving coverage of the campaign or responding to the initiatives of their opponents. The coding also indicated how treatment of parties, leaders, and issues varied across newspapers and across regions in Canada.

The study was designed in such a way as to ensure that most codes are purely objective—that is, not dependent on subjective decisions by coders. The study recorded, for instance, the first three parties, leaders, and issues mentioned in an article, in the order in which they appeared, as an indication of prominence. "First mentions" are a particularly valuable indicator of the issue agenda and the prominence of parties and leaders in the campaign. We also recorded the general emphasis of each article: primarily campaign-focused ("horse race"), or primarily issue-focused. This provides an indication of how much coverage is focused on polling results and stories about the campaign trail as opposed to policy issues.

Finally, we included one set of subjective codes for tone—positive, negative, or neutral—for parties and leaders. The specific instructions for coding the tone of media content were as follows: the default for all mentions is neutral; and a leader or party mention has to be clearly "good press" or "bad press" to be coded as such. (Note that this is similar to, for example, Brady and Johnston, 1987.) Put another way, unless the story was obviously and intentionally positive or negative, a mention of a leader or party was considered to be neutral. This is what you might call *latent* rather than *manifest* measurement of election-news content—it captures tone evident in the reporting of or commentary on a given event, rather than the negativity or positivity of the event itself. For that reason, careful attention was paid to training and reliability analyses for this indicator.

Let us consider this coding strategy in a bit more detail. The tone code does not simply reflect reports of leaders and parties criticizing policy platforms and records of competitors. Instead, our measure of an article's tone reflects critical and positive commentary of the main leaders and parties from sources *other than the main protagonists* of the campaign itself. For instance, reporting a Harper speech in which the Conservative leader objected to or attacked something about Paul Martin was considered neutral—just reporting the news. Reporting that speech and using it to further discuss Martin's failings, however, was considered negative. Our coders also noted tone when, for example, an economist issued an endorsement for a party's tax policy proposal, but not when another party leader attacked (or endorsed) it. The tone measure also captures assessments of leaders' and parties' performance in the campaign and in public-opinion polls. Reports of a party "surging ahead" in the polls were noted as positive. Conversely, stories noting "uninspiring" or "gaffe-prone" campaign performances were duly recorded as negative press. The overall result, then, was that mentions in news stories were predominantly neutral, and mentions in editorial and opinion pieces were mainly negative or positive. To be sure, the coders disregarded some of the subtle tone conveyed in articles and headlines, but then so do everyday citizens.

Our discussion of results will focus here on three exhibits—one tracking horse-race versus issue coverage during the campaign, another looking at the salience of specific issues, and finally a figure capturing the tone of coverage for parties and leaders. There is certainly much more to be said about these two elections; however, we suggest that our data on these fronts points to trends that are both substantively interesting and generalizable beyond these campaigns.

Note that, while the 2004 campaign was just six weeks long, the 2006 campaign lasted eight weeks, stretching over the Christmas holidays. In order to put results from both elections on the same graphs, we delay the starting point of the 2006 election by two weeks—in other words, week 3 for the 2006 campaign is week 1 for the 2004 campaign, and so on. Note also that this timing fits with commentators' impressions of the 2006 campaign; namely, that the pre-Christmas period was somewhat more subdued, and then the campaign started in full force following the holidays.

The Horse Race and Issues

Figure 7.1 shows the breakdown in coverage in terms of horse-race versus issue coverage for both the 2004 and 2006 election campaigns. Overall, roughly 55 percent of all coverage in 2004 was horse-race-focused, compared with 45 percent in 2006. The implication is that a voter looking through the newspaper is about as likely to see a story about the campaign—who's winning and who's losing—as they are to notice an article about the policy options presented by parties and leaders.

This presence of horse-race journalism is not a new development in Canadian politics, of course. Over the past 25 years or so, content analyses have frequently noted the prevalence of a "game frame" in coverage of Canadian election campaigns

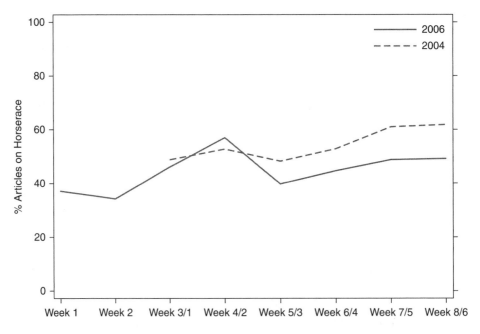

Figure 7.1 Horse-Race Coverage

Source: Media Observatory at McGill 2004 and 2006 Newspaper Election Study (http://www.media-observatory.mcgill.ca)

(e.g., Wilson, 1980; Fletcher, 1991; Mendelsohn, 1993). Our findings in this regard fit well with the conventional understandings of Canadian news media.

That being said, it is important to stress that the 2006 campaign did generate more issues-oriented coverage. The volume of horse-race coverage in 2004 is striking: after a brief period of policy discussion in week 2 of the campaign, horse-race coverage increased gradually to over 60 percent of all election articles. The space left for substantive policy discussion was, accordingly, relatively limited. In contrast, 2006 coverage of parties' policy proposals was not eclipsed by polls and campaign strategy. A slight majority of the 2006 election campaign's media cov⋯⋯ ⋯ policy-focused, and this wa⋯ ticularly true in the two ⋯⋯⋯ of ⋯⋯⋯⋯ be called the "pre-campaign" ⋯⋯ in this compar⋯⋯⋯, policy-driven campaign, however, regular ⋯⋯ would have ⋯⋯ about nine horse-race articles for every eleven policy arti⋯⋯

The horse-race emphasis does not vary by newspaper, though it does by article type. Looking at the two elections combined, news and opinion pieces were about 51 percent horse-race, while editorials were just 26 percent horse-race. Put differently, editorials are about one and a half times more likely than hard news stories to be about issues rather than about the race or strategy. In the same way, articles about the election o⋯ the front page were slightly more likely to be about the horse race than articles o⋯ subsequent pages (54 percent versus 47 percent). Note that this means that people who skim a newspaper, avoiding the editorial sections but briefly glancing at the front page, are exposed not just to less information but to *different* information. Specifically, horse race coverage will make up a greater proportion of the articles seen by these readers ⋯⋯ also Andrew, 2007).

The horse race–policy dichotomy does not entirely capture the ⋯⋯ or lack of policy issue coverage in a campaign. Table 7.1 shows ⋯⋯⋯⋯ ⋯⋯ The single most salient issue of these campaigns w⋯ ⋯⋯⋯⋯ ⋯⋯ ⋯⋯ corruption. The sponsorship scandal dominated ⋯⋯, and acc⋯⋯⋯⋯⋯ re-emerged as the most salient issue of the 2006 campaign's second half, aided by news that the RCMP was launching an investigation into a Liberal government decision on income trusts. Indeed, the overall salience of accountability and corruption in these two election campaigns is somewhat understated in Table 7.1. Observed weekly, accountability and corruption was the most discussed item in the press for four of the six weeks in the 2004 campaign, and it was the leading issue for five of the eight campaign weeks during the 2006 election. In effect, government *process* rather than specific government *policies* dominated ⋯⋯ two election

Note, ⋯⋯   news content, the
actual poli⋯   it in perspective, if
elections a⋯   includes not just a
commitmen⋯   care, education, the
environmen⋯   ; kind of policy was
addressed i⋯   2004, roughly three
in ten artic⋯

Definition of: bit, byte and gigabyte.	
Bit	A 1 or 0 (b) -----A bit is a small piece of information
Byte	8 bits = 1 byte
Gigabyte	1024 bytes = 1 gigabyte

Table 7.1 Leading Issues

Issue	2006	2004
Process		
Sponsorship Scandal, Income Trusts	7.9%	5.4%
Government/Leadership	3.5%	2.9%
Total	11.5%	8.3%
Policy		
Constitution, National Unity/Separatism	8.9%	5.1%
International Affairs/Defence	5.7%	4.2%
Social Issues/Programs	5.0%	3.3%
Taxes	4.8%	3.7%
Crime	4.7%	1.6%
Healthcare	4.0%	8.4%
Economy, Unemployment, Inflation, Trade & Industry	3.8%	2.1%
Same-Sex Marriage	3.4%	1.9%
Democratic Reform/Turnout	3.0%	3.4%
Environmental Issues	2.9%	2.3%
Immigration, Multiculturalism, Racism/Discrimination	2.7%	1.4%
Intergovernmental Relations	2.1%	1.3%
Deficit/Government Spending/Fiscal Responsibility	1.9%	2.6%
Education	0.8%	0.4%

Cells show percent of total first-issue mentions. For 2006, N = 4,255. For 2004, N = 3,224.
Source: Media Observatory at McGill 2004 and 2006 Newspaper Election Study (www.media-observatory.mcgill.ca)

This difference in policy coverage in the two campaigns is notable, and is primarily a product of the Conservative Party's strategy in 2006. Conservatives were more likely to feature in coverage of issues than the other parties in that election, due in large part to their strategy of introducing, in the early weeks of the campaign, almost one new policy per day. The same was not true for 2004, when the Conservative campaign was less proactive and the Liberal government was overwhelmed by ongoing charges of corruption. Indeed, 2004 was remarkable for a stunning lack of content on policy issues. The horse race accordingly overwhelmed issue coverage by a larger margin. We should not forget, however, that the 2004 election was the first since 1988 for which the outcome was uncertain, and one of the few that could reasonably fuel speculation about the intricacies of a minority government. It turned out that the horse race was one of the very few interesting elements of that campaign.

Tone of Coverage

What about the tone of the coverage? Figure 7.2 shows results for a combined "net tone" for parties and leaders. "Net tone" is (a) the number of *positive* mentions of the party or leader (e.g., "Liberals" or "Paul Martin") as a percentage of all mentions of that party or leader minus (b) the number of *negative* mentions of the party or leader as a percentage of all mentions of that party or leader. A value of zero accordingly indicates either entirely neutral coverage or an equal amount of positive and negative coverage. Positive values suggest more positive coverage than negative coverage; negative values suggest that more of the coverage of that party or leader was negative.

It is worth noting, first of all, that the tone of news coverage in these elections was predominately neutral. Looking over both campaigns, of the 5,763 mentions of either the Liberal Party or Paul Martin, 75 percent were neutral; for the 5,404 Conservative Party mentions, 81 percent were neutral. This is not to say that all the information being conveyed lacked entirely the content required for evaluations, of course—there will have been instances in which the Liberals or Conservatives had a good campaign stop or proposed a policy that some readers would approve of. Recall that the tone measures we use here focus on overt evaluations of candidates and parties on the part of the journalist. And, in this regard, it is apparent that positive and negative coverage is relatively rare. At least, this is true when looking at all articles combined. Looking across article types, there

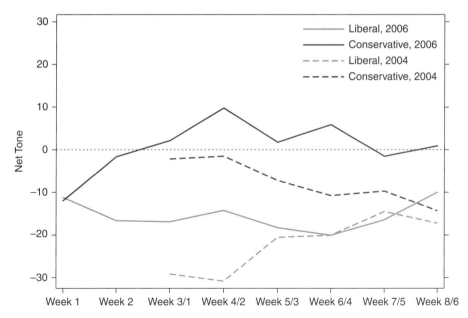

Figure 7.2 "Net Tone" for Liberals and Conservatives

Source: Media Observatory at McGill 2004 and 2006 Newspaper Election Study (http://www.media-observatory.mcgill.ca)

is clearly much more tone in editorial and opinion pieces. In both elections combined, roughly 81 percent of all news stories included no tone, but 40 percent of editorial pieces included evaluative judgments about parties or leaders, and 52 percent of opinion pieces included such judgments.

Looking at the direction of tone, it is evident that evaluative judgments were much more likely to be negative than positive. Roughly three-quarters of all "toned" judgments about leaders and parties in these campaigns were negative. This is partly illustrated in Figure 7.2—note that "net tone" is never above zero for the Liberals in either campaign, and is marginally positive for the Conservatives only in the middle weeks of the 2006 campaign. (Indeed the Liberals, and Paul Martin specifically, account for much of the negative coverage of these campaigns published in Canadian dailies.)

Were there systematic differences in tone across newspapers? Election campaigns tend to re-invigorate concerns about "media bias" among party leaders, political strategists, and journalists. While the word "bias" has negative connotations, partisan differences across newspapers can be seen to represent a healthy diversity of opinion among media outlets. (Though note that the argument valuing diversity in media outlets is premised on there being more than one newspaper within each regional market.) The trends identified here reflect the volume of negative or positive coverage of parties during the campaign—whether they reflect *bias* is perhaps another matter. We do note, however, that differences in the tone of news coverage do exist across newspapers, and—where trends in tone are evident in these data—these trends tend to match the partisanship reflected in editorial and opinion pieces. To give an example, in both elections, both the *National Post* and the *Calgary Herald* presented comparatively positive coverage of the Conservative Party. In 2006, the cumulative net tone for Conservatives over the campaign in the *Herald* was +8, compared to the seven-newspaper average of 0. The *Toronto Star*, in contrast, was the most negative about the Conservatives and comparatively more positive about the Liberals—or, more accurately given Liberal coverage in these campaigns, at least less negative about the Liberals. The *Star*'s net tone for Liberals in 2006 was –6, compared with the seven-newspaper average of –15.

In Summary

The 2004 and 2006 federal election campaigns were unique in some ways, but quite typical in others. The role that the sponsorship scandal played in both elections was clearly a unique feature; so, too, was the discussion of minority or coalition government, rare in Canadian federal politics, but especially prominent in the 2006 campaign. These elections followed a particularly prominent scandal for the long-governing Liberals, as well as a restructuring of the parties on the right. The partisan landscape was changing, as was the likelihood of majority governments. Process issues may have quite justifiably played a starring role.

That said, the relative predominance of horse-race coverage and the corresponding absence of policy content does not seem especially unique. Pundits have regularly criticized media for not supplying the kind of information required by a vote-decision-making public, and, regardless of the effect attention-grabbing poll results might have, few would support Kim Campbell's insinuation that election time is not the time to talk about serious issues. Active, representative government requires that voters make their policy preferences known to governments, if in no other way, then at least in the formation of those governments. Policies should thus play at least some role in election coverage—preferably a dominant one.

The prominence of negative over positive assessments was also not unique to these elections. Indeed, this trend has been identified not just in election coverage but in media content more generally. Whether the predominance of negative coverage is a problem is, however, another matter. Indeed, it may not be clear that horse-race coverage is entirely bad either. In the followings sections, we try to account for why we see so much horse-race coverage and negativity and make a case for the potential value of each.

ANOTHER POLL ABOVE THE FOLD: WHY SO MUCH HORSE-RACE COVERAGE?

A little more than half of the articles printed about the 2004 and 2006 elections focused on campaign activities, poll forecasts, and strategy. Canadian journalists were more likely to report how leaders and parties stood in the race, or to offer an interpretation of their behaviour, than they were to report policy positions. In short, "what" politicians said often took a back seat to "why" they said it and how well they (and the party they were affiliated with) were doing in the polls. Articles about the campaign and strategy also received more prominent coverage by newspapers than policy-oriented articles. People who occasionally read a front-page article were mostly exposed to information about the horse race. All of the papers presented the news about these elections in more or less the same way. The race clearly trumped policy.

On the surface, then, it seems as though newspaper coverage of these elections left something to be desired for responsible voters. Interpretive coverage of political events and projections of electoral outcomes, at least in theory, should not take precedence over the main issues. Policy information is certainly a prerequisite for successful modern democracy—it allows voters to make connections between their preferences and competing political options. But, in the elections studied above, responsible voters had to skip over almost three-quarters of the articles printed to find in-depth coverage of what the politicians and parties had to offer.

Horse-race-oriented news is not a new phenomenon in Canada, of course, or in other advanced industrial democracies (Graber, 1976; Jamieson, 1992; Patterson, 1993; Craig, 2000). Content analyses of Canadian media spanning almost three decades have noted the prominence of polls and strategy in coverage of politics during campaign and non-campaign periods (Wilson, 1980; Fletcher, 1981; Soderlund et al., 1984; Taras, 1990; Mendelsohn, 1993; Trimble & Sampert, 2004). Hence, the volume of horse-race journalism we observed during the 2004 and 2006 campaigns does not come as much of a surprise. The campaign content that preceded the elections of Trudeau, Clark, Mulroney, and Chrétien was, in this way, quite similar to the information supplied immediately before the elections of Paul Martin and Stephen Harper. While the saliency of policy domains changes from one election to another, Canadian voters have come to expect a consistent dose of this type of campaign journalism.

The persistence of horse-race-oriented content alone does not excuse the Canadian press from an audit in 2008, however. The fact remains that policy gets short shrift in articles published during campaigns. Why is this the case? There are several reasons to expect horse-race rather than policy coverage. In terms of the supply of horse-race information, we can look to the limitations and behaviours of both journalists and politicians. What parties and leaders say and do during a campaign is certainly related to the supply of horse-race or issue-focused media content, or, more to the point, the supply of issue content (see, for example, Flowers, Haynes, & Crespin, 2003). The increase of issue-oriented articles in 2006 can be linked to the Conservative Party's strategy of releasing one policy announcement per day during the first part of the campaign (Andrew et al., 2006; Waddell & Dornan, 2006). When politicians provided policy content in 2006, journalists covered it. In 2004, in contrast, the relative absence of policy articles in the press was partly driven by general reluctance of politicians, after the first week, to talk about much besides the faults of other parties and leaders (Goodyear-Grant, Soroka, & Maioni, 2004). Horse-race coverage is thus at least partly linked to the kinds of information that parties provide (or do not provide) in campaigns.

Even when politicians present new policy on the campaign trail, however, journalists can be limited in their capacity to write about it. Horse-race coverage may be a product

Filters
- Ownership of media
- Funding or advertising
- Sourcing (where do you get your news)
- Flack (letters, law suits, phone calls etc.)
- Ideologies or enemies

Substantivism vs. Instrumentalism: Substantivism is the theory that we humans are controlled by technology. That technology over time will run the economy and take over jobs. This theory believes that technology has the power. Instrumentalism is the theory concerning as an instrument or a significant part of out society. That technology has a key role in our society. However, it simply help things run smoothly and more effectively with the help of humans.

* POGG: Peace Order and Good Governance
* UBB: Usage Based Billing ⟶ or net
neu utrality.

Ideologies and Models: models
- Authoritarian: a form of social organization characterized by submission to authority. It is usually opposed to individualism and libertarianism. The press is subjected by the top elites and political beings, the elite decide what is published & diversity is wasteful.
- Libertarian: emphasize freedom, individual liberty, and voluntary association
- Communist/Totalitarianism: media encourages people to vote for "fluffy issues" rather than personal and real issues. This form is brainwashing people to think a particular way
- Revolutionary:
- Developmental

Canadian Press: Canadian Journalism
- Authoritarian
- Partisan Press (Mid to late 1880's): When the press is biased to one party in their information in their paper. Certain press are either considered liberal or conservative. Libs are Dems-Cons are Reps example - The Houston Chronicle is losing a lot of their readership because of the liberal partisan content.
- Objective Professionalism (Post WW2)
- Critical Journalism (Watergate)
- New Phase

who is most likely to form government and who is least likely. Perhaps it is attributed to a gaffe-free campaign by the leader, or a couple of well-received policies in the platform. In either case, such cues give undecided voters a good sense of who or what to look at first.

This means that candidates and parties who are portrayed by media as leading, or gaining ground, have an advantage in the weeks and days before an election (Ansolabehere & Iyengar, 1994). Voters might disregard (or at least pay less attention to) candidates, parties, and leaders who are not perceived to have a viable opportunity to win. At its worst, this means that candidates outside the mainstream will have a great deal of difficulty getting their message to voters. (For a particularly good example, see Meyrowitz, 1994.) Given the limited time voters have to assimilate a potentially huge volume of political information, however, it does seem sensible for voters to inform themselves about the policies and records of those thought to have the best chance of winning. (And shining a spotlight on the frontrunners might also lead to an extra degree of public scrutiny for those most likely to form the government.)

This is all speculative, of course. Our data cannot be used to explore how the so-called game frame was actually assimilated by Canadian voters. But, hypothetically speaking, the case for horse-race coverage is roughly as follows: By providing highly salient information about the viability of candidates, horse-race coverage can help voters more efficiently manage their news-gathering; in effect, it is a filtering mechanism that can help voters reduce the complexity of electoral choices.

MUST IT ALL BE SO NEGATIVE?

News content is dominated by the negative. Consider the well-known phrases, "If it bleeds, it leads" or "No news is good news." Or simply think about any recent newspaper or television news broadcast. Mass media over-emphasize the prevalence of violent crime (e.g., Altheide, 1997), and events involving conflict or crisis receive a greater degree of media attention (Shoemaker et al., 1991). U.S. networks regularly give more coverage to bad economic trends than to good ones (Harrington, 1989); the same trends are apparent in U.K. news coverage (Soroka, 2006). Indeed, that news tends to be negative is clear enough to any regular news consumer. And it is no less clear in our analysis of recent campaign coverage. Looking across all four major parties and leaders in the 2004 and 2006 campaigns, for every one positive mention there were almost three negative ones.

There is a growing body of work suggesting *asymmetry* in individuals' responses to—and in the reporting of—negative versus positive information. There is evidence, for instance, that negative information plays a greater role in voting behaviour (e.g., Campbell et al., 1960). U.S. presidents appear to be penalized electorally for negative economic trends but reap few electoral benefits from positive trends (e.g., Bloom & Price, 1975). In overall impressions of U.S. presidential candidates and parties, negative information seems to matter more than positive information (Lau, 1982). And negative campaigning appears to be a particularly powerful means of getting attention (though the actual impact of negative advertising is not clear; see, e.g., Lau et al., 2007; Fridkin & Kenney, 2004).

Why is this so? One account begins with the psychology literature on impression formation.[1] This work finds that unfavourable information has a greater impact on impressions than does favourable information across a wide variety of situations (e.g., Ronis & Lipinski, 1985). Several explanations have been given for this asymmetry. Most work suggests that impressions are formed based on an expectation, or reference point. These impressions can vary based on experience; however, individuals tend to be mildly optimistic, so the reference point tends, on average, to be slightly positive. In one conception, this simply means a shift in perspective: -4 looks much worse from an expectation of $+4$ than it does from an expectation of 0 (e.g., Helson, 1964). An alternative theory suggests that the asymmetry is driven by cognitive weighting—more attention is given to information that is regarded as unique or novel, which tends to be information that is more extreme (e.g., Fiske, 1980). So similarly, -4 is more extreme (and thus is given greater weight) if the expectation is $+4$ rather than 0. Both theories suggest that a mildly positive expectation leads individuals to view mildly negative information as very negative or particularly informative and react accordingly.[2]

The prominence of negative media coverage may be driven in part by this individual-level dynamic. Journalists are individuals, writing articles to appeal to other individuals. Journalists will thus regard negative information as more important, not just based on their own interests, but also on the interests of their news-consuming audience. Observed trends in media content are, in this view, a product of asymmetric reactions to information at the individual level.

Alternatively, it may be that media outlets' emphasis on negative news reflects one of their principle institutional functions in a democracy: holding current governments (and companies, and, indeed, some individuals) accountable. The notion of mass media as a "Fourth Estate" has been prominent both in the literature on newspapers (e.g., Schulte, 1981) and in the pages of newspapers themselves. Surveillance of this kind mainly involves identifying problems. We might, consequently, deduce that media emphasize negative information in part because it is their job to do so.

Asymmetry—viewed as a focus on monitoring and identifying problems—may thus be a standard attribute of representative democracy, not just for media but for voters as well. There is a body of political representational theory in which accountability for errors plays a central role. Ministerial responsibility in parliamentary systems focuses on this penalty-for-errors dynamic; so, too, do many accounts of "electoral responsibility." These notions of accountability fit well with early descriptions of asymmetry at the individual level: "the electorate votes against policies and incumbents to a greater degree than it votes for new policies and candidates" (Kernell, 1977, p. 51).

This accountability explanation need not be independent from the preceding psychological theories. A particular focus on the watchdog role of the press, and on accountability in governance more generally, may well be connected to the impression that negative information is a more critical indicator of government or candidate performance than is positive information. Asymmetry and accountability may be fundamentally intertwined. The existence of largely negative coverage should consequently not necessarily be viewed as a negative, normatively speaking; indeed, it may reflect a well-functioning media system. Mostly negative media content may be a typical and critical feature of representative democracy.

CONCLUSION

Our analyses reveal both similarities and differences between the 2004 and 2006 Canadian federal election campaigns. Practically speaking, the elections produced quite different outcomes. Media content reflected this difference. The Conservatives received more positive coverage in 2006, for instance. Relatedly, policy played a larger role in 2006, due in large part to the first two weeks of the pre-Christmas campaign, when the horse race played a comparatively small role. That said, the post-Christmas 2006 campaign looked much more like that of 2004; indeed, much more like many other campaigns. We have focused on two trends of media coverage evident in 2006 and 2004, and indeed in many other campaigns in Canada and elsewhere: (1) a predominance of horse-race coverage over policy content, and (2) the preponderance of negative rather than positive presentations of parties and leaders.

Whether either of these trends is good is another matter and one we have only partly addressed above. While the typical reaction has been to decry both horse-race coverage and negativity, however, we have tried to suggest several reasons why both may actually be useful. Horse-race coverage may help voters strategize; negative coverage may reflect the kind of monitoring function that media are supposed to perform in a democracy. And both may help newspapers attract an audience. Regardless of whether we accept these arguments, however, the prominence of both horse-race coverage and negativity suggest that both get attention from readers. The main goal of newspapers is to find an audience, after all. If, as political scientists, we want a public that is attentive to politics, then a campaign full of polling reports and overwhelmingly critical commentary may be the price we have to pay.

Media Journal Assignments

1. Examine the *National Post* and the *Globe and Mail* over a three-day period. How much coverage is there of federal politics? How much of it do you consider negative? Positive? Neutral? Can you determine differences between the two papers? Discuss how the evaluations of federal politics presented in these two newspapers may affect your understanding of politics, giving examples.

2. Utilizing newspaper databases, analyze three days of coverage of the last provincial election in your local paper. Was the coverage dominated by the horse race? What percentage of stories examined issues in detail? Do you think this information helped voters make up their minds on whom to vote for in the election?

Endnotes

1. This account draws heavily on Soroka, 2006.

2. Note that theories of *loss aversion* in economics make similar predictions: people will care more strongly about a loss than they do about a gain of equal magnitude. See Kahneman and Tversky, 1979.

References

Altheide, David L. 1997. "The News Media, the Problem Frame, and the Production of Fear." *Sociological Quarterly* 38 (4): 647–68.

Andrew, Blake C. 2007. "Media-Generated Shortcuts: Do Newspaper Headlines Present Another Roadblock for Low Information Rationality?" *Harvard International Journal of Press/Politics* 12 (2): 24–44.

Andrew, Blake, Antonia Maioni, & Stuart Soroka. 2006. "Just When You Thought It Was Out, Policy Is Pulled Back In." *Policy Options* 27 (3): 74–79.

Ansolabehere, Stephen & Shanto Iyengar. 1994. "Of Horse-Shoes and Horse Races: Experimental Studies of the Impact of Poll Results on Electoral Behaviour." *Political Communication* 11 (4): 413–30.

Blais, André, Elisabeth Gidengil, Richard Nadeau, & Neil Nevitte. 2002. *Anatomy of a Liberal Victory: Making Sense of the Vote in the 2000 Canadian Election*. Peterborough, Ont.: Broadview Press.

Bloom, Howard S. & H. Douglas Price. 1975. "Voter Response to Short-Run Economic Conditions: The Asymmetric Effect of Prosperity and Recession." *American Political Science Review* 69 (4): 1240–54.

Brady, Henry E. & Richard Johnston. 1987. "What's the Primary Message: Horse Race or Issue Journalism?" In *Media and Momentum: The New Hampshire Primary and Nomination Politics*, ed. Gary R. Orren and Nelson W. Polsby, 127–86. Chatham, N.J.: Chatham House.

Campbell, Angus, Philip E. Converse, Warren E. Miller, & Donald E. Stokes. 1960. *The American Voter*. Chicago: University of Chicago Press.

Craig, Richard. 2000. "Expectations and Elections: How Television Defines Campaign News." *Critical Studies in Mass Communication* 17 (1): 28–44.

Delli Carpini, Michael X. 2005. "News from Somewhere: Journalistic Frames and the Debate over 'Public Journalism.' " In *Framing American Politics*, ed. Karen Callaghan and Frauke Schnell, 21–53. Pittsburgh, Pa.: University of Pittsburgh Press.

Fiske, Susan T. 1980. "Attention and Weight in Person Perception: The Impact of Negative and Extreme Behavior." *Journal of Personality and Social Psychology* 38 (6): 889–906.

Fletcher, Frederick. 1981. "Playing the Game: The Mass Media in the 1979 Campaign." In *Canada at the Polls, 1979 and 1980: A Study of the General Elections*, ed. Howard R. Penniman, 280–321. Washington, D.C.: American Enterprise Institute for Public Policy Research.

———. 1991. *Reporting the Campaign: Election Coverage in Canada*. Toronto: Dundurn Press.

Flowers, Julianne F., Audrey A. Haynes, & Michael H. Crespin. 2003. "The Media, the Campaign, and the Message." *American Journal of Political Science* 47 (2): 259–73.

Fournier, Patrick, Richard Nadeau, André Blais, Elisabeth Gidengil, & Neil Nevitte. 2004. "Time-of-Voting Decision and Susceptibility to Campaign Effects." *Electoral Studies* 23 (4): 661–81.

Fridkin, Kim Leslie, & Patrick J. Kenney. 2004. "Do Negative Messages Work? The Impact of Negativity on Citizens' Evaluations of Candidates." *American Politics Research* 32 (5): 570–605.

Geer, John G. 2006. *In Defense of Negativity*. Chicago: University of Chicago Press.

Graber, Doris A. 1976. "Press and TV as Opinion Resources in Presidential Campaigns." *Public Opinion Quarterly* 40 (3): 285–303.

Goodyear-Grant, Elizabeth, Stuart Soroka, & Antonia Maioni. 2004. "The Role of the Media: A Campaign Saved by a Horserace." *Policy Options* 25 (8): 89–91.

Harrington, David E. 1989. "Economic News on Television: The Determinants of Coverage." *Public Opinion Quarterly* 53 (1): 566–74.

Helson, H. 1964. *Adaptation-Level Theory*. New York: Harper.

Jamieson, Kathleen Hall. 1992. *Dirty Politics: Deception, Distraction, and Democracy*. New York: Oxford University Press.

Kahneman, Daniel & Amos Tversky. 1979. "Prospect Theory: An Analysis of Decision under Risk." *Econometrica* 47(2): 263–91.

Kernell, Samuel. 1977. "Presidential Popularity and Negative Voting: An Alternative Explanation of the Midterm Congressional Decline of the President's Party." *American Political Science Review* 71 (1): 44–66.

Lau, Richard R. 1982. "Negativity in Political Perception." *Political Behavior* 4 (4): 353–77.

Lau, Richard R., Lee Sigelman, & Ivy Brown Rovner. 2007. "The Effects of Negative Political Campaigns: A Meta-Analytic Reassessment." *Journal of Politics* 69 (4): 1176–1209.

Mendelsohn, Matthew. 1993. "Television's Frames in the 1988 Canadian Election." *Canadian Journal of Communication* 18 (2): 149–71.

Meyrowitz, Joshua. 1994. "The (Almost) Invisible Candidate: A Case Study of News Judgment as Political Censorship." In *Controlling Broadcasting: Access Policy in North America and Europe*, ed. Meryl Aldridge and Nicholas Hewitt, 93–107. Manchester: Manchester University Press.

Patterson, Thomas E. 1993. *Out of Order*. New York: Knopf.

Ronis, David L. & Edmund R. Lipinski. 1985. "Value and Uncertainty as Weighting Factor in Impression Formation." *Journal of Experimental Social Psychology* 21 (1): 47–60.

Schulte, Henry H. 1981. *Reporting Public Affairs*. New York: Macmillan.

Shoemaker, Pamela J., Lucig H. Danielian & Nancy Brendlinger. 1991. "Deviant Acts, Risky Business and U.S. Interests: The Newsworthiness of World Events." *Journalism Quarterly* 68 (4): 781–95.

Soderlund, Walter C., Walter I. Romanow, E. Donald Briggs & R.H. Wagenberg. 1984. *Media and Elections in Canada*. Toronto: Holt Rinehart & Winston of Canada.

Soroka, Stuart N. 2002. *Agenda-Setting Dynamics in Canada*. Vancouver: University of British Columbia Press.

———. 2006. "Good News and Bad News: Asymmetric Responses to Economic Information." *Journal of Politics* 68 (2): 372–85.

Taras, David. 1990. *The Newsmakers: The Media's Influence on Canadian Politics*. Scarborough, Ont.: Nelson Canada.

Trimble, Linda & Shannon Sampert. 2004. "Who's in the Game? Framing of the Canadian Election 2000 by the *Globe and Mail* and the *National Post*." *Canadian Journal of Political Science* 37 (1): 51–71.

Waddell, Christopher & Christopher Dornan. 2006. "The Media and the Campaign." In *The Canadian Federal Election of 2006*, ed. Christopher Dornan and Jon H. Pammett, 220–52. Toronto: Dundurn.

Wilson, R. Jeremy. 1980. "Media Coverage of Canadian Election Campaigns: Horserace Journalism and the Meta-Campaign." *Journal of Canadian Studies* 15 (4): 56–68.

Chapter 8

Covering Muslim Canadians and Politics in Canada: The Print Media and the 2000, 2004, and 2006 Federal Elections

Yasmeen Abu-Laban and Linda Trimble*[1]

INTRODUCTION

It is extremely rare for the Prime Minister of Canada to publicly criticize decisions made by Elections Canada—after all, Elections Canada is the independent and non-partisan body set up by Parliament to take responsibility for all federal elections and referenda. Yet Prime Minister Harper did just that on September 9, 2007, when he declared, "I profoundly disagree" with Elections Canada's decision to allow Muslim women who wear the niqab (a head and face cover) to vote without showing their faces (CBC News, 2007a). Indeed, Canada's chief electoral officer, Marc Mayrand, was subsequently called before the Procedure and House Affairs Committee of the House of Commons to defend his decision. Mayrand said his decision rested on Charter rights, and he rejected any possibility of the Committee directing him to change his ruling. In Mayrand's view, an act of Parliament is required to override his discretionary authority, which is "designed much more for operational matters as opposed to dealing with some fundamental rights protected by the Charter, including the right to vote and freedom of religion" (CBC News, 2007b).

In this exchange, given "urgency" because of three federal by-elections taking place in the province of Quebec on September 17, 2007, there were some very notable silences. First, Prime Minister Harper chose not to discuss the fact that during every general election thousands of Canadians living abroad vote by absentee ballot. For those who simply mail in a ballot there is no formal requirement that these citizens "present" their face.

---

* This chapter significantly expands and updates an earlier article published by the authors as "Print Media Coverage of Muslim Canadians during Recent Federal Elections," *Electoral Insight* 8 (2) (December 2006): 34–42.

Second, the coverage did not focus on the fact that very few Muslim-Canadian women actually wear the niqab. In fact, in Quebec, the place of immediate concern for the exchange, it was estimated that a mere 50 Muslim-Canadian women cover up like this in the entire province, whose population is over 7.5 million; moreover, even those very few women who do cover their faces routinely agree to show them for identification purposes at banks, airports, and border crossings (Sara Elgazzar, cited in CBC News, 2007a). Not least, a glaring omission in the exchange stemmed from the fact that this was not an issue Muslim-Canadian organizations (or Muslim Canadians themselves) had ever asked to have placed on the agenda for public discussion or made an issue of themselves (*Globe and Mail*, 2007). Despite these omissions, the heated tone of the debate between the Chief Electoral Officer and the Prime Minister illustrates in microcosm form the politicization of religious difference that permeates Canadian politics—including electoral politics—today.

While the contemporary climate has spawned new considerations of such themes as the "reasonable accommodation" of religious minorities (see IRPP, 2007), when it comes to religion and politics, traditionally Canadian political scientists have been primarily interested in the impact of Christian religious faith on electoral politics. Specifically, political scientists analyzing electoral patterns from the 1950s onward have long debated the extent to which social background is relevant to vote choice in light of an important tendency for Catholics to support the Liberal Party (Meisel, 1956; Johnston, 1985; Blais et al., 2002; Blais, 2005; Bélanger & Eagles, 2006). Yet for the most part, religious groups have not been a sustained focus of attention within the media's coverage of Canadian federal elections. This may stem from a larger inclination toward secularism. Indeed, as Professor of Religious Studies Paul Bramadat observed, "the tendency in our society is to ignore religion only until some religious individual or group behaves, well, rather badly" (2005, p. 59). The September 11, 2001 attack on the United States, though perpetrated by a handful of individuals, was an event that brought religious divisions to the forefront, focusing attention on a large, heterogeneous, and transnational religious community: Muslims. Our chapter examines this heightened awareness of religious difference as it played out in Canadian print-media accounts during federal electoral campaigns.

Specifically, we analyze English-language print-media accounts of the 2000, 2004, and 2006 Canadian general elections that included discussions of Canadian Muslims. In addition to determining the quantity of coverage prior to and after September 11, 2001, we are also interested in evaluating the nature of the coverage. Assessing the nature of the coverage is important because the media form a key lens through which Canadian society and politics are viewed by most citizens. More specifically, the media are central in shaping, if not constructing, the beliefs people come to form about groups (like religious minorities such as Muslim Canadians) with whom they may infrequently interact (Henry & Tator, 2002, p. 5). We argue that, while the election coverage given to Muslim Canadians has increased over time, the nature of this discussion fails to fully capture the diversity of a community with deep historical roots in Canada, and thus fails to challenge negative stereotypes. In showing the significance of this argument and demonstrating it, we take a fourfold approach. First, we provide background information on the specific characteristics of Muslim Canadians and their political engagement. Second, we provide an overview of extant work on the media and Islam in Canada and elsewhere. Third, based on these reviews, we outline our methodology and hypotheses for the Canadian print-media accounts we examine. Fourth, we discuss in greater detail the specific findings that emerge from the media analysis.

MUSLIM CANADIANS AND THE MOSAIC

While for the purpose of analysis we choose to label a collectivity called "Muslim Canadians," this shorthand is used with the understanding that this is in fact a heterogeneous community, sustained through distinct waves of immigration dating back to the late nineteenth century (Abu-Laban, 1980, pp. 1–81). Muslim Canadians therefore exhibit important cohort differences (Abu-Laban, 1991, pp. 6–31). They are also differentiated in relation to different branches within Islam (Sunni, Shi'i, Druse, Ismaili, to name a few), as well as ethnicity, language, culture, class, and gender (McDonough & Hoodfar, 2005). As illustrated in Table 8.1, data drawn from the 2001 Census show that Muslims today comprise the largest non-Christian faith community in Canada, standing at 2 percent of the Canadian population.

In addition to the fact that the Muslim-Canadian grouping is projected to grow more rapidly than other non-Christian faith communities in Canada over the coming decade, it is notable that a 2004 Environics poll found that Canadians believed that

Table 8.1 Major Religious Denominations in Canada, 2001 (as a percent of population)	
Christian Faith Communities	
Roman Catholic	43.2
Protestant	29.2
Christian Orthodox	1.6
Christian, not included elsewhere	2.6
Non-Christian Faith Communities	
Muslim	2.0
Jewish	1.1
Buddhist	1.0
Hindu	1.0
Sikh	0.9
No Religious Affiliation	
No religion	16.2

Source: Adapted from Statistics Canada, "Religions in Canada, 2001 Census," Analysis Series, Catalogue No. 96f0030XIE2001015 (2003). URL: www12.statcan.ca/english/census01/products/analytic/companion/rel/contents.cfm

religious-based conflict will become more important than linguistic (French–English) or indigenous issues (Jebwab, 2005, p. 93). While such forecasts are impossible to verify except with the passage of time, we do know that since September 11, 2001, there has been a revival of essentialist arguments (which treat Muslims and other groups as undifferentiated) and posit a "clash of civilizations" between Christianity and Islam; we also know that Muslim Canadians (and those perceived as Muslim) have faced an increased risk of violence and discrimination by some co-citizens (Abu-Laban, 2002, pp. 459–82). Additionally, both Canadian citizens and non-citizens that are, or are perceived to be, Muslim have faced new forms of profiling by Canadian and American immigration and security officials, bringing new concerns relating to civil rights and human rights in North America (Abu-Laban, 2004; Arat-Koc, 2006). It has also been established that support for the September 11, 2001 attacks was virtually non-existent among Muslim Canadians (McDonough & Hoodfar, 2005, p. 137).

In response to the post–September 11 order and the U.S.-led "war on terrorism," Muslim-Canadian organizations and community leaders have developed new forms of organizing to attempt to counter stereotypes, fear, hate crimes, and racial profiling directed at Muslims generally, and to attempt to broaden dialogue both among Muslim Canadians and between Muslim- and non-Muslim Canadians (McDonough & Hoodfar, 2005, pp. 137–41). Thus, Muslim Canadians are not politically passive. However, it should also be noted that when it comes to participation in federal elections, the one available study suggests that voter turnout has been lower than that of Canadians overall, standing at only 42 percent in the 2000 election (compared to 61.2 percent of all Canadians), and improving somewhat in 2004 to 46.5 percent (compared to 60.9 percent of all Canadians) (Hamdani, 2005, pp. 1–9). Among Muslim Canadians, men are more likely to vote than women, and those of Arab origin appear to be more likely to engage in the electoral process than those of South-Asian origin (Hamdani, 2005, pp. 1–14). Compared to their numbers in the overall population, Muslim Canadians are under-represented as elected officials, though from the 1970s there were some men running and elected to office, and from the 1990s some women began to run and achieve success (notably, Muslim-Canadian women typically run for liberal or social democratic, rather than conservative, parties) (Hamdani, 2005, pp. 1–11).

The post–September 11 responses of Muslim Canadians have also involved attempts to directly shape artistic media representations. The television comedy *Little Mosque on the Prairie*, which premiered in 2007, finds humour in the interactions between Muslims and non-Muslims living in the small fictitious Canadian town of Mercy, Saskatchewan. In the words of its creator Zarqa Nawaz—a Muslim and mother of four based in Regina—the program aims to show "that Muslims can be funny and are just like everyone else" (CBC.caArts, 2007). Notwithstanding this rare example of attentiveness to ethnic diversity, the presence and persistence of stereotypes in the dominant U.S. and Canadian media remain a specific concern for the ongoing organizing of Muslim Canadians.

(MIS)REPRESENTING ISLAM AND MUSLIM CANADIANS: THE ROLE OF THE MEDIA

One of the earliest analyses of the way the media covers Islam was offered by the late Columbia University literary critic Edward Said. In his book addressing the role of the U.S. media in covering the Middle East after the Iranian revolution of 1979, Said (1981 [1997]) criticized what he saw as an escalating tendency to treat Muslims as homogenous, and to equate Islam with fundamentalism and a global threat. For Said, this was a misrepresentation that served to obscure the complexity of Islam, as well as Middle East politics. Film and artistic representations also garnered the attention of Jack Shaheen, who examined the representation of Arabs in television (1984) and, more recently, Hollywood films (2001). Shaheen's history of Hollywood cinema shows that Muslims and Arabs were treated as if they are one and the same, even though Arabs have many religious faiths and Muslims come from many ethnic backgrounds. Moreover, Arabs/Muslims have been treated as regular human beings in only five percent of over 900 Hollywood films. In Shaheen's words, "From 1896 until today, filmmakers have collectively indicted all Arabs as Public Enemy # 1—brutal, heartless, uncivilized religious fanatics and money-mad cultural 'others' bent on terrorizing civilized Westerners, especially Christians and Jews" (Shaheen, 2003, p. 172). Muslim and Arab women in Hollywood typically do not speak, and are cast as *femmes fatales* and/or oppressed rather than as "doctors, computer specialists, school teachers, print and broadcast journalists, or as successful well-rounded electric or domestic engineers" (Shaheen, 2003, p. 184).

There are some who counter that Hollywood and media representations of Muslims and Arabs are "variable and not necessarily insensitive or untruthful" (Mandel, 2001, p. 30). However, since the events of September 11, 2001, analyses of the media's coverage of Islam as well as Muslims tend to reinforce the overall findings of both Said and Shaheen. Nacos and Torres-Reyna (2007) looked at coverage in New York–based newspapers, as well as national American papers, before and after September 11. They pinpointed stereotyped messages about Islam and/or Arabs (as lazy, terrorist, suicide bombers, fanatic) and gendered stereotypes about female passivity. Their findings suggest that the *New York Times*, *New York Daily News*, *New York Post*, and *USA Today* coverage both quantitatively expanded and somewhat qualitatively improved in the immediate post-September 11 period as compared to prior to September 11; however, coverage slipped back into stereotyped discussions in the weeks leading up to the one-year anniversary (Nacos & Torres-Reyna, 2007, pp. 1–38). As well, their analysis suggests that the visual images six months prior to and six months after September 11 in *Time* and *Newsweek* magazines of Muslims and Arabs abroad were more numerous than images of them at home, and overall were negative, especially in *Time* (Nacos & Torres-Reyna, 2007, pp. 40–41). Similar negative and gendered stereotypes about Islam have also been found to permeate the discourses of major American television networks (CNN, ABC, CBS, NBC, and Fox) as well as the message board of CNN specifically (Martin & Phelan, 2002). These find echoes in the representation of Asian Muslims in the British press (Abbas, 2001); niqab (or burqa) images and captions on the internet

(Rantanen, 2005); and French-based television coverage of Muslims internationally and in France since 1979 (Deltombe, 2005).

Canadian media research on minorities (Muslim or otherwise) has revealed that ethnic minorities are both under-represented in media accounts and mis-represented (i.e., portrayed negatively) (Fleras & Kunz, 2001). As Karim (2003) shows, the misleading stereotypes identified by Said have been found in the Canadian media's treatment of Islam and global politics. Indeed, Karim asserts that today an "Islamic Peril" has come to replace the "Soviet threat" of the Cold War years (2003). Bullock and Jafri's (2000) examination of print coverage of Muslim women in the *Calgary Herald*, the *Globe and Mail*, the *Montreal Gazette*, the *Toronto Star*, and the *Vancouver Sun* between 1993 and 1997 found that they were presented as outsiders and as members of a grouping that does not promote "Canadian values," but rather advocates violence and the oppression of women. Yasmin Jiwani (2006) drew from international and domestic coverage in the *Gazette* (Montreal) in the weeks immediately following September 11, and demonstrated how stereotypes pervaded the international coverage of the Middle East, working to render Muslim women (particularly those who veil) as primitive and oppressed, and Muslim men as brutal (toward women) as well as envious of the West, irrational, untrustworthy, and simultaneously childlike and effeminate. The "voices of authority" in much of this coverage came from non-Muslim men living in the West. Likewise, Jiwani shows that stories involving issues relating to the backlash against Muslim minorities in the West/Canada also subordinated the voices of Muslims, especially those of Muslim women (see Jiwani in Chapter 17 of this book).

Such coverage carries implications for the level of understanding non-Muslim Canadians may have of Muslims in general and of Muslim Canadians in particular, accounting for why one national organization, the Canadian Islamic Congress, chooses to deliver an annual report on the Canadian French- and English-language coverage of Islamic issues. The Congress is attuned to the association of Islam with "extremism" and "terrorism" and with gendered stereotypes portraying Muslim women as lacking liberty and agency. Interestingly, their most recent report from 2004, available on their website, ranks newspapers from "bad" to "worst" (Canadian Islamic Congress, n.d.). Another national organization, the Canadian Council on American–Islamic Relations Canada, devotes much of its mission to media relations in order to "help shape an accurate understanding of Islam" (CAIR-CAN, n.d.). Our chapter looks at newspaper coverage of three separate national elections, and thus captures the coverage given to Muslim Canadians over time. As well, we determine how Muslim Canadians are treated as citizens, voters, and candidates within this reportage, considering the wide range of domestic and international issues and policies that may be addressed in partisan electoral debates.

METHODOLOGY AND HYPOTHESES

Our study examines Canadian newspaper coverage of Muslims during the last three national election campaigns (2000, 2004, and 2006). The selection of newspapers for this analysis reflects the demographic concentration of Muslim Canadians in specific cities.

Table 8.2 Concentration of Muslim-Canadian Population by Province, 2001

Canada	579,640
Ontario	352,530
Quebec	108,620
British Columbia	56,200
Alberta	49,045

Source: Adapted from Statistics Canada, "Religions in Canada, 2001 Census," Analysis Series, Catalogue No. 96f0030XIE2001015 (2003). URL: www12.statcan.ca/english/census01/products/analytic/companion/rel/contents.cfm

As shown in Table 8.2, Canadian Muslims are concentrated in certain provinces, and are most numerous in Ontario, followed by Quebec, British Columbia, and Alberta. Within these provinces, Muslim Canadians are further concentrated in Toronto, followed by Montreal, Vancouver, Ottawa, Calgary, and Edmonton. Combined, these six Canadian cities are home to 85.2 percent of the Canadian-Muslim population, with Toronto alone home to 43.8 percent of Muslim Canadians (Beyer, 2005, p. 240). Thus, in addition to addressing the two English-language "national" papers, the *Globe and Mail* and the *National Post*, we chose the largest English-language dailies in the cities with the largest Muslim populations: the *Gazette* [Montreal], the *Toronto Star*, the *Ottawa Citizen*, the *Calgary Herald*, the *Edmonton Journal* and the *Vancouver Sun*.

Using the Factiva and Canadian Newsstand databases, we conducted searches for election-news stories, including hard news, editorials, opinion pieces, and commentary, starting from the day the writ was dropped and ending one week after each election.[1] Any story with the word "Muslim" or "Islam" (or variation of Islam) was included in the sample if the topic was the Canadian election, regardless of whether or not the article identified Muslims in Canada as "Muslim Canadians."[2] This search yielded 67 articles: 13 from the 2000 election, 16 from the 2004 election, and 38 from the 2006 national election. Table 8.3 indicates which of the newspapers in our sample considered Muslim Canadians important to election coverage. The majority of the attention came from two newspapers, the *Globe and Mail* and the *Toronto Star*, which accounted for almost two-thirds of the stories overall and printed 94 percent of the articles mentioning Muslim Canadians published during the 2004 election. The other regional papers did not run stories mentioning Muslims or Islam in 2000 and 2004. Only the national papers and the *Toronto Star* included such stories. In 2006, the *Ottawa Citizen*, *Edmonton Journal*, (Montreal) *Gazette*, and *Vancouver Sun* ran a handful of stories, but none were printed in the *Calgary Herald* during any of the elections.

Both content analysis and critical discourse analysis techniques were used to examine Canadian newspaper coverage of Muslim Canadians during these three election campaigns. Content analysis employs "objective and systematic counting and recording procedures to produce a quantitative description of the symbolic content in a text"

Table 8.3 Number (percentage) of Stories Mentioning Muslims by Newspaper and Election

Newspaper	2000 Election N (% during election)	2004 Election N (% during election)	2006 Election N (% during election)	Row Total (%)
Globe and Mail	3 (23)	9 (56)	10 (26)	22 (33)
Toronto Star	3 (23)	6 (38)	12 (32)	21 (31)
National Post	7 (54)	1 (6)	4 (10)	12 (18)
Ottawa Citizen	0 (0)	0 (0)	6 (16)	6 (9)
Edmonton Journal	0 (0)	0 (0)	3 (8)	3 (5)
[Montreal] Gazette	0 (0)	0 (0)	2 (5)	2 (3)
Vancouver Sun	0 (0)	0 (0)	1 (3)	1 (1)
Calgary Herald	0 (0)	0 (0)	0 (0)	0 (0)
Column Totals	13 (19)	16 (24)	38 (57)	67 (100)

(Neuman, 2000, p. 293). A detailed coding instrument, including precise coding notes, was used to ensure consistency in measurement and coding (Manheim et al., 2005, p. 180). The structural characteristics of each news story were classified based on the newspaper in which it was published, the date of publication, the location in the newspaper, and the type of story (news, column, editorial). As well, for each article, we determined where Muslims or Islam were mentioned (in the headline or lead paragraph, for instance), established the role of Muslims or Islam in the story (integral, important, or tangential), and noted whether Muslims were directly quoted in the story. Substantive variables included the main focus of the story and several indicators of stereotyping. We gauged whether Muslims were depicted as homogeneous, identified only as a religious group, or cast as socially conservative or extremist in orientation. As well, we looked at the extent to which the news stories conveyed a message of inclusion of Muslim Canadians by identifying them as Canadians or Canadian citizens and as participants in federal elections.

While content analysis establishes what is written in the news articles, where it is placed, and the frequency with which it appears, thus identifying patterns in the coverage, it stops short of indicating what these patterns mean and what cognitive functions they perform. For example, when words like "terrorist" or "jihadist" are used in news articles mentioning Muslim Canadians, it is possible that journalists are associating Muslims with the events of September 11, 2001. But what are the associations? How are they structured? What sorts of semantic strategies, rhetorical devices, or narrative structures are used to communicate these associations? What sorts of evaluations are readers prompted to draw from the headline and the news report? Because of the questions left unanswered by content analysis, this method is ideally supplemented with a more conceptual approach to textual analysis (see van Zoonen, 1994, p. 73; van Dijk, 1991, p. 6). We chose critical discourse analysis (CDA), a qualitative method that analyzes how meanings are established and communicated through the semantic structures, organization, style, and rhetoric of news texts (van Dijk, 1991, p. 42). Guided by Teun van Dijk's approach in *Racism and the Press* (1991), we paid particular attention to those headlines and stories with Muslim Canadians as their central focus, examining the role and prominence of Muslim Canadians in each of the news stories, their relationship to the main topic of the story, and the ways in which they were described and evaluated. We used the principles and techniques of CDA to develop variables for the content analysis and to guide a holistic interpretation of the news texts. We analyzed the meaning structures of the texts and what they communicated about the role of Muslim Canadians in the election campaign.

Based on the literature about media coverage of elections and press treatment of Muslims and Islam, we developed four hypotheses to guide our study. *First, we anticipated that we would find more press attention to Muslim Canadians after 9/11, that is, in the newspaper coverage of the 2004 and 2006 election campaigns, because of the enhanced news value of the Muslim community.* The news value of an event, actor, or issue is assessed by editors based on its importance, proximity, timeliness, conflict, or unusualness (Scharrer, 2002, p. 395). The September 11, 2001 attacks on the United States brought religious differences to the forefront of news coverage in Canada, focusing attention on Muslims. But was this attention evident in news coverage of Canadian elections?

The U.S.-led "war on terror" was not overtly an election story unless political parties worked security issues or related foreign-policy concerns into their policy platforms. This is not surprising, as the literature on media coverage of election campaigns demonstrates that news media frame elections as games or horse races by focusing on who is winning, who is losing, and why (Cappella & Jamieson, 1997, pp. 37–57; Patterson, 1994, pp. 53–93; Trimble & Sampert, 2004, p. 53). Competitive parties and their leaders are, therefore, the focus of election coverage, and voters, activists, and citizen groups are typically sidelined by the press except when their ideas or behaviours have the potential to change the course of the game. Given the widespread application of the game frame in election coverage, we expected Muslim Canadians to be more visible and prominent when they were situated (or situated themselves) as part of the electoral "game"—as interested and potentially important participants in electoral politics. Thus, our *second hypothesis was that Muslim Canadians would be found to be more integral to and prominent in the press coverage of post 9/11 elections when their activities, or potential as a voting bloc, were relevant to the election campaign.* Similarly, because media coverage of elections evidences scant attention to substantive issues (see Trimble & Sampert, 2004), our *third hypothesis was that there was likely to be little coverage of the substantive policy concerns of Muslim Canadians in the post-9/11 environment, even when Muslims were the central focus of the story.*

The fourth hypothesis is drawn from the literature on the media treatment of Muslims that was overviewed earlier in this chapter. Both international and Canadian media studies have demonstrated that the news media characterize Muslims as a homogeneous group by failing to recognize or discuss the significant religious, linguistic, ethnic, cultural, class, and generational diversity within Muslim communities. As well, misleading stereotypes about Muslims and Islam have been found in Canadian media coverage of Islam and global politics, including the association of Muslims and Islam with religious fundamentalism and extremism, and the characterization of Islam as "global threat" (Karim, 2003). *Our fourth hypothesis reflected the expectation that Muslim Canadians would be found to be stereotyped by the news coverage. Stereotypes include being described or framed as a homogeneous entity, as a religious group, as socially conservative, and as extremist or fundamentalist.*

FINDINGS

When Are Muslim Canadians Included in Election News Coverage?

As predicted, Muslim Canadians or Islam were mentioned more often in election news coverage after the events of September 11, 2001. During the 2000 election campaign, only 13 stories were published in the eight papers over the course of the six-week campaign, 19 percent of the sample (see Table 8.3, above). This increased to 16 stories in 2004 (24 percent), and more than doubled, to 38, in 2006 (57 percent of the sample). While the overall number of articles is not large, the pattern over time confirms our expectation that there was significantly more coverage after September 11, 2001, than before. These results suggest that Muslims were of greatest interest to the newspapers during the 2006 election, but we argue that that was not in fact the case. Measures of prominence and importance in the news story are needed to determine when Muslim Canadians were considered interesting to Canadian press coverage of elections. For example, an article that mentions Muslims along with other religious groups at the end of a story about same-sex marriage conveys quite a different impression about the importance of Muslim Canadians to Canadian federal elections than does a profile of Muslim-Canadian candidates that names Muslims in the headline and lead paragraph and situates Muslims as the main topic of the news story.

We took three measures of prominence, noting whether or not Muslims or Islam were named in the headline, mentioned in the lead paragraph of the story, or quoted in the story. Headlines define the story. By summarizing the main topic of a news event, headlines signal to readers who or what is important in the story. Moreover, headlines are more likely than the body of a news story to be read, and recalled, by readers (van Dijk, 1991, p. 50). As well, because news stories are structured as pyramids, with "the most important, topical information" presented in the lead paragraph, mention of a particular actor or group in the lead paragraph communicates their relevance to the story. Our third measure of prominence is the appearance of direct quotations, as news stories typically report the opinions of major news actors about the main events in the story (van Dijk, 1991, p. 120). By quoting representatives of Muslim groups, reporters are indicating their newsworthiness and prominence in the news event (van Dijk, 1991, p. 152).

As Table 8.4 indicates, these measures illustrate substantial differences in the prominence of Muslims in the newspaper coverage of the three national elections. During the

Table 8.4 Measures of Prominence in Election News Stories, by Election

Measures of News Prominence	2000 Election N (%)	2004 Election N (%)	2006 Election N (%)	Row Total N (%)
Muslims or Islam mentioned in headline	0 (0)	5 (31)	6 (16)	11 (16)
Muslims or Islam mentioned in lead paragraph	0 (0)	5 (31)	7 (18)	12 (18)
Muslims or representatives of Muslim community quoted in the story	2 (15)	9 (56)	18 (47)	29 (43)

2000 election campaign, none of the stories mentioning Muslims or Islam named them in the headline or lead paragraph (see Table 8.4). Only two stories quoted Muslims or representatives of Muslim organizations (15 percent). As well, Table 8.4 shows that, while Muslims were mentioned in more news stories printed during the 2006 election than during the 2004 election, they were considerably less prominent in the 2006 election coverage. In 2006, representatives of Muslim organizations were quoted in almost half of the stories (47 percent), but Muslims or Islam were referred to directly in only 16 percent of the headlines, and mentioned in the lead paragraph in only 18 percent of the stories. In contrast, stories published during the 2004 election gave considerably more standing to the Muslim community, quoting representatives in more than half of the stories (56 percent). In almost one-third (31 percent) of the stories mentioning Muslims in 2004, they were named in the headline and in the lead paragraph.

The importance of Muslims or Islam to the news story also needs to be considered because editors and journalists can elevate minor topics to a lead status by manipulation of news structures. For instance, headlines are typically written by editors, who have the power to upgrade a less important topic by expressing it in the headline (van Dijk, 1991, p. 51). News stories mentioning Muslims or Islam were therefore coded based on the role they played in the story: *tangential* (merely mentioned, e.g., listed among other groups); *important* (but not the main focus); or *integral* (the main focus of the story). Table 8.5 emphasizes that Muslims were tangential to most of the stories in which they were mentioned in the 2000 and 2006 national elections; that is, to 92 percent of the stories in 2000 and 61 percent in 2006. They were not integral to any of the news stories about the 2000 election, and were integral to only 13 percent in 2006. In contrast, Muslims were important or integral to three-quarters (75 percent) of the news stories that mentioned them during the 2004 national election, and were tangential to only four (25 percent) of the articles.

Table 8.5 Importance of Muslims or Islam to the Main Topic of the Story, by Election

Importance of Muslims or Islam to the Main Topic of the Story	2000 Election N (%)	2004 Election N (%)	2006 Election N (%)	Row Total N (%)
Tangential to the main topic of the story	12 (92)	4 (25)	23 (61)	39 (58)
Important to the main topic of the story (but not the main focus)	1 (8)	7 (44)	10 (26)	18 (27)
Integral to the main topic of the story (focus of the story)	0 (0)	5 (31)	5 (13)	10 (15)

While we did not expect Muslim Canadians to be foregrounded in election news stories in 2000, even in stories that mentioned them, we were surprised by the differences between the coverage of the 2004 and 2006 elections. Why were Muslim Canadians considered by the media to be "in the game" in 2004, thus central to about a third of the news stories that included them? We hypothesized that Muslim Canadians were more integral to and prominent in the press coverage of post-9/11 elections when their activities were perceived to be relevant to the "horse-race" elements of the election campaign.

Muslim Canadians in the Election-News Frame

News topics are "semantic macro-structures" that "reduce the complex information of the text to its essential gist" (van Dijk, 1991, p. 72). By organizing information around a main topic, reporters communicate what the story is about, how it should be understood, and who is important to it. As outlined above, the literature on media coverage of election campaigns establishes that the main topic of most election news stories is the electoral game, or "horse race." We classified the news stories in our sample as fitting into a game frame or an issue frame. Those stories focusing on polling data, voting blocs, regional distribution of party support, and/or party appeals to particular groups of voters were coded as having a game focus. Stories with an issue focus featured discussion of election issues raised by parties or citizen groups, or included in party platforms, and we divided these into two broad issue categories: domestic policy and foreign policy/security issues. An "other" category captured the outliers, including a column printed during the 2000 election focusing on religious fundamentalism that mentioned the election only in

Table 8.6 Main Topic of News Stories Mentioning Muslims or Islam, by Election

Main Topic of Story	2000 Election N (%)	2004 Election N (%)	2006 Election N (%)	Row Totals N (%)
Domestic issues	0 (0)	2 (13)	6 (16)	8 (12)
Foreign Policy or security issues	1 (8)	3 (18)	7 (18)	11 (16)
The campaign game*	9 (69)	11 (69)	25 (66)	45 (67)
Other	3 (23)	0 (0)	(0)	3 (5)

* Includes a focus on the campaign "game" or horse race: who is winning, poll results, voting patterns, and campaign strategies for winning votes.

passing.[3] As Table 8.6 shows, the distributions across the three elections were similar. Very few of the stories featured either domestic or foreign policy as their main topic, though there was more attention to such issues in the 2004 and 2006 elections. The main topic of 67 percent of the news stories mentioning Muslims or Islam during these three elections was the electoral game (see Table 8.6). Therefore the distribution of news topics does not explain why Muslim Canadians were considered "in the game" in the 2004 election, but not in 2006.

Figure 8.1 supports our hypothesis about inclusion of Muslim Canadians in election coverage when their roles or activities were linked to the horse-race elements of the campaign. In particular, Figure 8.1 highlights dramatic changes in the portrayal of Muslims by election-news coverage over time. In the 2000 election, very few of the stories mentioning Muslims identified them as Canadian citizens (only 15 percent), or discussed their role as voters (8 percent). As we have seen, Muslims were tangential to the main topic of 12 election stories mentioning them. Muslim Canadians were mentioned in passing because of media attention to Canadian Alliance leader Stockwell Day's religious views and the Liberal Party's election strategy of situating Day's fundamentalism as a threat to Canadian values. Eight of the 13 articles published in 2000 mentioned Muslims as one of several religious groups in the context of stories about religion in politics. For instance, five of these quoted or referred to Liberal MP Hedy Fry's assertion that a comment by Stockwell Day ("Jesus Christ is the God of the whole universe") was "an insult to every Muslim, Buddhist, Sikh, everybody who believes in other religions."[4] Most of the remainder of the stories mentioning Muslims in 2000—four in total— represented an effort to rebut assertions of racism on the part of the Canadian Alliance Party. Alliance leader Stockwell Day contended that the party was not racist because it was "open to immigrants and members of ethnic groups" and featured "candidates from the Jewish, Chinese, Sikh and Muslim communities."[5] The only 2000 election story mentioning Muslim Canadians in the context of a substantive policy or election issue

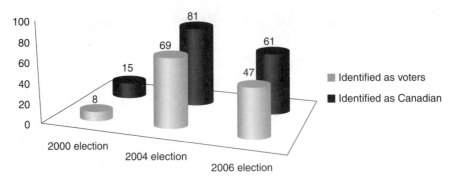

Figure 8.1   Percentage of Stories Identifying Muslims as Voters, Canadians, by Election

was an article published in the *Toronto Star* that discussed Stockwell Day's unequivocal support of Israeli policies and quoted the executive director of the Canadian Arab Federation as saying that "Day's comments are something that will go with us to the polling stations."[6]

In contrast, post-9/11 election coverage tended to describe Muslims as Canadians by referring to their Canadian-based organizations by name or by mentioning their participation in Canadian elections as voters or candidates. Muslims were explicitly identified as Canadian citizens in 81 percent of the coverage in the 2004 election, but only in 61 percent in 2006. Moreover, 69 percent of the articles mentioning Muslims in 2004 identified them as voters, or as a voting bloc, compared to 47 percent in 2006. In the 2004 election, Muslims were identified as voters in 82 percent of the stories whose main topic was the electoral game. However, in 2006, Muslim Canadians were described as voters in less than half (48 percent) of the stories with the electoral game as the central topic. In sum, Muslim Canadians were included, to a modest extent, in the election news frame in 2004 when they were identified as, and appealed to as, Canadians—and as voters.

The emphasis on Muslims as Canadian citizens and active electoral participants in 2004 was due to the coverage offered by the *Globe and Mail* and the *Toronto Star*, which produced 15 of the 16 articles mentioning Muslims during the first election held after the events of September 11, 2001 (94 percent of the 2004 sample). Several of the articles published during the 2004 election suggested Muslim Canadians had the power to shape electoral outcomes in key constituencies. Headlines such as "Why Muslims should vote,"[7] "Muslims urged to go to the polls"[8] and "Muslims urged to get connected"[9] indicated that the role of Muslim-Canadian voters was taken seriously by the *Globe and Mail* and *Toronto Star*. In addition to reporting on the Canadian Islamic Congress's voting drive, the *Globe and Mail* published a column by the president of the Congress, Mohamed Elmasry, urging Muslims to "cast an informed vote."[10] The *Toronto Star* also ran a number of stories about the so-called "ethnic vote," and described the efforts of various Muslim candidates, including NDP candidate Monia Mazigh,[11] to win election. A news story in the *Globe and Mail* about the importance of the "immigrant vote" to the 2004 election noted the growing size of the Muslim-Canadian community and quoted political scientist Henry Jacek: "I think, since 9/11, they are extraordinarily political. They are sensitive to the security measures in North America . . . I think a lot of them are going to vote."[12] Yet very few of these stories discussed the post-9/11 policy concerns of Muslim Canadians.

While Muslim Canadians may be included in the frame as voters under particular circumstances, such as appeals to the community to exercise its franchise strategically, the dominance of the game frame tends to divert attention from substantive campaign issues or policy claims. Indeed, less than a third of the coverage mentioning Muslims focused on domestic or foreign policy debates (see Table 8.6, above). Our third hypothesis, that little attention would be paid to the substantive policy concerns of Muslim Canadians in the post-9/11 environment, even when Muslims were the central focus of the story, was supported. Only four stories (6 percent of the sample) included quotes by representatives of Muslim-Canadian organizations speaking directly to policy issues of concern to their communities. One of these articles was the column written by the president of the Canadian Islamic Congress mentioned above. In it, Mohamed Elmasry observed that "the issues most on the minds of Canadian Muslims, [are] issues that have not been so far debated in this campaign."[13] Another example, a story published by the *Toronto Star* in 2006, reported on an all-candidates debate hosted by Muslim groups, but instead of leading with quotes from leaders of Muslim-Canadian organizations it featured the views of non-Muslim candidates and political officials on the anti-terrorism bill and security certificates.[14] There were a few stories that raised questions about policies directly affecting Muslim Canadians, such as anti-terrorist legislation and racial profiling, but these did not quote or paraphrase Muslim Canadians. As van Dijk notes, in press reports racialized minorities are seldom "speakers and definers of their own reality," or even seen to have "an opinion about majority actions and policies" (1991, p. 154). Moreover, ethnic minorities "often speak in the Press through mediation . . . [through] white politicians, lawyers, etc." (van Dijk, 1991, p. 154). This was certainly the case for Canadian election coverage of the electoral interests of Muslim Canadians. For instance, critiques of the Canadian government's national security certificate system, "under which several Muslim men have been detained under secret evidence," were described in the press through the quoted assertions of Bloc Québécois leader Gilles Duceppe.[15] Moreover, while the assertions of non-Muslim party leaders and candidates that Muslim Canadians had been targeted by anti-terrorism legislation and that security certificates had been reported without qualification, journalists and headline writers distanced themselves from similar views expressed by the Muslim-Canadian community by placing the allegation in quotation marks (see van Dijk, 1991, p. 154). For example, the headline about the debate on Muslim-Canadian issues read: "Muslims 'targeted,' debate hears."[16] In sum, Muslim Canadians were quoted when they had something to say about their community as a voting bloc, and not when they had opinions about policy issues or party platforms. On policy matters, the interests of Muslim Canadians were interpreted by non-Muslim candidates and party leaders.

Stereotypes and Misrepresentations

Based on the literature about media coverage of Muslims, we examined each of the news stories for damaging mischaracterizations and stereotypes. We expected to find that Muslim Canadians were stereotyped by being described or framed as a homogeneous entity, as a singular religious group, as socially conservative, and as extremist or fundamentalist. One of the dominant misconceptions about Muslims is that they are homogeneous in their faith, ethnicity, language, and culture. Table 8.7 indicates that this one-dimensional portrayal of Muslims was firmly embedded in the election-news stories. Overall, 84 percent of the election coverage homogenized Muslims. This trend was particularly evident in the 2000 election, in which every story mentioning Muslims approached them as a homogeneous group. As noted, Muslims were merely mentioned in most of these stories as one of several religions with members whose views were relevant to the campaign. Unsurprisingly, 77 percent of the stories mentioning Muslims or Islam during the 2000 election presented Muslims solely through the lens of religion.

The 2004 and 2006 elections featured a very different portrayal of Muslim Canadians, as illustrated in Table 8.7. While the complexity and diversity of Muslim Canadians continued to be largely ignored by news reports, election-news articles did not position Muslims as solely a religious community, as they did in 2000. Approximately two-thirds of the coverage in 2004 and 2006 characterized Muslims as voters, as members of political organizations, as candidates, or as concerned citizens. However, it should be noted that even these stories that described Muslim Canadians as Canadian voters tended to frame their electoral participation through their religiosity. For example, an election story printed in 2004 by the Globe and Mail, titled "Muslims urged to go to the polls," began with these sentences: "It's 6:20 p.m. and the chanting of the muezzin begins to echo through this sprawling West-end Toronto mosque. . . . It's the call to prayer, and . . . increasingly a call to vote."[17] Similarly, a story mentioning NDP candidate Monia Mazigh noted that, "should she win, [she] will become the first Muslim woman to sit in Parliament wearing her hijab scarf."[18] Also typical of this emphasis on religion was a 2004 election article titled "On a vote and a prayer; Religious groups spurred toward political activism."[19] Moreover, some Muslim candidates were unhappy with their representations as Muslims first, candidates second. "I'm a Muslim, of course," said Liberal candidate Omar Alghabra. "But also I'm a male, an engineer, a Liberal. All of that is part of my identity."[20] Yasmin Ratansi, the first Muslim woman elected to the House of Commons, had a similar view: "I have never run as a Muslim or a woman. I have run as a competent businesswoman or professional. I never hyphenate myself. I'm a Canadian."[21]

Very few of the articles cast Muslim Canadians as socially conservative, with the highest percentage (21 percent) published during the 2006 election, when Muslims and other religious groups reacted to the same-sex marriage issue. Typical of such coverage was this assertion: "some of the strongest opposition to same-sex marriage is among the country's Chinese, Muslim, Sikh and other Asian voters and their religious leaders."[22] Winning votes from such communities was constructed as key to Conservative candidate wins in suburban Ontario ridings.[23] There was little nuance in the presentation of religious groups,

Table 8.7 Portrayal of Muslims in Canadian Election-News Stories, by Election

Portrayal of Muslims in the news story*	2000 Election N (%)	2004 Election N (%)	2006 Election N (%)	Row Totals N (%)
Muslims portrayed as a homogeneous group	13 (100)	13 (81)	30 (79)	56 (84)
Muslims described only as a religious group	10 (77)	5 (31)	14 (37)	29 (43)
Muslims depicted as socially conservative	1 (8)	1 (6)	8 (21)	10 (15)
Muslims associated with extremism	3 (23)	1 (6)	11 (29)	15 (22)

* Note that these are not mutually exclusive portrayals, as Muslims may have been depicted in more than one, if not all, of these ways within a single news story.

including Muslims, despite assertions by some Muslim leaders that the community's stance was more complex and heterogeneous than news reports made it out to be. The executive director of the Council on American–Islamic Relations (Canada), Riad Saloojiee, said "media reporting on Islam has been like an electric jolt for many, and if we don't represent what Islam is, our faith is going to be hijacked by narrow-minded bigots and extremists."[24]

The association of Muslims and Islam with extremism was evident in the 2000 election coverage, but sharply revealed in 2006. While in 2004 Muslims were linked with extremism in only one article (6 percent), three articles (23 percent) associated Islam with religious fundamentalism during the 2000 election.[25] In 2006, 11 articles, almost a third of the total number of articles mentioning Muslims, depicted them as radicals, even as terrorists. Much of this increase in 2006 came from seven articles, almost a fifth of the stories mentioning Muslims or Islam, reporting the (false, as it turned out) accusation that a Liberal candidate, Omar Alghabra, described his nomination win as a "victory for Islam."[26] Similarly, two articles identified a political party supporter as a "suspected terrorist."[27] More ominously, a *National Post* columnist opined that "radical Islamists have declared war on all secular democracies, including Canada," and thus they constitute a "world-wide Islamo-fascist threat to democracy" courtesy of "a war the jihadists deliver to your doorstep."[28] This example is indicative of the *National Post*'s approach to the Muslim-Canadian community, as 42 percent of this paper's election articles associated Muslims/Islam with extremism, compared with 9 percent of *Globe and Mail* stories and 14 percent of *Toronto Star* stories. Words like "fascist," "jihadist," and "terrorist" invoke readers' knowledge scripts, tapping into negative assumptions and prompting dangerous and misleading representations of Muslims and Islam. For example, even though the stories reporting the unfounded allegations that Liberal candidate Omar Alghabra had declared his nomination win a "victory for Islam" included vehement denials and rebuttals from the candidate, associations with religious fundamentalism had been clearly drawn. Even in articles about Muslim voters, anger and possible retribution against "the weak" was suggested. For instance, the first sentence of a *Globe and Mail* article titled "Influence of Muslim voters is growing" said: "The political fate of three vulnerable cabinet ministers may depend on whether the Liberals can calm angry Arab and Muslim community groups between now and January 23."[29] Anger was linked to the increased political mobilization of Muslim-Canadian organizations and tied to electoral outcomes in key Ontario ridings, thus suggesting retribution by Muslim voters and organizations.

Overall, the news stories mentioning Muslim Canadians afforded little opportunity to educate Canadians about the heterogeneity of this community or to challenge negative stereotypes of Muslims. Election articles homogenized Muslim Canadians, and while few articles portrayed Muslims as solely a religious group, most framed Muslim-Canadian political interests as firmly rooted in and expressed through a faith stance. A great deal of the coverage of the 2000 and 2006 elections lumped Muslims in with other religious organizations in discussions of the role of religion and politics or as part of a constellation of groups opposing same-sex marriage. Most disturbingly, post-9/11 coverage, especially in 2006, associated Muslim Canadians with extremism and terrorism. As mentioned above, Liberal candidate Omar Alghabra suffered the consequences of the news value of such association. The false accusation that he had declared his nomination win a "victory for Islam" became the subject of a news release by an anti-Islam organization and was widely reported in the Canadian press. Despite a retraction and an apology, and Alghabra's election win, newspaper readers are more likely to remember the "smear" than the truth.

CONCLUSION

Our analysis of the 2000, 2004, and 2006 elections demonstrates that there has been an increase over time in the amount of newspaper coverage given to Muslim Canadians during federal election campaigns, which we suggest can be related to the impact of September 11, 2001. Overall, our findings indicate that, while increased media attention has afforded new recognition of Muslim Canadians as voters and candidates, the dominant game frame of election coverage presents both opportunities and constraints for portraying the complexity of Canadian Muslims. As such, while the English-language treatment of Muslim Canadians during elections, particularly the 2004 election, opened up modest opportunities to contemplate the role of Muslims as voters, there was very little space devoted to contesting negative portrayals and reflecting the diversity of a community with deep historical roots in Canada. In fact, the 2006 coverage stands out for reinforcing long-standing stereotypes. Thus, while media representations are not static, and may shift in some periods, a long-standing pattern found in the Canadian and international coverage of Islam and Muslims has proven to be tenacious.

Analysts like Karim H. Karim have shown that, in covering global events, the Canadian media have homogenized and stereotyped Muslims, and in the process constructed an "Islamic peril." As it stands, at least in the English-language Canadian electoral press coverage we addressed, the game frame presents mixed results for re-examining this and other negative portrayals. Given the importance of the media in shaping the views Canadians hold of each other, the limitations of the game frame need to be considered by journalists, community activists, politicians, and citizens seeking better understanding of Canadian society. More broadly, we suggest that the media in all its complexity (from print journalism to television, film, and the internet) demands the attention of political scientists as well as all those seeking more accurate representation of Canada's multicultural diversity.

Media Journal Assignments

1. Over a one-week period, monitor how racial minorities are depicted on CTV's *National News with Lloyd Robertson*. How do we see racial minorities? Are they in positions of authority? How many reporters are members of racial minorities? How does this fit with Abu-Laban and Trimble's critique of the coverage of minorities in the media?

2. Over a three-day period, compare the 7 to 10 p.m. television schedule on CBC with that of CTV to determine how racial minorities are depicted in entertainment television programming. Are racial minorities present or are they ignored? Are their characters complex or one-dimensional? Are there differences between the programs carried by CTV and the CBC?

3. During the 2006 general election, sociologist Cecil Foster wrote a newspaper article criticizing the role of media pundits and commentators covering the election. He asked a simple question: "Have you noted that not one of these regular talking heads, at least on my television, is what we may call a visible-minority Canadian?" In his view, visible minorities were confined to "explaining" their "presumed community" to "real Canadians," or were cast as recent immigrants trying to understand the Canadian political scene, since they had presumably "just arrived from their land where there is no democracy." Monitor three days of news coverage on the 6:00 news on CBC and CTV to determine if Foster's complaint is a valid one. Source: Cecil Foster, "Visible Minorities Being Shut out of Political Messaging," *Guelph Mercury*, January 14, 2006, p. A8.

Endnotes

1. Specifically, utilizing the Factiva Database, our search dates for the 2000 election were from October 22 to December 4, 2000; for the 2004 election, May 23 to July 5, 2004; and for the 2006 election, November 30, 2005, to January 30, 2006.

2. The search terms employed were "election and federal and Muslim"; "election and Muslim"; "candidate and Muslim"; "vot* and Muslim"; "election and federal and Islam*"; "election and Islam*"; "candidate and Islam*"; "vot* and Islam*."

3. John Grey, "Fear not the fundamentalist politician," *Globe and Mail*, November 8, 2000, p. R2.

4. See, for instance, Jack Aubry, "Day accused of insulting other religions: Liberal derides 'insult,'" *National Post*, November 18, 2000, p. A12.

5. Shawn McCarthy, "Alliance candidate quits over remarks," *Globe and Mail*, November 20, 2000, p. A1.

6. "Canada doesn't need Mideast quarrels," *Toronto Star*, October 26, 2000, p. 1.

7. Mohamed Elmasry, "Why Muslims should vote," *Globe and Mail*, June 7, 2004, p. A19.

8. Katherine Harding, "Muslims urged to go to the polls," *Globe and Mail*, June 4, 2004, p. A8.

9. Leslie Scrivener, "Muslims urged to get connected," *Toronto Star*, May 23, 2004, p. A7.

10. Mohamed Elmasry, "Why Muslims should vote," *Globe and Mail*, June 7, 2004, p. A19.

11. Monia Mazigh was described as "the woman who campaigned tirelessly to free her husband Maher Arar from a Syrian jail." Kim Lunman, "Undeterred in 'McGuinty country,'" *Globe and Mail*, June 7, 2004, p. A6.

12. Gloria Galloway, "Sikhs reach beyond Liberals as political influence grows; Canadian-born children of immigrants are switching allegiance, poll suggests," *Globe and Mail*, May 25, 2004, p. A9.

13. Mohamed Elmasry, "Why Muslims should vote," *Globe and Mail*, June 7, 2004, p. A19.

14. Isabel Teotonio, "Muslims 'targeted,' debate hears; Community's issues ignored: Organizer Liberal defends security certificates," *Toronto Star*, January 14, 2006, p. A7.

15. For instance, Tu Thanh Ha, "Duceppe dances around questions," *Globe and Mail*, January 5, 2006, p. A6.

16. Isabel Teotonio, "Muslims 'targeted,' debate hears; Community's issues ignored: Organizer Liberal defends security certificates," *Toronto Star*, January 14, 2006, p. A7.

17. Katherine Harding, "Muslims urged to go to the polls," *Globe and Mail*, June 4, 2004, p. A8.

18. Erin Anderssen, "'Childish' party leaders fail to connect on real issues," *Globe and Mail*, June 17, 2004, p. A9.

19. Leslie Scrivener, "On a vote and a prayer," *Toronto Star*, June 26, 2004, p. A29.

20. Andrew Chung, "Pro-Islamist words dubbed a 'smear'; 'Victory for Islam' raises hackles. Liberal fiercely denies he said it," *Toronto Star*, December 23, 2005, p. A1.

21. Christian Cotroneo, "Commons still lacks diversity; Election didn't substantially boost minorities," *Toronto Star*, January 25, 2006, p. A9.

22. Christopher Waddell, "Media watch," *Globe and Mail*, December 6, 2006, p. A7.

23. For example, Heba Aly, "Tories say stand on gay marriage tightens race in Brampton," *Globe and Mail*, December 23, 2005, p. A15.

24. Leslie Scrivener, "Muslims urged to get connected," *Toronto Star*, May 23, 2004, p. A7.

25. Two articles discussed a Liberal candidate who allegedly attended an "Islamic rally with signs reading 'Death to Israel.'" This was discussed in a *National Post* editorial (November 16, 2000, p. A19), which declared, "Every party attracts its share of nuts."

26. Glen McGregor, "'Mixing of religion and democracy' stirs controversy: Group claims Liberal Toronto-area candidate said nomination was 'victory for Islam,'" *Ottawa Citizen*, December 21, 2005, p. A5. Despite the controversy, which Omar Alghabra feared would "derail" his campaign, he was elected in Mississauga-Erindale.

27. Elizabeth Thompson, "Suspected terrorist endorses Bloc," *Ottawa Citizen*, December 6, 2005, p. A4; also, Tu Thanh Ha, "Duceppe dances around questions," *Globe and Mail*, January 5, 2006, p. A6.

28. Robert Fulford, "Do not disturb," *National Post*, December 31, 2005, p. A17.

29. Jeff Sallot, "Influence of Muslim voters is growing," *Globe and Mail*, December 19, 2006.

References

Abbas, Tahir. 2001. "Media Capital and the Representation of South Asian Muslims in the British Press: An Ideological Analysis." *Journal of Muslim Minority Affairs* 21 (2): 245–57.

Abu-Laban, Baha. 1980. *An Olive Branch on the Family Tree: The Arabs in Canada.* Toronto: McClelland & Stewart.

Abu-Laban, Sharon McIrvin. 1991. "Family and Religion among Muslim Immigrants and Their Descendants." In *Muslim Families in North America*, ed. Earle H. Waugh, Sharon McIrvin Abu-Laban, and Regula B. Qureshi, 6–31. Edmonton: University of Alberta Press.

Abu-Laban, Yasmeen. 2002. "Liberalism, Multiculturalism and the Problem of Essentialism." *Citizenship Studies* 6 (4): 459–82.

———. 2004. "The New North America and the Segmentation of Canadian Citizenship." *The International Journal of Canadian Studies* 29 (1): 17–40.

Arat-Koc, Sedef. 2006. "Whose Transnationalism? Canada, 'Clash of Civilizations' Discourse, and Arab and Muslim Canadians." In *Transnational Identities and Practices in Canada*, ed. Vic Satzewich and Lloyd Wong, 216–40. Vancouver: University of British Columbia Press.

Bélanger, Paul & Munroe Eagles. 2006. "The Geography of Class and Religion in Canadian Elections Revisited." *Canadian Journal of Political Science* 39 (3): 591–609.

Beyer, Peter. 2005. "Appendix: Demographics of Religious Identification in Canada." In *Religion and Ethnicity in Canada*, ed. Paul Bramadat and David Seljak, 235–40. Toronto: Pearson Longman.

Blais, André. 2005. "Accounting for the Electoral Success of the Liberal Party in Canada: Presidential Address to the Canadian Political Science Association." *Canadian Journal of Political Science* 38 (4): 821–40.

Blais, André, Elisabeth Gidengil, Richard Nadeau & Neil Nevite. 2002. *Anatomy of a Liberal Victory*. Peterborough: Broadview Press.

Bramadat, Paul. 2005. "Re-Visioning Religion in the Contemporary Period: The United Church of Canada's Ethnic Ministries Unit." *Canadian Diversity* 4 (3): 59–62.

Bullock, Katherine H. & Gul J. Jafri. 2000. "Media (Mis)representations: Muslim Women in the Canadian Nation." *Canadian Woman Studies* 20 (2): 35–40.

CAIR-CAN. (n.d.) "About Us." Available at www.caircan.ca/aboutus.php (accessed January 3, 2008).

Canadian Islamic Congress. (n.d.) *2004 CIC Medea Research Report*. Available at www.canadianislamiccongress.com/rr/rr_2004.php (accessed January 3, 2008).

Cappella, Joseph N. & Kathleen Hall Jamieson. 1997. *Spiral of Cynicism: The Press and the Public Good*. New York: Oxford University Press.

CBC.caArts. 2007. "CBC's Little Mosque to Break New Ground." January 4. Available at www.cbc.ca/arts/tv/story/2007/01/03/little-mosque.html (accessed January 3, 2008).

CBC News. 2007a. "Harper Slams Elections Canada Ruling on Veils." 9 September. Available at www.cbc.ca/canada/story/2007/09/09/harper-veil.html?ref=rss (accessed October 1, 2007).

———. 2007b. "Electoral Officer Says He Won't 'Juggle' Fundamental Rights over Veil Issue." 13 September. Available at www.cbc.ca/canada/story/2007/09/13/mayrand-veil.html (accessed 1 October, 2007).

Deltombe, Thomas. 2005. *L'Islam imaginaire: La construction médiatique de l'Islamophobie en France, 1975–2005*. Paris: La Découverte.

Fleras, Augie & Jean Lock Kunz. 2001. *Media and Minorities: Representing Diversity in a Multicultural Canada*. Toronto: Thompson Educational Publishing.

Globe and Mail. 2007. "Editorial: Why Make Veils an Issue?" September 11, A20.

Hamdani, Daood. 2005. *Muslim Women: From Polling Booths to Parliament*. Canadian Council of Muslim Women, March 2005.

Henry, Frances & Carol Tator. 2002. *Discourses of Domination: Racial Bias in the English-Language Press*. Toronto: University of Toronto Press.

IRPP (Institute for Research on Public Policy). 2007. *Policy Options* 28 (8) (September).

Jebwab, Jack. 2005. "Muslims and Multicultural Futures in Western Democracies: Is Kymlicka's Pessimism Warranted?" *Canadian Diversity* 4 (3): 92–96.

Jiwani, Yasmin. 2006. *Discourses of Denial: Mediations of Race, Gender and Violence*. Vancouver: University of British Columbia Press.

Johnston, Richard. 1985. "The Reproduction of the Religious Cleavage in Canadian Elections." *Canadian Journal of Political Science* 18 (1): 99–113.

Karim, Karim H. 2003. *Islamic Peril: Media and Global Violence*. Montréal: Black Rose Books.

Mandel, Daniel. 2001. "Muslims on the Silver Screen." *Middle East Quarterly* 8 (2): 19–30.

Manheim, Jarol B., Richard C. Rich, Lars Willnat & Craig Leonard Brians. 2005. *Empirical Political Analysis: Research Methods in Political Science*. 6th ed. New York: Pearson Education.

Martin, Patrick & Sean Phelan. 2002. "Representing Islam in the Wake of September 11: A Comparison of U.S. Television and CNN Online Messageboard Discourses." *Prometheus* 20 (3): 263–69.

McDonough, Sheila & Homa Hoodfar. 2005. "Muslims in Canada: From Ethnic Groups to Religious Community." In *Religion and Ethnicity in Canada*, ed. Paul Bramadat and David Seljak, 133–53. Toronto: Pearson Education.

Meisel, John. 1956. "Religious Affiliation and Electoral Behaviour: A Case Study." *Canadian Journal of Economics and Political Science* 22 (4): 481–96.

Nacos, Brigitte L. & Oscar Torres-Reyna. 2007. *Fueling Our Fears: Stereotyping, Media Coverage, and Public Opinion of Muslim Americans*. Lanham, Md.: Rowman & Littlefield.

Neuman, W. Lawrence. 2000. *Social Research Methods: Qualitative and Quantitative Approaches*. 4th ed. Toronto: Allyn & Bacon.

Patterson, Thomas E. 1994. *Out of Order*. New York: Vintage.

Rantanen, Pekka. 2005. "Non-documentary Burqa Pictures on the Internet: Ambivalence and the Politics of Representation." *International Journal of Cultural Studies* 8 (3): 329–51.

Said, Edward W. 1981 [1997]. *Covering Islam: How the Media and the Experts Determine How We See the Rest of the World*. rev. ed. New York: Vintage Books.

Scharrer, Erica. 2002. "An 'Improbable Leap': A Content Analysis of Newspaper Coverage of Hillary Clinton's Transition from First Lady to Senate Candidate." *Journalism Studies* 3 (3): 393–406.

Shaheen, Jack G. 1984. *The T.V. Arab*. Bowling Green: Bowling Green University Popular Press.

———. 2001. *Reel Bad Arabs: How Hollywood Vilifies a People*. New York: Olive Branch Press.

———. 2003. "Reel Bad Arabs: How Hollywood Vilifies a People." *Annals of the American Academy* 588 (July): 171–93.

Trimble, Linda & Shannon Sampert. 2004. "Who's in the Game? The Framing of the Canadian Election 2000 by the *Globe and Mail* and the *National Post*." *Canadian Journal of Political Science* 37 (1): 51–71.

van Dijk, Teun. 1991. *Racism and the Press*. London and New York: Routledge.

van Zoonen, Liesbet. 1994. *Feminist Media Studies*. London: Sage.

Chapter 9
Polling in Canada: Calling the Elections

Christopher Adams[1]

INTRODUCTION

Current Liberal Party pollster Michael Marzolini of Pollara Research used to tell a story about his first meeting with Jean Chrétien. The Liberal leader was told "this is Michael Marzolini, he is a pollster," upon which Chrétien waved Marzolini over to his office chesterfield. After a few moments of awkward silence, Chrétien asked when the work would begin. Apparently he thought Marzolini was an "upholsterer," not a "pollster." This chapter will show what pollsters do when they aren't asked to mend the couches of our political leaders. These social researchers examine public perceptions about everything, including consumer brands and political parties and their leaders.

The discussion begins with how survey research techniques, including election polling, developed in the United States. Following is an account of how polling began to be used in Canada. It will be shown how polls are used by the press to *capture* the mood of Canadians, and by party strategists to find ways to *change* their mood. The final part of the chapter deals with new trends facing the industry, as well as how tools other than polling, such as focus groups, are effectively used by political strategists. A major theme of this chapter is that the media's relationship to political polling should be understood within the context of historical developments in the hugely profitable worldwide marketing industry.

AMERICAN ELECTIONS AND POLITICAL POLLING

In 1935, a new species—the polling firm—was born when George Gallup opened a one-room office equipped with a single desk, a telephone, and a typewriter. The new company, located across the street from Princeton University in Princeton, New Jersey, was called the American Institute of Public Opinion. Gallup hoped Princeton's prestige would rub off on his start-up business (Moore, 1992, pp. 47–57). Americans first encountered Gallup through his weekly column "America Speaks!" which was picked up by media clients, including the *Washington Post*, during the firm's first year. Until the 1930s, the media tended to rely on sporadically organized "straw polls" to measure American attitudes.

Such polls are surveys based on unreliable sampling, poor interviewing standards, or mail-in surveys from readers. These offered, at best, a rough sense of the public's mind on political issues and voter preferences, but were notoriously inaccurate when used to predict electoral outcomes.

In 1916, the widely read magazine *Literary Digest* began conducting national polls during presidential elections based on very large samples. Survey respondents were selected from such sources as readership lists and, in later years, telephone directories and automobile registrations. The idea was to reach as many people as possible. With Herculean effort, in each of the 1928 and 1932 presidential elections, over 20 *million* mail-out ballots were issued to homes across the United States. While in retrospect these sampling methods may appear generally primitive, the *Digest's* results were surprisingly accurate at the national level. In both the 1928 and 1932 presidential elections, the two polls came within 1 percent of the actual vote (Moore, 1992, p. 32).

Because he believed the *Digest's* polls were based on questionable sampling techniques and under-representing key segments of the American population, Gallup felt he could do better. Putting his money where his mouth was, Gallup promised to refund his media clients' money if his polls for the 1936 presidential election were less accurate than the *Digest* poll. The *Digest* predicted a victory for Republican presidential candidate Alf Landon based on over 2.25 million mail-in ballots. Gallup, however, foretold a Democrat victory for President Franklin Roosevelt based on mere thousands of interviews. The *Digest* was out by an embarrassing 19 percentage points. Gallup's results, on the other hand, were within seven percentage points, and he had correctly predicted a victory for FDR.

What hurt the accuracy of the *Digest's* polling numbers was the reality that by 1936 the United States was in the depths of a severe economic depression and the voting public had become politically divided along socio-economic lines. Upper-income Americans had formed a clear preference for the Republicans, while those in lower income brackets tended to favour the "New Deal" Democrats. In effect, the *Digest's* sampling methodology was skewed toward gathering the opinions of well-off citizens rather than those with lower incomes who supported the Democrats' social-welfare promises (and who tended not to appear on many of the mailing lists used by the *Digest*) (Moore, 1992, pp. 46–47).

Gallup's success was based on using samples that included predetermined "quotas" for different segments of the population. This involved ensuring that a sufficient number of interviews would be conducted with American voters from all regions and important socio-demographic categories. The lesson learned from 1936, which still holds today in the market-research industry, is that understanding public opinion is best achieved not by interviewing as many people as possible, but by ensuring that the survey sample represents the full population being studied.

Gallup was not alone in using the 1936 election to demonstrate the efficiency of modern survey techniques to predict elections. Archibald Crossley's polling work for the Hearst newspaper chain matched Gallup's numbers, while Elmo Roper's polling work for the American magazine *Fortune* showed national results within 1 percent of the actual outcome. With only a fraction of the sample used in the *Digest* poll, ranging from

4,000 to 5,000 interviews, Gallup, Crossman, and Roper were successful because they implemented new sampling measures to ensure that members of different social segments would be sufficiently represented in the results (Lachapelle, 1991, p. 7). By the 1940s, survey research (with its reliance on quota sampling) would be further refined by the introduction of what came to be known as "probability sampling." For most studies, this means that each member of the population has an equal probability of being surveyed. For example, if two people in a group of 20 people are to be randomly selected for an interview, we would say that the probability of being selected is one in ten. Therefore, assuming that random-sample techniques are being employed to study voters in a particular country, every eligible voter in the research population—the national electorate—has an equal probability of being selected (Babbie, 2004, pp. 186–91).

The early successes of Gallup and others created a bond of trust between pollsters and the American media. Survey results were published with increasing regularity in the daily press. However, this relationship changed with the 1948 presidential election, when disaster struck. Gallup, Roper, and many other pollsters were so confident that Republican Thomas Dewey would defeat President Truman—and the media was so confident in the pollsters—that prominent newspaper and magazine articles were published based on these false predictions. The problem was not that their numbers were any less accurate than in 1936, it was that they incorrectly predicted President Truman's defeat. Many years later, the pollster for the *Los Angeles Times*, John Brennan, remarked, "doing polling is like being in the airlines . . . people only remember the crashes" (Moore, 1992, p. 313). Few would forget the 1948 fiasco and the media's distrust of the polling industry's techniques lasted until 1960.[2]

During the highly competitive U.S. presidential election of 1960, in which Democratic candidate John F. Kennedy narrowly defeated Republican candidate Richard Nixon, another influential pollster made a name for himself. Louis ("Lou") Harris broke new ground by providing direct polling services to the successful Kennedy campaign. Rather than giving his client simple "horse-race" analysis of who was winning and who was losing, Harris provided strategic advice regarding the views of key segments of the population, and identified where the campaign should focus its energy. In this way, polls proved effective for fashioning the leader's image and platform. They answered such questions as what the party should do to attract women voters, blue-collar voters, minority voters, or suburbanites. In this sense, political polling had evolved into "marketing research." Just as research could be used to shape strategies for selling consumer products, so too could polls be used to win over political shoppers (swing voters) and profoundly influence electoral outcomes.

TECHNOLOGY AND INDUSTRY DEVELOPMENTS

Opinion polling is often thought of as a tool designed for politicians and the media. Yet during the late 1940s and 1950s, the polling industry's growth was strongly tied to a postwar economic boom that brought with it growing consumer spending, economic productivity, and the implementation of new government programs. Public-opinion research organizations were needed for more than simply measuring voter preferences and attitudinal change among citizens; they were to provide market research. Teenagers, employees, soldiers, teachers, voters, university students, managers, housewives, and just about everyone else could be studied, which was especially important for national and international firms as they entered new and less familiar markets. Therefore, firms such as automobile companies, advertising agencies, the music industry, lobbyists, soap producers, and major retailers turned to research consultants to help better understand what consumers wanted or did not want. It was here that real money could be made, and as a result the industry blossomed.

Until the 1980s, survey research was extremely labour intensive. Most surveys were collected through mail-out surveys, personal encounters with respondents (otherwise called "intercept" interviews), or telephone interviewing. Each interview generated a completed paper survey, often numerous pages in length. Therefore, a two-page survey of 1,000 respondents produced 2,000 pages that were shipped to a central location for processing. Consider this: if each page contained responses to 15 different questions, a total of 30,000 answers would need to be read and transferred to tally sheets. These results would then be converted into summary tables and statistics calculated manually. In the 1950s, computer processing began to be used and surveys were "key punched" and translated onto computer cards for processing (Burns & Bush, 2006, p. 43).

The advent of personal computers in the 1980s liberated research analysts from their reliance on large-scale mainframe computers. Desktop computers equipped with sophisticated statistical programs such as SAS and SPSS became easily affordable. With a few keystrokes, instant statistical calculations could be produced. Computers were also increasingly used to manage sample lists, call-back scheduling procedures (to reduce "non-response bias," which occurs when respondents are not available for interviewing), and quality-control measures. A significant industry milestone was the introduction of Computer Assisted Telephone Interviews (CATI). Equipped with a telephone headset, a keyboard, and a screen, interviewers were now tied directly into the polling firm's computer system during the interview. CATI determined how the questionnaire would appear on the interviewers' screens. This rendered obsolete the paper and pen surveys, which were error-prone and involved a cumbersome process of keypunching the recorded responses. Furthermore, the new system eliminated the need to ship surveys from place to place when doing national studies (Burns & Bush, 2006, pp. 251–52).

Not surprisingly, the market-research industry works hand-in-hand with the marketing and advertising industry, which collectively generates an estimated annual $20 billion in revenues worldwide. Over the past ten years considerable consolidation has occurred. Now, two-thirds of survey industry revenues are accrued to only 25 firms, most of which are based in Europe or the United States (Honomichl, 2005, p. 10). None of these major survey companies are located in Canada; however, that does not mean that Canadian pollsters have been inactive or without influence on the world stage.

Major Issues:

- **Concentration**: is a process whereby progressively fewer individuals or organizations control increasing shares of the mass media.Contemporary research demonstrates increasing levels of consolidation, with many media industries already highly concentrated and dominated by a very small number of firms.
- Worldwide phenomenon of mega media ownership
- Struggle between public service media and private broadcasting
- Private broadcasting is being lobbied out of existence
- Cross Media Ownership
  - No media should be allowed to own all forms of media
  - People can now own TV, radio, newspaper, magazines etc.
  - People can own many different areas of media
- Vertical Integration (Prevent growth of competition)
- Digitalization
  - Specialization and customization of media
  - Fragmentation of audiences
  - National existence at risk.

Technology – Background information
- First radio message in the world began in Canada: "Is it snowing there?"
- First radio station started in Montreal
- Technology is more than apparatus and machine devices
  - It involves people at work, organization, etc.
- Way of ordering information and connecting people
- Technology involves apparatus, techniques of operation and social institutions

his team at Columbia University and another team led by Angus Campbell and Philip Converse at the University of Michigan, a number of Canadian-based researchers were working on studies regarding Canadian voters (Kanji & Archer, 2002). In 1965, Peter Regenstrief, a pollster for the *Toronto Star*, produced *The Diefenbaker Interlude*, which was a comprehensive study that demonstrated that Canadian voting is largely determined by such social groupings as occupation, ethnicity, and language (Regenstreif, 1965). In that same year, John Meisel launched the first of what are now called the Canadian Election Studies (CES) in consultation with Philip Converse. Since then, and following each subsequent federal election, the CES has been the definitive public source for understanding Canadian voter attitudes and behaviours (Gidengil, 1992). Because the CES initially involved enormous amounts of labour, technical support, and access to mainframe computers, significant government funds and university-based institutional resources were required. The CES continues to require extensive support in the form of telephone field-centre support and analysis and is conducted during and after each federal election. Regarding the 2004 CES, 4,300 interviews were conducted during the election. Added to this were post-election interviews with 3,100 individuals and a mail-back survey of 1,500 respondents (CES/ÉÉS, 2004).[4]

The Media and Campaign Strategies

It is one thing to examine voter attitudes and behaviours from an academic perspective and quite another to use survey data to win elections. As Harris's success providing polling services to the Kennedy campaign illustrates, effective campaigning requires pollsters who can precisely identify where the "swing voters" (that is, those who are willing to switch their loyalty from one party to another) are to be found. In effect, campaign polling is action-oriented. According to Canadian Liberal Party pollster Michael Marzolini, "Party pollsters try to 'shift the needle' by determining which hot buttons can be pushed and levers pulled that will both solidify the party's core vote and draw support from the other parties" (Marzolini, 2006, p. 257).

One of the first times that modern polling was used in Canada for political ends was during the Second World War. Conscription, or what Americans would refer to as "the draft," seriously divided the country between pro-conscription forces in English-speaking Canada and anti-conscription forces in Quebec. Gallup suppressed the release of its own poll, which revealed serious divisions on the issue, due to pressures from the Liberal wartime government. At the same time, the government was paying Gallup to run a series of secret polls on this and other wartime issues (Hoy, 1989, p. 10). One publicly released poll that shook the national political scene occurred in September 1943, when Gallup reported that the Co-operative Commonwealth Federation (the precursor to today's NDP) held a slight lead over both the Liberals and the Conservatives (Brodie & Jenson, 1980, pp. 204–9). Fearful of a postwar electoral defeat, the Liberals commissioned a series of polls in 43 ridings leading up to the 1945 election. Thanks to the comprehensive polling information and the extensive marketing research of the party's advertising agency, Cockfield, Brown, the party was repositioned as a reformist-oriented party and thereby re-elected in the 1945 federal election (Whitaker, 1977, pp. 228, 232).

When Louis St. Laurent took over as the Liberal leader, Cockfield, Brown continued to guide the party to further victories. According to Reginald Whitaker, St. Laurent was an advertiser's "dream" in that he was "the perfect human material for the image merchants. The prosperous, dull . . . 1950s found their personalization in the paternal, authoritative, kindly figure of 'Uncle Louis.' Cockfield, Brown lent their best efforts to the careful cultivation of this image; in a real sense, the elections of 1949 and 1953 were the first Canadian elections dominated by a consciously manipulated media image of the party leader" (Whitaker, 1977, p. 237). Much of Cockfield, Brown's work was done for free, in the expectation of being awarded with numerous government contracts. It is estimated that during the 1950s, when the Liberals were in power, annual government billings by Cockfield, Brown were in the range of $1.5 million to $2 million. Indeed, after the Liberals' loss of power in 1957, the agency was no longer willing to provide research and other consultancy services without payment (Whitaker, 1977, pp. 251–52, 262).

While advertising agencies worked their magic on the Liberals, the Progressive Conservatives also began using polls to fashion their own strategies, only with less success. The PCs' 1953 federal campaign was said to be based on a pre-election poll of 3,000 Canadians conducted by McKim Advertising, which reported that voters were more concerned about taxes than other issues. One party strategist, Dalton Camp, was doubtful, saying the results were unreliable because the interviews had been conducted just prior to the announcement of a federal budget while the media had been focusing on taxes. He argued that it was only natural that this issue would appear in the results as a "top-of-mind" concern. Camp would later comment that the poll was "primitive research . . . employed to advance poor strategy" (Camp, 1970, pp. 99–100). Indeed, his concerns were unheeded and the survey results proved to be a disastrous guide when the PCs took only 51 seats to the Liberals' 170.

A funny thing happened on the way to the voting station in the 1957 election. Late in the campaign, the Gallup organization predicted a win for the Liberals based on 48 percent of the vote compared to the PCs' 34 percent. The polling results, coupled with a sense that the Liberals were indestructible, led many journalists to inaccurately predict a Liberal major-ity against John Diefenbaker's PCs. When the votes were counted, the Liberals held only 106 seats (with 42.3 percent of the vote, close to 6 percent less than the Gallup forecast), and the PCs held 112 (with 39 percent of the vote, 5 percent more than the forecast) (Meisel, 1962; Bickerton et al., 1999, p. 213). Reminiscent of the Truman vs. Dewey fiasco of 1948, *Maclean's* magazine included in its post-election commentary an erroneous refer-ence to the Liberal "victory," which was said to have been framed and hung over the bed of the newly elected prime minister (Hoy, 1989, p. 19).

In the early 1960s, there were rumours that Kennedy's personal dislike for Diefenbaker was sufficiently intense to have him "smuggle" his pollster Harris into the country to help with the Liberals' 1962 election campaign. Help was again given in the 1963 campaign and then by U.S. pollster Oliver Quayle in the 1965 and 1968 campaigns (Adams, 2007, p. 12; Hoy, 1989, p. 22). At the same time, the PCs were only willing to commission one national poll per election due to party president Dalton Camp's view was that it "was too expensive to do more. I used to run the national office for $30,000 a month in the mid-1960s. A poll then would cost $20,000. That was big money then" (Hoy, 1989, p. 25).

Following the 1972 election, in which the Liberals were very nearly defeated, Keith Davey (otherwise known as the "Rain Maker," a metaphor for his ability to produce election victories based on effective strategies, even when things looked difficult for the party) secured Toronto-based Martin Goldfarb to serve as the Liberals' official pollster. Goldfarb introduced a national daily poll involving 1,000 telephone interviews, which began two weeks into the campaign. Because long-distance telephone costs were high, interviews were done by local interviewers. The completed surveys were shipped to Toronto at the end of each night, and by noon the next day, the data would be processed and analyzed. Goldfarb claims that it was the first time in either the United States or Canada that this type of national election polling had been accomplished, and, in a strange kind of historical role reversal between the two countries, both he and Keith Davey were invited to New York to advise Democratic Party strategists on their innovative technique (Goldfarb, 2007).[5]

Goldfarb represented both old and new elements for the Canadian research industry. National parties would no longer have to resort to the questionable polling skills of advertising agencies or import American experts. Yet he also represented the older system of political favouritism represented by Cockfield, Brown because his firm was well positioned to win federal government projects. For example, in 1977, four national polls, three for the federal Finance department and one for the Secretary of State regarding federal bilingualism, were said to have netted his firm $210,000. In 1980, Goldfarb Consultants was reported to have received over $1.3 million in contracts during the previous eight years (Hoy, 1989, pp. 123–25).

By the mid 1970s, and after a series of losses to the Liberals, the PCs had yet to find a reliable pollster. In 1977, this changed with the discovery of Allan Gregg, who stood in sharp contrast to his more conservative-looking colleagues in the industry or in the party that would adopt him. Gregg was a young graduate of Carleton University, often publicly sporting sneakers, a pierced ear, and long hair. With his new firm, Decima Research, Gregg was hired by the PCs' national-campaign chairman, Lowell Murray, to direct the party's polling for the 1979 federal election (Courtney, 1981, p. 129). After Joe Clark's PC minority-government victory, Gregg's national reputation was established and he remained the party pollster during and after the 1984 Brian Mulroney landslide. This lasted until 1993, when the PCs lost power to the Liberals under Jean Chrétien. Following the path established by his predecessors, Gregg's Decima Research was able to win numerous lucrative contracts with the federal government. According to one report, during Mulroney's final years in power, federal government departments were spending a total of $64 million a year, with much of the work going to Decima Research (Rounce, 2006, pp. 146, 148).

During the 1980s, a number of other pollsters became well known nationally. Two examples are Michael Adams, who formed Environics, and Angus Reid, with his Winnipeg-based Angus Reid Group. Both effectively used a media-oriented strategy to attract new clients, not unlike that used by George Gallup in the 1930s. Environics linked up with the *Globe and Mail* and Quebec's respected newspaper *Le Devoir*. In the meantime, Angus Reid developed an early relationship with Izzy Asper and his developing network of CanWest Global TV, and then later developed a national profile by providing polling to the Southam newspaper chain (which included such major newspapers as the *Gazette* [Montreal] and the *Ottawa Citizen*). In 1989, Reid sold a controlling interest of his firm to Southam. It was the first and only time in Canada that a media company owned a major polling company, raising concerns about collusion between the two industries. Reid later purchased it back, with the support of his employees, in the early 1990s, and then sold his firm again in 2000 at a price exceeding $60 million to Paris-based Ipsos. The firm then

Globalization in the Media: Prominent Figures in Media
- Peter and David Thomson Control the CTV Global Media
- Leonard Asper controls Can West Global (A Canadian Company): went bankrupt in the late 2009, sold its broadcasting assets to Shaw Communications and newspaper assets were sold to Postmedia Network
- P.K. Peladeau controls Quebecor
- Rogers family owns Rogers
- Greenberg Brothers owns Astral Media
- Astral Media was founded by the Jewish Greenberg brothers: Ian, Harold, Harvey and Sidney, they founded Astral Media in 1961.
- Astral media is the largest radio broadcast in Canada with 83 radio stations in 8 different provinces.
- Also has TV and newspaper media outlets
- Some of their board of directors brothers are up and comers to take over Can West Global
- Started off in photography

based Viewpoints Research—turned to Comquest, which had helped the provincial wings of the party win victories in Saskatchewan and Ontario (Whitehorn, 1997, p. 95).

In the 2006 federal election, each major party used different strategies for their national campaigns. The Conservatives turned to two individuals for their national polls:

Priming and Framing: Commercial Pressure Points
- Dumbing down news to try and reach the larger amount of people
- Serious discussion is driven out by media that is quick stimulating and entertaining
- 8 second sound bites used frequently
    - 8 seconds should capture everything
    - Politicians need to put policy into two sentences

Advertising
- Want cross media coverage (Television, newspapers, blog, etc.)
- Specialized audiences
    - Advertisers have become embedded in the media
- Invasion of tabloids
    - Need to fill a 24 hour news cycle
    - Screaming gets substituted for analysis
- Tobacco prohibited on TV and Radio
- No limit on adds on the radio but the TV has a limit

News Trends:
→ Personalization
→ Dramatization
→ Fragmentation

became linked to merit. Except in rare circumstances, research firms now have to work through an open-bidding system to qualify for large government contracts.[6] As an illustration of this, the Liberals' polling firm, Pollara Research, won close to $1.5 million in federal-government contracts during the 2001–02 year, while at the same time other firms, many of which were either non-partisan or associated with other parties, were awarded contracts that in total exceeded those of the Liberal pollsters. These included Ekos Research ($4.5 million), Environics ($3.6 million), and Ipsos-Reid ($3.5 million) (Rounce, 2006, p. 153).

Another factor that has since changed the industry's relationship to government was the Quebec advertising scandal that unfolded during the final years of the Chrétien government (in which it was discovered that payments had been made to the federal Liberal Party by Quebec-based advertising agencies in exchange for government contracts). Questions began to be raised about the awarding of public-opinion research contracts. After examining the matter, the Auditor General issued a report in 2003 stating that the procedures for awarding opinion-research contracts had been properly implemented. However, in Ottawa there remains a high level of sensitivity to issues of trust and accountability, which research firms ignore at their peril (Rounce, 2006, p. 154).

Media Coverage and Federal Elections

It might surprise some to hear that most polls are never released to the public. In the same way that corporations such as Wal-Mart or Canadian Tire are careful to guard the results of their customer-satisfaction or brand-awareness research, Canadians rarely see the work done for political parties. What the public does see are results from studies that are either commissioned directly by the media or done for public-relations purposes by companies and organizations. Because of this, elections provide pollsters with an opportunity to exhibit their skills publicly when predicting the public's intentions (voting preferences), while newspapers and television networks compete with each other in advising the public on who is winning or losing the horse race.

Most firms see media work as reputation-enhancing rather than profitable. When a national television or newspaper chain uses a pollster's results, it signifies that his or her work is trustworthy, which in turn helps attract corporate clients. Pollara's Marzolini writes that, when working for the media, it is usually not for immediate profit. "Most polling firms subsidize their clients, spending far more money collecting data than could be reimbursed by their sponsors. Most work [to build] . . . name-recognition and profile, trusting that this will assist their firm's marketing efforts. Others poll out of pride and reputation, wanting to demonstrate their accuracy and analysis and hoping to be the firm with the most accurate poll of the election. There are very few opportunities other than elections and referendums in which pollsters can prove the accuracy of their craft" (Marzolini, 2006, p. 256).

The process by which polls are developed for the media can be complicated and is usually planned well in advance of a national election being called. The major networks and newspaper chains usually know who their research suppliers will be. To save money, and to maximize exposure for their polls, television networks and newspapers often enter a partnership arrangement for the duration of the election. A typical example of how a media provider and a polling firm will work together is illustrated by the case of the 2006 federal election. Prior to the election being called, discussions were conducted between the *National Post* and Darrell Bricker, who heads the Public Affairs division at Ipsos-Reid. These were aimed at establishing 1) the polling budget; 2) the questions that were to be asked during the campaign; 3) the number of interviews to be conducted to sufficiently cover the country and all major regions; 4) the frequency of the polls; and 5) the timing by which Ipsos-Reid would provide results from each poll to *National Post* editors so that their staff could meet their deadlines for the targeted date of the poll's release (Bricker, 2007).

Election polling can be a very stressful process for everyone in a research firm due to many factors. Such factors include: 1) meeting the narrow timelines for each of the "field windows" (the time periods in which all the surveys commence and end) that are allotted for conducting national polls—these often exceed 1,000 interviews per wave, which is considered a moderately large-scale survey project in the industry; 2) the need to analyze the data, especially as the findings pertain to regional and socio-demographic segments in the population such as women, suburbanites, and specific age groups; 3) preparing a comprehensive news release for those journalists who have been assigned to the story; and 4) having available the firm's senior pollster, such as Darrell Bricker of Ipsos-Reid or Allan Gregg, who was with the Strategic Counsel during the 2006 election, for a series of newspaper and on-camera interviews. As election day nears, polling firms are called upon daily by their media client to discuss the polling trends, and then on election day their senior analyst is usually found in one of the national network's television studios to provide analysis as the voting results are counted. For example, Bricker provided on-camera analysis for Kevin Newman in national Global-TV studios, while Gregg was in the CBC studios with Peter Mansbridge. The work does not end there. The day after there is extensive media coverage regarding which of the polling firms (and their media clients) most accurately predicted the election.

Table 9.1 provides an overview of how many of the major firms were used by the national media during the 2006 federal election. Two firms, SES Research and the Strategic Counsel, provided daily results to their clients, while others, such as Decima and Pollara, were in the field less frequently (Waddell & Dornan, 2006; Marzolini, 2006). The full extent to which polls were used and released through the media during the 2004 and 2006 federal elections is shown in a website maintained by Professor Andrew Heard, who teaches in the Political Science department at Simon Fraser University. This site (which can be found at www.sfu.ca/~aheard/elections/) proved invaluable during the 2006 election for many journalists, academics, campaign workers, and voters who wanted to better understand both the day-to-day developments as the election unfolded and its outcome.

Table 9.1 Polling Firms, Media Clients, and the 2006 Federal Election

Polling Firm	Polling Activity/Frequency	Media Client
SES Research	Daily polling	CPAC
Strategic Council	Daily polling	Globe and Mail CTV
Ipsos-Reid	Weekly during the first half, increased frequency in second half of election	National Post
Ekos Research	Weekly, then daily in the last two weeks	Toronto Star
Decima Research	Less than weekly during the first half, increased frequency in second half of election	Canadian Press
Pollara Research	Less than weekly during the first half, increased frequency in second half of election	Reuters Rogers Media
Environics	Polling not publicly released. Frequency uncertain.	CBC

Source: Based on Waddell and Dornan (2006) and Marzolini (2006).

Levelling the Playing Field: The Costs of Election Polling

Considerable financial resources are required to pinpoint the salient issues among voters and identify the areas of weakness among competing parties and the messages that will most likely sway specific segments of the population. In order to help level the playing field, at least with regard to curbing the excesses of election spending, a new Canada Elections Act (Bill C-2) was introduced in 2000. This new legislation addressed concerns regarding "third-party spending" (that is, monies spent by individuals, businesses, or organizations rather than by the parties themselves, thereby allowing parties to circumvent the spending limits) (Massicotte, 2006, p. 197). In 1993, Parliament set a $1,000 ceiling on third-party spending, which was struck down by the courts as being an infringement on free speech. New regulations were put into place requiring that third parties register with the chief electoral officer while limits to spending for each third party were $3,000 per riding and $150,000 overall. After a series of court challenges, the Supreme Court upheld the law in 2004. This means that third parties must continue to register with the chief electoral officer, and the extent to which they can fund such expenses as opinion polls is limited (Massicotte, 2006, p. 199).

In 2003, Bill C-24 (an Act to Amend the Canada Elections Act and the Income Tax Act) was given royal assent. New ceilings on contributions relating to nomination campaigns, leadership campaigns, and elections were put into place, and the definition of election expenses was expanded to include opinion polling. The effect is that campaign directors now have to include polling in their budgetary calculations. Furthermore, and perhaps more significant for the party system as a whole, Bill C-24 includes measures by which the federal government now reimburses political parties that win 2 percent of the national vote (or 5 percent in ridings in which they field candidates) at a rate of $1.75 per vote (Massicotte, 2006, p. 206). Such new funds will no doubt have a long-term impact on party budgets and the extent to which polling is purchased in the future.

Concerns have also been raised about how much the public should be exposed to polls during elections. For example, some argue that polls can cause voters to switch their preferences if they think that their first choice has a poor chance of winning. With reference to what is usually termed "strategic voting," there is evidence it negatively influences "third parties" such as the NDP in both federal and provincial elections (Cutler et al., 2004, pp. 1–3). However, the strategic-voting effect that public polls might cause begs the question: Does this not also suggest that publicly released polls enhance the democratic process by allowing voters to better understand how their vote can be effectively used? In 1998, the Supreme Court ruled that the public has a right to access this information. It thereby ruled that polls could be released at any time during an election. Subsequently, the Election Act of 2000 only prohibits polls on the day of the election. The Act, however, ensures that news reports regarding election polls must now identify the survey's sponsor, the polling firm, the dates upon which the interviews were conducted, the sampling method, and the margin of error (Massicotte, 2006, p. 200). Such measures help to ensure that a minimum of standards are in place for reporters who might not always understand the technical side of polling research.

A broader concern regarding how polls are used is their influence on decision making among leaders and within government. The claim is that more attention is paid to polling numbers than to principles, ideas, or the views of party members. Furthermore, policy becomes aimed at short-term rather than long-term goals due to the public's fickleness. British prime minister Winston Churchill remarked during World War II, "Nothing is more dangerous than to live in the temperamental atmosphere of a Gallup Poll; always taking one's temperature . . . there is only one duty . . . and that is to try to be right and not fear to do so" (quoted in Lowi, 1981, p. 163). American political scientist Theodore Lowi counters by arguing that polling provides insights into the public's mind that might otherwise be unobtainable: "survey research . . . can help make citizens less gullible, group leaders less strident, and politicians less deceitful" (Lowi, 1981, p. 172).

CHALLENGES FACING THE INDUSTRY

A major challenge currently faces the polling industry in North America, and it relates to non-response bias. That is, are those who are answering the surveys any different than those not responding to surveys? Are respondents increasingly only those who are readily available to be interviewed? Those who don't mind responding to telephone calls? Those who enjoy answering questions? Naturally, if fewer and fewer Canadians respond to pollsters, then the threat of non-response bias will increase. This problem is increasing in two ways.

First, due to the ubiquity of modern polls, as well as telephone-sales calls (rather than research-related calls), many potential respondents now screen their calls or simply decline to be surveyed. To overcome this, pollsters need to ensure that their surveys are brief, are conducted by well-trained interviewers, that call-back procedures are used if the respondent is busy or not available, and that the survey includes a good opening statement.

The second threat pertains to the changing nature of telecommunications. Until recently, virtually any citizen (with the exception of those living in poverty or in very remote communities) could be reached via a land-line telephone. However, many now opt to use cellular telephones as their primary residential line, or even internet-based calling (otherwise known as VOIP). Reaching these individuals through traditional sampling methods is difficult. Furthermore, these alternative communication avenues have a higher usage rate within specific segments of the population, such as younger people. To counter this problem, polling firms can apply a number of tools. One that is commonly used is to weight the data so that under-represented segments within the surveyed population are made to reflect their proper proportion within the general population (for example, if young adults are found to be under-represented in the survey results, those who have these characteristics and who were interviewed would be "weighted" up). Other tools include obtaining sample lists of people who have cellphones, building a panel of citizens who have agreed to be interviewed in the future, or using online surveys to augment the telephone-survey methodology.

Some take an extreme position by arguing that emerging online-research techniques are superior to telephone-based methodologies. Since selling his firm to Ipsos, Angus Reid now operates an online-research firm that was able to more accurately predict the popular support in the 2007 Quebec provincial election than his telephone-based competitors (Angus Reid Strategies, 2007). Most national firms now offer sophisticated online polling services to their clients. This includes Ipsos-Reid and Decima Research (which was purchased in 2007 by Harris Online). However, concerns continue to be raised regarding the extent to which this relatively new technique can consistently capture the opinions of all parts of Canadian society, including those in lower-income or less technically attuned households. Common wisdom in the industry is that different methodologies suit different research objectives (Popiel, 2007). With regard to surveying the general population concerning their voting intentions, telephone surveys continue to be the most commonly used and relied-upon methodology.

THE QUALITATIVE DIMENSION

The discussion in this chapter has focused on the quantitative side of social research, which involves understanding the attitudes of large populations (in this case, the electorate) by asking questions about voter preferences. One widely recognized shortcoming to quantitative analysis is that survey researchers find it difficult to get at the underlying reasons why certain voters prefer one party (or candidate) over another. To deal with these questions, research firms are often asked to provide *qualitative* research findings based on focus groups.

In a typical study, respondents that fit a specific attitudinal and socio-demographic profile are recruited to attend a focus-group session. For example, if the Conservative Party was interested in developing a strategy to win more ridings in the suburbs around Toronto (otherwise known as the "905 Beltway"—where the Liberals performed well in the 2006 Federal Election), it might recruit women from the region who report having voted in the previous election and do not feel committed to any particular party.

The focus group, consisting of eight to ten representatives from the targeted voter segment being studied, would be moderated by a professional researcher who would guide the discussion for close to two hours. This discussion would explore the underlying reasons for choosing certain candidates and parties over others. The moderator might ask participants to imagine what the perfect candidate might be like, or to articulate their top two issue areas and then explain why they are important. Individuals are then able to discuss these issues in an open fashion. Party strategists in the backroom watch closely to see on what points their campaign ideas might be resonating and to see what ideas could be incorporated into speeches, platforms, and advertising.

Rather than rely on focus groups, some strategists turn to audience testing. This usually involve recruiting large groups (sometimes over 100) to a central location, where respondents are given hand-held devices featuring a dial that can be moved from left (meaning that the respondent is giving a low score) to right (signifying a high score). The technology is usually referred to as a Portable Audience Response System (PARS), which monitors participant attitudes when shown television commercials, radio materials, or a pre-recorded speech. During the time in which they are exposed to the materials being tested, respondents move the dial from moment to moment as their feelings about what they see (or hear) change. This allows the researcher to identify specific words, phrases, sounds, and images that the audience identifies as positive or negative. Because each hand-held dial is distinctly identified in the system, the researcher can segment the audience's responses according to such things as gender, whether they voted for a specific party in the previous election, income, education level, preferred radio station, and so on. An example of how this would be useful is that the audience testing might reveal that higher-income women liked a particular advertisement while lower-income men did not.

CONCLUSION

This chapter has provided an overview of the polling industry as it developed in the United States and later in Canada. It can now be considered a sophisticated and mature industry, servicing media providers, political parties, government agencies and departments, and the corporate world. Each decade has brought about industry-related techniques and technologies, such as CATI and online surveys, and it is now doubtful that any political party could put forward an effective campaign strategy without using public-opinion research. Likewise, newspapers and television networks continue to compete with each other by turning to the polling industry during each national campaign.

Media Journal Assignments

1. Monitor your daily newspaper over a one-week period. How often do you see polling information utilized? What types of polls are being conducted and how is the information used by the media? Is the information provided helpful for you as a news consumer? Provide examples to illustrate the benefits and problems with polling data.

2. Go online and find five different online surveys. Would you consider these polls to be effective ways to gain information? Why or why not?

Endnotes

1. The author would like to thank two of his colleagues at Probe Research Inc., Scott MacKay and Kevin MacDougald, for their insightful comments on earlier versions of this chapter.

2. For this election and predictions of Truman's defeat, including audio and video clips, see PBS online: www.pbs.org/wnet/historyofus/web13/segment5_p.html.

3. These accounts are based on the author's experiences while working as a senior project manager at Goldfarb Consultants in Toronto from 1995 to 1997 and as vice president of the Angus Reid Group until shortly after the firm's purchase by Ipsos.

4. Access to the CES data and supporting literature is available at http://ces-eec.mcgill.ca.

5. These facts are derived from an interview by the author with Martin Goldfarb, August 29, 2007.

6. Projects are usually awarded through two avenues: by a call for suppliers to submit proposals on a project-by-project basis, or through what are called "standing offers." A standing offer is available to firms that have been placed on a limited list of pre-approved suppliers. The process is handled through Public Works and Government Services Canada in a politically neutral manner. The system allows federal departments to hire firms on the list without going through a competitive bidding process. When this happens, the costs for the project have already been established in the original standing offer. For public-opinion research, the federal government usually limits this list to a short list of accredited firms for qualitative work (focus groups), and a second list for quantitative work (surveys). Due to the lengthy and complicated process of qualifying for the standing offer, many firms are not eligible. All federal-government projects that are open for bidding (including standing offers) can be viewed at www.merx.com.

References

Adams, Michael. 2007. "Political Polling Research in Canada." *Vue: The Magazine of the Marketing Research and Intelligence Association* (March 2007): 10–13.

Allen, Barbara. 2006. "How Ottawa Buys: Procurement Policy and Politics Beyond Gomery." In *How Ottawa Spends, 2006–2007,* ed. G. Bruce Doern, 95–115. Montreal: McGill-Queen's University Press.

Angus Reid Strategies. 2007. News Release. March 28. www.angusreidstrategies.com.

Babbie, Earl. 2004. *The Practice of Social Research.* 10th ed. Belmont, Ca.: Wadsworth/Thompson Learning.

Bickerton, James, Alain Gagnon, & Patrick Smith. 1999. *Ties That Bind: Parties and Voters in Canada.* Toronto: Oxford University Press.

Bricker, Darrell. 2007. Communications with this chapter's author, November 12, 2007.

Brodie, Janine, and Jane Jenson. 1980. *Crisis, Challenge and Change: Party and Class in Canada.* Toronto: Methuen.

Burns, Alvin & Ronald Bush. 2006. *Marketing Research.* 5th ed. Upper Saddle River, N.J.: Prentice-Hall.

Butler, Peter. 2007. *Polling and Public Opinion: A Canadian Perspective*. Toronto: University of Toronto Press.

Camp, Dalton. 1970. *Gentlemen, Players and Politicians*. Toronto: McClelland & Stewart.

CES/ÉÉS. 2004. *Canada Election Study/Étude Électoral Canadienne*. Available at http://ces-eec.mcgill.ca.

———. 2006. *Canada Election Study/Étude Électoral Canadienne*. Available at http://ces-eec.mcgill.ca.

Converse, Jean. 1987. *Survey Research in the United States: Roots and Emergence, 1890–1960*. Berkeley: University of California Press.

Courtney, John. 1981. "Campaign Strategy and Electoral Victory: The Progressive Conservatives and the 1979 Election." In *Canada at the Polls, 1979 and 1980: A Study of the General Elections*, ed. Howard Penniman, 121–51. Washington: American Enterprise Institute for Public Policy Research.

Cutler, Fred, Patrick Fournier, Greg Lyle & Stuart Soroka. 2004. "The 2003 Ontario Election: Campaigns, Advertising, Debates, Bandwagons, and Issue Importance." Paper presented to the CPSA, June 2004.

Ellis, Faron & Keith Archer. 1997. "Reform at the Crossroads." In *The Canadian General Election of 1997*, ed. Alan Frizzell and Jon Pammett, 111–34. Toronto: Dundurn Press.

Gallup, George & Saul Rae. 1940. *The Pulse of Democracy*. New York: Simon & Schuster.

Gidengil, Elizabeth. 1992. "Canada Votes: A Quarter Century of Canadian National Election Studies." *Canadian Journal of Political Science 25* (June 1992): 219–48.

Goldfarb, Martin. 2007. Personal interview with the author. August 29.

Honomichl, Jack. 2005. "Honomichl Global Top 25." Special Supplement, *Marketing News*, August 15.

House of Commons, Standing Committee on Public Accounts. 2005. *Management of Public Opinion Research: Report of the Standing Committee on Public Accounts*. June 2005.

Hoy, Claire. 1989. *Margin of Error: Pollsters and the Manipulation of Canadian Politics*. Toronto: Key Porter Books.

Johnston, Richard. 1985. *Public Opinion and Public Policy in Canada*. Toronto: University of Toronto Press.

Kanji, Mebs & Keith Archer. 2002. "The Theories of Voting and Their Applicability to Canada." In *Citizen Politics: Research and Theory in Canadian Political Behaviour*, ed. Joanna Everitt and Brenda O'Neill, 160–83. Don Mills, Ont.: Oxford University Press.

Lachapelle, Guy. 1991. *Polls and the Media in Canadian Elections: Taking the Pulse*. Toronto: Dundurn Press.

LeDuc, Lawrence. 1975. "The Measure of Public Opinion." In *Canada at the Polls: The General Election of 1974*, ed. Howard Penniman, 209–41. Washington: American Enterprise Institute for Public Policy Research.

Lowi, Theodore. 1981. *Incomplete Conquest: Governing America*. New York: Holt Rinehart & Winston.

Massicotte, Louis. 2006. "Electoral Legislation Since 1997: Parliament Regains the Initiative." In *The Canadian Federal Election of 2006*, ed. Jon Pammett and Christopher Dornan, 196–219. Toronto: Dundurn Press.

Marzolini, Michael. 2006. "Public Opinion and the 2006 Election." In *The Canadian Federal Election of 2006*, ed. Jon Pammett and Christopher Dornan, 253–82. Toronto: Dundurn Press.

Meisel, John. 1962. *The Canadian General Election of 1957*. Toronto: University of Toronto Press.

Moore, David. 1992. *The Super Pollsters: How They Measure and Manipulate Public Opinion in America*. New York: Four Walls Eight Windows.

Page, Christopher. 2006. *The Roles of Public Opinion Research in Canadian Government*. Toronto: University of Toronto Press.

Popiel, Stephen. 2007. "On-Line and Off-Line Market Research: How Revolutionary?" Presentation to the Online Conference of the Marketing Research and Intelligence Association, Toronto.

Regenstrief, Peter. 1965. *The Diefenbaker Interlude: Parties and Voting in Canada, An Interpretation*. Toronto: Longmans.

Robinson, Daniel. 1999. *The Measure of Democracy: Polling, Market Research and Public Life, 1930–1945*. Toronto: University of Toronto Press.

Rounce, Andrea. 2006. "Ottawa's Spending on Public Opinion Research: Implications for Democratic Governance." In *How Ottawa Spends, 2006–2007*, ed. G. Bruce Doern, 138–61. Montreal: McGill-Queen's University Press.

Waddell, Christopher & Christopher Dornan. 2006. "The Media and the Campaign." In *The Canadian Federal Election of 2006*, ed. Jon Pammett and Christopher Dornan, 220–52. Toronto: Dundurn Press.

Warren, Kenneth. 2001. *In Defence of Public Opinion Polling*. Boulder, Colo.: Westview Press.

Whitaker, Reginald. 1977. *The Government Party: Organizing and Financing the Liberal Party of Canada, 1930–58*. Toronto: University of Toronto Press.

Whitehorn, Alan. 1997. "Alexa McDonough and Atlantic Breakthrough for the New Democratic Party." In *The Canadian General Election of 1997*, ed. Alan Frizzell and Jon Pammett, 91–110. Toronto: Dundurn Press.

Woolstencroft, Peter. 1997. "On the Ropes Again? The Campaign of the Progressive Conservative Party in the 1997 Federal Election." In *The Canadian General Election of 1997*, ed. Alan Frizzell and Jon Pammett, 71–90. Toronto: Dundurn Press.

Zolf, Larry. 2003. "Martin's Pollster." CBC News Viewpoint, July 7. Available at www.cbc.ca/news/viewpoint/vp_zolf/20030707.html (accessed August 20, 2008).

Part III
Intersections: Citizens, Media, Politics

Mainstream media are often accused of closing off possibilities for citizen participation in politics. Because "media construct the public sphere of information and opinion and control the terms of their exchange," political reality is shaped according to the priorities and perspectives of corporate and government elites and citizens are constructed as passive spectators, as consumers of politics rather than as active participants in democratic governance (Mazzoleni & Schulz 1999, pp. 250–51). But citizen groups and social-movement organizations can fight back by using new media to engage in online citizen journalism. In 2006, *Time* declared the "person of the year" to be "You"—as in all of the ordinary people who create their own media by contributing to YouTube and Wikipedia, MySpace, and Facebook. *Time* waxed lyrical about the internet, asserting that the web is about "the many wresting power from the few." As *Time's* editors put it, for "seizing the reins of the global media, for founding and framing the new digital democracy, for working for nothing and beating the pros at their own game, TIME's Person of the Year for 2006 is you" (Grossman, 2006).

This section of the book looks at the ways in which citizens and civil-society groups use media to get their messages across to the public, politicians, and governments. Chapters 10 and 11 document the limitations of traditional media and explore the potential of new media, particularly the internet, to shake up elite control of political communication and deepen democracy. Framing of social movements and their issues by the mainstream news media, and attempts by groups to shape their own representations through the media, are explored in Chapters 12 and 13. The first two chapters of this section challenge *Time* magazine's Pollyanna-like prognosis about the revolutionary potential of new media. Citizen-generated news produced on weblogs, networking sites, discussion forums, and media-sharing sites constitutes the background noise of mediated politics, maintains **Curtis Brown**, a Manitoba-based blogger, journalist, commentator, and political science student. A graduate of the University of Regina's School of Journalism, he began his reporting career in Saskatchewan before shifting to the political beat with the *Brandon Sun*. Brown later served as the *Sun's* editorial-page editor, and in the spring of 2005 launched a political blog, Endless Spin Cycle (http://endlessspin.blogspot.com), which he continues to update as this book goes to press. Curtis writes regular columns for the *Winnipeg Free Press* and the *Brandon Sun*, and is currently working on a Master's thesis that explores how partisan blogs frame media coverage of the federal Conservative government.

In Chapter 10, "White Noise: The Blogosphere and Canadian Politics," Brown maps the landscape of political blogging in Canada, offering a typology of blogs and outlining their rapid proliferation over the past decade. He provides several examples of blog power, showing how information that politicians and governments want to keep under wraps can be brought to light through artful web placement and publicity. Blogs now have an impact on journalism, politics, and public opinion, Brown contends, and blog-based "citizen journalism" is proliferating, but no one really pays attention until traditional media sources replay (and reformulate) their content. As a result, while the blogosphere does allow citizen pundits to bypass traditional media filters, invariably their voices have little impact until they are mediated by the large media corporations, which continue to control much of news production and dissemination.

Curtis Brown's argumentation is echoed in Chapter 11, "Great Expectations: The Internet and the Changing Nature of Democratic Politics," by **Graham Longford** and **Steve Patten**. Longford and Patten outline the potential of the internet and new information and communications technologies (ICTs) to enhance the nature and perform-ance of democratic politics by building virtual communities of engaged citizens who share information, engage in meaningful democratic deliberations, participate in e-governance, and challenge elite control of political communications. The internet has, they argue, facilitated alternative politics by allowing activists to initiate protests, hold virtual meet-ings, and disseminate information by sending mass emails, uploading videos on YouTube, or posting on linked websites. However, these campaigns are fleeting or exist on the margins of power, and the reality of citizen politics via the internet has fallen far short of expectations. As the authors demonstrate, new media are increasingly owned and controlled by "old media": the multinational conglomerates that run television, newspapers, newsmagazines, radio, and web browsers. Moreover, political and economic elites dominate cyberspace and, rather than promoting e-governance or facilitating genuine citizen participation in political decision making, they use their web presence to feed the mainstream media's appetite for good quotes and dynamic visuals. Longford and Patten fear what will happen if the internet is not regarded (and protected) as a public good. Without equality of access and freedom from colonization by corporations or the state, they argue, the internet will do little to enliven democracy or re-engage disenchanted citizens.

In Chapter 12, "Social Movements and the Media," **Miriam Smith** provides histor-ical and contemporary examples of social movement interactions with the media, documenting the importance of political communication to their formation, expansion, and success. Like Longford and Patten, Smith is optimistic about the potential of ICTs to promote certain forms of democratic activism and to politicize and contest the power of the mainstream media. Because social movements are determined to challenge and ultimately transform social, economic, and political institutions, values, and behav-iours, they have used both mainstream and alternative media to reach specialized and mass audiences. Social-movement organizations have developed and published their own forms of communication to members and interested publics, but the success of these movements often hinges on their ability to capture the attention of larger audiences—audiences capable of pressuring corporations and governments to make change. Since such audiences are largely under the control of mainstream media, some movement organizations have become adept at staging media events and pandering to news values. Smith itemizes the strategies available to social movements when engaging with the media, noting also the risk of losing control over the framing of issues; attention can come at the cost of movement legitimacy. The alternative, activism through the internet and other forms of new media, facilitates transnational and cross-movement links, and, in Smith's view, allows activists to "bounce back" when established media close off opportunities for dialogue and dissent.

The risks of losing the struggle with the news media to name and frame a movement's political ideals and goals are clearly illustrated in Chapter 13, "'Too Broke to Answer the Phone': Reporting the 'Death' of the National Action Committee on the Status of Women." **Angela Failler**'s account of media representations of the decline of Canada's once large and influential feminist organization underlines Stuart Allen's contention that news is a profoundly ideological construction, as reporting invariably advances some truth-claims and disregards or minimizes others (Allan, 2004, p. 4). Failler argues that the ideological positioning of corporate mass media in Canada is elitist, sexist, racist, and conservative, and as a result feminists have always had to contend with media marginalization of their claims and misrepresentations of their objectives. The National Action Committee (NAC) has been framed as alternately powerful enough to constitute a threat to the public good, or on the brink of death, too weak to imperil dominant power relations. For instance, the election of Sunera Thobani, the first woman of colour to serve as president of the NAC, was constituted as illustrative of the organization's alleged ability to represent "all" women. In contrast, prematurely and derisively reporting the "death" of the NAC undermined the organization's legitimacy and may have hastened its demise.

Angela Failler ends her chapter with the observation that the NAC "missed the internet revolution." What difference would it have made had the NAC been able to mobilize on the web, engaging in direct and unmediated dialogue with supporters, coalition partners, and women's organizations around the world? Would the NAC have survived? Do the new media create independent spaces for citizen activism and interest mobilization, or do they serve to merely entrench elite interests and corporate media power?

References

Allan, Stuart. 2004. *News Culture*. 2nd ed. London: Open University Press.

Grossman, Lev. 2006. "Time's Person of the Year: You." *TIME Magazine* Online, Wednesday, December 13. Available at www.time.com/time/magazine/article/0,9171,1569514,00.html (accessed June 28, 2008).

Mazzoleni, Gianpietro & Winfried Schulz. 1999. "Mediatization of Politics: A Challenge for Democracy?" *Political Communication* 16: 247–61.

Chapter 10

White Noise: The Blogosphere and Canadian Politics

Curtis Brown

The mosquito ring tone emits a shrill, piercing sound that most people over the age of 20 cannot hear. Because of a biological condition called presbycusis, or aging ear, only children and teenagers can hear the 17-kilohertz squeal students download to their cellphones in order to keep their teachers from detecting when a text message has arrived in the middle of class (Vitello, 2008). It is only when this high-pitched sound grates enough on a pair of prepubescent ears that the tone's existence is pointed out to the adult in the room and, as a result, the cellphone ends up locked away in the teacher's desk.

This piece of sonic technology—originally designed by a Welsh firm as a way for shopkeepers to drive away teenaged loiterers from their storefronts—works much like the communications tools that are transforming our media, our politics, and our democracy. The blogosphere, the all-encompassing network of webpages that allows anyone with an opinion to share it with the world, is very much like the mosquito tone in that it is virtually undetectable to the average person unless someone who is aware of it points it out. Even though surveys of Canadian citizens show that they are more likely to read blogs than Americans and Europeans (comScore, 2006), it would appear that most citizens pay little attention to the content produced by bloggers and other would-be online "citizen journalists" until traditional media sources bring it to their attention (Drezner & Farrell, 2008). While new forms of electronic communication have certainly changed how information about politics, government, and other institutions flows between decision makers and citizens, these methods have not lived up to their hype as a participatory and egalitarian tool for engaging all citizens in public debate.

The reality is that when online tools like blogs, discussion forums, social networking sites like Facebook, and media-sharing websites like YouTube are adapted to politics, they become the white noise playing in the background of political discussion. On any given day, bloggers discuss the minutiae of political life while the rest of the population goes about its business. It is only when the discussion catches the interest of reporters plugged into this network that they, like the teenagers who can hear the piercing screech of the mosquito ring tone, disseminate the information to a wider audience that is largely tuned out. Graham Longford and Steve Patten make this case in greater detail in Chapter 11, but as a journalist who first discovered Canadian political blogs in 2004 and started my own blog about Manitoba and federal politics in the spring of 2005, I can certainly state that this has been true of my experience.

To provide an example, my blog, Endless Spin Cycle, features a piece of hidden HTML code that allows me to track who visits my website, where they came from, and where their computer is located. Over two typical days—Tuesday, June 24, 2008, and Wednesday, June 25, 2008—nearly 20 percent of my traffic came from people working at computers inside the Manitoba Legislature, making this the single biggest repository of people who read my work. Another 12 percent of my readership over these two days came from other government offices, including the House of Commons, the City of Winnipeg, the federal Treasury Board Secretariat, and the U.S. Department of State. A smaller yet still significant number of hits came from newsrooms, such as those of the *Winnipeg Free Press*, the *Brandon Sun*, the *Winnipeg Sun*, the CBC, and CTV. About 15 percent of the readers on these two days clicked on my blog after following a link on another local blog, which demonstrates how the blogosphere works as a network of continual point and counterpoint between its contributors. While it is impossible to know exactly who is reading from these locations, or from others, as only the IP address is recorded, this evidence offers a partial demonstration of how the blogosphere tends to be an elite rather than a communitarian forum for discourse. If my experience is indicative, then I am largely writing for those whose occupation demands that they pay attention to politics. While I do know that there are interested citizens from outside these political, bureaucratic, and journalistic circles who read what I write, it does not take long before it emerges that these people already have a strong interest in politics. Many of the complete strangers I came to know as a result of my efforts on the web later started their own blogs, volunteered on campaigns, and/or ran for office. In other words, these were not ordinary citizens, but rather deeply engaged political individuals with a strong desire to join the club.

In Manitoba (and this is probably true of anywhere in Canada), political blogs seem to fall into four basic categories. The first kind of blog is what Jane Singer calls j-blogs, which are written by journalists and columnists like me. These online soapboxes are extensions of our professional work, allowing us to post short, pithy observations and material that might not fit into a regular news story or column in something approaching real time. Sometimes blogs are used by editors to explain the journalistic process to their respective audiences, or to discuss the reasons why some editorial decisions are made. The blogging format has been adapted by media outlets, yet the medium challenges professional norms of traditional journalism such as fairness, balance, and non-partisanship (Singer, 2005). While this is less of a challenge for writers like me who are expected to express political opinions, it is more challenging for reporters who must attempt to cover an issue even-handedly for the next edition or newscast and then offer an instant opinion on the same issue for their blog. Even if a reporter is scrupulously fair to both sides of his or her story, the subjects of the piece may perceive a bias based on the contents of a reporter's blog.

The second type of blog is the political-activist blog. These bloggers tend to openly support a particular political party and use their blog as a way of pumping up their teammates and attacking political opponents. Many of these blogs are organized into communities of partisan bloggers, such as the Blogging Tories (Conservatives), Liblogs (Liberals) or the Blogging Dippers (NDP). Some of these bloggers are anonymous, but many of them—and certainly many of the better-read ones—do sign their name to their work. These blogs are more prevalent at the national level, and are discussed in further detail in the rest of this chapter.

The third type of blog is the anonymous-observer blog. Some of these bloggers hide their identity because blogging publicly may have professional or personal repercussions. These bloggers may have a particular political point of view, but because they are anonymous they are more likely to be more diffuse in their criticism and praise of political figures. Some of these bloggers offer thoughtful perspectives and balanced critiques, but others use their anonymity as a cover to launch blistering *ad hominem* attacks against individual political and journalistic figures. One of the earliest Manitoba bloggers, The Black Rod, has been doing this by acting as a self-appointed watchdog of Manitoba media outlets, particularly the *Winnipeg Free Press*. Another example is the blog Blackberry Addicts, a group blog that was run by a number of New Democratic Party members in the lead-up to Manitoba's 2007 election. This blog, which became dormant after the election, was openly partisan and anonymous. Its authors attacked several targets in the months leading up to the campaign, but its favourite rhetorical punching bag appeared to be Hugh McFadyen, the Progressive Conservative Party leader. "Baby Huey," as the blog's authors called him, was painted in a negative light on a near-daily basis leading up to and throughout the election campaign. While it isn't exactly clear just how this blog may have framed media coverage of McFadyen, the Tories, or the NDP, the blog's authors made it clear their intent was to put their own pro-NDP spin on whatever was being said about the governing party by rebutting "the know-nothing, open-mouth nonsense that generally passes for political punditry in Manitoba" (Blackberry Addicts, 2006).

The fourth and final type of blog is what I call the transformative-discourse blog. Sadly, these blogs are a rarity in the Canadian political landscape. These blogs are typically written by individuals who write to draw attention to issues in their neighbourhoods and local communities that may be overlooked or dealt with in less detail by the mainstream media outlets. Usually, these bloggers are upfront about their identity and do not view politics through a specific partisan prism. Their motivation to blog is both cathartic (it allows them to express opinions about issues that they feel must be heard) and heuristic (it creates a dialogue that seeks to solve common problems). Some of the best examples of transformative-discourse blogs in Winnipeg deal with issues facing local neighbourhoods, such as urban decay, heritage preservation, crime, housing, etc. Examples of Canadian blogs that fall into these four categories are outlined in Table 10.1.

Blogs have come a long way in Canadian politics in very little time. While the internet first began playing a role in Canadian politics in the late 1990s, its impact was

Table 10.1

J-Blogs	Political-Activist Blogs
Inkless Wells (http://blog.macleans.ca/category/blog-central/national/inkless-wells/)	The Calgary Grit (http://calgarygrit.blogspot.com)
	Stephen Taylor (www.stephentaylor.com)
CBC Editor's Blog (www.cbc.ca/news/canada/editorsblog/)	Warren Kinsella (http://warrenkinsella.com)
Susan Delacourt on Politics (http://thestar.blogs.com/politics/)	Small Dead Animals: The Roadkill Diaries (www.smalldeadanimals.com)

Anonymous-Observer Blogs	Transformative-Discourse Blogs
The Black Rod (http://blackrod.blogspot.com)	Rise and Sprawl (http://riseandsprawl.blogspot.com)
The Tea Makers (http://teamakers.blogspot.com)	Christopher Leo's blog (http://blog.uwinnipeg.ca/ChristopherLeo/)

never as widely felt as it was in the United States. In the 2000 election, Canadian political parties started to use their websites as sophisticated and interactive tools to contact voters, thus making them more than the online pamphlets they had been to that point (Small, 2007). Some Canadians also began turning to online discussion forums to talk about politics—though, as Harold Jansen and Royce Koop discovered in their comparison of discussion boards during the 2000 federal election and the 2001 British Columbia election, this medium is dominated by a small and very active number of participants (Jansen & Koop, 2005). The authors found that individuals posting on these two boards tended to skew discussion in a particular ideological direction, as well as post far more negative than positive items about particular parties, their candidates, and their leaders.

Blogs, which appeared in the mid 1990s, first emerged as sources of Canadian political commentary shortly after the turn of the millennium. For the most part, the evolution of the Canadian blogosphere lagged behind that of the United States, where bloggers had already played a role in the downfall of Republican Senate Majority Leader Trent Lott after he publicly praised Strom Thurmond's segregationist policies (Bloom, 2003). But it wasn't until the spring of 2005 that the ability of blogs to act as an alternative source of information was fully realized by journalists and the Canadian public.

During the commission of inquiry into the federal government's sponsorship program, Justice John Gomery placed a publication ban on the testimony of Jean Brault, the former president of the Groupaction advertising agency and one of the central figures in the sponsorship scandal. While Canadian media outlets could not publish the details of Brault's testimony, Ed Morrissey, a conservative blogger based in Minneapolis, received details of the testimony and published them on his website,

Captain's Quarters. Under the heading "Canada's Sponsorship Scandal Breaks Wide Open," Morrissey reported that Brault told the commission about how his advertising firm had received "hundreds of thousands of dollars in bogus transactions," some of which was funnelled back to the Liberal Party in the form of "untraceable cash donations." Morrissey also reported that Brault explained how he hired "employees" who were actually working for the Liberal Party's Quebec wing. In addition to publishing these statements, Morrissey suggested that

> If the Gomery Commission can corroborate Brault, then the reek of corruption goes through all levels of the Liberal party and may explain their ability to out-campaign the Conservatives. After all, they've siphoned off hundreds of millions of government dollars to promote their own party and to guarantee their monopoly on power. They hijacked the Canadian tax base to fund their own campaigns and hide the financial trail. (Morrissey, 2005)

Because he was writing from the United States and was thus was all-but-impossible to prosecute for violating a court-ordered publication ban, Morrissey was able to report Brault's stunning testimony before the CBC, CTV, the *Globe and Mail*, or any other Canadian media outlet could publish or broadcast this information. Canadians dying to know what Brault had said in that Montreal courtroom could log on to Morrissey's blog and learn most of the explosive details. Thanks to the "borderless blogosphere," any Canadian with internet access could link to any of the news aggregator websites or partisan blogs in both countries linking to Morrissey's post (Adamson, 2005). After five days, Canada's bloggers and Canadian journalists were finally allowed to provide their

Zakaria: Another war in the Middle East by: Fareed Zakaria
1. Obama says a nuclear Iran would set off an arms race in the Middle East. But a nuclear North Korea has not led the two countries directly threatened by its weapons South Korea and Japan—to go nuclear. Saudi Arabia and Egypt did not go nuclear in response to Israel's developing a large and robust arsenal of nuclear weapons.
2. Obama has explains that nuclear Irean would be a problem like India and Pakistan with their nuclear weapons. But India and Pakistan went to war three times in 30 years before they had nuclear weapons. Since they went nuclear, they have been strained and have not fought a war in 40 years.
3. Iran's weapons could fall into the hands of terrorists, say the President. But would a country that has labored for decades to pursue a nuclear program and suffered huge sanctions and costs to do so then turn around and give the fruits of its efforts to a gang of militants?
4. This kind of reasoning is part of the view that the Iranians are mad, messianic people bent on committing mass suicide. When General Martin Demspey explained on my CNN program last month that he viewed Iran as a "rational action," he drew howls of protest.

2006). According to Taylor, the Conservative Party required the blogosphere to deliver its message free of the media filter:

> Conservatives gather around blogs for warmth in a cold and hostile media environment. From this small hopeful light in the darkness, conservatives spread the message to others open to positive change and re-establishment of our country's pride. This is the grassroots and this is our time. (Taylor, 2005)

Taylor's words proved prophetic, as Conservative bloggers put their new-found clout to work as Canadians geared up for another federal election. As Wayne Chu (2007) noted in his analysis of the 2006 campaign, bloggers aggressively publicized evidence of suspicious trading activity prior to the Liberal government's November 23, 2005 decision not to tax income trusts. Many blogs linked to a comment on Stockhouse, an internet forum for investors, posted six hours before then–finance minister Ralph Goodale announced the decision not to tax income trusts at a press conference (Tomlinson, 2005). While bloggers linked to this and other evidence, it was not until December 27, 2005, that the RCMP announced, in a letter sent to NDP MP Judy Wasylycia-Leis, that it was investigating allegations of insider trading. At that point, the issue became a major media story, and in post-election analysis it was viewed as a defining moment in the campaign.

Did blogs make a difference in terms of how the story was played? The evidence is unclear. While the media did not pay a great deal of attention to the allegations until the RCMP announcement in late December 2005, several weeks after the income-trust decision was announced, blogs may have provided journalists with a ready-made frame to present the issue to their audiences once it was considered newsworthy. Blogs may have contributed to what Doris Graber termed "media facts" that morph into "politically significant feelings and attitudes" (Graber, 1984, p. 73). In this case, the fact that the RCMP were investigating Goodale and the Department of Finance was enough to convict the Liberals in the court of public opinion and at the ballot box, even though, in the end, the RCMP did not charge either Goodale or any other political actor as a result of their investigation (Bronskill, 2007).

Following the election, blogs enjoyed even more prominence as the Prime Minister's Office and members of the Parliamentary Press Gallery fought over how journalists on Parliament Hill would be able to cover the new Conservative government. The PMO instituted a new policy for press conferences that required reporters to put their names on a list in order to be allowed to ask questions of the Prime Minister or Cabinet ministers (Vongdouangchanh, 2006). Many journalists protested this move and walked out of press conferences where the new rule was imposed. As a result, Prime Minister Stephen Harper temporarily boycotted the national press gallery (Panetta, 2006), and spoke favourably of blogs as a media form that could be "helpful for democracy" by limiting the perceived power of the professional journalists stationed on Parliament Hill (Libin, 2006).

In this climate, did blogs supplant the mainstream media as a prime source Canadians could turn to for information on politics? The evidence suggests not. However, it would seem that blogs play a threefold role as they evolve in the Canadian political context.

First, the format has been mimicked, as many more political reporters blog now than ever before. The four major Toronto-based daily newspapers—the *Globe and Mail*, the *Toronto Star*, the *National Post*, and the *Toronto Sun*—all offer blogs by some of their senior reporters as media outlets experiment with this new medium. Second, bloggers act as a watchdog for traditional journalists, drawing public attention to their errors and lapses in judgment. Third, bloggers can use their power—and at times, their partisanship—to collectively fixate on a particular issue until it becomes impossible to ignore.

A perfect example of this second and third function of bloggers came in late 2007. On December 13, former Prime Minister Brian Mulroney appeared before the House of Commons ethics committee to testify about payments he received from German business-man Karlheinz Schrieber. During Mulroney's testimony, Liberal MP Pablo Rodriguez asked the former prime minister if he had recently lobbied the then–industry minister, Maxime Bernier, or anyone else in the Conservative government, on behalf of Quebecor, whose board Mulroney sat on, regarding an upcoming wireless spectrum auction. Later that after-noon, CTV NewsNet pundit (and former Liberal MP) Jean Lapierre claimed that "the CBC" had asked Rodriguez to put those questions to Mulroney. Within hours, the Conservative Party's news release attacking the CBC was reproduced on several Conservative blogs. The following day, Conservative Party campaign manager Doug Finley sent a letter to CBC Ombudsman Vince Carlin asking for an investigation. The CBC announced on December 14 that it had launched an internal inquiry, which was reported by the Canadian Press (Canadian Press, 2007). However, Conservative-affiliated bloggers posted frequently about the subject throughout December and January, with many of them demanding that the CBC employee who wrote the questions be identified and that the results of the investigation be made public. One Blogging Tory, Steve Janke, posted seven different items attacking the CBC and the Liberals in the initial week after the accusation was made (Janke, 2007). These posts reiterated the issues raised in news releases sent out by the Conservative Party on December 17 and January 3 and echoed comments critical of the CBC that Finley had made in a fund-raising letter that had been sent to Conservative supporters in late December. While these blogs on their own likely merely acted as a parti-san echo chamber for what the Conservative Party was saying on the issue, they may have reinforced the pressure on the CBC to take the unusual step of identifying the offending reporter, Krista Erickson, by announcing on January 21, 2008, that she was being reassigned from Ottawa to Toronto. At this point, most major Canadian news outlets both reported the story and identified Erickson as the reporter who had written the questions (*Globe and Mail*, 2008; Canwest News Service, 2008). Had the Conservative Party and its affiliated bloggers not made as much noise about this matter, it is doubtful other media outlets would have reported the issue to the extent that they did. While this shows how bloggers can act to frame how journalists cover stories, it also exposes the limits of their influence. If reporters had chosen to simply ignore what bloggers were saying, would the story have been covered the same way, with Erickson being identified? It's highly doubtful.

A recent and lesser-known example from Manitoba illustrates how something that appears in the blogosphere or on YouTube has little to no public impact until mainstream media outlets shine a light on it. On April 24, 2008, Progressive Conservative MLA Heather Stefanson rose in the Manitoba Legislature to ask the provincial water steward-ship minister, Christine Melnick, a routine question about walleye fishing in Dauphin Lake. Members of nearby First Nations communities had been exercising their treaty rights and catching walleye out of season on the tributaries that feed the lake, and Stefanson asked Melnick whether she would use her powers to ban all fishing on the tributaries. When Melnick responded, she noted that the government was providing "sustenance" to First Nations residents under their treaty rights (Legislative Assembly of Manitoba, 2008a). When Melnick said the word "sustenance," another Progressive Conservative MLA, Leanne Rowat, yelled out "Wine and beer?" across the aisle that separates NDP MLAs from PC MLAs. Though this catcall—one of many barbs MLAs toss out during the back-and-forth of the daily Question Period—was not recorded in *Hansard*, it could be heard on the live video recording broadcast on the Legislature website and a local cable-access network.

To someone who does not follow Manitoba politics, this would seem like a strange, nonsensical, and potentially racist comment to make in the course of a debate on First Nations fishing rights. Within a couple of hours, an 85-second clip of the exchange was posted on YouTube. Within 12 hours, it was posted on two Manitoba blogs, Just Damn Stupid and Pissing In The Tent (Just Damn Stupid, 2008; Cotton, 2008). While the authors of these two blogs commented negatively on Rowat's catcall, what was interest-ing is that none of Winnipeg's major media outlets immediately publicized the remark. Was it because they didn't hear it? Were they covering up the fact that an MLA may have uttered a racial slur on the floor of the Legislature? It turns out it was for neither reason; rather, the event passed unnoticed because the reporters who were in the press gallery that day understood that the context of Rowat's "wine and beer" catcall following the word "sustenance" carried a far different meaning. A year earlier, a government minister had defended receipts for wine and beer purchased for a dinner meeting as "sustenance" (Welch, 2008a). Since then, Rowat called out the phrase "wine and beer" whenever one of the NDP government's ministers used the phrase "sustenance" in the Legislature. She soon came to wish she had chosen her words more carefully.

These bloggers continued to post on the issue after the exchange in the House on April 24. On Wednesday, April 30—six days after the original exchange in the Manitoba Legislature—Aboriginal and Northern Affairs Minister Oscar Lathlin spoke publicly about Rowat's comment, describing it as "offensive to Aboriginal people and . . . an affront to members of this House" on the floor of the Manitoba Legislature (Legislative Assembly of Manitoba, 2008b). That same day, the head of the Southern Chiefs Organization, Grand Chief Morris Shannacappo, also demanded during an interview with the CBC that Rowat not only apologize, but also resign her post as Aboriginal affairs critic (CBC, 2008). Though Rowat claimed to have apologized privately to Lathlin and another Aboriginal MLA, Culture Minister Eric Robinson, Lathlin demanded a public apology from both Rowat and Progressive Conservative leader Hugh McFadyen. Suddenly, what was once an inside joke in the Legislature exploded into a very public racial spat. The following day, May 1, the *Winnipeg Sun* published a photo of Rowat on its front page along with a story detailing Lathlin's call for an apology as well as—for the first time—details of the original "wine and beer" comment (Turenne, 2008a). The *Winnipeg Free Press* also published its first story on the incident, albeit without a photograph (Welch, 2008a). On May 2, McFadyen appeared once again on CBC Radio to defend Rowat and explain her comment, while both the *Sun* and the *Free Press* published a number of commentaries in their pages and on their websites during the following few days (see Welch, 2008a; Brodbeck, 2008; Turenne, 2008b; Engstrom, 2008), almost all of which defended Rowat and attacked Lathlin and the NDP government for trying to paint Rowat and the Progressive Conservatives as racist.

There are some eerie parallels between this incident and the Lott situation, in which bloggers kept Trent Lott's inflammatory comments from fading away. Still, these incidents demonstrate the limited influence blogs and websites such as YouTube actually have. Until the elite media covered either story, it had little traction beyond the limited audiences who read the blogs. Once reporters and editors at the mainstream media outlets made the issue part of their news agenda—or, to be more accurate, once events such as Lathlin's point of privilege or Lott's public apology dictated that they could no longer ignore them—the original incident became newsworthy. As Drezner and Farrell (2008, p. 3) put it when describing the Lott affair, "blogs were not a causal variable in explaining Lott's downfall, but they were an important intervening variable." So, even if a tree falls in the blogosphere and a reporter hears it crash, it does not actually make a discernible sound until that reporter or his or her editor decides that the public should hear the sound as well. Or, to go back to the original example, journalists are like the teenagers who can hear the squeal of the mosquito tone and decide to draw everyone else's attention to its presence. Up to that point, it's just background noise.

In spite of this, blogs and other forms of new electronic media such as YouTube, Facebook, etc. have already demonstrated their ability to transform Canadian politics. Besides forcing politicians and media figures to be more answerable for their comments and actions, these online tools allow those not lucky enough to own a printing press or a journalism degree to register their observations and opinions in the public domain. For those who use their blogs to publish transformative discourse about their neighbourhoods and the issues they face in their everyday lives, this web-based media can be used to share ideas and organize like-minded individuals around a common cause. For the most part, however, the Canadian political blogosphere is a dissonant battleground of partisan opinion and private interest. The keystrokes tapped out by partisan bloggers on their keyboards and blogging journalists on their BlackBerries are the barely audible drumbeats setting the tempo of political combat. The blogosphere itself may be a revolutionary tool in the history of communication and democracy, but it merely acts as one more mediating force in Canadian politics—and a mostly indiscernible one at that.

References

Adamson, Rondi. 2005. "Borderless Blogs Vs. Canada Press Ban." *Christian Science Monitor*, April 30. Available at www.csmonitor.com/2005/0413/p09s01-coop.html (accessed June 12, 2008).

Blackberry Addicts. 2006. Available at http://blackberryaddicts.blogspot.com (accessed on June 25, 2008).

Bloom, Joel. 2003. "The Blogosphere: How a Once-Humble Medium Came to Drive Elite Media Discourse and Influence Public Policy and Elections." Paper presented to the 2003 annual meeting of the American Political Science Association, Philadelphia, August 2003.

Brodbeck, Tom. 2008. "'Wine' whine fizzles." *Winnipeg Sun*, May 2, 5.

Bronskill, Jim. 2007. "'Sheer Agony' followed income trust allegations." *Globe and Mail*, May 16. Available at www.theglobeandmail.com/servlet/story/RTGAM.20070516.wnadeaugoodale0516/BNStory/ Front (accessed June 12, 2008).

Canadian Press. 2007. "CBC investigates question's origins." *Toronto Star*, December 15. Available at www.thestar.com/News/article/285888 (accessed June 10, 2008).

Canwest News Service. 2008. "CBC pulls Ottawa reporter: Krista Erickson helps Grit MP." *Windsor Star*, January 22, A7.

CBC. 2008. Canadian Broadcasting Corporation. "MLA's Wine and Beer Comment Sparks Allegations of Racism." CBC.ca, April 30. Available at www.cbc.ca/canada/manitoba/story/2008/04/30/ wine-and-beer.html (accessed June 2, 2008).

Chu, Wayne. 2007. "Of Blogs and Broadcasters: The Influence of Web Logs in Political Campaigns." Paper presented to the Canadian Political Science Association, Saskatoon, June 2007.

comScore Media Matrix. 2006. "The Score: Blogs Gain Media Acceptance Worldwide." Press Release, December 14. Available at www.imediaconnection.com/content/12750.asp (accessed June 10, 2008).

Cotton, James. 2008. "Wine and Beer." PITT: Pissing in the Tent. Available at www.pissinginthetent.com (accessed June 25, 2008).

Drezner, Daniel & Henry Farrell. 2008. "The Power and Politics of Blogs." *Public Choice* 134 (2008): 15–30.

Engstrom, Kevin. 2008. "Shameless Smearing." *Winnipeg Sun*, May 4, 6.

Flanagan, Tom. 2007. *Harper's Team: Behind the Scenes of the Conservative Rise to Power*. Kingston: Queen's-McGill Press.

Globe and Mail. 2008. "CBC Reporter reassigned for feeding Mulroney-Schreiber hearing questions." January 21. Available at www.theglobeandmail.com/servlet/story/RTGAM.20080121.wcbcreport0121/BNStory/Entertainment/home (accessed June 10, 2008).

Graber, Doris. 1984. *Processing the News: How People Tame the Information Tide*. New York: Longman.

Janke, Steve. 2007. "The Conservatives are demanding answers to allegations of Liberal-CBC collusion." Angry in the Great White North, December 17. Available at http://stevejanke.com/archives/ 249570.php (accessed June 18, 2008).

Jansen, Harold & Royce Koop. 2005. "Pundits, Ideologues and Ranters: The British Columbia Election Online." *Canadian Journal of Communication* 30: 613–32.

———. 2006. "Canadian Political Blogs: Online Soapboxes or Forums for Democratic Dialogue?" Paper presented to the Canadian Political Science Association, York University, June 2006.

Just Damn Stupid. 2008. "Bet This Won't Show Up in Hansard." April 24. Available at http://justdamnstupid.blogspot.com/2008/04/bet-this-wont-show-up-in-hansard.html (accessed June 25, 2008).

Kinsella, Warren. 2001. *Kicking Ass in Canadian Politics*. Toronto: Random House Canada.

———. 2007. *The War Room*. Toronto: Dundurn.

Legislative Assembly of Manitoba. 2008a. *Hansard* 60 (30b) (April 24, 2008): 1021–1125.

———. 2008b. *Hansard* 60 (33) (April 30, 2008): 1389–1450.

Libin, Kevin. 2006. "'I've Got More Control Now': Exclusive interview: Prime Minister Stephen Harper explains why the press gallery's fighting him—and why it's backfiring." *Western Standard*, June 19, 15.

Morrissey, Ed. 2005. "Canada's Corruption Scandal Breaks Wide Open." Captain's Quarters, April 2. Available at www.captainsquartersblog.com/mt/archives/004220.php (accessed June 12, 2008).

Panetta, Alexander. 2006. "PM to shun Ottawa journalists, saying they're biased against him." *Toronto Star*, May 25, A7.

Singer, Jane. 2005. "The Political J-Blogger: Normalizing a New Media Form to Fit Old Norms and Practices." *Journalism* 6 (2): 173–98.

Small, Tamara. 2007. "Canadian Cyberparties: Reflections of Internet-Based Campaigning and Party Systems." *Canadian Journal of Political Science* 40: 639–58.

Taylor, Stephen. 2005. "Blogging Is Grassroots." Stephen Taylor: Conservative Party of Canada Pundit, April 28. Available at www.stephentaylor.ca/2005/04/ (accessed June 12, 2008).

Tomlinson, Kathy. 2005. "Online Posts Suggest Leak in Income Trust Case." CTV.ca, December 7. Available at www.ctv.ca/servlet/ArticleNews/story/CTVNews/20051207/whistleblower_incometrusts_ 20051207/20051207?hub=TopStories (accessed June 10, 2008).

Turenne, Paul. 2008a. "Chiefs target Tory." *Winnipeg Sun*, May 1, 3.

———. 2008b. "MLA's a heckler, not a racist." *Winnipeg Sun*, May 2, 11.

Vitello, Paul. 2006. "a ring tone meant to fall on deaf ears." *New York Times*, June 12. Available www.nytimes.com/2006/06/12/technology/12ring.html (accessed June 12, 2008).

Vongdouangchanh, Bea. 2006. "Reporters strike war footing with PMO, but Harper won't be dictated to by national media." *Hill Times*, February 27. Available at www.thehilltimes.ca/html/index.php?display=story&full_path=/2006/february/27/pmo/&c=1 (accessed December 5, 2007).

Welch, Mary Agnes. 2008a. "Tory leader unfairly tarred as racist: Leader." *Winnipeg Free Press*, May 1, A5.

———. 2008b. "Two weeks of pent-up griping." *Welch's Gripe Juice—Winnipeg Free Press Blog Central*. May 2. Available www.winnipegfreepress2.com/blogs/welch/?p=45 (accessed May 30, 2008).

Wells, Paul. 2006. *Right Side Up*. Toronto: McClelland & Stewart.

Chapter 11

Great Expectations: The Internet and the Changing Character of Democratic Politics

Graham Longford and Steve Patten

INTRODUCTION

The years just prior to the dawn of the twenty-first century were marked by great expectations regarding the impact of the internet and other new information and communications technologies (ICTs) on the character and practice of democratic politics. The prevailing assumption was that access to new ICTs and computer-mediated communications would change partisan behaviour while improving government services and access to information. More fundamentally, it was anticipated that a new age of egalitarian news and information dissemination and internet-based public dialogue would empower ordinary citizens and deepen democracy. This chapter examines the impact of the internet on the character of democratic politics. Following a review of the new ICTs and the nature of early expectations regarding their consequences for democratic politics, the chapter addresses the actual impact of the internet in three broad areas: (1) governments, political parties, and electoral democracy; (2) opportunities for deliberative democracy; (3) alternative politics and social movements. While it will be clear that some dimensions of democratic life have benefited from popular access to the internet, this has not been the case for other dimensions of democracy. Democratic practices have not changed as anticipated. Moreover, as is so often true in political life, the process of integrating the internet and new ICTs into democratic politics has been shaped by the character of existing social, political, and economic institutions and power relations.

THE CHANGING CHARACTER OF ICTS

The free flow of information and communication is "democracy's oxygen" (Winter, 1997). As such, numerous advances in democratic politics have coincided with the development of the institutional and technological infrastructures for the production and distribution of information, including the constitutional protection of free speech and the free press, and improvements in information and communications technologies (ICTs) (Bimber, 2003). The ICTs of historic importance to democracy include the printing press, the postal service, the telegraph and telephone, and radio and television. A common theme in the social histories of early ICTs is the sense of disappointment experienced by those with grand hopes that ICT-driven democratic developments would be truly revolutionary (Marvin, 1990; Standage, 1998). This chapter examines the democratic expectations and actual consequences of a range of new ICTs.

By "new ICTs," we refer to a cluster of digital and network technologies that includes personal computers, modems, software, and the internet, and the various applications that run on them, including email, the World Wide Web, and peer-to-peer networks. Also part of this cluster are cellular telephones, digital audio and video recorders, and mobile computing devices that are increasingly internet-enabled and compatible. What marks these technologies as "new" is not simply their recent emergence but, more importantly, the break they have introduced in relation to previous ICTs like newspapers, radio, and television in terms of the former's quantitative and qualitative effects on the production, circulation, and discussion of information. New ICTs have facilitated the emergence of the so-called "new media" of digital platforms for the production and distribution of knowledge, information, and cultural content—that is, web portals and sites, search engines, wikis, social-networking sites, weblogs, podcasts, audio and video streaming— and the organizations and enterprises that operate them, including MSN, Google, Wikipedia, Facebook, and YouTube. New media platforms and enterprises have been touted as alternative sources of knowledge and information that challenge the increasingly commercialized old media of newspapers, radio, and television. By allowing consumers to bypass the editorial bias and news filtering of the traditional media, the new media allow "disintermediation" between raw news content and those who consume it. Admittedly, however, enthusiasm for the new media's ability to bypass traditional media is partially tempered by recognition of the extent to which the new media *are* the old media insofar as many popular new media properties have been acquired from the traditional media by multinational conglomerates.

The new ICTs have enabled a worldwide explosion in the production of information. The proliferation of digital content on computer hard drives, CDs, DVDs, and the web is rapidly outstripping content produced in older formats such as books, newsprint, and film and video. Global daily email traffic has surpassed 31 billion messages (Lyman & Varian, 2003), while the World Wide Web now comprises over 11.5 billion pages and is growing rapidly (Gulli & Signorini, 2005). This explosion of information has been enabled by the low cost and relative ease with which digital content can be duplicated and transmitted. Older technologies such as print, radio, and television require substantial capital invest- ments in equipment, and the costs of producing content are high. Historically, such cost factors limited participation in the production and distribution of news and information to large commercial and public institutions such as private and public media enterprises. Personal computers, the internet, and new ICTs allow a wider range of individuals and groups to engage in producing and distributing news and information. They also allow news and information to be shared much more widely and quickly. While the old media emphasized the unidirectional broadcast of news and information to passive readers/listeners/viewers, the new ICTs enable multi-modal forms of communication, including communications that are one-to-one (email), one-to-many (a webpage), and many-to-many (online discussion forums and social networking sites). There is also greater opportunity for interactivity and collaboration between information producers and consumers. Indeed, with the rise of user-generated content sites like MySpace, YouTube, and Facebook, the distinction between producer and consumer has collapsed into the category of the user. The cumulative impact of these changes in news and information dissemination should not be underestimated. But, prior to assessing their political consequences, it is worth recalling some of the early enthusiasm regarding the democratic implications of new ICTs.

GREAT EXPECTATIONS: ICTS AND DEMOCRATIC POLITICS

In the mid 1990s, optimism about the capacity of new ICTs and the internet to transform existing processes of social and political interaction and information sharing produced a wave of utopian speculation about a coming era of technologically driven democratization (Levin, 2002; Winner, 1997). Expectations were high that the new-media revolution would transform democratic politics. Observers writing from a variety of perspectives speculated that, by facilitating the exchange of politically relevant news and information and creating new opportunities for political action, the internet would promote a new, more democratic civic ideal.

Commenting on the internet and mainstream electoral politics, Daniel Weitzner characterized the internet as "a vast new forum for political discourse and activism which allows genuine interaction between voters and elected representatives" (cited in Levin, 2002, p. 81). Enthusiasts of referenda and direct democracy claimed that online decision-making and participation had the potential to enable a new form of plebiscitarian e-democracy (Barney, 1996). More radical democrats and liberal communitarians argued that the internet's greatest potential lay in its capacity to build virtual communities of politically engaged internet citizens—netizens—coming together to identify and deliberate on issues of the day. Howard Rheingold (2000), for example, wrote that computer-mediated communication and networked "cybercommunities" would provide citizens the leverage needed to challenge the political and economic elite's monopoly on powerful communications media. Finally, from the ideological right, influential libertarian futurists went even further. In the boldly subtitled *A Magna Carta for the Knowledge Age*, Dyson, Gilder, Keyworth, and Toffler (1994) argued that new ICTs would close the gap between information-rich citizens and those who lacked information and knowledge, flatten organizations, enhance individual freedom and local decision-making, and, in the end, allow the power and authority of centralized government and entrenched bureaucrats to "melt away" as newly empowered citizens take full advantage of their capacity to self-govern.

An important theme in the early literature on ICTs and politics was the impact of the internet on the production and distribution of political information. Sanguine observers argued that lowering the cost of information production opened the door to a greater diversity of information and opinion by ensuring that new voices would find expression in a more vibrant and inclusive public sphere. Lawrence Grossman (1995) wrote of an emerging "Electronic Republic" in which new ICTs and unmediated interaction with political news ensured a more reflexive and politically powerful process of public-opinion formation. Still others argued that improved access to the means of producing, distributing, and receiving information would allow ordinary citizens and civil society groups to become broadcasters and publishers capable of sidelining the powerful barons of the mass media. As political weblogs and independent media became more popular, scholars of "public journalism" began to speculate about the emergence of something even more empowering: "the public's journalism" (Witt, 2004).

As the twenty-first century dawned, the new ICTs and the internet were losing their novelty and more sober assessments of their consequences for democratic politics were being written. Still, expectations were high that politics would be done differently in the internet era. As such, optimists remained confident that low-cost information production, egalitarian public conversations in cyberspace, and new opportunities for political action would transform and deepen democracy.

GOVERNMENTS, POLITICAL PARTIES, AND ELECTORAL DEMOCRACY IN THE ERA OF THE INTERNET

The internet and digital technologies related to websites, listservs, and electronic-data records are altering the political and business practices of both political parties and our elected governments. In Canada and many other jurisdictions, governments have begun to use the internet for the dissemination of program information and the delivery of services. Political figures have also discovered that the internet is a convenient tool for bypassing the mass media when publicizing new initiatives and accomplishments (Alexander, 2001a; Fountain, 2001; Margetts, 1999). In both cases, however, the information being made available is mostly standard program information or propaganda, and the services provided online (such as passport applications) are typically related to programs that are organized for citizens as mere consumers of government services (Longford, 2004). Efforts to utilize the internet to stimulate citizen engagement and involvement with the policy-making process have been half-hearted and disappointing—in other words, citizens are being served, but not empowered (Longford & Hurrell, 2006). Political parties have also embraced new ICTs and established a presence on the web. However, new ICTs tend to be utilized for tasks such as voter identification and fundraising, and partisan websites are little more than virtual campaign brochures that offer only limited interactive features; new technologies have not often created meaningful space for the politically engaged to participate in democratic dialogue (Hurwitz, 1999; Small, 2007). Little of this has served to improve the character and quality of electoral democracy.

When the Canadian government embraced new ICTs in the late 1990s it claimed they would streamline the delivery of public services and facilitate interactive communication and public consultation (Alcock & Lenihan, 2001; Richard, 1999). The 1999 Government On-line (GOL) project—an initiative that made vast quantities of information available on the government's main internet portal (www.canada.gc.ca)—was touted as an antidote to civic malaise that would transform the relationship between governments and citizens to a degree not seen since the birth of the welfare state (Treasury Board of Canada Secretariat, 2000). While it is true the federal government now enjoys a significant online presence—roughly 70 percent of Canadians have used the federal government's website in the past year, and online transactions now account for roughly one-third of all interactions between citizens and government (Statistics Canada, 2007)—the GOL initiative has been most successful in relation to serving citizens as consumers of existing government services and programs, such as registering a business or accessing information about public benefits. It has failed to effectively address the needs of citizens as active observers of and participants in the political process. Of course, the Canadian government is not alone in this respect. A comprehensive study of 270 municipal websites in California found very few sites containing features that might effect meaningful change in local governance. Indeed, even the most innovative sites were "more entrepreneurial than participatory" (Cavanaugh, 2000, p. 231).

To be fair, the federal government has experimented with using the internet to enable more participatory forms of policy deliberation, including "e-consultations" in areas such as foreign policy, health care, climate change, and defence. Unfortunately, these initiatives have been ad hoc, producing uneven and often unrepresentative results (Longford & Hurrell, 2006). Too often, e-consultations have taken the form of online-feedback exercises in which governments collect information and reaction from citizens in response to predetermined policy options. Government, rather than citizens, identifies the issues, frames the agenda and debates, and delimits the range of policy options. Moreover, the relationship between citizen consultations and actual policy-making decisions tends to remain unclear, a long-standing weakness of Canada's system of public consultations (Patten, 2001). An online consultation by the Romanow Commission on the Future of Health Care in Canada (2001–02) offers an example of the limits of such exercises. On the surface, the Commission's e-consultation was a success, with over 36 million hits to the Commission's website and tens of thousands of online surveys and consultation workbooks completed. But feedback was limited to responding to four predetermined policy options, and respondents were highly unrepresentative of the Canadian population (Jackson et al., 2002). On the whole, few federal e-consultations have resulted in genuinely democratic citizen engagement, which Phillips and Orsini identify as "interactive and iterative processes of deliberation among citizens . . . and between citizens and government officials with the purpose of contributing meaningfully to specific public policy decisions in a transparent and accountable way" (Phillips & Orsini, 2002, p. 3).

Malina (2003) has made the useful distinction between e-government and e-governance. Whereas the more status quo–oriented e-government is top down, involves governments communicating to citizens, and is primarily about administration and service delivery, e-governance is horizontal, aims at fostering civic communication, and facilitates citizen input in government policy-making. Canadian government initiatives in the use of new ICTs are closely aligned with the former, resembling little more than administrative reforms inspired by the market-oriented efficiency principles of the new public management. Although governments have experimented with innovations that could provide more democratic and participatory forms of policy deliberation, such as e-consultations, there is a limited commitment to developing these vehicles of e-governance.

As with governments, political parties initially adopted new ICTs to streamline operations, reduce overhead, and automate functions such as compiling and updating voter records (Kippen, 2000; Alexander, 2001b). Beginning in the 1990s, however, political parties in Canada began to explore the technologies' democratic possibilities. The populist-leaning Reform Party of Canada, for example, conducted a series of "tele-democracy" experiments during its party-leadership campaigns (Barney, 1996; Cross, 1998). Toward the end of the 1990s, all the major parties began to establish websites and exploit the new media to communicate with supporters and voters during and between election campaigns. But the 2000 election signalled the real watershed in the emergence of internet campaigning; in that election the use of web-based tools and communications became an integral part of campaigning (Small, 2007). Canadian parties are now using applications such as blogs, video-sharing, and user-generated social-networking sites to establish a web presence and get their message out. As an indication of the growing importance of the net, the popular video-sharing site YouTube became a new zone of partisan contestation in 2007 (Infoscape Research Lab, 2007). This was particularly evident during Ontario's fall election, when both provincial parties and partisan bloggers made active use of video sharing on YouTube.

Taking stock of the impact of new ICTs on partisan electoral politics, one is struck by the gap between the rhetoric of ICT enthusiasts and the reality of their use. A decade ago, Reform Party leader Preston Manning suggested that experiments in tele-democracy marked initial steps toward "building the Athens of the twenty-first century," a polity in which technology facilitated widespread citizen participation, engagement, and deliberation (Barney, 1996). Instead, as a handful of recent studies of the use of new ICTs in Canadian politics has shown, citizens remain disengaged and genuine deliberation is the exception rather than the rule (Barney, 2000; Barney, 1996; Carty et al., 2000; Cross, 1998; Small, 2007). In the case of the Reform Party's tele-democracy experiments, Cross found that the act of participating was highly atomized and privatized: "Not only do most [tele-]voters not meet the candidates, but they have little opportunity to communicate with other voters with different experiences from their own" (Cross, 1998, p. 143). Barney found the majority of the Reform Party's early initiatives involving new ICTs to be manipulative, elite-dominated, and of little or no value in terms of educating citizens, eliciting meaningful opinion, or building social capital among citizens (Barney, 1996). Even today, partisan websites appear to offer little more than virtual campaign brochures, providing a technologically advanced means of distributing the candidate's bio, photo, speeches, and policy statements (Small, 2007). Ironically, considering that the web was touted as allowing parties and candidates to make an end run around the news media in order to speak in a direct, unmediated fashion to voters, partisan websites are increasingly being developed to meet the mainstream news media's desire for campaign clips, sound bites, policy statements, and up-to-the-minute reaction to events. As Small's analysis of campaign websites from the 2004 federal election revealed, "the internet and websites are mainly used to amplify traditional methods of campaigning" rather than to push the boundaries of innovation in democratic participation and deliberation (Small, 2007, p. 654). To the extent that campaign websites are interactive, such features serve as tools for gathering data on supporters, recruiting volunteers, and soliciting financial contributions. They are not places of democratic dialogue and deliberation. While user-generated content sites like YouTube have been touted as potential tools for the democratization of electoral communications, their use closely resembles campaign-style advertising, and viewership is low (Infoscape Research Lab, 2007).

Perhaps more significant than the partisan use of new media to communicate with voters is the growing use of new ICTs for back-office purposes such as the collection and analysis of large databases of voter profiles and preferences, and their use in targeting and customizing partisan communications for strategic voting blocks and swing voters. Modern election campaigns are sophisticated exercises in voter identification, mobilization, and social control through agenda-setting and issues management. Very few voters would be familiar with the term "data mining," but electronic-data records are an increasingly important aspect of electoral democracy (Alexander, 2001b; Flanagan, 2003; Howard, 2005). Modern political campaigns rely on sophisticated database technologies that enable strategists to monitor the mood of voters, track party supporters, identify swing voters, solicit donations, coordinate get-out-the-vote activities, and customize political messages that can be delivered to target audiences electronically. Flanagan (2003) refers to this as the rise of the "database party." Today the governing Conservative Party maintains a database—called the Constituent Information Management System (CIMS)—containing the names of over 2 million Canadians (Canadian Press, 2007). In the United States, where data mining is more advanced, political campaigns combine public data—such as voters lists—with a range of commercially available data that is obtained through public-opinion and marketing surveys, internet spyware, and subscription lists, among other means. By cross-referencing these lists, Howard (2005) estimates political parties have profiled 4 in 10 American voters in exhaustive detail.

Data-mining techniques allow political campaigns to customize and target their political messages to a degree previously unimaginable. While conducting national advertising campaigns on television, parties can simultaneously target specific groups of voters with essentially private email communications that travel below the radar of scrutiny by the media or rival parties (Carty et al., 2000). In the fall of 2007, the federal Conservatives sent unsolicited Rosh Hashanah greetings via email to an undisclosed number of Jewish Canadians as part of their effort to woo socially conservative voters from minority ethnic and religious communities (Canadian Press, 2007). A number of commentators have warned of the fragmentation of the national public sphere, as "a series of highly focused, private conversations among voters, interest groups and politicians" replace the collective, public conversation that has characterized electoral politics in the past (Carty et al., 2000). While Flanagan celebrates the achievements of database parties, critics lament their democratic deficits. According to Whitaker, for example, such parties place little value on the traditional ideals of grassroots mobilization and citizen engagement around a set of ideas and issues. Instead, the focus is on using technology and telemarketing techniques to appeal to targeted populations in swing ridings, and this represents "the decline of deliberative, negotiated democracy and its replacement by unmediated telemarketing" (Whitaker, 2001, p. 21).

NEW OPPORTUNITIES FOR DELIBERATIVE DEMOCRACY?

A quarter of a century ago—before the transformations in ICTs that allowed widespread access to high-speed internet, user-friendly email programs, and a virtual explosion in the number and variety of political websites and weblogs—Benjamin Barber (1984) speculated that new information technologies had the potential to enhance civic awareness by increasing public access to information and facilitating participatory dialogue and deliberation across great distances. His vision was of the enrichment of democratic governance through computer-mediated interpersonal discussions and new forms of public debate. Of course, in these early years, Barber was not alone in assuming the internet would provide new opportunities for the enhancement of deliberative democracy.

Deliberative democracy involves rational, open-minded debate leading to collective decision-making (Dryzek, 2000). Strong democrats contend that deliberative democracy requires free and informed public deliberation in the context of a rich and politically lively "public sphere" (Habermas, 1989). In this context, the public sphere is understood as the social sites that act as a buffer between the state and the economy and the private realm. A vibrant public sphere creates social spaces for citizens to share information and viewpoints, while negotiating the collective understandings that define the shared text of civic life. The public sphere is home to the civic conversations that allow a broad range of citizens to realize their capacity to influence the norms and values that dominate contemporary politics. It is not surprising, therefore, that the issue of the internet's capacity to enliven deliberative democracy is typically framed in terms of its potential to transform the public sphere. As a forum for social communication, cyberspace transforms the public sphere by revolutionizing the "constellation of communicative spaces" in which information and ideas circulate, possible collective futures are debated, and political wills are expressed (Dahlgren, 2005).

Prior to the internet, the communicative spaces of the public sphere included public squares, community halls, and social meeting places—such as pubs and coffee houses—as well as the associational life of social and community groups (Oldenburg, 1989), and the many moments of information and opinion dissemination via the mass-communication news media and smaller-scale alternative media. In recent years, access to mass-media information sources has become so essential to participation in public dialogue that print media, radio, and television are sometimes identified as the place where "the public" is created and given its being (Hartley, 1992; Shulz, 1997).

The internet transforms the public sphere by expanding the number and reach of communicative spaces and creating new contexts for the identification and formation of a complex mosaic of overlapping and interconnected spheres for public deliberation. Communication in cyberspace via websites, listservs, weblogs, and other means transcends physical space and creates opportunities for alternative news sources that challenge the hegemony of territorially bound public life mediated by traditional mass-media institutions (Keane, 1995). Perhaps most significant for the public sphere, however, the internet contributes to the "pluralizing of the public" by creating numerous new opportunities for groups of citizens interacting in cyberspace to reflexively define themselves as "counter-publics" who articulate political discourses and identities that exist as alternatives to the homogenizing influence of the dominant discourse and identity of "the public" (Chambers, 2005; Warner, 2002).

The combination of a proliferation of communicative spaces, shared information, and alternative media, and the emergence of reflexive counterpublics could generate the sort of vigorous and diverse political life and public sphere that is associated with deliberative democracy in heterogeneous societies (Kellner, 1995; Poster, 1995). Unfortunately, ordinary people are not significantly more politically engaged or better informed than they were prior to the explosion of news and information on the internet—nor has the public sphere been politically enlivened. Instead, reflecting what Pippa Norris (2001) has called the "reinforcement effect," citizens who were already politically engaged now use the internet to seek out additional information and connect with others who are equally politicized, while the politically disengaged majority remain disengaged. As Peter Dahlgren (2005, p.151) explains, "the use of the Net for political purposes is clearly minor compared with other purposes to which it is put. The kinds of interaction taking place can only to a small degree be considered manifestations of the public sphere; democratic deliberation is completely overshadowed by consumerism, entertainment, non-political networking and chat, and so forth. Further, the communicative character of the political discussion does not always promote the civic ideal; much of it is isolated (and at times unpleasant), and its contribution to democratic will formation cannot always be assumed."

Why has the internet failed to enliven deliberative democracy? Essentially, as Barber (2000/2001) observed in his more recent—and less sanguine—work on the issue, in the absence of conscious political choices to the contrary, the internet will tend to mirror the relatively apolitical, stratified, and commercialized society in which it exists. It is our contention, moreover, that the failure to make choices that would allow the internet to contribute to the enhancement of deliberative democracy began with the lack of popular and official commitment to the internet as a public good. In making this claim we are using the term "public good" in its normative political sense. The internet has certain properties of "publicness" in that it is associated with a well-functioning public sphere, and the benefits of ensuring generalized access to the net extend beyond individual-level benefits to include broader social benefits. Defining the internet as a public good suggests that it would be unjust to allow lack of access to exacerbate existing social inequalities. There should, in other words, be social rights of access to the internet—and market forces or commercial imperatives should not determine the distribution of internet access. There are three important anti-democratic consequences of our failure to strengthen the public sphere by defining the internet as a non-commercial public good. First is the emergence of what is called the digital divide. Second is the fact that attention and influence within the communicative spaces of cyberspace reflect pre-existing social hierarchies and fail to effectively challenge the foci and orientation of the traditional mass media. Third is the corporate colonization of the internet. Each of these is addressed in turn.

The digital divide is typically understood as the gap between those with regular and effective access to the internet and those without such access. Beyond that, however, it is a gap between the info rich and the info poor, and between those with the capacity to engage in the public conversations and political life of cyberspace and those who are excluded from this important new dimension of the public sphere (Clement & Shade, 2000; Warschauer, 2003). Not surprisingly, the digital divide parallels the existing stratification of social and economic status and affluence. While over two-thirds of the Canadian population have access to the internet at home, rural/remote and Aboriginal communities, along with disabled and low-income Canadians, continue to face significant barriers in accessing and making effective use of computers and the internet. Internet access among the wealthiest 20 percent of Canadian households exceeds 80 percent, whereas only 30 percent of low-income households were connected as of 2004 (Statistics Canada, 2004). Similarly, while over 30 percent of Canadian university graduates use the internet to obtain political information, the rate for those without post-secondary education is closer to 10 percent. Interestingly, even among those with access to the necessary computer technology, internet-based political participation is socially skewed. Research regarding large online public deliberations (Albrecht, 2006) and internet-based political debate (Cammaerts & Van Audenhove, 2005) confirms what is known about which citizens are most likely to contact government online (Bimber, 1999): political participation in cyberspace is skewed by educational attainment, socio-economic status, and gender. Rather than being characterized by free and equal access, the virtual public sphere of cyberspace is dominated by the already politically active. As those who participate in public discussions and debates are given an additional venue for their civic engagement, info-rich citizens are made info-super-rich, while the info poor remain as they were (Bimber, 2003; Gidengil et al., 2004). Those lacking access to the internet are absent from the cyberspace-based dimensions of public life and less able to influence the norms and values that govern in civic life and shape expressions of popular political will.

Political weblogs would seem to be an ideal venue for innovative political discussions that highlight the independent views of citizens. The fact that blogs have become increasingly interactive—with opportunities to leave comments and link to one another—should allow the political blogosphere (that is, the sum total of political blogs and their interconnections) to challenge the mainstream mass media's capacity to define the focus and character of public debate. According to Tanni Haas (2005), however, in addition to being populated by an unrepresentative slice of primarily male, privileged, and politically active citizens, the political blogosphere is dominated by subject matter, information, and opinion that reproduces, rather than departs from, the discourse of mainstream news media. There are hundreds of active political blogs in Canada. But, as with the mainstream media, there is a clear hierarchy that allows a select group of influential bloggers to set the agenda for most others. Furthermore, many of the top bloggers are either journalists employed by major news organizations, political professionals with ties to the party leaders, or long-term political activists with deep roots in partisan politics. Describing the blogosphere's relationship to the mainstream media as derivative and parasitic, Haas argues that "the primary contribution of politically oriented weblog writers consists in linking to and commenting on pre-existing, internet-based mainstream news reporting and commentary" (2005, p. 389). To the extent that political blogs do depart from the foci and norms of the mass media, it is often to delve into the minutiae of party politics and partisan competition—and frequently in an uncivil manner (Elmer, 2007). While often interesting, political weblogs make no more than a limited contribution to public political dialogue.

Concerns regarding commercialization and corporate colonization of the internet go to the heart of the idea of the public sphere and deliberative democracy. To the extent that the communicative spaces of cyberspace are a part of the public sphere, they must be substantially free of control and manipulation by power hierarchies associated with the state or the economy. As information is increasingly commodified and innovation and control of the internet is left to markets, this goal becomes progressively less attainable. Lincoln Dahlberg's (2005) examination of corporate colonization of cyberspace and the marginalization of critical communication demonstrates how large corporate portals and commercial media websites dominate online attention—cyberspace's most valuable resource. The data are striking: the list of the most-visited U.S. websites reads like a who's who of major e-commerce and media conglomerates, including Yahoo!, Fox, the *New York Times*, Amazon, MSN, Google, Time Warner, e-Bay, Viacom, and CBS (comScore, 2007a). The experience here in Canada is similar, with the additionally troubling fact that only a single Canadian-owned and operated web property, Quebecor Media's Canoe Network, cracked the top 10 list of websites visited by Canadians (comScore, 2007b). These patterns go against the vision of cyberspace as an alternative to the mass media.

Many internet users rely on search engines such as Google News and Yahoo! News to access news and information. While there is no doubt that these services improve access to the diverse universe of alternative news sources that have come into existence over the past decade, the search-selection criteria favour mainstream mass-media and commercial websites. Search engines systematically prioritize certain types of sites and information at the expense of others, leading to a narrowing of the internet's value as a means by which to give voice to alternative perspectives and increase the communicative spaces that constitute the public sphere. The search-engine corporate model, it must be remembered, is based on expanding the capacity to generate ad revenue (MacPhail, 2007). Introna and Nissenbaum (2000, p. 178) have argued that allowing the continued evolution of search engines to be guided by market ideology and commercial interests is "at odds with the compelling ideology of the Web as a public good." Of even more concern, however, is a campaign by major American internet service providers, like AT&T, Verizon, and Comcast, to win the right to interfere with the flow of internet traffic so that information and sites that are most profitable to them would be delivered more quickly or prominently to subscribers. The principle that is at stake here is network neutrality—that is, that a free and open internet is threatened when corporations are allowed to privilege certain data with faster and higher-quality service or greater prominence. A non-neutral internet would permit service providers to engage in commercially motivated interference with subscribers' access to the content and applications of their choosing, creating a two-tier internet of fast lanes and slow lanes, with access to the fast lanes based on ability to pay. A two-tier internet threatens to marginalize alternative, non-commercial, educational, and community-based websites (Longford, 2007; Scott et al., 2006). When American telecommunications legislation that would protect network neutrality was introduced in 2006, corporate interests lobbied for amendments that would privilege free-market rights over network neutrality. While the U.S. Federal Communications Commission (FCC) recently forced AT&T to adhere to network neutrality as a condition of regulatory approval for its $82 billion merger with BellSouth (Reardon, 2006), network neutrality has yet to be enshrined in U.S. legislation. The situation in Canada is similar, with major internet service providers (ISPs) opposed to network-neutrality protection, and the Minister of Industry refusing to consider network-neutrality legislation (Longford, 2007).

Internet service providers in the United States and Canada, including AT&T, Comcast, Bell, Telus, and Rogers, have taken advantage of the current uncertainty over the legal status of network neutrality to install and deploy technology that enables them to discriminate against and even block certain internet content. While much of this internet traffic interference is commercially motivated, on more than one occasion ISPs have engaged in content blocking that is tantamount to political censorship. In August 2007, for example, U.S. broadband provider AT&T muted a song containing lyrics critical of President Bush during a live Pearl Jam concert webcast (Kramer, 2007). In one of the more notorious cases of political censorship by an ISP, Canada's Telus blocked subscribers' access to Voices for Change, a website that was being operated by unionized employees with whom it was in the midst of a labour dispute (Open Net Initiative, 2005). The network-neutrality debate raises important issues about the consequences of allowing commercially motivated market forces to influence the development and architecture of the internet. Without a firm commitment to the development of the internet as a public good, market forces will privilege commercial models—such as the "two-tier internet"—that maximize the profits that can be made from the internet and new media; little regard will be paid to the accessibility and diversity of the online public sphere.

For the internet to contribute to deliberative democracy, cyberspace must be a realm of reflexive citizen engagement. We must, therefore, be concerned that corporate colonization of cyberspace is resulting in increased prominence for consumer services and infotainment at the expense of politically lively public dialogue: "The corporate domination of attention not only marginalizes many voices but also promotes the constitution of participants as individualized-instrumental consumers rather than critical-reflexive citizens" (Dahlberg, 2005, p. 170). If, indeed, we experience the internet as atomized consumers rather than engaged citizens, the internet's contribution to deliberative democracy is minimized. It is a matter of considerable concern that our internet experiences may sometimes promote the very sort of cyberbalkanization that is detrimental to the public sphere (Putnam, 2000; Sunstein, 2001). There is an obvious tension here. The capacity for the internet to facilitate the emergence of a diverse range of counterpublics is a democratic response to heterogeneity. The fact that there are new opportunities for groups of citizens interacting in cyberspace to work out internal issues and reflexively define their collective political identities is a positive development—something that has long been recognized as essential to a more democratic public sphere (Fraser, 1992). But, at the same time, the internet's capacity to foster hyper-atomization goes further, potentially undercutting the shared-text and common-public culture that is essential to a well-functioning public sphere. To date, the internet has not created the sorts of linkages between individuals and groups that a shared public sphere requires. Indeed, there is the very real possibility that the internet is serving to fragment the public sphere by isolating individual consumers and allowing distinct communities of interest to congeal as disparate islands of political communication—a consequence that most certainly runs counter to the enrichment of deliberative democracy (Galston, 2003).

ALTERNATIVE POLITICS, SOCIAL MOVEMENTS, AND THE INTERNET

One of the most exciting consequences of the internet for democratic politics has been its capacity to create new spaces for the flourishing of alternative media and new opportunities for political organizing and action by social-movement organizations. Alternative political movements, particularly progressive movements of the ideological left, have a long tradition of publishing news and opinion periodicals and newsletters that aim to inform and mobilize their core activists while also reaching out to potential new supporters. Prior to the emergence of new ICTs, however, these were typically amateurish-looking publications with very limited circulations. The costs and technical challenges associated with publishing high-quality mass-circulation periodicals were simply prohibitive. The number and range of publications that challenged the priorities and analysis of mainstream corporate media began to grow with the birth of the New Left and the flourishing social-movement politics in the 1960s and 1970s. But the real explosion in alternative media occurred when the internet facilitated a dramatic reduction in the cost and effort associated with the production and distribution of alternative media (Deibert, 2002).

The goal of alternative media is to provide counter-information to that offered by the mainstream corporate-news media while also building activist communities capable of engaging in effective political actions. The leading examples of internet-based alternative media provide more than access to news stories that are written on topics or from perspectives that are marginalized by the mainstream press. They also offer advice for political activists, information on political campaigns and events, and space for interactive dialogue between activists. Indymedia.org is certainly the best known of the progressive alternative media on the internet. Indymedia was established as an Independent Media Centre (IMC) to provide grassroots coverage of the protests that coincided with the meetings of the World Trade Organization (WTO) in Seattle in 1999 (Juris, 2005). Its initial goal was to facilitate the sharing of non-corporate coverage of the protests. Using open-publishing software that allows individual activist-journalists to contribute information, images, and news stories that are instantly available on the Indymedia webpage, the Seattle IMC helped to bring activists' perspectives on the WTO protests to the world. Indymedia is now a global network of over 140 interlinked weblogs in 50 countries—in recent years it has been visited by between 500,000 and 2,000,000 readers each day (Haas, 2005). In Canada, Rabble.ca was launched by progressive journalists and activists involved in planning protests during the state-sponsored meetings on the Free Trade Area of the Americas (FTAA) in Quebec City in 2001. While Rabble provides an interactive discussion forum, information on upcoming events, and other services for progressive activists, the central focus of the website is news stories and columns written by progressive Canadian journalists and columnists. While some of these are written for Rabble.ca, many are simply reproduced from the publications that employ these writers.

Dorothy Kidd (2003) and others who are enthusiastic about the transformative potential of internet-based alternative media and the IMCs associated with Indymedia.org contend that open-publishing and grassroots web networks empower progressive activists by reversing the hierarchy that normally separates the producers of news (journalists and editors) from consumers of news. Henshaw-Plath refers to this as "using technology to disintermediate the authority and power structure of the editor" (cited in Juris, 2005, p. 201). In practice, however, the largest and most influential alternative media websites tend to retain traditional roles for editors. The main features on Rabble.ca, for example, are editor-selected columns by established progressive journalists who are also read in the mainstream news media. Even in the case of Indymedia.org, the prominent centre column of the webpage is now reserved for features that are screened by a small working group from the Seattle collective that manages the website. According to Haas (2005), the decision to establish procedures for the selection of the content in the centre column resembles the gatekeeping methods of mainstream news organizations.

All the same, there is no doubt that these leading alternative-media websites have expanded the reach of critical-news coverage while also serving as a hub for information sharing among progressive activists.

Internet-based networking is now an essential feature of alternative politics. While the majority of activist websites tend to reach rather small audiences, and most of the people who are politically active on the web were already politically active before becoming engaged in cyberspace, it is clear that new ICTs make political action easier, faster, and potentially more universal (Van Aelst & Walgrave, 2002). Modern ICTs lower the obstacles to collective action by providing a space for political identity formation and strategy development. Most striking has been the use of the internet by the movement against neo-liberal globalization to influence international forums, treaty negotiations, and meetings. While the most frequently referenced case involves the use of the internet to organize and publicize the protests that disrupted the Seattle meetings of the World Trade Organization in 1999, "the battle for Seattle" actually followed on the heels of an even more impressive effort by many of the same social-movement organizations to successfully disrupt OECD negotiations toward a Multilateral Agreement on Investment (MAI) in 1997 and 1998 (Smith & Smythe, 2001). Canadian groups like the Council of Canadians were among the social-movement organizations that played a key role in this truly international political campaign. As nodes of strategic coordination, mobilization, and information dissemination within a global network of 600 organizations from over 70 countries, the Council and other organizations became part of an electronically networked movement capable of consolidating knowledge, expertise, and resources with impressive flexibility and speed (Deibert, 2002). Over a number of months, the quiet and secretive process of negotiating the MAI was brought to public attention, and the potential consequences of an agreement were opened up to scrutiny by civil society. Many of the claims being made about the MAI negotiations were unverifiable (Ayres, 1999); still, information was diffused rapidly, and public-opinion polls soon revealed growing popular concern about the consequences of the MAI. As key countries withdrew their support for the negotiations, agreement was eventually made impossible. While the campaign waged by these networked social movements was certainly not the only reason for the failure of the MAI, grassroots exploitation of internet technology for political opportunity was an important contributing factor (Smith & Smythe, 2001).

By linking people and information in unprecedented ways, the internet has produced new forms of political organizing and action. In the summer of 2007 the organization Students for a Free Tibet borrowed a page from the Greenpeace political-action manual when they rappelled down the Great Wall of China and unfurled a large banner that read "One World, One Dream, Free Tibet 2008." What was unique about this political action was that it was videoed by cellphone and almost instantly transmitted to New York and posted on YouTube. Even in China—a country committed to blocking the free flow of information regarding the movement for Tibetan independence—a social-movement organization was able to use new ICTs to give a small-scale protest global reach (Gandhi, 2007). The media picked up on the story, segments of the YouTube video were shown on national television news, and a small-scale protest was turned into a significant political statement.

In the United States, what is now known as MoveOn.org emerged in 1998 as a grassroots email petition encouraging politicians to "move on" from highly personal and partisan politics to more pressing issues of concern to ordinary people. Within days, this email campaign had produced a petition with hundreds of thousands of signatures. Today, MoveOn.org has 3.3 million members who are linked through a website and regular email updates. No longer the grassroots initiative it was a decade ago, MoveOn.org has spawned two organizations: MoveOn Civic Action (a non-profit organization focusing on education and advocacy), and MoveOn Political Action (a registered political action committee that lobbies in Congress and campaigns for the election of progressive candidates). MoveOn still uses the internet for web-based political petitions, but has also taken on the task of challenging the conservative media's interpretation of key political issues with interesting, informative, and often humorous videos that are watched by hundreds of thousands of viewers on YouTube. On two occasions, MoveOn used the internet to organize "Virtual Marches on Washington" to protest the ongoing war in Iraq. On the days of these virtual peace marches, anti-war activists flooded the White House and U.S. Congress with thousands of faxes, emails, and phone calls (Perrone, 2003). Now a significant voice for progressive Americans, MoveOn would simply not exist without the internet.

The capacity of the internet to allow social movements to transcend space while disseminating information and mobilizing counterpublics is a significant development for political protest in the context of democratic politics. While internet-based political actions don't amount to anything close to a meaningful disruption of the structural power of state and corporate actors, successful organizing—particularly in cases like the MAI— demonstrate the extent to which the internet can facilitate the realization of "interstitial power" operating at the margins and in relation to specific issues (Deibert, 2002).

CONCLUSION

There is no doubt that the internet and other new ICTs have altered the character of democratic politics. The effects can be seen in the realm of formal electoral politics and the delivery of government service, as well as in web-based public dialogue and social-movement campaigns. Computer-mediated communication and the new media are reshaping the practice of democracy. Unfortunately, the opportunities for the deepening of democracy offered by the internet and new ICTs remain unrealized, often because they run counter to the inclinations or interests of entrenched political and commercial interests. Little more than a decade ago there were great expectations for an ICT-driven democratic transformation; today it is clear that in the absence of popular and official commitment to the internet as a public good capable of deepening democracy, the great expectations of early enthusiasts will remain expectations dashed.

Media Journal Assignments

1. Utilizing Curtis Brown's list found in Chapter 10, monitor two of the j-blogs and two of the political-activist blogs over a one-week period to determine how active these websites are. What kind of information did you find on these sites? Were they informative? Discuss.

2. Go to the *Winnipeg Free Press* online website at www.winnipegfreepress.com and compare the features of this site to the Canwest chain's website at www.canada.com. What are the differences between the two sites? What are the similarities?

3. Check out one of the following public-activism websites—Oxfam (Oxfam.ca), No Dirty Gold (nodirtygold.org), Make Poverty History (makepovertyhistory.ca), and Avaaz.org. Briefly outline the central goals of the organization, and discuss the ways in which the organization uses email and/or other forms of electronic communication (e.g., web-based petitions) to carry out its activism.

References

Albrecht, S. 2006. "Whose Voice is Heard in Online Deliberation? A Study of Participation and Representation in Political Debates on the Internet." *Information, Communication & Society* 9: 62–82.

Alcock, R. & D. Lenihan. 2001. *Opening the E-Government File: Governing in the 21st Century.* Changing Government Series, Vol. 2. Ottawa: Centre for Collaborative Government. Available at www.ppforum.ca/common/assets/publications/en/cg2-opening%20the%20e-government%20file.pdf (accessed September 22, 2008).

Alexander, Cynthia. 2001a. "Cents and Sensibility: The Emergence of e-Government in Canada." In *How Ottawa Spends 2000–2001: Past Imperfect, Future Tense*, ed. L. Pal, 185–209. Toronto: Oxford University Press.

———. 2001b. "Digital Leviathan: The Emergence of e-Politics in Canada." In *Party Politics in Canada*, 8th ed., ed. H. Thorburn and A. Whitehorn, 460–76. Toronto: Prentice-Hall.

Ayres, J. 1999. "From the Streets to the Internet: The Cyber-Diffusion of Contention." *Annals of the American Academy of Political and Social Science* 566: 132–43.

Barber, B. 1984. *Strong Democracy: Participatory Politics for a New Age*. Berkeley, Ca.: University of California Press.

———. 2000/2001. "Electronic Democracy: Which Technology for Which Democracy? Which Democracy for Which Technology?" *International Journal of Communications Law and Policy* 6: 1–8.

Barney, D. 1996. "Push-button Populism: The Reform Party and the Real World of Teledemocracy." *Canadian Journal of Communication* 21: 381–413.

———. 2000. *Prometheus Wired: The Hope for Democracy in the Age of Network Technology*. Vancouver: University of British Columbia Press.

Bimber, B. 1999. "The Internet and Citizen Communication With Government: Does the Medium Matter?" *Political Communication* 16: 409–28.

———. 2003. *Information and American Democracy: Technology in the Evolution of Political Power*. New York: Cambridge University Press.

Cammaerts, B. & L. Van Audenhove. 2005. "Online Political Debate, Unbounded Citizenship, and the Problematic Nature of a Transnational Public Sphere." *Political Communication* 22: 179–96.

Canadian Press. 2007. "Harper's Jewish Mailing List Draws Privacy Inquiry." CTV.ca, October 11. Available at www.ctv.ca/servlet/ArticleNews/story/CTVNews/20071011/mailinglist_pm_071011/20071011?hub=Politics (accessed on December 16).

Carty, R.K., W. Cross, & L. Young. 2000. *Rebuilding Canadian Party Politics*. Vancouver: University of British Columbia Press.

Cavanaugh, J.W. 2000. "E-Democracy: Thinking About the Impact of Technology on Civic Life." *National Civic Review* 89: 217–27.

Chambers, S.A. 2005. "Democracy and (the) Public(s): Spatializing Politics in the Internet Age." *Political Theory* 33: 125–36.

Clement, A. & L. Shade. 2000. "The Access Rainbow: Conceptualizing Universal Access to the Information/Communications Infrastructure." In *Community Informatics: Enabling Communities with Information and Communications Technologies*, ed. M. Gurstein, 1–20. Hershey, Pa.: Idea Group.

comScore. 2007a. "comScore Media Metrix Releases Top 50 Web Rankings for October." Press Release, November 26. Available at www.comscore.com/press/release.asp?press=1902 (accessed December 4, 2007).

———. 2007b. "comScore Releases Top Canadian Web Rankings for October." Press Release, November 26. Available at www.comscore.com/press/release.asp?press=1918 (accessed December 4, 2007).

Cross, B. 1998. "Teledemocracy: Canadian Political Parties Listening to Their Constituents." In *Digital Democracy: Policy and Politics in the Wired World*, ed. C. Alexander and L. Pal, 132–48. Toronto: Oxford University Press.

Dahlberg, L. 2005. "The Corporate Colonization of Online Attention and the Marginalization of Critical Communication?" *Journal of Communication Inquiry* 29: 160–80.

Dahlgren, P. 2005. "The Internet, Public Spheres, and Political Communication: Dispersion and Deliberation." *Political Communications* 22: 147–62.

Deibert, R. 2002. "Civil Society Activism on the World Wide Web: The Case of the Anti-MAI Lobby." In *Street Protests and Fantasy Parks: Globalization, Culture and the State*, ed. D. Cameron and J. Stein, 88–108. Vancouver: University of British Columbia Press.

Dryzek, J. 2000. *Deliberative Democracy and Beyond: Liberals, Critics, Contestations*. Oxford: Oxford University Press.

Dyson, E., G. Gilder, G. Keyworth, & A. Toffler. 1994. *Cyberspace and the American Dream: A Magna Carta for the Knowledge Age*. The Progress & Freedom Foundation. Available at www.pff.org/issues-pubs/futureinsights/fi1.2magnacarta.html (accessed November 18, 2004).

Elmer, G. 2007. "Canadian political blogosphere undergoes transition." *Hill Times*, November 12, 13.

Flanagan, T. 2003. "Database Party: The 2002 Leadership Campaign for the Canadian Alliance." *Canadian Parliamentary Review* 26.

Fountain, J. 2001. *Building the Virtual State: Information Technology and Institutional Change*. Washington D.C.: Brookings Institution Press.

Fraser, N. 1992. "Rethinking the Public Sphere: A Contribution to the Critique of Actually Existing Democracy." In *Habermas and the Public Sphere*, ed. C. Calhoun, 109–42. Boston: MIT Press.

Galston, W. 2003. "If Political Fragmentation Is the Problem, Is the Internet the Solution?" In *The Civic Web: Online Politics and Democratic Values*, ed. D. Anderson and M. Cornfield, 35–44. Lanham, Md.: Rowman & Littlefield.

Gandhi, U. 2007. "Censors powerless against the Net." *Globe and Mail*, August 9, A12.

Gidengil, E., A. Blais, N. Nevitte, & R. Nadeau. 2004. *Citizens*. Vancouver: University of British Columbia Press.

Grossman, L. 1995. *The Electronic Republic: Reshaping Democracy in the Information Age*. New York: Penguin.

Gulli, A. & A. Signorini. 2005. "The Indexable Web Is More than 11.5 Billion Pages." Paper presented to the International World Wide Web Conference, May 10–14, Chiba, Japan. Available at www.cs.uiowa.edu/~asignori/web-size/ (accessed December 1, 2007).

Haas, T. 2005." "From 'Public Journalism' to the 'Public's Journalism'? Rhetoric and Reality in the Discourse on Weblogs." *Journalism Studies* 6: 38–396.

Habermas, J. 1989. *The Structural Transformation of the Public Sphere: An Inquiry into a Category of Bourgeois Society*. Cambridge, Ma.: MIT Press.

Hartley, J. 1992. *The Politics of Pictures: The Creation of the Public in the Age of Popular Media*. New York: Routledge.

Howard, P.N. 2005. "Deep Democracy, Thin Citizenship: The Impact of Digital Media in Political Campaign Strategy." *Annals of the American Academy of Political and Social Science* 597: 153–70.

Hurwitz, R. 1999. "Who Needs Politics? Who Needs People? The Ironies of Democracy in Cyberspace." *Contemporary Sociology* 28: 655–61.

Infoscape Research Lab. 2007. "Code Politics: Federal Party Leaders and Partisans on YouTube Spring 2007." Available at www.infoscapelab.ca/videopolitics (accessed on December 6, 2007).

Introna, L. & H. Nissenbaum. 2000. "Shaping the Web: Why the Politics of Search Engines Matters." *Information Society* 16: 169–85.

Jackson, K., S. Zagon, R. Jenkins, & J. Peters. 2002. *Public Input on the Future of Health Care: Results from the Consultation Workbook*. Prepared for the Commission on the Future of Health Care in Canada.

Juris, J. 2005. "The New Digital Media and Activist Networking within Anti-Corporate Globlization Movements." *ANNALS of the American Academy of Political and Social Science* 597: 189–208.

Keane, J. 1995. "Structural Transformations of the Public Sphere." *Communication Review* 1: 1–22.

Kellner, D. 1995. "Intellectuals and New Technologies." *Media, Culture & Society* 17: 427–48.

Kidd, D. 2003. "Becoming the Media: The Global IMC Network." In *Representing Resistance: Media, Civil Disobedience, and the Global Justice Movement*, ed. A. Opel and D. Pompper, 224–50. Westport, Conn.: Praeger.

Kippen, G. 2000. *The Use of New Information Technologies by a Political Party*. Vancouver: SFU-UBC Centre for the Study of Government and Business.

Kramer, S. 2007. "AT&T Silences Pearl Jam; Gives 'Net Neutrality' Proponents Ammunition." Forbes.com. Available at www.forbes.com/2007/08/09/att-pearljam-music-tech-cx_pco_0809 paidcontent.html (accessed December 4, 2007).

Levin, Y. 2002. "Politics after the Internet." *Public Interest* 149: 80–94.

Longford, G. 2004. "Rethinking the Virtual State: A Critical Perspective on e-Government." In *Seeking Convergence in Policy and Practice: Communications in the Public Interest*, vol. 2, ed. M. Moll and L. Shade, 109–40. Ottawa: Canadian Centre for Policy Alternatives.

———. 2007. "'Network Neutrality' vs. 'Network Diversity': A Survey of the Debate, Policy Landscape and Implications for Broadband as an Essential Service for Ontarians." Toward a Broadband Research Agenda for Ontario Working Paper, Ministry of Government Services (Ontario) and the Knowledge Media Design Institute, University of Toronto.

At http://kmdi.utoronto.ca/broadband/programs/Files/longford_paper.pdf (accessed December 4, 2007).

Longford, G. & C. Hurrell. 2006. "Online Citizen Consultation and Engagement in Canada." In *Encyclopedia of Digital Government*. ed. A. Anttiroiko and M. Malkia, 1261–67. Hershey, Pa.: Idea Group.

Lyman, P. & Varian, H. 2003. *How Much Information? 2003*. School of Information Management and Systems, University of California at Berkeley. Available at www2.sims.berkeley.edu/ research/projects/ how-much-info-2003/ (accessed December 1, 2007).

MacPhail, W. 2007. "The Google plot: It all ads up." Rabble.ca. November 15. www.rabble.ca/news_full_story.shtml?sh_itm=97fd12495ad54afb255148c03aba1838&rXn=1& (accessed November 18, 2007).

Malina, A. 2003. "E-Transforming Democracy in the U.K.: Considerations of Developments and Suggestions for Empirical Research." *Communications: The European Journal of Communication Research* 28: 135–55.

Margetts, H. 1999. *Information Technology in Government: Britain and America*. London: LSE/ Routledge.

Marvin, C. 1990. *When Old Technologies Were New: Thinking about Electric Communication in the Late Nineteenth Century*. New York: Oxford University Press.

Norris, P. 2001. *Digital Divide: Civic Engagement, Information Poverty, and the Internet Worldwide*. Cambridge: Cambridge University Press.

Oldenburg, R. 1989. *The Great Good Place : Cafés, Coffee Shops, Community Centers, Beauty Parlors, General Stores, Bars, Hangouts, and How They Get You Through the Day*. New York: Paragon House.

Open Net Initiative. 2005. "Telus Blocks Consumer Access to Labour Union Web Site and Filters an Additional 766 Unrelated Sites." OpenNet Initiative Bulletin 010. August 2. http://opennetinitiative.net/bulletins/010 (accessed December 4, 2007).

Patten, S. 2001. "Democratizing the Institutions of Policy-Making: Democratic Consultation and Participatory Administration." *Journal of Canadian Studies* 35 (4): 221–39.

Perrone, J. 2003. "Virtual protesters bombard Washington." *Guardian* [Electronic Version]. February 26. Available at www.guardian.co.uk/world/2003/feb/26/politics.antiwar (accessed, September 22, 2008).

Phillips, S. & M. Orsini. 2002. *Mapping the Links: Citizen Involvement in Policy Processes*. CPRN Discussion Paper No. F/21. Ottawa: Canadian Policy Research Networks.

Poster, M. 1995. "CyberDemocracy: Internet and the Public Sphere." Available at www.hnet.uci.edu/mposter/writings/democ.html (accessed October 3, 2004).

Putnam, R. 2000. *Bowling Alone: The Collapse and Revival of American Community*. New York: Touchstone.

Reardon, M. 2006. "FCC approves AT&T-BellSouth merger." CNET News.com. December 29. Available at http://news.com/FCC-approves-ATT-BellSouth-merger/2100-1036_3-6146369.html (accessed November 8, 2007).

Rheingold, H. 2000. *The Virtual Community: Homesteading on the Electronic Frontier*. rev. ed. Cambridge: MIT Press.

Richard, É. 1999. "Tools of Governance." In *Digital Democracy: Discourse and Decision Making in the Information Age I*, ed. B. Hague and B. Loader, 73–86. London: Routledge.

Scott, B., M. Cooper, & J. Kenney. 2006. "Why Consumers Demand Internet Freedom: Network Neutrality: Fact vs. Fiction." Free Press, Consumer Federation of America, and Consumers

Union, May. Available at www.freepress.net/docs/nn_fact_v_fiction_final.pdf (accessed December 4, 2007).

Shulz, W. 1997. "Changes of Mass Media and the Public Sphere." *Public* 4: 57–69.

Small, Tamara A. 2007. "Canadian Cyberparties: Reflections on Internet-Based Campaigning and Party Systems." *Canadian Journal of Political Science* 40: 639–58.

Smith, P. & E. Smythe. 2001. "Globalisation, Citizenship and Technology: The Multilateral Agreement on Investment (MAI) meets the Internet." In *Culture and Politics in the Information Age*, ed. F. Webster, 184–206. London: Routledge.

Standage, T. 1998. *The Victorian Internet: The Remarkable Story of the Telegraph and the Nineteenth Century's On-Line Pioneers.* New York: Walker.

Statistics Canada. 2004. "Household Internet Use Survey 2003." *Daily*, July 8. Available at www.statcan.ca/Daily/English/040708/d040708.pdf (accessed December 4, 2007).

———. 2007. *Connecting with Canadians: Assessing the Use of Government On-Line*, by C. Underhill and C. Ladds. Catalogue No. 56F0004MIE-No. 015. Ottawa: Statistics Canada.

Sunstein, C. 2001. *Republic.com.* Princeton N.J.: Princeton University Press.

Treasury Board of Canada Secretariat. 2000. "Speaking Notes for the Honourable Lucienne Robillard, President of the Treasury Board." Address to The International Council for Information Technology in Government Administration, Ottawa, Canada. September 18. Available at www.tbs-sct.gc.ca/pres_speech2000/0918_e.html (accessed November 7, 2004).

Van Aelst, P. & S. Walgrave. 2002. "New Media, New Movements? The Role of the Internet in Shaping the 'Anti-globalization' Movement." *Information, Communication & Society* 5 (4): 465–93.

Warner, M. 2002. *Publics and Counterpublics.* New York: Zone Books.

Warschauer, M. 2003. *Technology and Social Inclusion: Rethinking the Digital Divide.* Cambridge Mass.: MIT Press.

Whitaker, R. 2001. "Virtual Parties and the Decline of Democracy." *Policy Options* (June): 16–22. Available at www.irpp.org/po/archive/jun01/whitaker.pdf (accessed December 7, 2007).

Winner, L. 1997. "Cyberlibertarian Myths and the Prospects for Community." *Computers and Society* 27: 14–19.

Winter, J. 1997. *Democracy's Oxygen: How Corporations Control the News.* Montreal: Black Rose Books.

Witt, L. 2004. "Is Public Journalism Morphing into the Public's Journalism?" *National Civic Review* 93: 49–57.

Chapter 12

Social Movements and Media

Miriam Smith

INTRODUCTION

On June 29, 2007, First Nations organized a National Day of Protest against the failure of governments to implement treaties and to recognize Native land claims. In anticipation of Native blockages of road and rail traffic in Central Canada, rail service was cancelled between Toronto and Montreal and Highway 401 in eastern Ontario was closed by the police. This protest resulted in a public debate in the media on the legitimacy of such forms of action. Many voices in the media called for First Nations to respect the law. Others were more sympathetic to the idea that First Nations had been unable to achieve their goals through the courts and through negotiation with government, and therefore saw the National Day of Protest as a legitimate expression of grievances, even if it resulted in inconvenience or economic loss to others (CBC News, 2007).

The media are central to the way in which social movements reach their audience—including those inside their own movements, as well as outsiders, the public, and potential allies. Social movements such as the environmental movement and the women's movement and national movements such as First Nations have used the media to draw attention to their demands, goals, and values. Traditionally, print media such as newspapers and newsletters provided a means for social-movement activists to communicate with each other and with their bases. With the advent of mass media, such as television and radio, social movements were able to capture public attention using images that conveyed their messages, sometimes shocking the public or attempting to capture its sympathy.

The environmental movement in Canada, especially Greenpeace, has mastered the art of direct action—that is, engaging in direct efforts to stop environmentally damaging actions through open challenges to governments and corporations. The sight of Greenpeace's *Rainbow Warrior* setting off in 1978 to stop nuclear testing sent a vivid message that caught the public's attention and was the first in a long line of Greenpeace actions that were in part designed for television and mass media through the production of the telling image that would convey the message. With the rise of the internet and digital communication, social movements have been able to build global and transnational alliances and networks as never before. Movements such as the anti-globalization movement have brought together activists from many countries to oppose international trade and security agreements. These new transnational actions and alliances have been made possible in part by the rise of electronic media and the internet, and media elites themselves have often played a role, enabling direct access to media channels and popularizing such movements (Waters, 2004). Moreover, in the past decade, we have seen important new social movements that have challenged the mainstream media in Canada and proposed alternative sources of activist-based and web-based media as a means of circumventing corporate control of newspapers, radio, and television. Some of the most recent social movements have politicized the role of the media by criticizing the established media and arguing that corporate concentration of media has led to a narrowing of perspective. Instead, these new movements have proposed home-grown news and grassroots publishing through the internet as an alternative means of accessing news.

In this chapter, I will examine the ways in which Canadian social movements have used the media, as well as the new ways in which the media themselves are being politicized, questioned, and contested in new forms of activism. In the first section of the chapter, I will define the meaning of the term *social movement*, before going on to consider the ways in which media contribute to the development of the political and social identities that are a precursor of social-movement action. In the second section, I will discuss how social movements use their own media to build themselves up and establish a sense of collective identity among their constituents. In the third section of the chapter, I will explore specific strategies used by social movements to build themselves, capture public attention, and achieve their goals. Finally, I will examine new forms of media such as the internet, the effects of these new forms on social movements, and the new movements that are using grassroots media strategies to question corporate concentration of the media in Canada.

WHAT ARE SOCIAL MOVEMENTS?

Social movements and political protests provide an alternative means for citizens to participate in politics. In voting, citizens express their preference for one team of political leaders or another through voting for a candidate. At the local level, in cities and localities, these political leaders usually run as individuals, while at the provincial and federal levels voters choose between candidates who are running for specific political parties, such as Liberals, Conservatives, Greens, Bloc Québécois, or New Democrats. This form of politics is territorially defined because voters can only support the candidates and parties in their particular riding. These parties and candidates may not represent the specific views of citizens on many issues. A voter may be forced to support a party that shares his or her liberal views on social issues but is much more conservative on fiscal issues. Alternatively, a voter might choose a party that represents his or her views on fiscal and social issues but not on the environment.

In contrast, by participating in group politics, citizens can choose to support specific groups—such as environmental groups, feminist groups, anti-globalization groups, or anti-war groups—that reflect their views and values. Social movements are most commonly defined as "purposive collective actions whose outcome, in victory as in defeat, transforms the values and institutions of society" (Castells, 1997, p. 3). That is, social movements are actions undertaken collectively by people in groups (*collective action*). They are not random actions, such as hanging around on a street corner or in a park. Rather, they are *purposive*, meaning that they have a goal or purpose. Finally, the purpose of the group or collective action is to change society in some way. This could mean that a given group is aiming to change government policies or the ways in which citizens and institutions carry out their everyday activities—in other words, it is attempting to change social practices. Environmental movements, for example, may have many different targets. They may aim to encourage people to recycle, or they may aim to ensure that Canada keeps its commitments under the Kyoto Protocol.

Canadian Content Rules: CRTC Controversies
- Websites rules
- Al Jazeera

CBC 1929 Aired Commission recommended the creation of a national radio broadcast network. A major concern was the growing influence of American radio broadcasting as U.S.-based networks began to expand into Canada.
- Radio has just started and a lot of American stations were being beamed into Canada
- 1932 CBC was created by the Canadian government

→ Governance : 12 boards of directors
→ Expenditures: $1.8 billion dollars
→ Ombudsmen: check for accuracy, integrity and fairness in the CBC operations
→ Building Blocks:
　　　- CRTC: Canadian Radio-television and Telecommunications Commission is a public organisation with mandate as a regulatory agency for broadcasting and telecommunications. It was created in 1976 when it took over responsibility for regulating telecommunication carriers.
　　　- Canadian Ownership: Anything over 35% requires permission from the CRTC because they provide laws and provides licensing.
　　　- Canadian Content
　　　- Funding and taxes
　　　- Control of foreign programming

However, the environmental movement challenges the model of unbridled economic growth and looks for ways to shift our economic models and way of life toward a sustainable future (McKenzie, 2002). Similarly, the women's movement taps into a sense of collective identity among women that is mobilized in politics in many different ways. Feminists of the 1960s and 1970s put forth the slogan, "The personal is political," and in so doing challenged the traditional boundaries of politics on the left and on the right (Dobrowolsky, 2008).

Social movements often use radical tactics to protest, as in the case of the First Nations' protest in June 2007 and other Native road blockades. In recent years environmental groups have also engaged in direct actions, such as members chaining themselves to trees in order to prevent clear-cut logging, or—very famously by Greenpeace—sending out boats to challenge nuclear testing in the ocean or to challenge hunting and fishing practices. In 1970, a group of women marched from Vancouver to Ottawa to push for abortion rights for women and, once inside the House of Commons, chained themselves to the visitors' gallery, recalling the actions of the British suffragettes who chained themselves to the gates of Parliament demanding the right to vote. In the 1930s, unemployed men marched to Ottawa in the "On-to-Ottawa Trek" to protest the conditions in work camps for the unemployed set up by the government (Armour & Stanton, 1990); Palmer, 1992). In Quebec City in 2001, major demonstrations and protests occurred against globalization. These instances of demonstration and protest have occurred throughout Canadian history and form an important part of the history of Canadian politics.

THE MEDIA AND COLLECTIVE IDENTITY

In his book *Imagined Communities*, Benedict Anderson (1983) discusses the role of print media in the development of national identity. Anderson argues that nations are "imagined communities" that cannot exist before people have an awareness of the political space they inhabit and the presence of other people and other citizens in the same space, especially people they cannot see and places they have never visited. This media space is familiar to us, but prior to the rise of print media and the emergence of literacy in the West people did not have a sense of a common political space. Anderson's book discusses the role of print media in creating the common sense of political identity necessary for the establishment of the stability of the nation-state and the emergence of nationalism as a political force. The same can be said for social movements. Because social movements are collective actions, they rest on the assumption of political communication. Hence, the media are central to the very existence of social movements.

One of the earliest examples of a social movement in Canada was the temperance movement. This was a large mass movement that arose throughout the colonies of what is today Canada, including Upper and Lower Canada and the Maritimes, in the 1830s and 1840s. The movement's aims were to convince people to stop drinking or at least reduce their consumption of alcohol, and to support public policies that would encourage abstinence from alcohol. Long before Mothers Against Drunk Driving, the temperance movement encouraged people to reflect on their consumption of alcohol and to consider the social and economic consequences of that consumption. Yet at the same time, the movement was very much a mass collective action, with fiery leaders (mainly preachers and other religious figures) who would hold large-scale gatherings in small towns and rural areas, enjoining people to "take the pledge" of abstinence from alcohol. In this way, the movement typified many of the features of contemporary social movements in that it aimed to change government policy as well as social practices and tapped into a sense of personal identity by asking people to pledge to change their behaviour. While much of the activity of the temperance movement was achieved through personal speaking tours given by movement leaders, the emergence of print media also assisted the widespread dissemination of literature promoting the goal of the movement. In particular, as historical research has shown, the movement used printed sermons and speeches, which were often reproduced in the broadsheets and newspapers of the day and circulated widely (Noel, 1995). The relatively high level of literacy in the British North American colonies was one of the preconditions for the rise of the temperance movements in the same way that, as Anderson argued, the emergence of print media was essential to the creation of a sense of common national community. Many other social movements of this historical period also depended on print media for the dissemination of their ideas. For example, the movement to abolish slavery and the slave trade in the British Empire and the United States was a transatlantic social movement that relied on the dissemination of information through newspapers and letters (Keck & Sikkink, 1998).

Modern social movements have also relied to an important extent on print media. The social movements of the 1960s, such as the women's movement, the anti-war movement, and the nationalist movements in Quebec and English-speaking Canada, often developed forms of media of their own that served to build a sense of common political identity. Nationalist movements in Quebec and English-speaking Canada developed new sources of political communication such as magazines and newsletters, which were used to disseminate movement news. Feminist communities often produced local newsletters and broadsheets with a small-scale circulation within the movement. The archive of the Canadian women's movement at the University of Ottawa preserves hundreds of newsletters and periodicals produced by women's groups from all regions of Canada in the 1960s and 1970s. These newsletters and small magazines were one of the primary means through which social movements of this period discussed political questions, developed strategies of action, and communicated a common sense of movement identity. In this way, print media continued to provide the vital infrastructure through which social movements produced and developed a sense of common purpose and political identity. These media were self-produced and largely self-financed; they were produced by movement activists for other movement activists.

At the same time, during the 1960s and 1970s, many social-movement organizations attempted to develop new forms of print media that would reach outside the social movement to a general audience. These forms of media, then, were not just produced by the movement for the movement, but were strategically designed to appeal to the audience of the social movement—the general public, government policy-makers, or sympathetic allies of the movement. In the United States, for example, the women's movement established its own mass circulation magazine, Ms., which featured the writings of prominent feminists such as Gloria Steinem and Betty Friedan. In English-speaking Canada, left-wing nationalists, socialists, and social democrats of the late 1960s and 1970s founded or revived publications such as the *Canadian Forum*, *This Magazine*, and the *Canadian Dimension*, which served as mass-circulation periodicals for the labour, socialist, and left-wing nationalist movements of the period. The gay liberation movement in Toronto established North America's most intellectual queer periodical, *The Body*

Politic, which, from its first issue in 1971 until it ceased publication in 1987, put forth an uncompromising vision of gay liberation.

The media, therefore, play important roles in terms of the development of social movements. These roles include:

- creating a political space in which activism can occur (e.g., print media and the emergence of the nation-state; the internet and the emergence of cyberspace)

- creating a common sense of political identity through media that is aimed at the constituency of the social movement itself (e.g., a gay liberation newspaper; a website for feminist activists)

- influencing public opinion and winning allies outside the movement (e.g., capturing media attention through television or mainstream newspaper coverage)

These roles are not mutually exclusive. When social movements attempt to build up their own constituencies through developing their own media, they may also enlist sympathetic allies from outside the community. For example, in the case of the gay and lesbian movement, *The Body Politic* was primarily produced for the gay and lesbian community. And yet, when the police attacked *The Body Politic* and the periodical was charged with obscenity, many allies from outside the lesbian and gay community defended it. When the mainstream media pays attention to social-movement activities, it may encourage people to join movements and assist in the development of social awareness of the movement's aims and goals. An excellent example of this is provided by the environmental movement. Greenpeace specializes in using the media to draw attention to environmental causes. By engaging in direct-action tactics, Greenpeace is able to capture media attention and has raised consciousness regarding environmentalism (Dale, 1996). By going out in their boats to the sites of hunting activities or nuclear testing, Greenpeace activists provide arresting images of a small group of environmentalists challenging powerful governments and industries.

Many studies of social movements have shown the importance of capturing the attention of mainstream media for their success, whatever their target. Social movements that are aimed at changing corporate behaviour, such as the use of child labour and sweat shops in developing countries, have succeeded in capturing the attention of mainstream media, leading to boycotts of Nike and other corporations. Through actions such as these, corporate behaviour has been changed. In Canada, there is no doubt that the Oka stand-off in the summer of 1990 drew the attention of Canadians to Native issues as never before. Photographs appearing in many newspapers during the crisis symbolized the tension between Aboriginal peoples and non-Aboriginal Canadians and galvanized politicians into action. In the wake of the Oka crisis, the Mulroney government established the Royal Commission on Aboriginal Peoples, which conducted a wide-ranging inquiry into Aboriginal political issues in Canada and heard from a substantial number of First Nations. In the United States, the civil rights movement of the 1950s and 1960s was successful in capturing the attention of the mainstream media, with the result that the sit-ins that began in Greensboro in 1960 spread throughout the Southern states, setting into motion a train of events that finally brought segregation to an end in that country. Because of the media attention paid to these events, blacks in the cities in which there was media coverage heard about what was happening elsewhere and social movement activism spread throughout media hot spots. At the same time, the depiction of the repression faced by protestors and movement activists in the South, including the brutal water cannons and dogs that were used on protestors, helped to galvanize white public opinion, especially in the North, against segregation (Andrews & Biggs, 2006). These examples show how media coverage helps build social-movement constituencies and helps social movements to achieve their goals—whether these goals are building public awareness, changing social practices, changing public policy, or changing all three.

MEDIA AND SOCIAL MOVEMENT STRATEGY

There are many strategic challenges for social movements in using the media. Because social movements are not monolithic organizations, it is often difficult for social-movement leaders to control the way messages are presented to media. Large and diverse movements, such as First Nations or the environmental movement, may have many different voices, relatively decentralized organizational networks, and less well-resourced organizations than competing business groups and corporations that regularly access the media. In social movements, the leaders cannot control the grassroots, and in some the grassroots are out in front of the leadership in exploiting media opportunities. For example, in the case of the First Nations protest of June 2007, there were many debates within First Nations communities regarding the necessity and wisdom of this form of protest. For weeks prior to the protest, the government and the leader of the Assembly of First Nations, Phil Fontaine, sparred in the media over the government's handling of First Nations issues. However, the demonstration was not called, organized, or controlled by the Assembly of First Nations; in fact, it was Mohawk leader Shawn Brant who was responsible for setting up the blockades on Highway 401. The action of blocking the highway and forcing the closure of rail lines in Central Canada was a huge media story in Southern Ontario. On the Day of Protest, the coverage by Reuters and the Canadian Press typified the ways in which Mohawk leader and protest organizer Shawn Brant was depicted in the mainstream media. According to Reuters, Brant was a "dissident leader," arguing for "a campaign of economic disruption" in the face of Aboriginal poverty and the lack of government action on land claims. Brant stated that militancy was the only way for First Nations to achieve their goals. While Reuters did not give Brant a chance to develop his own arguments and claims, the news agency framed his comments by providing data on Aboriginal poverty and problems with the lands claims process (Sibonney, 2007). Both Reuters and the Canadian Press emphasized the disagreement among Native leaders, as the Chief of the Assembly of First Nations, Phil Fontaine, called attention to the many peaceful protests that went on across the country rather than focusing attention on the actions of Brant. He also framed First Nations demands in a way that would appeal to other Canadians, stating, "We are looking for the basic necessities of life that come with being Canadian—clean drinking water, decent housing, education and health care. We are looking for equality of opportunity so we can get good jobs and support ourselves and our families. We are looking to control our own destinies. Improving our lives won't only be good for us, First Nations people, it will be good for Canada" (Canadian Press, 2007). In the end, though, because of the way the demonstrations were handled by First Nations and by the police, there was substantial public sympathy for First Nations, and many non-Aboriginal citizens indicated their support for First Nations actions.

In addition to the fact that social movements are constituted out of decentralized networks that may face strategic challenges in remaining "on message" with the media, movement organizations that are well organized, unified, and coherent must often choose between accessing the mainstream media, using alternative media, or building their own. Movements may find that the pursuit of media attention dictates the strategies they use. That is, social movements may engage in direct action such as demonstrations as a means of capturing media attention.

As was seen in the case of the First Nations' protests, a confrontational protest using direct-action tactics will garner more attention from the media than a quiet presentation to government. When environmentalists chain themselves to trees or rural protesters block highways or city streets with farm machinery, these actions are likely to appear on the news and win attention from the public. However, the price of such actions may also involve a loss of public sympathy if they are depicted as simply disrupting traffic or inconveniencing the public. In the case of the Day of Protest, Native leaders negotiated with police to end the blockade of Highway 401, thus ensuring that travellers would not be inconvenienced on the highway. Clearly, there was a risk of loss of public sympathy, and Phil Fontaine tried to counter this by appealing to the interests of other Canadians in resolving the problems faced by First Nations.

Furthermore, when social movements undertake action for the purpose of gaining the attention of mainstream media, they must accept the fact that they may be depicted by journalists and media in a way that undercuts the legitimacy of their message (see Kielbowicz & Scherer, 1986). That is, they may be depicted negatively. Social movements that do not engage in direct action may have a very difficult time in accessing the media at all. A large-scale study of social movements shows that simply obtaining media coverage for their activities is very challenging. Also, they are more likely to reach a media audience with a protest or action if their issue is already in the news (McCarthy et al., 1996).

Another way the media may influence the choices of strategy by social movements is through the evolution of new media technologies. The creation of new forms of media may open up new strategic possibilities for social-movement activism. Since the 1960s, there has been acceleration in the speed of communication and a concentration in the ownership of media resources. The rise of digital technologies, cable television, and the internet have changed the way media are used. These technologies have given consumers more choice and control over what they read, listen to, or watch. At the same time, many critics have argued that corporate concentration has led to less choice in the mainstream media and, increasingly, on the internet as well, as Longford and Patten discuss in

Chapter 11 (see also Taras, 2001). For social movements, increased concentration of media may close off channels of access. However, it is also true that new technologies place more power not only in the hands of the public or the consumer of media, but also in the hands of social movements. It is easier for social movement activists to gather information from all over the world, to communicate with policy experts—whether in the legal, technical, or scientific worlds—or to network with each other. The rise of global and transnational social-movement organizing and the increasingly important role of non-governmental organizations in international political debate is one result of the changes in the media and in communications that have affected social movements.

These global and transnational forms of organizing have become increasingly important in the Canadian context in recent years. Whether over issues such as the expansion of free trade to the Americas, the post-9/11 Peace and Prosperity Initiative, or other intergovernmental and international agreements on global trade and security, the anti-globalization movement has opposed these agreements and sought to highlight their negative consequences for Canada's political independence as well as for social justice and the environment. The Quebec and English-speaking Canadian anti-globalization movements have strong international links. In 1995, the Quebec women's movement organized the "Bread and Roses" March Against Poverty, a protest in which women from all over Quebec marched to Quebec City to contest neo-liberal government policies and demand government action to end poverty for women and children. This type of march has many echoes in Canadian history, perhaps most notably in the Abortion Caravan of 1971 and the On-to-Ottawa Trek of the 1930s discussed previously. The Quebec women's movement's "Bread and Roses" march was very successful in capturing public attention, and in later years similar marches were held. While the initial march had some support from women's groups around the world, the action eventually evolved into the World March of Women, held on International Women's Day in different locations around the world (World March of Women, 2007). The same groups are also involved in the World Social Forum, an international meeting that has been held regularly to promote global social justice and women's and environmental issues (Conway, 2004). Drawing on local traditions, the World March of Women exemplifies social-movement action and activism in the global era, in which transnational links are forged through new media and especially through electronic media and the internet. In the case of the World March of Women, groups from around the world are able to communicate much more easily than they would have been able to do prior to the advent of the internet, facilitating awareness of developments and actions in diverse locations, as well as providing a means for coordinating international and transnational action.

For this reason, some new social movements have focused on putting out their own media messages using new technology. Rather than relying on the established print or television media to put their message across, some social-movement activists have argued that movements cannot rely on the mainstream media to get their message out. In the 1970s and after, Christian evangelical groups used newsletters and mass mailings to reach their adherents and to encourage organizational efforts and solicit donations to their cause. These new organizational techniques were particularly noteworthy in the United States, as was the term "moral majority," which was used to depict the supposedly large-scale public support for traditional and conservative religious values. These methods were also used in Canada by groups such as the Evangelical Fellowship of Canada (Reimer, 2003). With the rise of the internet, this form of grassroots strategy has become easier. On the one hand, some social-movement organizations have professionally created websites that invite citizens to contribute, almost as a form of consumerism. The Greenpeace website, for example, allows the viewer to "join" Greenpeace by giving a credit card number. Such websites often sell products that allow consumers to show their adherence to the values of the movement organization through purchases of items such as branded coffee mugs, hats, and bumper stickers (Greenpeace Canada, 2007). At the same time, the internet can also be used to release information to shame governments and corporations into action. For example, Amnesty International has expanded its traditional pre-internet campaigns of letter-writing to governments on behalf of political prisoners to mass internet campaigns asking the public to email in support of its causes (Amnesty International Canada, 2007). The internet allows social movements to control the messages they convey and to have access to a mass audience traditionally controlled by the major media. However, as was the case with newsletters in the past, social movement leaders and activists must decide how the interests of the movement are best served and to what extent it may be worthwhile to dilute the message of the movement or to compromise movement goals in order to obtain mainstream media coverage. The rise of the internet undercuts this debate to some extent, given that social-movement leaders cannot control what activists post. The internet truly enables the grassroots to circumvent the leadership of social movements.

The mainstream media may block, distort, or facilitate the impact of social movements (Carroll & Ratner, 1998). Social movements may try to frame their values, goals, and actions in ways that will maximize the likelihood of positive coverage or facilitation of their aims by the mainstream media (Ryan et al., 2001). When social movements are blocked or when their message is distorted by the mainstream media, they may choose to build and create their own media, especially given the accessibility of the internet. In doing so, they may reach a smaller audience, but they may be better able to control the presentation of their message. The internet provides a ready vehicle for groups that wish to democratize the media. A number of scholars have suggested that the internet opens up new possibilities for democratic debate and dialogue because it enables dissenting and alternative voices to be heard. Nevertheless, internet access is still not ubiquitous, especially for Canadians living in rural areas.

MOVEMENTS CHALLENGING MEDIA

Many critics have long argued that the mainstream media function to contain dissent and to defuse social-movement activism and protest (Gitlin, 1980). However, other research shows that mainstream media can provide openings for new viewpoints and beliefs of social movements that may differ greatly from majority views. For example, Sharon Stone has shown how the mainstream media in Canada have depicted the issue of violence against women, arguing that the feminist movement was able to get its message across and that the dominant corporate media are not monolithic in their reproduction of existing political and social views (Stone, 1993). Recent analyses of media coverage of events such as the massive demonstrations that occurred against neo-liberal globalization in Seattle in 1999 show that even the most mainstream media sources were sympathetic to the protestors and clearly depicted the distinction between the minority of protestors, who engaged in violent action, and the vast majority, who did not (Rojecki, 2002). Further, some analysts have suggested that the demise of the Cold War opened up new media spaces for dissent; however, the effects of 9/11 may have shifted the terrain once more toward a binary "us vs. them" mentality, which reduces the media capacity to express and cover dissenting voices. Nonetheless, it has been argued that the advent of the internet has given social movement activists a new self-reliance and an ability to bounce back, even when media depictions are negative (Rojecki, 2002). Analyzing the impact of anarchists at the Seattle protest and their use of media, Owens and Palmer emphasize that anarchists were able to use the internet to fight back against negative publicity of their actions in the protests, mounting a campaign on the web in their own defence (2003, pp. 335–8).

In recent years, there has also been a rise of social movements that contest the power of mainstream media. William Carroll and Robert A. Hackett (2006) term this form of movement activity "democratic media activism." While there have long been protest campaigns to reform the media, in this era of heightened corporate concentration of media ownership, media activists especially contest the structure of corporate-controlled media, and critique media content. Organizations such as Ad Busters shed a new critical light on our consumption of media, arguing that big-media dominance leads to political apathy, disengagement, consumerism, and environmental degradation. On the other side of the coin, evangelical and conservative groups have also engaged in democratic media activism by contesting the media's depictions of sex, drugs, or gay content. However, as Carroll and Hackett emphasize, there is an important difference between "democratization through the media (the use of media, whether by governments or civil society actors, to promote democratic goals and processes elsewhere in society), and democratization of the media themselves" (2006, p. 84). Carroll and Hackett's research shows that democratic media activists are concerned not only with changing the content of media, but also with advocating for reform of the rules and regulations that govern media, such as the rules for funding Canadian television, ensuring Canadian content, or regulating satellite radio reception. In addition, democratic media activists are interested in building alternative media and in empowering citizens to criticize and evaluate the media (Carroll & Hackett, 2006, pp. 87–88). As the media become more dominant and play an increasingly important economic role in post-industrial economies such as Canada, social movements that challenge the structure, content, and actions of the mainstream media are likely to be increasingly important in Canadian politics.

CONCLUSION

Social movements are a means by which citizens may make their voices heard in politics beyond the electoral system. In addition to voting and participating in election campaigns, many Canadians come together in groups and movements that represent their particular values, beliefs, and identities, whether these identities are oriented toward progressive causes such as social justice and the environment or toward traditional values such as those of the Christian evangelical movement. The media play an important role in social-movement politics and pose many dilemmas for movements and activists. While the mainstream media may close off opportunities for social-movement access or distort their messages, access to media has often been critically important for social-movement success. Access to media enables social movements to reach a broad audience and to gain sympathetic allies and political support. The rise of the internet and the increased speed of communication in the global era have opened up new possibilities for social movements to use media to create a sense of their own community, to solidify the bonds of collective identity, and to reach new audiences. New social movements have emerged that have challenged the dominance of media in our culture and the consumer-driven dynamic and restricted political choices posed by corporate concentration of media. The media is the lifeblood of social-movement action just as it is the lifeblood of other forms of politics in the contemporary era.

Media Journal Assignments

1. Visit the website of one of the organizations discussed in this chapter, such as the World March for Women, Greenpeace Canada, or Amnesty International Canada. Discuss the ways in which the organization is using its web presence to forward its social-movement values. How does it mobilize to take advantage of a changing media environment? Do you think this new form of communication offers new opportunities for citizen groups, or barriers to their mobilization efforts? Provide examples and discuss.

2. Analyze the media coverage of a social movement (e.g., environmentalism or the women's movement) either on television or in your local newspaper over a one-week period. Is adequate coverage provided or are these organizations largely ignored? Do the media present a full examination of the demands of social movements or is the coverage provided simply event-oriented?

References

Amnesty International Canada. 2007. "About AI Canada." Available at www.amnesty.ca/about/index.php (accessed August 2008).

Anderson, Benedict. 1983. *Imagined Communities: Reflections on the Origin and Spread of Nationalism*. London: Verso.

Andrews, Kenneth T. & Michael Biggs. 2006. "The Dynamics of Protest Diffusion: Movement Organizations, Social Networks, and News Media in the 1960 Sit-Ins." *American Sociological Review* 71 (October): 752–77.

Armour, Moira & Pat Stanton. 1990. *Canadian Women in History: A Chronology*. Toronto: Green Dragon Press.

Ayers, Jeffrey M. 1998. *Challenging Conventional Wisdom: Political Movements and Popular Contention against North American Free Trade*. Toronto: University of Toronto Press.

Canadian Press. 2007. "Protests block 401, rail lines." June 29. Available at www.thestar.com/printArticle/230885 (accessed August 2008).

Carroll, William & Robert A. Hackett. 2006. "Democratic Media Activism through the Lens of Social Movement Theory." *Media, Culture and Society* 28 (1): 83–104.

Carroll, William & R.S. Ratner. 1998. "Media Strategies and Political Projects: A Comparative Study of Social Movements." *Canadian Journal of Sociology* 24 (1): 1–34.

Castells, Manuel. 1997. *The Power of Identity*. Oxford: Blackwell.

CBC News. 2007. "Aboriginal Day of Action Unfolds Peacefully." June 29. Available at www.cbc.ca/canada/story/2007/06/29/aboriginal-action.html (accessed August 2008).

Conway, Janet. 2004. *Identity, Place, Knowledge: Social Movements Contesting Globalization*. Halifax: Fernwood.

Dale, Stephen. 1996. *McLuhan's Children: The Greenpeace Message and the Media*. Toronto: Between the Lines.

Dobrowolsky, Alexandra. 2008. "The Women's Movement in Flux: Feminism and Framing, Passion, and Politics." In *Group Politics and Social Movements in Canada*, ed. Miriam Smith, 159–80. Peterborough: Broadview Press.

Gitlin, Todd. 1980. *The Whole World Is Watching: Mass Media in the Making and Unmaking of the New Left*. Berkeley and Los Angeles: University of California Press.

Greenpeace Canada. 2007. *Support Greenpeace*. Available at www.greenpeace.org/canada/en/support-greenpeace (accessed August 2008).

Harrison, Trevor. 2008. "The Populist and Christian Evangelical Movements: A Comparison of Canada and the United States." In *Group Politics and Social Movements in Canada*, ed. Miriam Smith, 203–24. Peterborough: Broadview Press.

Keck, Margaret & Kathryn Sikkink. 1998. *Activists Beyond Borders: Advocacy Networks in International Politics*. Ithaca, N.Y: Cornell University Press.

Kielbowicz, Richard B. & Clifford Scherer. 1986. "The Role of the Press in the Dynamics of Social Movements." *Research in Social Movements, Conflict and Change* 9: 71–96.

McCarthy, J.D., C. McPhail, & J. Smith. 1996. "Images of Protest: Selection Bias in Media Coverage of Washington, D.C. Demonstrations." *American Sociological Review* 61: 478–99.

McKenzie, Judith I. 2002. *Environmental Politics in Canada: Managing the Commons into the Twenty-First Century*. Don Mills, Ont.: Oxford University Press.

Noel, Jan. 1995. *Canada Dry: Temperance Crusades before Confederation*. Toronto: University of Toronto Press.

Owens, Lynn & L. Kendall Palmer. 2003. "Making the News: Anarchist Counter-Public Relations on the World Wide Web." *Critical Studies in Media Communication* 20 (4): 335–61.

Palmer, Bryan. 1992. *Working-Class Experience: Rethinking the History of Canadian Labour, 1800–1991*. Toronto: McClelland & Stewart.

Reimer, Sam. 2003. *Evangelicals and the Continental Divide: The Conservative Protestant Subculture in Canada and the United States*. Montreal and Kingston: McGill-Queen's University Press.

Rojecki, Andrew. 2002. "Modernism, State Sovereignty and Dissent: Media and the New Post–Cold War Movements." *Critical Studies in Media Communication* 19 (2): 152–71.

Ryan, Charlotte, Kevin M. Caragee, & William Meinhofer. 2001. "Framing, the News Media, and Collective Action." *Journal of Broadcasting and Electronic Media* 45 (1): 175–82.

Sibonney, Claire. 2007. "Poverty the focus of Canada-wide native protest." Canada.com, June 29. Available at www.canada.com/topics/news/national/story.html?id=bd61f2dd-0a80-4fc9-af3f-01698fb6e099&k=90824&p=1 (accessed August 2008).

Stone, Sharon. "Getting the Message Out: Feminists, the Press, and Violence against Women." *Canadian Review of Sociology and Anthropology* 30 (3): 377–401.

Taras, David. 2001. *Power and Betrayal in the Canadian Media*. Peterborough: Broadview Press.

Waters, Sarah. 2004. "Mobilising against Globalisation: Attac and the French Intellectuals." *West European Politics* 27 (5): 854–74.

World March of Women. 2007. *Our Actions*. Available at www.marchemondialedesfemmes.org/actions/en (accessed August 2008).

Chapter 13

"Too Broke to Answer the Phone": Reporting the "Death" of the National Action Committee on the Status of Women

Angela Failler

INTRODUCTION

In October 2006, Stephen Harper's Conservative government made drastic funding cuts to the budget of Status of Women Canada, the single agency within the federal government that exists to uphold Canada's accountability to the principles of gender equality set out in the Charter of Rights and Freedoms and in the United Nations' Convention on the Elimination of All Forms of Discrimination against Women. In response to the cuts, prominent journalist and social activist Judy Rebick (2006) wondered whether this move was be tantamount to "a nail in the coffin of women's equality." But women's equality, or feminism—the movement behind the push for women's equality—has been pronounced "dead" time and time again—particularly in the mainstream media. What do these repeated pronouncements signal? What purpose do they actually serve? The aim of this chapter is to explore the media's use of "death" as a discursive frame in the representation of the feminist movement in Canada. News coverage of the National Action Committee on the Status of Women (NAC), Canada's largest feminist organization, is given as the primary example toward this aim. A secondary aim of the chapter is to evaluate NAC's ability to "talk back" through the media in an effort to get its messages across to citizens and politicians. Questions that structure this discussion include: How has NAC, as a feminist activist organization, made use of the media? What factors contribute to its effectiveness (or lack thereof) in media relations? Has NAC been able to take advantage of the changing media environment and new forms of communications such as the internet? Or have these developments been a barrier to NAC's mobilization, perhaps even contributing to its perceived "death"? Through the example of NAC, this chapter highlights both the conflicts and the creative potential generated in the complex relationship among citizen groups, media, and political struggle.

FEMINISM AND THE MEDIA

Investigating NAC's relationship to the media is benefited by placing it within the broader context of the relationship between feminism and the media. Before doing so, however, the terms "feminism" and "the media" are clarified independently for their use in this chapter.

Feminism

Feminism is an incredibly diverse (and, yes, alive!) movement with distinct local, national, and transnational formations and histories. But generally, feminism can be understood as a set of ideas and practices geared toward social justice that is mobilized through political activism, intellectual debate, cultural and creative production, community service, and personal relationships. Together, feminist thought and feminist action work to address a myriad of issues, including, but not limited to the omission of women and marginalized persons[1] from official accounts of history; the exclusion of women and marginalized persons from decision-making processes involving government, law, and public policy; the discounting and misrepresenting of women's and marginalized persons' experiences in what counts as "knowledge" and "culture"; and the discrimination and abuse faced by women and marginalized persons within the social institutions of religion, marriage, family, labour, health care, education, law, government, and the media. In short, feminism offers criticisms of past and present injustices, as well as alternatives for a better, more equitable future.

Taking its lead from the struggles of everyday life, feminism puts theories that identify inequalities into practice toward making social change. The kinds of theories and practices that feminists employ vary greatly, as do the philosophical and political traditions that feminists draw upon. This is reflected in distinctions often made between different types of feminism, such as socialist feminism, liberal feminism, radical feminism, lesbian feminism, anti-racist feminism, eco-feminism, poststructuralist feminism, psychoanalytic feminism, postcolonial feminism, transnational feminism, and so forth. Thus, referring to feminism in the plural—as "feminisms"—has become a meaningful way to capture the wide-ranging and prolific work of this movement.

Feminisms in North America are now said to be in their "third wave." Among other things, this characterization acknowledges the continuity of the third wave with the first and second waves that came before it. The first wave of feminism is best known for the gains of certain basic, formal equalities for women such as the right to vote, to own property, to be considered "persons" under the law and, therefore, to be entitled to the rights, freedoms, and protections guaranteed by constitutions such as the Canadian Charter of Rights and Freedoms. Although these are important stepping stones, second-wave feminists came to recognize that the formal gains of the first wave did not necessarily translate into substantive equality for women, nor did they necessarily improve the quality of women's everyday lives.

For example, that women were allowed to run for public office did not mean that they would achieve equal representation in government, or that their concerns would be adequately addressed by governmental policies. Sexism, it was understood, ran deeper and more pervasively than this. Moreover, second-wave feminists began to notice that equality measures did not, in fact, benefit all women equally; that is, while some white, middle-class, heterosexual, and able-bodied women benefited, women who were marginalized on account of their race, class, sexuality, age, or disability faced additional barriers preventing them from accessing such benefits.

Building on second-wave feminism, a key concept in the development of third-wave feminism is "intersectionality." Intersectionality recognizes that our lived experiences cannot be reduced to or explained by singular identifications such as gender. Instead, as individuals we are constituted multiply and simultaneously by gender, race, class, language, sexuality, nationality, age, and other social differences. Intersectionality also recognizes that distinct systems of domination—including sexism, racism, heterosexism, ageism, and class discrimination—intersect with each other in particular ways to determine who occupies positions of privilege and power in any given context. For example, where a white, middle-class woman may not occupy a position of power within a room dominated by white, middle-class men, this same woman may indeed be among the powerful in a roomful of women from various backgrounds. Thus, the concept of intersectionality is used to move away from the assumption that all women's realities and, therefore, needs, are the same. Feminists currently employ an intersectional analysis, for instance, to evaluate the impact of the intensification of global capitalism on women's lives. In this case, sexism, imperialism, racism, and global economics are seen to intersect with each other, creating conditions of exploitation particularly for poor women, indigenous women, women of colour, and immigrant women.

In Canada today, feminism encompasses a wide range of activities organized both formally and informally for the purposes of advocacy, research, lobbying, networking, crisis response, and cultural production. They include but are not limited to women's community groups, sexual assault centres, arts organizations, feminist publishing groups, women's studies programs in colleges and universities, women's health organizations, legal-action groups, governmental agencies, and women's caucuses within larger associations such as labour unions. "Coalitions" are also formed between various feminist groups as a way of building a politic across a broad spectrum of communities. Moreover, feminist organizations range from local, provincial, territorial, and regional to national and international in scope. Although some of the smaller and less formal organizations run on the resources of volunteer membership, most feminist organizations in Canada rely upon government or institutional grants as well as significant fundraising. This arrangement, however, puts them in a precarious position, since they are perpetually subject to funding cutbacks. A reason feminist groups are especially vulnerable in this regard is that their mandates often include challenging the practices of the very institutions or structures they work within and rely upon financially—as will be seen in the case of the National Action Committee on the Status of Women in relation to the federal government.

Nevertheless, feminist groups continue to make a difference in people's lives and are critical players in Canada's democratic process.

The Media

Media, in the broadest sense, are the means by which messages and information are communicated. According to this definition, everything from telephone to radio, television, film, video, newspapers, books, magazines, advertisements, street signs, architecture, art, music, dance, photography, computer games, text messages, and the internet could be considered media. When referred to as "*the* media," however, what is usually being described are mass media. Mass media are forms of communication that are widely disseminated and received and, because of this capacity, are thought to have a significant influence in society. Traditionally, mass media included television, radio, newspapers, magazines, popular music, and cinema—although new interactive media that utilize internet and digital technologies are being recognized for their mass potential as well. The media being looked at in this chapter with regard to the National Action Committee on the Status of Women are primarily print and broadcast news media. The internet is also discussed as an emerging site for the circulation of political opinion.

The media play a central, albeit controversial, role in politics. Citizens depend on "the news," in particular, to be informed of current issues and events in order to knowledgably participate in public debate. As well, the media are expected to serve as a monitor to protect citizens against serious abuses of power by publicizing political processes. However, as media scholar Douglas Kellner points out, this "dual democratic function" grows out of an idealized notion of a free press that is able to report on affairs of the state without the interference of government or other influential power players (Kellner, n.d.). The main problem with this notion, and the reason why Kellner and other critical media scholars consider it idealistic, is that it assumes it is possible for the media to somehow be outside of or immune to the very culture that produces mass media. Instead, the media are quite clearly embedded within political and cultural powers, and the information conveyed to the public is shaped accordingly. For instance, as media production and regulation are increasingly organized in line with profit-oriented business models, the potential to serve in the public's interest is compromised. Aside from the publicly funded Canadian Broadcasting Corporation (CBC) and a few surviving independent and community broadcasters, the majority of news and entertainment media in Canada are owned and operated by a handful of large, private conglomerates, including Canwest Global Communications, CTVglobemedia, Rogers Communications Inc., and Shaw Communications Inc. Within these conglomerates, the allocation of resources for media production is determined by their shareholders and advertisers, whose stakes are primarily in the business sector rather than the social sector (Lorimer et al., 2008). As such, the "news" offered through these venues can be assumed to reflect, first and foremost, corporate priorities that are also typically politically conservative.

Despite their obvious corporate bias, mainstream news media still purport to uphold the values of balance, objectivity, and non-partisanship. British media scholar Jonathan

Bignell (2002) calls this the construction of a "mythic climate of opinion." That is, through the use of certain codes and framing techniques, news producers create the sense that a diversity of views is being represented even when it is not. The effect of the mythic climate of opinion, according to Bignell, is that it "reduces the potential for the viewer to intervene with his or her own discourse about the events reported in the news, and instead passively aligns the viewer with the news institution presenting the news" (2002, p. 123). In other words, rather than encouraging public debate, the mythic climate of opinion undermines the need for it by making audience members feel as if their personal concerns are either outside of what is relevant or that they are already being addressed, however cursorily. What Bignell's analysis suggests is that the impetus for mainstream news sources to be perceived as balanced and objective is less about a commitment to the principles of fairness and freedom of expression than it is an attempt to draw as wide an audience as possible for the purpose of maximum circulation and profit. Far from carrying out the democratizing function of making political manoeuvres visible to the public, from a critical perspective the mainstream news media actively *obscure* the way in which dominant power is reproduced by entrenching status quo views.

Given these conditions, the mainstream media become a problem or hurdle for citizens and citizen groups who are seeking to publicize views that run counter to the conservative, hegemonic politics of the corporate elite. Feminists, for instance, have always struggled with exclusion from and misrepresentation by the media. Subject to the harshest of caricatures, they are rarely portrayed by the mainstream media in a positive light; instead, the media construct stereotypes and distortions that make both individual feminists and feminist politics easily dismissible by an otherwise potentially sympathetic public. Numerous scholars have characterized this treatment of feminists by the media as part of a general "backlash" against feminism. Susan Faludi (1991), for one, observes that the media are particularly hostile toward feminists or feminism during periods when women's advancements—or even the prospect of women's advancements—are sensed to be a threat to existing power hierarchies. At times like these the media circulate rhetoric on "post-feminism" or the "death of feminism," claiming that women have "made it" and that therefore feminism is unnecessary or anachronistic even when the realities of women's lives are testament to the fact that sexist discrimination and abuse persists. High-profile examples include the *Harper's Magazine* feature from 1976 titled "Requiem for the Women's Movement," the *New York Times Magazine* article from 1982 titled "Voices from the Post-Feminist Generation," and the much publicized *TIME Magazine* cover and accompanying story from 1998 with its provocative title, "Is Feminism Dead?" (Yu, 1999).

Needless to say, feminism's relationship to the media is ambivalent at best. Yet this has not stopped feminists from continuing to engage with media, or from producing their own independent and counter-cultural forms of media. For instance, third-wave feminists (also sometimes referred to as "young feminists") have popularized the making and distributing of feminist zines[2] in both print and online versions, many of which respond specifically to the negative impact of the mainstream media on young women's perceptions of themselves and the culture(s) they live in. The Canadian magazine *Shameless: For Girls Who Get It* and the U.S. magazine *Bitch: Feminist Response to Pop Culture* both aim to reach out to young feminist readers who feel "ignored by mainstream media" (*Shameless Magazine*, 2007). The scholarly journals *Feminist Media Studies* and *Camera Obscura: Feminism, Culture, and Media Studies* offer forums for critical, academic engagement with the media. And Rabble.ca, a Canadian online news site, incorporates political commentary by several regular contributors whose views are explicitly feminist (although the site defines itself as "progressive," rather than "feminist" per se).

Notably, one of the founders of Rabble.ca is former National Action Committee on the Status of Women president Judy Rebick. Rebick's media experience serves to remind us that NAC's relationship to the media has not developed only from a distance. Indeed, several of NAC's key organizers were or are media "insiders" themselves, by virtue of having worked in the media industry. Their simultaneous involvement with these two often at-odds institutions adds an interesting layer to understanding how NAC has been characterized by the media, as well as how NAC has, at times, been able to utilize the media as a platform for political mobilization.

BACKGROUND TO NAC

In 1967, the Canadian federal government under the leadership of Liberal prime minister Lester B. Pearson set up a Royal Commission on the Status of Women (henceforth referred to as "the Commission"). The Commission was created in response to increasing pressure from women's groups demanding that an investigation into the conditions of Canadian women's lives be undertaken. Laura Sabia, then president of the Canadian Federation of University Women, promised to march 2 million women on Parliament Hill if the government failed to act (Rebick, 2005). So, in 1968, the Commission began sending representatives across the country to collect briefs from local and provincial women's groups, many of whom had organized subcommittees on matters they deemed important in anticipation of the Commission's hearings. In 1970, the Commission released its report, making 167 recommendations for changes to laws and policies in areas that fell under the purview of the federal government, including family law, employment, child care, birth control, education, and the Indian Act (Cross, 2000). The Commission understood these changes to be a crucial step toward improving the greater equality of women in Canada.

The year after the Commission's report, a coalition of women's groups formed the National Action Committee on the Status of Women. NAC's first mandate was to lobby the government on the Commission's recommendations in order to ensure their implementation.[3] As well, NAC developed policy initiatives beyond those outlined in the report, as it felt the Commission did not substantively address violence against women or the barriers facing women with disabilities, lesbians, or aboriginal, immigrant, and visible-minority women (Vickers et al., 1993). NAC's expanding membership, from 32 or so groups at its inception to more than 650 by the mid 1990s, meant that the range of issues and strategies it pursued also expanded and shifted in focus. In its earlier phases, NAC was outspoken on the patriation of the Canadian Constitution, the North American Free Trade Agreement

(NAFTA), the Charlottetown and Meech Lake accords, abortion, child care, maternity leave, custody rights, divorce legislation, employment equity, women's representation within labour unions, poverty, pornography, sexual assault on military women, and violence against women in general. Into the 1990s, NAC began to address the impact of globalization on women's lives and the rights particularly of marginalized women, including immigrant and refugee women, women of colour, aboriginal women, lesbian women, and women with disabilities.[4]

Not surprisingly, NAC's growth has occasionally necessitated periods of significant restructuring, including turning a critical eye on its own practices with respect to inclusivity. Through affirmative action policies, for example, it has made efforts to move women of colour into leadership positions within its organization (Rebick, 2005). As well, since the late 1990s NAC has been working to integrate young women's previously unheard voices into its mandate (Monsebraaten, 1998; Armstrong, 1998; Rundle, 1999; Williams, 2006).

NAC's expansion has also translated into increased financial pressures since, far from keeping up with the organization's growth, government funding has dwindled over time. Once supported by the Women's Program of the federal government agency Status of Women Canada, a succession of cutbacks beginning in the mid 1980s with Brian Mulroney's Conservative leadership saw NAC's budget eroded. In a 1989 *Globe and Mail* article, NAC president Lynne Kaye was quoted as calling the cutbacks a "retaliatory measure" on the part of the Conservative government, introduced because NAC had "fought to hold the government to its commitment to end discrimination against women in all its forms" (*Globe and Mail*, 1989). In other words, NAC felt that its funding was being withdrawn precisely for holding the government accountable to its promises on women's equality. Cutbacks peaked in 1998 under Jean Chrétien's Liberals when NAC lost its core funding entirely after funding criteria changed to an emphasis on "projects" rather than ongoing organizational support. In an interview with Joan Grant-Cummings, who was president of NAC at the time, Ann Decter, writer for the Canadian feminist magazine *Herizons*, describes the implications of the shift from core to project-based funding as follows: "Core funding keeps an organization alive to do the work of its chosen mandate. Project funding means the funder has approval of each particular project, and so begins to gain control over an organization's priorities" (Decter, 1998, p. 19).

Reluctant about what it thus saw as a strings-attached funding process, NAC nevertheless got in line to submit project proposals for consideration by Status of Women. However, the tenuous nature of this funding meant that ultimately NAC came to rely upon community fundraising events, membership fees, and donations in order to stay afloat (Decter, 1998). Despite its efforts, NAC fell into debt. No longer able to maintain salaries or host annual meetings, by 2004 it finally cut off its answering machine because there were literally no paid staff members left to answer the phone (Carmichael, 2004).

Even so, with its national office effectively closed, remaining executive members formed an advisory council to plan for NAC's future. In 2005, a plenary session was held in Ottawa to strategize new directions, and in 2006 an annual general meeting was held for the first time since 2001, when the organization's current president, Dolly Williams, was elected.

As of September 2007, however, NAC reports that it continues to struggle due to Status of Women funding restrictions that were re-entrenched with Stephen Harper's Conservative government cutbacks announced by the Minister of Status of Women, Bev Oda, in October 2006 (C. Power, personal communication, September 25, 2007). These cutbacks not only affect NAC's potential to access federal support, but have resulted in the closure of 12 regional Status of Women offices and countless other organizations and front-line services, including women's shelters (Status Report, 2006).[5] Subsequently, NAC has put into place rebuilding strategies that are less dependent on government funds, while at the same time calling for the restoration of core funding to women's advocacy, lobbying, and research groups that rely on this support for basic operations. NAC is also seeking funding to acquire the resources necessary to revise and update its website, which has been "under construction" since 2001 (C. Power, personal communication, September 25, 2007).

Media visibility is one way in which the public perception of an organization or political group is shaped. During its most recent rebuilding phase, NAC has been especially low profile, if not altogether absent, in the mainstream news media. References to the ongoing efforts of the remaining executive, new president, volunteers, and membership of more than 600 groups that NAC still maintains are barely to be found. Along with the loss of its federal funding and the closure of its national office, media invisibility has undoubtedly contributed to the current sense of NAC's demise. The remainder of this chapter thus examines the ways in which NAC has been made visible or invisible in the media over the years. Politically conservative, sexist, and racist power relations are shown to play a major role in shaping the news media's repeated reports of NAC's so-called "death."

THE NEWS MEDIA'S SPIN ON NAC: "DEATH" AS A DISCURSIVE FRAMEWORK

Like other modes of cultural production (cinema, literature, theatre, etc.), news production is a form of storytelling (Lorimer et al., 2008). In other words, making news involves a series of choices about what stories to tell and how to tell them. Thus, the news is not a mirror of reality; nor is it simply an objective gathering of content or events. Rather, what appears to us as the news is subject to a strategic process of selection, or "gatekeeping," which determines what is included and what is left out. Gatekeeping decisions are made by different actors in the news-making chain, including news directors, editors, and sometimes journalists themselves, but they are also heavily influenced by owners of news organizations and other stakeholders, such as advertisers, whose interests are primarily to maintain allocative and operational control over the news process in order to maximize profit (Lorimer et al., 2008).[6] Further to this, in order to maintain profit-making as their priority, news organizations tend to support political efforts that will not stand in the way of their business orientation. Not surprisingly, the result is a mutually supportive relationship between the commercial, mainstream news media and corporate-minded, conservative political players. Hence, the mainstream news is a highly constructed version of social reality that, most of all, reflects the political orientations and interests of news organizations and their elite stakeholders. The interests of the general public, unfortunately, are considered mainly for how they might be "spun" in order to be rendered profitable. This strategic news "spinning" toward profit reflects what cultural theorist Raymond Williams observes of what has become of the ideal of freedom of expression under the pressure of increasing commercialism: "Freedom," he writes, "amounts to the freedom to say anything you wish, provided you can say it profitably" (1989, p. 88).

Central to the process of news spinning is the application of journalistic conventions to the presentation of news content or events. Journalistic conventions consist of various framing, coding, and editing techniques that function to shape and construct the news according to particular norms and values (Bignell, 2002). Examples of these techniques include (but are not limited to) the strategic framing of camera shots, narrative voiceovers, and print layouts; the ordering and appearance of news stories; the selection of words, catchphrases, and headlines; the choice of certain "official sources" or "experts" as consultants; and the use of "consensus cues" to encourage the reader's/viewer's identification with the perspectives of the news creators (Aday et al., 2005). According to communications theorist George Gerbner, within the context of the corporate mainstream media, journalistic conventions work toward cultivating a stable set of images that uphold the status quo, as well as editing out those perspectives or voices that challenge it (Jhally, 1997). In other words, the media rarely offer a critical view of social reality but instead reinforce dominant ideas, existing relations of power, current structures of inequalities, and accepted cultural norms and stereotypes in their portrayal of "the way things are."

How is the status quo cultivated in the mainstream news media's "spin" on NAC? A critical survey of Canadian newspaper coverage from approximately the 1980s to the present reveals that, due to its allegiances to conservative interests, the mainstream news media cannot tolerate NAC's feminist, democratizing efforts or its challenges to the status quo and has, therefore, found ways to render it dismissible. Through the use of particular discursive framing, linguistic codes, and editorial selectivity, NAC is portrayed as either threatening to the public good[7] or perpetually on the brink of death. Either way, it is delegitimized as a political voice and, as such, can be dismissed by news audiences and the mainstream public. While NAC has a few, occasional "friends" among contributors to the news media, portrayals of NAC generally fail in their ability to understand or communicate the methods and aims of feminist political activism, instead relying upon myths, stereotypes, and distortions of the work feminists and feminisms do.

The question we might begin by asking, then, is not just *why* but *how* is it that the media construct the death of an organization or movement that is actually alive? There are three particular "events" that appear, repeatedly, in the mainstream press coverage of NAC over the years: (1) funding cuts, (2) internal conflicts, and (3) an ongoing question as to whether NAC is relevant to "average" Canadian citizens, particularly women. These events are consistently interpreted in such a way as to suggest that the organization is about to die, or deserves to die, on account of them. In other words, when these three issues are raised in mainstream news coverage, they are presented as harbingers of NAC's death. In order to analyze the media's reporting of NAC, a closer look at its treatment of these three issues is required.

Funding Cuts

Both supporters and critics of NAC understand cuts to funding by the federal government to be detrimental to the organization. This funding, issued through the government agency Status of Women Canada, has been used to maintain many of NAC's basic operations, including staffing, communications, research, the organizing of lobbying and outreach events, and costs associated with hosting meetings and convening delegates from women's groups across Canada. Beyond these pragmatic uses, however, government money also gives the advantage of perceived legitimacy. That is, when an organization such as NAC has the support of an "official" authoritative body such as the state, it is more likely to be seen as legitimate by the mainstream. The state's authoritative power to confer legitimacy becomes particularly apparent in the way in which the mainstream media subsequently represent NAC when the state *rescinds* its financial support. For example, upon the announcement of federal budget cuts to NAC in 1989, the *Toronto Star*, Canada's largest daily newspaper, ran a lengthy article by Carol Goar titled "National Action Committee's tactics sophomoric: Why Tories spurn feminist group." In it, Goar gives a long list of "tactical errors" she opines NAC has made that, in her view, justify the Conservative government's cutbacks. Among the tactical errors she cites is that "[NAC] is out of step with the prevailing philosophy in Ottawa" (Goar, 1989). Well, certainly NAC *was* "out of step" with the prevailing Conservative government's philosophy. It opposed many of the government's main policy initiatives, including those on privatization and military spending, as well as Brian Mulroney's proposals in the Charlottetown Accord and the Free Trade Agreement with the United States, arguing that they were detrimental to the potential for women's equality in Canada (Rebick, 2005). Goar's failure to recognize NAC's oppositions as either measured resistance or democratic participation, instead characterizing them as "tactical errors," is telling; it reveals an investment in the authoritarian notion that if you are not in line with the state's politics you are not a legitimate political player, and if you are not a legitimate political player *within these terms* you are not deserving of either state or public support. There is no room or imagination for resistance here. Goar's account simply serves to reinforce the status quo by presenting the ruling political regime as the only viable political option.

It is interesting to note that where mainstream critics such as Goar see funding cuts to NAC as evidence of its failures or as a precursor of its death, NAC members and allies have interpreted them as evidence of its *effectiveness* as a political agitator and, in this light, as a retaliatory measure on the part of the government. In 1990, for instance, former NAC vice-president Marjorie Cohen anticipated that "if NAC ever became really politically effective, they could expect vicious repercussions" (Petten & Jefferson, 1995, p. 20). Indeed, when later that same year NAC representatives gave a critical report on the status of women in Canada at a United Nations meeting on worldwide discrimination against women, its annual federal funding was subsequently cut by a third (Petten & Jefferson, 1995). Of course, this perspective is de-emphasized in the mainstream press. Instead, what is emphasized for general consumption is the idea that NAC has brought funding cuts and their associated difficulties upon itself by wasting taxpayers' money and "generous grants" from government programs on its unaccounted for, so-called "questionable" agendas (Francis, 1999).

Internal Conflict

A second "tactical error" that Goar and others in the news repeatedly cite as cause for NAC's demise is the existence of internal conflicts and a diversity of opinions within its ranks. Admittedly, NAC has had recurring tensions within its membership over issues such as regional representation and whether marginalized women's voices were being heard on particular issues. It has had rifts over key debates such as the Meech Lake Accord, where it became clear that francophone Québécois feminists had different stakes than English-Canadian feminists did in the proposed treaty, resulting in the Fédération des femmes du Quebec splitting from NAC in 1989 to pursue its politics independently (Rebick, 2005). And on occasion NAC has endured major upheavals where, for instance, disagreements over organization and strategy at its 1988 AGM led to the last-minute withdrawal of a presidential candidate and the resignation of most of its paid staff (Rauhala, 1988). What is significant, however, is the way in which the mainstream news media interpret and represent these events predominantly in negative terms, as chronic divisiveness, fractioning, instability, self-contradiction, and general incompetence. Headlines appearing in the *Globe and Mail* after the 1988 AGM, for example, read "Feminist flagship rocked by feuding" (Rauhala, 1988) and "Partnership in peril" (*Globe and Mail*, 1988), while the *Toronto Star* reported how NAC "exploded . . . with bitter in-fighting, tears and predictions of self-destruction" (Dunphy, 1988).

It is not considered that NAC's "conflicts" may, at least in part, be related to the stress of being under constant threat of funding cutbacks, or of being continually undermined by government and media backlash, or of having to accomplish most of its work on a volunteer basis with a volunteer executive committee, including its presidents, who went unpaid until 1993 (and then unpaid again in the late 1990s when NAC lost its core funding entirely). Instead, the mainstream news chooses to focus on details that can be construed as internal failures, remaining noticeably silent on NAC's many successes. After all, successes, especially feminist successes, are not as newsworthy or sensational as conflict (especially feminist conflict). Decter echoes this when she observes, "NAC operates under the scrutiny of a mainstream media quick to magnify any whiff of disagreement between feminists" (1998, p. 19). This kind of scrutiny and its resulting negative media attention has significant implications for NAC, since even the slightest suggestion of perceived disagreement can serve as ammunition for critics who are looking for reasons to insist upon its illegitimacy. In her commentary after the controversial 1988 AGM, *Globe and Mail* writer Ann Rauhala (1998) makes this implication obvious by suggesting that NAC try to appear "cooperative" so that the Tory government would not use its internal "fighting" as an excuse to withdraw its financial support (which it did anyway in the months that followed).

Equating NAC's internal tensions and conflicts with failure or death, the mainstream press fails to imagine (or deliberately ignores) the possibility of their productivity; that is, that tensions and conflicts may signal an active and dynamic political process. Upon being consulted about their own views on the 1988 AGM controversy, Lorraine Greaves (NAC's drop-out presidential candidate) and Lynne Kaye (her left-standing opponent, with whom the "in-fighting" was said to have broken out) *both* stated that the fallout was less catastrophic than the media had portrayed (Anderson, 1988). In fact, Kaye expressed the feeling that NAC had emerged stronger because of its "open dissent" (Dunphy, 1988), and Greaves ultimately described the split as "constructive" (Rauhala, 1998). In a rebuttal to the *Globe and Mail's* inflammatory coverage of the AGM events, a letter to the editor titled "Splits healthy sign" offers a similar view. It suggests that the divisions in the NAC are not a disaster but should be viewed as healthy because they demonstrate that

> women—including even feminists—differ among themselves on political and social
> issues just as much as men do ... Recognition of that fact ... would be a sign of
> political maturity ... (Addington 1988)

What the author of this letter to the editor matter-of-factly points out is that difference is integral to political processes and, as such, the *Globe's* criticism of NAC on the basis of internal differences only demonstrates its limited perspective on the subject.

This limited perspective—the inability to recognize pluralism or diversity as a strength rather than a weakness—speaks to the general inability or refusal on the part of mainstream political structures and mainstream media to recognize political voices other than those that represent singular, universalizing ideals (which, incidentally, are not flexible or nuanced enough to appreciate the reality of social differences—or intersectionality—in people's lives, but instead privilege only those who are closest to the universal norm of idealized subjectivity: white, Christian, heterosexual, able-bodied, middle-class, and male). News media, in particular, seem befuddled by the prospect of multi-vocality. Perhaps, given the constraints of journalistic conventions that limit content to the most easily digestible sound bytes, a plurality or diversity of opinions emanating from what is assumed to be one homogenous movement ("feminism" or "the women's liberation movement") is experienced simply as information overload. In other words, perhaps feminism is just too darn complicated (!) to be represented in all its nuances given the pressures for journalists to produce stories almost instantaneously in order to meet contemporary standards of newsworthiness. Or, what is equally likely is that feminism appears less threatening and more easily dismissible if it can be lumped into one over-generalized perspective.

Corresponding to its insistence on being able to relate to feminism as a singular perspective is the media's demand that there be a single leader to represent and interview. Even better, of course, would be if that leader was young and "photogenic" (which implicitly means white, middle-class, and heterosexual), since "a party leader's cheekbones and fashion sense were more newsworthy than her policy pronouncements" (Vickers et al., 1993, p. 57). Despite anti-feminist rhetoric stereotypically equating feminism with unattractive women,[8] the press nonetheless managed to find media-worthy NAC leaders, particularly in the figures of Chaviva Hošek and Judy Rebick (Hošek was president of NAC from 1984 to 1986 and Rebick from 1990 to 1993). The media were drawn to Hošek, interpreting her as traditionally feminine, attractive, and intelligent—but in an easy, "non-threatening" way (Goddu, 1999). Rebick, on the other hand, was "media savvy," having learned, in her words, how to "play that game" in order to get media attention (as cited in Goddu, 1999). And she did. The media almost exclusively turned to Rebick as NAC's spokesperson during her tenure as president and beyond (Goddu, 1999). In a typical case, the Montreal *Gazette* ran a headline that read "Rebick's actions spur sharp debate in women's movement" (cited in Goddu, 1999). Referring to the "no" vote NAC had endorsed on the Charlottetown Accord referendum in 1992, the headline held Rebick solely responsible despite the fact that the endorsement had been made collectively by NAC and that Rebick, personally, had leaned toward the "yes" side of the debate. Of the paper's assumption that the "no" vote was necessarily her own, Rebick speculates that "The media could not relate to a non-patriarchal structure where the leader is not the one to make the decision" (cited in Goddu, 1999). In other words, the media failed to understand how the president of a political organization did not ultimately wield authoritarian power over the rest of its membership.

NAC as a "Special Interest Group" or "NAC doesn't speak for me": Racist Backlash

After Judy Rebick's presidency ended in 1993, NAC's media visibility dropped considerably. Some attributed this drop to the stepping down of Rebick, whose outspokenness and strategic engagement with the media had garnered the organization at least a certain amount of publicity. However, the drop also coincided with two other crucial events: the rise to leadership positions of women of colour within NAC, and the apparent rise of sentiment among certain women that NAC was no longer relevant to them. Toronto freelance writer and editor Lisa Rundle[9] is clear about the inter-implications:

> Essentially, I think after Judy Rebick left and women of colour and young women started to get positions of power, the media started to ignore NAC . . . In part, it's that Judy Rebick was particularly media savvy and knew how to spin things. In part, it was the bias of the mainstream media that marginalized a group with women of colour at the helm, assuming it no longer spoke to women generally somehow. (Personal communication, August 14, 2007)

As Rundle points out, it was not the fact of Rebick's stepping down alone that spurred the media's sudden disinterest in NAC. Rather, it was also significant that Rebick's successor was Sunera Thobani, the first woman of colour in NAC's history to hold the position of president. And while her election marked a positive growth for NAC in terms of its own representational politics and being a catalyst for membership expansion with the subsequent joining of several immigrant and refugee women's organizations, Thobani was met with thinly disguised racism and outright contempt by both politicians and the media. Upon the acclamation of her presidency, for instance, Conservative MP John MacDougall stood up in Parliament and charged Thobani with being an illegal immigrant (Landsberg, 2001). The media followed suit by calling into question how Thobani, as an immigrant woman of colour, could possibly represent the interests of Canadians (Goddu, 1999).

Both political conservatives and the mainstream media, in other words, had great difficulty imagining Thobani as the "new face" of Canada's women's movement. This difficulty revealed deep biases surrounding notions of, first of all, who was considered legitimately Canadian (presumably not immigrant women or women of colour) and, correspondingly, whose interests were seen to best represent Canadian women's interests "*in general*" (again, presumably not immigrant women or women of colour). The fault of this "in general" proviso is in the assumption that, first, all Canadian women's interests can or must be represented homogeneously in order to launch a viable political movement and, second, that these interests are best defined by the experiences of privileged, white, Anglo, middle-class, heterosexual women (to the exclusion of "other" women's experiences).

In their study on the representation of women in television news, Lana Rakow and Kimberlie Kranich describe how these assumptions are built into news-making: "When reporters and editors think of women, they think of white women; when they think of feminists, they think of white women" (1991, p. 19). Whiteness, that is to say, functions as the default norm in the imaginative construction of the identificatory categories "women" and "feminists" in the media. As a result, and as Thobani herself observed of the way in which she was treated by journalists who were women, in particular, "They had a really hard time seeing themselves reflected in this movement if it was being led by this woman who was so unlike them" (as cited in Goddu, 1999). The racism inherent to the construction of the categories "women" and "feminists" thus functioned to undermine Thobani and each successive NAC president who was a woman of colour as somehow exceptional and/or irrelevant to the interests of Canadian women "in general"—this, in spite of contrary evidence such as the fact that during Thobani's term as president, NAC, along with the Canadian Labour Congress, organized the largest mobilization in history of women across Canada at the National Women's March Against Poverty in 1996 (Molgat & Cummings, n.d.).

These racist constructions also manifested in the complaints of several conservative and (supposedly) liberal white women featured in the media through this period, who declared that (post–Judy Rebick) NAC no longer "spoke to them" and therefore they could no longer support NAC as an organization.[10] In the *Globe and Mail*, for example, Diane Allen reported that because she was "white, middle-class, able-bodied and heterosexual" she was "made to feel guilty" by NAC's "politically correct standards." Moreover, she complained, NAC's policies and decision-makers "excluded and alienated the majority of Canadian women" (Allen, 1995). Clearly presuming that *she*, as a white, middle-class, able-bodied, and heterosexual woman, represented the majority of Canadian women, Allen's complaint only serves to reveal how Thobani's presidency and the prioritizing of the needs of poor and racially marginalized women was incompatible with *her* vision of feminism; that is, a feminism that exists solely for the mobility of white, upper-middle-class women such as herself—those women, in her view, that *really* matter. Ironically, Allen began her article by charging that it is NAC that promotes a "narrow view of Canadian womanhood" (1995, p. A22).

In another display of ignorance and xenophobia, *Calgary Herald* columnist Diane Francis (later with the *National Post*) wrote in 1999 that Ottawa should revoke NAC's funding on the basis that, as she believed, NAC supported "Marxist guerrillas . . . murderous armies of thousands . . . [living] off levies paid to them by drug traffickers . . . [and] terrorizing peasants who side with the rule of law (Francis, 1999). To make this absurd imaginative leap—from the idea of NAC as a once merely "unaccountable" organization (in her words again) to one that engages in illegal guerrilla warfare through the use of "drug and also kidnap revenues," Francis claimed that NAC has been "hijacked by minority groups and refugees with an agenda that has absolutely nothing to do with the status of women, or the status of anyone for that matter, living in Canada." She added, "The cause of these guerrillas is not where my tax dollars should be going" (1999, p. A17). Conflating the interests of minority groups and refugees with terrorism, as she did in this characterization, Francis clearly saw the prioritizing of non-white and refugee woman as "deadly" for her notion of feminism. Moreover, as she completely ignored the transnational relations involved in the production of the state and its citizenry, Francis allowed herself to think that immigrant women are not really women (nor are they really Canadian). Rather, in her mind, the identities "woman" and "immigrant" were mutually exclusive, aptly demonstrating Rakow and Kranich's point about how "when [reporters] think of women, they think of white women; when they think of feminists, they think of white women" (1991, p. 19). In addition, because the politics surrounding the status of immigrant and refugee women did not represent Francis's *own* interests—as she so thinly disguised them in her statement that "The problem with this activist women's organization is that it was hijacked by persons of a certain political persuasion, which is opposite to mine" (Francis, 1999)—they were not worthy of her support. In sum, Francis's version of both feminism and social reality displayed a total lack of awareness of the way in which her privilege was founded upon the racialized hierarchy she invoked in order to dismiss the relevance of minority groups and refugee groups. Put differently, her problematic commentary relies on the foreclosure and denial of "other" subjectivities in order to prop up a weak claim to being marginalized by NAC and its "politically correct" agenda.

Also central to resisting women of colour in positions of power, and to taking seriously the conditions of the lives of marginalized women in Canada, is the construction of NAC (and feminism itself) as a "special interest group." There are many examples of this construction in the mainstream news media, including Michael Coren's story from the *Financial Post* (1998), which lends itself obviously. In yet another diatribe on the perceived "failures" of NAC, Coren writes, "Then we have the fact that while contemporary feminism wants to be important it marginalizes itself by its radicalism. Race and sexuality have become more central issues than gender as organizations such as NAC show their obsession with lesbianism and, as one member termed it, 'the class domination of white women'" (1998, p. 17). Once again, that critics such as Allen and Coren identify NAC's attention to race and sexuality (that is, its attention to non-white and non-heterosexual women) as constituting its failure to be relevant to "average" Canadian women further uncovers the white-centric, heteronormative bias implicit to dominant, status-quo conceptions of political subjectivity (that is, who is considered a deserving subject in the public sphere), as well as the limitations of portrayals of feminism in the media. By constructing an image of NAC as obsessive, fringe activists whose agenda is "overrun by special interest groups" (Carlyle, 2002, p. 14), mainstream news producers have attempted to dismiss NAC, or perhaps feminism in its entirety, as a political movement to be taken seriously.

NAC AS A MEDIA PLAYER IN A CHANGING MEDIA ENVIRONMENT?

Suffice it to say, NAC has borne the brunt of the mainstream news media's backlash more frequently than it has appeared in a positive light. Occasionally, however, NAC supporters and executive members have themselves taken up the defensive by responding to negative coverage in, for example, letters to the editors of national newspapers. As well, in one standout, proactive instance, NAC organized a televised debate with the federal election candidates of 1984 where well-known feminists posed questions to the candidates "as if women mattered" to the political process.[11] Initially, the debate boosted NAC's public profile, having drawn, according to Doris Anderson, "a bigger national audience than the Stanley Cup playoffs" that year (1988, p. F1). Nevertheless, in subsequent years the "women's debate," as it became known, was met with increasing resistance, such as the time when Brian Mulroney would only agree to the debate upon the condition that the television networks themselves hosted it rather than NAC, which he characterized as a "special interest group" (*Toronto Star*, 1988). By 1997, the spirit of the debate was undermined even further as Jean Chrétien refused to participate altogether, followed by the withdrawal of all other federal party leaders (who sent substitutes in their place) with the exception of the NDP's Alexa McDonough (Canadian Press, 2007). The debate that year did not even make national television, but instead appeared on the subsidiary parliamentary channel (Davy, 1997).

From its very inception, NAC identified the media as an important site of mobilization, where, for instance, at the Strategy for Change conference of 1972, a "Mass Media Impact" workshop was offered to conference delegates among only a half-dozen or so other choices (Molgat & Cummings, n.d.). Despite this acknowledgment, NAC has never had sufficient funds to develop its communications or media strategies beyond the basic functioning needed to run the organization. Instead, its resources have been prioritized for grassroots activism and lobbying efforts. Thus, while NAC supporters and NAC members have had worthwhile suggestions for development on this front—such as Urshad Manji's idea that NAC publish zines, host a campus radio show, and launch an "umbrella" website linking all member groups to encourage networking between older and newer generations of feminists (Rundle, 1999)—there remains a sense that NAC's potential in this regard has not been realized. Or, to put it as succinctly as NAC's youngest president-elect Denise Campbell did (her brief term incidentally cut short in 2001 by budgetary constraints), "NAC missed the internet revolution" (cited in Carmichael, 2004). Precisely what this means for NAC today is yet to be fully known since the organization is still in the midst, as mentioned earlier, of applications to secure funding to put toward this very task—upgrading and updating its website, enhancing its online networking capacities. What is clear, however, is that by and large the resistance NAC has been met with from the mainstream media as well as politically conservative power players has kept it on the periphery of Canadian politics. Yet it continues to strategize new ways of engaging the public and creating social change.

CONCLUSION

There are still many unanswered questions as to how NAC will proceed from here, given the current (ongoing) conservative, anti-feminist political culture in Canada. This chapter has focused on the ways in which the media contribute to this culture by misrepresenting the work that NAC does and by cultivating status quo interpretations that aim to dismiss feminist efforts as illegitimate and irrelevant. In particular, it highlights how the mainstream news media have constructed NAC's "death" as a means for dismissal. Through particular discursive framings, editorial choices regarding whose opinions are consulted and represented, and journalistic "spinnings," news sources have told a similar story over and over since NAC's establishment over 35 years ago: that NAC does not deserve public support because a) it represents "fringe" or "radical" interests, not the interests of so-called "average" Canadians; b) it is incoherent and ineffective on account of internal differences and plurality; and c) it is not in line with popular or dominant political philosophies (that, incidentally, conceive of citizenship and subjectivity from an elitist, white-centric, masculinist viewpoint). Moreover, by repeatedly casting feminism as a homogenous, overgeneralized movement that is perpetually on its deathbed, the mainstream media deny citizens information about the contribution of feminist activism to Canadian politics. In this sense, the media not only *reflect* the sexist, racist, and homophobic dynamics of the conservative culture more broadly; they actively *create and reproduce* these dynamics. It is for precisely this reason that feminists insist on calling attention to the media as a crucial site of political engagement.

Media Journal Assignments

1. Utilizing Failler's reference list as a starting point, research feminist online blogs to determine how they are different from other blogs. How is the feminist movement being articulated online? Provide examples if possible.

2. Keep track over a one-month period of the number of times you read or hear about feminism either online, in the newspaper, on television, or in magazines. Is the treatment of feminism complimentary? Is it derisive? How does this shape how you view feminism?

3. Access the website of a feminist organization and determine how it uses media as resistance to challenge conservative, corporate, or patriarchal interests.

Endnotes

1. By "marginalized persons" I am referring to those who are most vulnerable to systemic and everyday discrimination in Canada: women, racial minorities, immigrants, Aboriginal people, non-heterosexual people, transsexual and transgendered persons, the elderly, children, persons with disabilities, and poor and working-class people.

2. Zines, an abbreviation of "fanzines," are self-published works that typically have low or no budgets and a small circulation. In print form they are produced by assembling and photocopying original and borrowed material including images, poetry, rants, and other expressions that are generally "anti-establishment" in spirit. Among young feminists, zines are considered a "do-it-yourself" form of counter-cultural production (Stasko, 2001). "E-zines" are the online version of print zines, which,

in Krista Scott-Dixon's terms, "share the spirit of the witty tourism of girl culture" as a form of feminist political activism (2001, p. 303).

3. In "Report on the Royal Commission on the Status of Women: Where Are We after Thirty Years?" (2000), Legal Director of the Ontario Women's Justice Network Pamela Cross observes that, while the work of the Commission was groundbreaking for its time and made a real difference in some women's lives, 30 years later many of its recommendations, especially those dealing with women in the "most vulnerable situations," had yet to be implemented or had been only partially implemented. As for some of the recommendations that were, in her words, "implemented on paper and in theory," Cross argues that their effectiveness remains debatable.

4. It should be noted that, while NAC has begun to support these women, it has not always explicitly done so. This shift has come in large part as a result of both internal and external criticisms by those who felt that NAC remained rooted in the priorities of white, middle-class, heterosexual, and able-bodied women.

5. Another case in point: As a direct result of funding cuts to women's groups by Stephen Harper's Conservative government in 2006, the National Association of Women in the Law (NAWL) announced in September 2007 that it was being forced to lay off its entire staff and shut down its national office after 33 years of feminist engagement with the law in Canada. (See NAWL's 2007 press release titled "Harper government working to silence women").

6. According to Lorimer, Gasher, and Skinner (2008), "allocative control" refers to the allocation of both labour and capital resources to a news organization by publishers, shareholders, and directors. "Operational control" refers to the management and dispersal of these resources, once allocated, *within* the news organization. This work is done primarily by editors and producers (pp. 243–44).

7. In 1970, then Federation of Women Teachers of Ontario staff member Kay Sigurjonnson remembers journalists responding to the report of the Royal Commission of the Status of Women as if it was a joke (Rebick, 2005, p. 27). Judy LaMarsh, who was a Liberal cabinet minister at the time, describes reaction to the report by the national press as "scathing" (Vickers et al., 1993, p. 53). This defensive hostility on the part of the news media can be seen, for example, in an article run by the *Toronto Star* in December 1970 describing the Commission's report as "more explosive than any terrorists' time bomb" (Westell, 1970, p. 13). Aligning the Commission's report with "terrorism," the article effectively constructs feminism and its efforts (in this case, the effort to reveal the conditions of Canadian women's lives as *women* saw them) as inherently threatening to the general public; a characterization that would set the tone for the mainstream media's representation of the Canadian feminist movement, including NAC, henceforth.

8. Conservative American political commentator Rush Limbaugh, for example, is known for having stated, "Feminism was established to allow unattractive women easier access to the mainstream of society" (Media Matters for America, 2005).

9. Lisa Rundle is co-editor of *Turbo Chicks: Talking Young Feminisms* (2001) and a columnist for *Herizons* magazine on young women and feminism.

10. See, for example, Margaret Wente's "The sad decline of NAC" (1995), as well as the *Globe and Mail*'s feature "Completely NACkered" (1998).

11. I am borrowing this phrase from the title of Jill Vickers et al.'s book, *Politics As If Women Mattered: A Political Analysis of the National Action Committee on the Status of Women* (1993).

References

Aday, S., Livingston, S., & Hebert, M. 2005. "Embedding the Truth: A Cross-Cultural Analysis of Objectivity and Television Coverage of the Iraq War." *Harvard International Journal of Press/Politics* 10 (1): 3–21.

Addington, R. H. 1988. "Splits healthy sign." [Letter to the editor]. *Globe and Mail*, May 28, D7.

Allen, D. 1995. "The end of NAC." *Globe and Mail*, February 9, A22.

Anderson, D. 1988. "Action committee in crisis—again." *Toronto Star*, July 30, F1.

Armstrong, J. 1998. "NAC fights to attract new blood: National women's group has settled internal battles but has to deal with cuts in funds." *Globe and Mail*, June 8, A3.

Bignell, J. 2002. *Media Semiotics*. 2nd ed. Manchester and New York: Manchester University Press.

Canadian Press. 2007. "Election 97, Election Notebook: Wondering where the boys are." *Globe and Mail*, May 17, A12.

Carlyle, E. 2002. "NAC attack." *Canadian Dimension* 36 (1): 14–17.

Carmichael, A. 2004. "Canada's national women's organization can't afford to answer phone." Canadian Press NewsWire, March 7. Available from ProQuest database (579732691) (accessed July 30, 2007).

Coren, M. 1998. "Feminism is still alive and kicking but its result is ambiguous as best: Contradictions riddle women's movement." *Financial Post*, July 9, 17.

Cross, P. 2000. "Report on the Royal Commission on the Status of Women: Where Are We after Thirty Years?" November 2000. Available at www.owjn.org/issues/equality/thirty.htm (accessed August 12, 2007).

Davy, D. 1997. "Women's issues are a no-show." *Hamilton Spectator*, May 29, A10.

Decter, A. 1998. "Working from the Ground Up: An Interview with Joan Grant-Cummings." *Herizons* 12 (1): 17–19.

Dunphy, C. 1988. "New leader 'optimistic' feminists will close ranks." *Toronto Star*, May 24, G1.

Faludi, S. 1991. *Backlash: The Undeclared War against American Women*. New York: Doubleday.

Francis, D. 1999. "Women's group doesn't represent women or women's issues: Ottawa should nix National Action Committee on the Status of Women by saying no to its funding demands." *Calgary Herald*, July 18, A17.

Globe and Mail. 1988. "Partnership in peril." [Editorial]. May 23, A6.

———. 1989. "The federal budget: Retaliation seen in cuts to NAC." April 29, A11.

Goar, C. 1989. "National Action Committee's tactics sophomoric: Why Tories spurn feminist group." *Toronto Star*, May 20, D4.

Goddu, J. 1999. "'Powerless, public-spirited women,' 'angry feminists,' and 'The muffin lobby': Newspaper and magazine coverage of the Canadian Advisory Council on the Status of Women, the National Action Committee on the Status of Women, and REAL Women of Canada." *Canadian Journal of Communication* 24 (1). Available at www.cjc-online.ca/viewarticle.php?id=507&layout=html (accessed September 23, 2007).

Jhally, S., director. 1997. *The Electronic Storyteller: Television and the Cultivation of Values*. (Motion picture.) Northampton, Mass: Media Education Foundation.

Kellner, Douglas. (n.d.) "The Media and Social Problems." Available at www.gseis.ucla.edu/faculty/kellner/ (accessed July 21, 2007).

Landsberg, Michelle. 2001. "Unmasking bigotry behind the hysteria." *Toronto Star*, October 14. Available at http://lists.econ.utah.edu/pipermail/rad-green/2001-October/001117.html (accessed October 9, 2007).

Lorimer, R., M. Gasher, & D. Skinner. 2008. *Mass Communication in Canada*. 6th ed. Toronto: Oxford University Press.

Media Matters for America. 2005. "The 'Truth' according to Limbaugh: Feminism established 'to allow unattractive women easier access to the mainstream of society.'" August 16. Available at http://mediamatters.org/items/200508160001 (accessed October 4, 2007).

Molgat, A., and J. Grant Cummings. (n.d.) "Herstory." Available at www.nac-cca.ca/about/his_e.htm (accessed August 6, 2007).

Mitchell, A., L.B. Rundle, & L. Karaian. 2001. *Turbo Chicks: Talking Young Feminisms*. Toronto: Sumach Press.

Monsebraaten, L. 1998. "Feminists make room for next generation: Women under 30 seek more power on NAC executive." *Toronto Star*, June 6, A6.

NAWL/ANFD. 2007. National Association of Women and the Law. September 20. "Harper government working to silence women." Available at www.nawl.ca/ns/en/Actions/20070920 Press.html (accessed September 30, 2007).

Petten, A. & L. Jefferson. 1995. "NAC: Issues and Strengths." *Canadian Dimension* 29 (5): 19–21.

Rakow, L. F. & K. Kranich. 1991. "Women as Sign in Television News." *Journal of Communication* 4 (1): 8–23.

Rauhala, A. 1998. "Feminist flagship rocked by feuding." *Globe and Mail*, May 21, D1.

Rebick, J. 2005. *Ten Thousand Roses: The Making of a Feminist Revolution*. Toronto: Penguin Group.

———. 2006. "A nail in the coffin of women's equality?" Rabble.ca, October 16. Available at www.rabble.ca/politics.shtml?sh_itm=55866db5d908c2e8a628bf3e48e6956c&rXn=1& (accessed July 21, 2007).

Rundle, L. 1999. "Who needs NAC? . . . If feminists don't start asking some tough questions . . . we may end up leaving our women's movement in the hands of its critics." *This Magazine* 32 (5): 24–29.

Scott-Dixon, K. 2001. "Girls Need eZines: Young Feminists Get On-line." In *Turbo Chicks: Talking Young Feminisms*, ed. A. Mitchell, L.B. Rundle, and L. Karaian, 302–8. Toronto: Sumach Press.

Shameless Magazine. (n.d.) "About *Shameless*." Available at www.shamelessmag.com/about/ (accessed November 6, 2007).

Stasko, C. 2001. "Action Grrrls in the Dream Machine." In *Turbo Chicks: Talking Young Feminisms*, ed. A. Mitchell, L.B. Rundle, and L. Karaian, 275–83. Toronto: Sumach Press.

Status Report. 2006. "Oda finally confirms termination of HALF of SWC workforce." Statusreport.ca, November 29. Available at www.statusreport.ca/?q=node/96 (accessed September 19, 2007).

Toronto Star. 1988. "Tories want 4 TV debates by party leaders." August 27, A5.

Vickers, J., P. Rankin, & C. Appelle. 1993. *Politics As If Women Mattered: A Political Analysis of the National Action Committee on the Status of Women*. Toronto: University of Toronto Press.

Wente, Margaret. 1995. "The sad decline of NAC." *Globe and Mail*, February 4, A2.

———. 1998. "Completely NACkered." *Globe and Mail*, June 9, A16.

Westell, Anthony. 1970. "Report is more explosive than any terrorists' time bomb." *Toronto Star*, December 8, 13.

Williams, A. 2006. "A Gap in the Movement: Should Young Women Revive Canada's Near-Dead National Feminist Body?" *This Magazine* 39 (5): 18–21.

Williams, R. 1989. *Resources of Hope: Culture, Democracy, Socialism*. Ed. Robin Gable. London: Verso.

Yu, C. 1999. "Dead in name only: The term 'feminism' may be out of fashion, but its attitudes are still alive and kicking." *Alberta Report* 26 (4): 24–26.

Part IV
Wagging the Dog? Media and Public Policy

In the 1997 film *Wag the Dog* (Levinson, 1997), Dustin Hoffman takes on the role of Stanley Motss, a Hollywood film producer hired by the White House to deflect a presidential sex scandal. Motss works with Conrad Brean, played by Robert DeNiro, a tired and cynical Whitehouse spin doctor who needs to protect the president's re-election chances by diverting media attention to a newer and bigger event—a war. Not a real war, but a made-for-television war complete with villains and heroes, victims and martyrs. With the aid of the latest technology, plus a few actors and a film crew, Motss and Brean create and feed the story to the media, even providing a logo and a theme song to define the narrative. DeNiro's character is the ultimate spin doctor, the tail that has the power to wag the media dog with impunity. *Wag the Dog* is obviously a black comedy and in no way depicts reality, but the film makes us uncomfortably aware of how thin the line can be between putting a positive spin on events and concocting out-and-out lies and manipulations.

A *spin doctor* is a media-relations and communications consultant employed by public- or private-sector clients to battle with the press for "control of the dominant media frame" (Fox, 1999, p. 101). Spin doctors present and interpret events and issues to the news media in ways that are designed to "maximize the benefit and minimize the damage to a politician" (Nesbitt-Larking, 2007, p. 337). They are particularly active during election campaigns, but are busy during non-election periods as well. In Canada, there are a number of communications strategists housed in the Prime Minister's Office; these overtly partisan appointees work full-time to control how the media report policy issues of concern to the government and cover government ministers, especially the prime minister. Once a week, the *Hill Times*, a weekly newspaper dedicated to covering the happenings on Parliament Hill, publishes a column called "The Spin Doctors." In the column, media strategists from each of the four major parties react to a question set by the paper, and their responses illustrate the different ways in which the parties are "spinning" the issues. That the media resist partisan interpretations is acknowledged by the spin doctors themselves. One of the Liberal Party's well-known backroom boys, Warren Kinsella, provides expert advice on how to deal with the media in his book *Kicking Ass in Canadian Politics* (2001). Kinsella cautions that spin should be done with some caution as "fancy talk simply won't work" with reporters.[1]

The chapters in this part of the book discuss the struggle for control of mediated political events and issues, examining the roles of both political and media actors in raising the profile of—and framing—public policy issues. The section begins with journalism instructor **Robert Bragg's** confrontations with spin doctors during his tenure at the *Calgary Herald*. Bragg's 26 years of journalism experience include 2 years at CKUA Radio and 24 at the *Calgary Herald*, including 13 years on the *Herald* editorial board as an editorial writer and columnist. As a reporter at the *Herald*, Bragg covered municipal, provincial, and federal politics, and as an editorial writer he specialized in political and social commentary. Since 1999 he has been a member of the Journalism faculty at Mount Royal College's Centre for Communication Studies, teaching courses on journalism, media history, and theories of communication. In Chapter 14, "Encountering Spin: The Evolution of Message Control," Bragg outlines the three-step process used by the spin doctor for former U.S. president Ronald Reagan—"Control the message. Keep it simple. Repeat it, endlessly"—and elaborates this with examples from his experience as a journalist confronting political message control. Bragg argues that the journalist's job of distinguishing truth from deception is becoming increasingly difficult because of media convergence and the increased sophistication of political parties and governments in controlling the media. As a result, media consumers become more cynical about the messages they are being asked to accept. However, Bragg does sound a moderately hopeful note, suggesting that representative (or activist) journalism may have an important role to play in challenging social stereotypes such as misrepresentations of mental illness.

Alasdair Roberts echoes Bragg's concern with media access to political information, detailing the obstacles faced by journalists when they seek information that is unfettered and unfiltered by communications managers. Chapter 15, "Spin Control: The Struggle over Access to Information," outlines the workings of Canada's Access to Information Act (ATIA), which is meant to facilitate media (and citizen) access to government documents. However, Roberts outlines a troubling culture of secrecy by detailing the government tactics for denying or avoiding requests for information from the media. He describes both formal and informal methods of resisting those requests, including changes to bureaucratic practices, manipulation of records, and the rise of an oral culture within the government that makes accessing information much more difficult. Roberts calls for amendments to the ATIA that will create a culture of access, but he is not optimistic about the possibilities for legislative reform or changes to the behaviour of those who control access to government information. One of Roberts's examples is the recalcitrance of officials in Public Works and Government Service Canada to release information relevant to the Gomery Inquiry into the sponsorship scandal; embarrassed by the scandal, officials tagged media requests for documents and subjected them to an intense and deeply politicized approval process.

In Chapter 16, "Framing Gomery in English and French Newspapers: The Use of Strategic and Ethical Frames," **Anne-Marie Gingras**, **Shannon Sampert**, and **David Gagnon-Pelletier** examine the media depiction of the Gomery Commission hearings into the federal government's mismanagement of public funds through the so-called Sponsorship Program, designed in the wake of the 1995 Quebec sovereignty referendum to promote the federal government's visibility through communications initiatives such as event advertising. When an auditor general's report revealed significant mismanagement of public funds, the Prime Minister called a Commission of Inquiry; led by Mr. Justice John Gomery, its public hearings were widely reported in the press and the Gomery Commission became a media event. As Gingras, Sampert, and Gagnon-Pelletier's chapter shows, that news media constructed the sponsorship issue as a "scandal" illustrates journalistic resistance to being "spun" by government. In their coverage of the Commission hearings, journalists displayed their unwillingness to parrot the government's version of events when informing Canadians of the extent and implications of the scandal. This study is unique in Canadian political-communications research because it documents differences in French- and English-Canadian newspaper coverage of an important national-policy issue. The authors reveal that English-language newspapers were more likely to employ a straightforward strategic frame, while French-language papers offered more nuanced and balanced coverage and emphasized the moral and ethical dimensions of the scandal. These differences, argue Gingras, Sampert, and Gagnon-Pelletier, reflect the cultural context within which these media organizations produce the news.

In Chapter 17, "Covering Canada's Role in the 'War on Terror,'" **Yasmin Jiwani** performs a textual analysis of the *Globe and Mail*'s construction of the events following the September 11, 2001 terrorist attacks on the World Trade Center and the United States Pentagon. She suggests that the *Globe* mirrored the approach of American newspapers by deploying binaries of "us" (the U.S. government and its citizens, and, by extension, the "West") versus "them" (the terrorists, or the "Rest"). The nationalistic discourses that emanated from the *Globe* in the first week following the attacks upheld Canada's position as an ally of the United States rather than a potential site of opposition. Moreover, Jiwani argues, Canada's national newspaper uncritically accepted the rise of state power through increased surveillance, detention, and deportation of Muslims and the necessity of security certificates. Jiwani identifies the people and policy choices that were obscured by the dominant narrative and exposes the gendered and racialized assumptions structuring media discourses. In her conclusion, she notes that consumers of news are not easily duped by mainstream representations of the "truth," and citizens turned to other sources of information to understand the events of and after 9/11.

In the film *Wag the Dog*, the spin doctors create a martyr—Sgt. William Schumann, or "good old Shoe"—who is "rescued" from the hands of the alleged terrorists and flown home to the United States for a hero's welcome. Shoe is the subject of the theme song for this fictitious "war on terror," a song that becomes the anthem of the nation, inspiring American teens to lob their old shoes over power lines around the nation. While the power of the state to inspire and cultivate jingoistic patriotism is parodied in the film and finds echoes in Canadian news mediations of politics, the chapters in this section show that media and citizens have the capacity to interrogate, contest, and resist the official versions of policy issues and events.

Endnote

1. Or, in the words of one of the politicians Kinsella quotes in the book, "You can't shine shit" (Kinsella, 2001, p. 193).

References

Fox, Bill. 1999. *Spinwars: Politics and New Media*. Toronto: Key Porter Books.
Kinsella, Warren. 2001. *Kicking Ass in Canadian Politics*. Toronto: Random House Canada.
Levinson, Barry. 1997. *Wag The Dog*. New Line Cinema.
Nesbitt-Larking, Paul. 2007. *Politics, Society and the Media*. 2nd ed. Peterborough: Broadview Press.

Chapter 14

Encountering Spin: The Evolution of Message Control

Robert Bragg

INTRODUCTION

> Control the message.
>
> Keep it simple.
>
> Repeat it, endlessly. (Starowicz, 1995)

It's a succinct, three-step formula articulated best by William "Bill" Deaver, former U.S. president Ronald Reagan's media advisor. Deaver was the man who worked closely with B-movie star Reagan to help transform him, first into the Governor of California, and ultimately into the president best known as "the Great Communicator." In a 1995 interview, Deaver was clear about his role and how he viewed the media, especially U.S. network television:

> If I produced good television, the [networks] loved it. If I gave them a picture that was entertaining, attractive, amusing, dramatic, I'd make the evening news every night. I did their work for them. (Starowicz, 1995)

Visually attractive staging, irresistible to television, helped convey simple messages within the context of an overall information strategy. These were the essential elements of Deaver's approach. "It was having a strategy, and the media didn't have a strategy," Deaver said. Its success in setting the news agenda and in reinforcing Reagan's popular image as the "Great Communicator" meant it soon became a widely imitated approach for politicians to take toward journalists. It was seized on and consciously implemented by the Progressive Conservatives in their Canadian federal election campaign of 1988, for example (Starowicz, 1995).

Of Deaver's three steps, the first—Control the Message—is the most difficult for people who work in media, whether they are journalists, public relations workers, politicians, celebrities, or, as sometimes happens, ordinary working people. To whoever is involved in the daily workings of the media in whatever capacity, the issue of message control is fundamental. In the practice of journalism this involves, but is not limited to, "news judgment"—choosing what is, and what is not, newsworthy. It also includes the pressures for and against hyping, highlighting, downplaying, ignoring, or suppressing particular messages or sets of messages, also known as agendas.

When I began addressing this issue with young would-be journalists in my classes at Mount Royal College, it forced me to reflect on my years as a journalist, to re-examine my personal career history in light of some of the larger news events and historical happenings that created the context within which I worked. I began my career in 1965 reporting for a campus newspaper, the *Gauntlet*, at the University of Calgary, and later, the University of Alberta's *Gateway*. I also spent a couple of postgraduate years in Alberta public broadcasting as an announcer-producer for the province-wide radio network CKUA. However, the bulk of my work as a journalist was performed for the *Calgary Herald*.[1] For the *Herald* I covered beats such as city hall, the provincial government, and federal politics before joining the *Herald* editorial board, an assignment that included the privilege of writing a personal column.

My professional journalism career extended from 1973 to 1999, from the mid–Cold War era to well beyond into the days of postmodernism and the dot-com bubble. A lot of news has come and gone, from Watergate to the World Wide Web. News media have expanded, proliferated, transformed, mutated, and fragmented in various ways. What rough beast is now slouching toward (or away from) what some might call "reality" is anyone's guess. As the late James W. Carey, professor emeritus at Columbia University's School of Journalism, put it, "Reality is up for grabs" (Carey, 1989, p. 25). And a key reason reality itself is now problematic—"up for grabs"—and why journalists are caught in the mega-scrum to find out and report on often very elusive and confusing situations is because of the struggle to "control the message." Journalists now, more than ever before, are at the centre of that struggle.

In undemocratic environments, where force of arms is a first resort for political rulers rather than rule of law, the importance of journalists in this reality-defining process is quickly established. What is a first order of business for any dictator—whether long established or newly minted? Suppression of an independent press. Shooting the messenger. Ask journalists in Mexico, Nigeria, the Philippines, or Russia (Committee to Protect Journalists, 2007) if they are seen as a threat to the powers that be. The answer is obvious. It's not quite so obvious in our media-rich, open society, yet the issue presents itself here as well: but rather than soldiers, secret police, public fiats, television-station takeovers, jailings, bannings, disappearances, assassinations, and executions, the methods for controlling the message here are relatively subtle and multi-faceted. In Canada and the United States, message control involves a struggle over the message itself, rather than the bodies and lives of working journalists.

From my own history, I can draw examples that help trace the evolution of what have today become sophisticated methods of exerting message control, maintaining message control, and extending message control into a larger exercise of power within our democratic society. I would argue that such methods have evolved over the past several decades from observed successes and failures in message control, including creating a myth as a way of insuring a particular ongoing interpretation of an issue; avoiding conflicting signals by staying "on message"; changing the subject to avoid discussion of difficult or uncomfortably controversial issues; and realizing the enduring power of stigma and stereotype. These are methods I encountered in my work as a journalist—encounters that revealed early versions of what have evolved into a repertoire of deliberate, systematic message-control procedures used daily as key ways communications advisers, bureaucrats, and politicians seek control over what the public sees, hears, and understands. The cases that follow are prototypical of some, not all, of the message-control methods now deployed in the media arena.

CASE 1: CREATE A MYTH

State of the News Media 2010:
1. Internet
   - Originators
   - Aggregators
   - Commentators/Opinion
2. **Civic Journalism**: the practice "is both a philosophy and a set of values supported by some evolving techniques to reflect both of those in journalism. At its heart is a belief that journalism has an obligation to public life – an obligation that goes beyond just telling the news or unloading lots of facts. The way we do our journalism affects the way public life goes aka done by pro journalists
3. **Advocacy Journalism**: that intentionally and transparently adopts a non-objective viewpoint, usually for some social or political purpose. Because it is intended to be factual, it is distinguished from propaganda. Meaning, it write journals and editorial pages advocating or criticizing and in favour of certain things
4. **Gonzo Journalism**: is a style of journalism that is written without claims of objectivity, often including the reporter as part of the story via a first-person narrative. Written subjectively and often including the report in the story
5. **Checkbook Journalism**: is the form of journalism where the essential characteristic is that the journalist pays the subject of the work money for the right to publish his story. Meaning, pay people to tell their story
6. **Parachute Journalism**: the practice thrusting journalists into an area to report on a story in which the reporter has little knowledge or experience. The lack of knowledge and tight deadlines often result in inaccurate or distorted news reports, especially during breaking news. Meaning, put them in a country in a short time and get them to tell their story

Western Canadian economy, federal ignorance of Alberta's point of view, and callous, if not quite malevolent, disregard for the well-being of Westerners generally. In Alberta, "the NEP" became a key term for controlling the parameters of public debate. By repeating it endlessly, alternative interpretations were suppressed while the salient message—that Ottawa and, by extension, Central Canada would never be trusted—was pounded home.

In fact, the NEP in retrospect was a political move in a complex game that played out between Ottawa and Alberta during the 1970s and early 1980s. The driving force was the rapidly rising international price of oil, pushed upward by the Organization of Petroleum Exporting Countries (OPEC) cartel. Sharp price increases in 1973 and again in 1979 had sparked oil booms in resource-rich Alberta and near-recession conditions in manufacturing-based, oil-dependent Eastern Canada. The political fallout automatically pitted the vote-rich East against the oil-rich West.

The political antagonism was further clarified with the rise and fall of Joe Clark's short-lived minority Progressive Conservative government. Clark's government fell in 1980 over a budget proposing oil and gasoline price hikes. The victorious Trudeau government's first post-Clark budget included the NEP. The political position of the Lougheed government made eminent sense as a bargaining position. What was in question was the severity of the Alberta response, which not only stigmatized the NEP as a policy, but alleged that it was tampering with the fundamental rights of the province over its own resources. By repeatedly characterizing the NEP as a "takeover," Alberta's leading politicians and media not only attacked the substance of the policy but created the conditions for a suspicion of Confederation itself. It was not surprising to see an upsurge in Western separatist sentiments in the wake of the campaign against the NEP. "A poll conducted in 1981 showed that forty-nine percent of Albertans supported separation from Canada" (University of Calgary, 2007).

The clarity of public debate on oil-economy questions was further muddied by the global recession of 1982, when soaring interest rates and a complex host of factors led to the collapse of Alberta's boom. The economic hardships suddenly inflicted on Alberta were conveniently, if inaccurately, all attributed to the National Energy Program rather than to the more difficult to understand but crucially important effects of international economic conditions (University of Calgary, 2007).

In fact, Lougheed and Trudeau had reached a rapprochement on the policy by September 1981, when the two leaders signed off on an agreement on a modified NEP. The severe global recession the following year hit the oil economy worldwide. The collapse in Texas was as bad as that in Alberta. It had much more to do with the global oil surplus, sparked again by OPEC's expanded production plus a spate of new oil discoveries. The downward spike in Alberta was tracking the world economy more than responding to a made-in-Ottawa energy policy.

By 1987 in Alberta the NEP had taken on the status of unquestionable myth—shorthand for all the ills the "feds" could foist on the province. Despite the election of a federal Progressive Conservative government in 1984 and a subsequent rollback of many NEP provisions, the NEP was still regarded as the mechanism by which the province was systematically robbed of "foregone revenues" of billions of dollars. On April 12, 1987, my *Herald* column noted that Trudeau and Lougheed had indeed hoisted champagne glasses in a classic photo op in honour of their 1981 negotiated agreement to a modified NEP.

I was arguing that, despite this agreement, the myth of the NEP and the evil federal government remained strong in Alberta in defiance of the facts. The 1984 advent of a Tory government that abolished the NEP and established the world oil price for Alberta crude had failed to dent the myth of Alberta as victim of the NEP. According to the myth, "Ottawa is responsible for the world grain surplus, the fracturing of OPEC and the subsequent collapse of world oil prices" (Bragg, *Calgary Herald*, April 12, 1987, p. A4).

My assertion that Lougheed had agreed to the NEP in September 1981 was met with a long, detailed April 23 Letter to the Editor from former Alberta energy minister Merv Leitch, who, on behalf of Lougheed, asserted that what had been agreed to in September 1981 had "resulted in substantial changes in the NEP to the benefit of Albertans" (Leitch, *Calgary Herald*, April 23, 1986, p. A6). He claimed that my assertion to the contrary was simply untrue. Such heavyweight response to my column showed me how the myth served to underpin the provincial political agenda. Although my column had little ripple effect, it reconfirmed the mythical status of the National Energy Program as the culprit in Alberta's economic collapse of 1982. To this day it retains a tremendous power to invoke the spectre of federal interference in the "free-market" economy of once-again-booming Alberta.[3] As Halloween tricks go, the NEP still has the status of a frightening mask.

CASE 2: CONTROL THE MESSAGE
Brian Mulroney is Running for Leadership of the Progressive Conservative Party
1983

I first encountered Brian Mulroney in late April 1983 when he was in the thick of a 12-candidate race for leadership of the federal Progressive Conservative Party. The 44-year-old Montreal lawyer had flown into Calgary in search of delegate support, to spread his message, and to turn on his considerable charm in the heart of the West. As one of the race's front-runners, Mulroney had at last come to the home province of his chief rival, Joe Clark—the image-challenged Tory leader who was nevertheless widely perceived as the man to beat.

Mulroney had lost once to Clark in the 1976 leadership race, and was subsequently seen by many as a key instigator of the anti-Clark faction within the PCs—the faction that stubbornly refused to endorse Clark's leadership during the 1982 convention review. Clark's failure to receive the self-designated target of two-thirds of the delegates in that review (he fell 1 percent shy) prompted his decision to gamble on a leadership race as a way to ultimately unite the Tories and then defeat the hated Liberals.

By April 1983, that race was in full swing. Mulroney and Clark were locked in a nationwide battle for delegates—the designated official electors who would gather in convention in June in Ottawa to pick the person with the best chance of defeating the long-ruling but increasingly fatigued Grits in the next federal election. For Brian Mulroney, in the spring of 1983, the universe, at least his corner of it in federal Canadian Tory circles, appeared to be unfolding as it should. But that did not mean that there was not still work to be done. For Mulroney, that work included finding ways to win the support of Western Tories, despite being a lawyer from Quebec. To do that, Mulroney chose to go on the offensive against Clark in Alberta. To avoid sounding as though he was from head office on a disciplinary visit to the Calgary branch of the party, he used Quebec itself as his key.

Choosing Calgary as the venue for laying into Clark over the controversial delegate selection battles then raging in Quebec was a clever way to kill two birds with one diatribe. My report in the next day's *Herald* said, "Brian Mulroney attacked Joe Clark Thursday for accepting support from Quebec separatists in his Tory leadership campaign." By such a blatant tactic Mulroney got to distance himself literally and figuratively from his own ties to Quebec sovereignists. "You don't get to be leader of this country by playing footsie with the Parti Québécois," Mulroney said, denying in the next breath that any PQ members were working on his campaign, as Clark had asserted earlier that week (Bragg, *Calgary Herald*, April 29, 1983, p. A1). Mulroney painted Clark as a desperate and disruptive opportunist, unfit to lead a national party, much less the country.

On the positive side, Mulroney portrayed himself as a latter-day Sir John A. Macdonald—the Tory of the old school who would unite the party and the country through an alliance of the East (Ontario and Quebec) with the West (Alberta et al.). He told a Calgary audience of 800 curious Tories that he wanted to revive Sir John A.'s "grand alliance" of French and English, of East and West, to prevail in the election and prevent the party from becoming "doomed to opposition" (Bragg, *Calgary Herald*, April 29, 1983, p. A1). To that end, Mulroney claimed that he himself offered the best chance of winning seats in Quebec—in stark contrast to the Clark-led Tories' humiliating 1980 election defeat, which saw the PCs elect only one Quebec MP.

At his ensuing press conference, Mulroney claimed to have twice as many Quebec delegates as Clark (none of them with PQ ties, of course), and then, in what became in hindsight an ironical statement, Mulroney condemned Clark for pledging to negotiate on power-sharing with the provinces and promising compensation to Quebec if it chose to opt out of future constitutional amendments (Bragg, *Calgary Herald*, April 29, 1983, p. A1).

So far, so good. The future Tory leader, and future two-term majority prime minister, had presented a professional political face to Calgary Tories. He had delivered clear messages that simultaneously undercut his opponent and displayed his own positive attributes—his ability to win in Quebec, his telegenic personal appearance, his articulate public-speaking style, and his ability to come across as an all-around charming person. Clark, in contrast, had been painted as a loser desperately and irresponsibly seeking separatist support in Quebec to cling to power in Ottawa.

In that same press conference, however, Mulroney showed his quirky ability to undermine his own position by forgetting to stay on the message. It happened in an instant when a female journalist stood to ask a question about Mulroney's position regarding women's rights. Perhaps it was Calgary's high altitude, or perhaps it was simply Mulroney's urge to show off his informal charm, but, whatever the cause, his response was certainly one that a candidate's media trainer in today's world of message control would certainly have coached against.

Instead of dealing respectfully and directly with the question, Mulroney leapt off his message track and invited the reporter for a drink to discuss the question privately. The innuendo did not go unnoticed. News accounts the next day—print and broadcast—highlighted Mulroney's gaffe. It gained as much attention as his attack on Clark—his allegations of separatist influence in his chief rival. It distracted from his promise to deliver Quebec to the Tories while raising an uncomfortable question about his ability to handle politically and culturally sensitive issues.

In a few seconds of glibness Mulroney had jeopardized his carefully delivered campaign message. By going "off message" he came close to turning his successful mission into a failure, and, in hindsight, foreshadowed the loose-cannon aspect of his personality that would later land him, as prime minister, in political hot water.[4]

Despite such a stumble, Mulroney went on to win the leadership race and the subsequent 1984 federal election—the first of his back-to-back majorities. And there were times when Brian Mulroney's ability to change the course of a line of media enquiry actually helped him sell his policies to the Canadian public. Consider, for instance, the 1988 "free trade election."

CASE 3: WHEN IN DOUBT, CHANGE THE SUBJECT
Brian Mulroney and the Free Trade Election
1988

The federal election of 1988 was ostensibly fought on the issue of free trade. The incumbent Tories, under Prime Minister Brian Mulroney, were in favour of a negotiated agreement with the United States in the form of a free trade agreement (FTA). The Liberals and NDP were opposed. The clearly drawn battle lines on the federal political stage were equally apparent in the alignment of various political pressure groups from professional lobbyists to outspoken gadflies such as *Canadian Encyclopedia* publisher Mel Hurtig. On the pro-FTA side were the Business Council on National Issues, the Canadian Manufacturers Association, the C.D. Howe Institute, and the Fraser Institute. On the anti-FTA side stood the likes of the Council of Canadians, the National Farmers Union, and the Canadian Labour Congress.

The "free trade election" in the fall of that year revealed the deep and complex relationship between Canada and the United States. Opponents of the FTA condemned the pact (negotiated in 1987 and set to come into effect in 1989) as a sell-out that would tie Canada much more closely to the American economy, society, and culture. They argued it would permanently cement our dependency and ratify our colonial status in North America. Proponents, on the other hand, painted glowing pictures (in well-financed promotional campaigns) of Canada's rising trade and export opportunities, the assertion that "Canadians are ready to compete" with American businesses for lucrative continental trade opportunities.

During the election campaign, the voices pro and con escalated as the November voting day approached. The federal Liberals, under leader John Turner, deplored the deal and drew a stark picture, epitomized in a television "attack ad" showing the eager hand of the Tories using a pencil to literally erase the forty-ninth parallel on a map of North America. In that scenario, Canada literally disappeared. Polls found the Tories hard-pressed to close the sale on the FTA. The majority of Canadians weren't buying into it. As the leading salesman for the deal and the man with the majority government at stake, Mulroney had the most to lose. To win the crucial vote, the Tories decided to adjust their media strategy.

I got a taste of this in miniature when the Prime Minister came to call at the *Herald* editorial board. As one of the editorialists assigned to the FTA issue, I had generally tended to criticize the pact as a bit too much of a pig in the poke. I had attempted to maintain objectivity and avoid oversimplifying a complicated economic and political trade agreement. It proved challenging for journalists and the general public to keep the issue's pros and cons in perspective; this was particularly true during an election campaign, when views are easily polarized. By the time Mulroney arrived in Calgary, I had more questions (for both sides) than convincing answers from either. The smoke and mirrors were, as often happens in elections, clouding rather than clarifying the genuine issues of true concern to the public.

On the day of the Prime Minister's noon-hour visit, after the usual security clearance, police inspections, sniffer-dog walk-throughs, etc., Mulroney and a few aides settled comfortably into the plush chairs of the *Herald* boardroom to chat with assembled reporters, photographers, and editorialists. A light lunch awaited the PM's dining pleasure. Coffee and the "good china" were on display on the sideboard. Mulroney was asked, "Would you like a sandwich?" to which he replied "No thanks . . . perhaps later, thank you." Mulroney, charming as ever, politely declined any food. Instead, the assembled, increasingly hungry gathering held a polite but platitudinous 25-minute discussion. Soft questions about the West, Quebec's aspirations, and the prospects of another majority were fielded, as the publisher, the editor-in-chief, editorial board members, and reporters took turns asking the Prime Minister for his quotable views.

This delayed my task—to ask at least one free trade agreement question. I wanted to ask about the current issue raised by free trade opponents charging that Canada would face heavy pressure under the agreement to "harmonize" our social programs, such as medicare and welfare programs, with the United States in order to "level the playing field" in terms of economic competition. It was not a tough question but I never got a chance to ask it. Just as my turn to ask a question arrived, as I cleared my throat and opened my mouth, the Prime Minister, ever polite, interrupted, "I'll take that sandwich now."

As if on cue, the hungry crowd at the table acted as if they had been given a licence to stand in unison to take a break for something to eat. The press portion of the meeting quickly dissolved into small talk; lunch was served. The crowd in the room converged on the side table to fill plates with sandwiches, fill cups with coffee, and take a break. Ten minutes later, sandwich tucked away, the Prime Minister's handlers announced that his tight schedule meant Mulroney must be moving to his next stop—a busy road trip for the PM, you see. The issue of the free trade agreement was not going to dominate the *Herald*'s version of his visit. My impression at the time, one I still believe, is that Mulroney had a deliberate strategy to play down, and, if possible, avoid the FTA as a topic. He would also have known from whom questions on that topic would likely come and so used his visit to stay with topics that would highlight his leadership skills and charming manner and, incidentally, put free trade off the discussion agenda. I think he timed the lunch break to aid in this strategy, which was also made easier by the formal trappings of such a prime ministerial visit to an editorial board. It meant that the meeting was not so much a press conference (although news would be generated simply by the fact of Mulroney's visit to the *Herald*) as it was a state visit in miniature, combined with a photo opportunity. It meant the room was crowded with *Herald* executives as well as news gatherers, with handlers and briefers as well as photographers and security. Persistent questioning on a specific topic was virtually impossible; questioners instead strove to show respect for the man and his high office.

This vignette also shows, in miniature, the shifting Tory election strategy with respect to the FTA. As the polls at that time showed "no sale" on free trade, then ducking the question and changing the subject to a more promising issue made good political sense. The Tories won the "free trade" election essentially by deciding *not* to talk about free trade, and to highlight instead the skills of their charming leader.

By December 1988 Mulroney had his new majority safely in hand. The FTA would soon become law. In a post-election analysis, I discovered that the advertising agency that had advised the Tories on strategy had deliberately turned the focus from the FTA (where the Grits were strong and gaining on their pro-Canada, anti-FTA platform) to the question of leadership (where Mulroney compared favourably in the polls with the stumble-prone Liberal leader John Turner).[5] In other words, the secret to Tory success with the public was: *Change the subject*. That meant moving away from the FTA issue and training their sights on a different, more vulnerable, target. It meant attacking the leadership skills of John Turner and comparing them with the skill of the country's current prime minister. Polls showed the Grits were weaker than the Tories on leadership questions, despite having the best of it in opposing the FTA. Changing the subject worked to deflect the issue—not only in the *Herald* boardroom but in determining the outcome of the 1988 federal election. By not focusing on the FTA, by changing the subject, Mulroney won the election and made sure the deal went through.

CASE 4: OPENING THE DOORS ON MEDIA AND THE POWER OF STIGMA

The World Psychiatric Association's Fight against the Stigma of Schizophrenia

In the summer of 1997, I engaged in a form of advocacy journalism that departed from traditional "objective" reportage common to daily newspapers at the time. My stories were part of my participation in a two-year "Open the Doors" project organized and funded by the World Psychiatric Association (WPA) and psychiatrists at the University of Calgary's medical school. It engaged a range of medical and mental-health professionals, health activists, caregivers, communications specialists, a Chicago-based ad agency, and, at the centre of the action, "consumer/survivors"—that is, people with schizophrenia.

The project, fundamentally a communications endeavour, aimed to tackle the complex and contradictory problem of the stigma of mental illness (specifically schizophrenia). Every time the adjective "schizophrenic" is used it dehumanizes persons with the illness. The adjective "schizoid" is equally pejorative. Adding to the confusion, these terms are often used colloquially to describe an average person attempting to cope with intellectual or emotional contradictions (being of two minds = schizophrenic) rather than someone dealing with the complex set of mental conditions that characterize schizophrenia in the medical sense. On a more profound level, conflict-hungry news media tend to report sensational or conflict-centred stories that consistently associate schizophrenia (and other mental illnesses) with violent, bizarre, erratic behaviour. Success stories involving consumers, survivors, treatments, medications, or therapies find little space in the mainstream media. This is the stigma attached to the condition of schizophrenia. Media portrayals of schizophrenia—trivializing colloquialisms, sensationalist focus on violence, insensitive dehumanization—convey, recapitulate, and reinforce this stigma (Wahl, 2003, p. ix).

Such mediated stigma makes it that much more difficult to organize support, raise awareness, drum up research funding, and conduct scientific medical research into the illness. In turn, this makes it a major challenge to clear away the misconceptions to establish solid medical, research-based knowledge about the illness. Stigmas reflect fear and ignorance. Fear and ignorance prevent research, and lack of research permits the conditions for fear and ignorance to continue. And the circle goes round and round. It was this vicious circle that sparked the World Psychiatric Association campaign to attempt to reduce stigma, raise awareness, and, in the long run, make it easier to raise support, inspire and fund research, and improve the medical and social conditions under which people with schizophrenia now live.

As an editorial writer for the *Herald* for the previous decade, I had been writing opinion pieces and news analyses for years, but had never taken what could be described as an "engaged" stand on any issue. I had never gone beyond expressing a personal bias in an opinion column or endorsing the corporate editorial stands taken on behalf of the

Herald. These latter unsigned items on the editorial page were (and still are) considered the official voice and position of the *Calgary Herald*.[6]

From this background it was for me then a significant step out of character to take on the role of a *"representative journalist"* in a public project involving a variety of representative groups as well as an advertising agency. It was a challenging exercise and experience for a journalist schooled in the "don't-join-parties-don't-sign petitions" ways of the craft to become personally engaged in not only describing and advocating for change but attempting to develop a media strategy that would help effect change. Is this how journalists move into public relations, or was I still practising journalism? This question kept cropping up as I got deeper into the project.

My engagement was on two levels. One was as a journalist, writing stories and analyses of schizophrenia and its accompanying stigma. I wanted to humanize the illness, bring it into perspective, and explain the issues involving its onset and treatment. Here I felt comfortable, doing what I had traditionally done, attempting to write as accurately and fairly as possible about a significant social issue. On another level, I played the role of media representative, contributing my insights as a journalist practitioner to the effort to develop a strategy for combating, or even dispelling, mediated stigma. On this front I was swimming in unknown waters. I found myself drifting toward some kind of communications-consulting role, which had a disconcerting effect on my view of myself as a journalist, but which may have, in the long run, improved my work because it improved my awareness of the impact my chosen career can have on people.

The "Open the Doors" project was included in an analysis of media portrayals of mental illness done in 2005 by Soraya Roberts for the *Ryerson Review of Journalism* (Roberts, 2005). Her story, "Lost in Translation," references the 1995–97 anti-stigma campaign, including "surveying the *Calgary Herald's* coverage of mental illness for the duration of 18 months" as well as providing journalists with "in-depth information on mental illness ... and exposure to patients, then record[ing] how the coverage changed." As I told Soraya when we discussed the campaign, our "view was that media weren't going to change unless they got feedback. A way to do that is on a case-by-case basis over time, responding to the negative and positive" (Roberts, 2005).

As the *Ryerson Review of Journalism* reported, the Calgary World Psychiatric Association campaign showed modestly positive results: "News stories—accurate descriptions of diagnoses, profiles of people with mental illnesses, and human-interest pieces—increased in number, and the quality of reporting also improved." This proved to be short-lived, however. As the report indicated, "a series of highly charged cases—a shooting on Parliament Hill in Ottawa, subway-pushing cases in Toronto and New York, and the Prime Minister (Jean Chrétien) being attacked by a man with schizophrenia—hit the headlines and the *Herald's* coverage regressed to its previously stigmatizing form" (Roberts, 2005). Dishearteningly, the results were short-term, localized, and, seemingly, erased the instant a high-profile act of violence occurred that involved a person with schizophrenia. The stigma remains entrenched and thus news coverage requires constant vigilance from the people who are most impacted by it to attempt to give the media feedback on the ways it reinforces this vicious cycle.

CONCLUSION

Since these events took place, the process of message control has become much more sophisticated and more consciously directed. It has penetrated the practices and procedures of every level of politics, from school boards to the Prime Minister's Office. The rise of "spin," along with the advent of communications consultants and media training, shows the response from the political half of the equation. On the media side, journalists face an accelerated scramble for ratings and readers in a 24/7 globalized news world. Because large audiences can no longer be easily assembled in a mosaic of cable, online, broadcast, satellite, and print media, there is a tendency to emphasize impact and sensation over content and importance. The result tends to skew news coverage toward the visually compelling and dramatically engaging. If these elements are lacking, it becomes tempting for competing news outlets to manufacture them in order to hook audiences.

In a parallel development, the business of advertising has been struggling to rise above its own "clutter" in the multi-channel, multi-media environment. The Catch-22 problem remains: to find a way out of the clutter invariably involves creating more clutter. Recent gimmicks include trucks loaded with billboard scrolls, electronic video billboards, and ubiquitous product placement in television programming and Hollywood films. People who go out to the movies have to sit through 20 minutes of commercials in advance of the movie. Now there are reports of paid "word-of-mouth" campaigns, where people are hired to promote products to their friends and acquaintances without disclosing their sponsorship arrangement. (Walker, 2004, p. 68)

To look back on the past quarter century, from my perspective, is to look back on a simpler, less controlled time—a time when journalists had more control over the gathering and dissemination of news. It was also a time before "convergence," when clear distinctions could be made between print and broadcast journalism. Today, I see many contenders for control over those message(s) that regularly attract public attention. I see a spectrum of contenders vying with journalists for that control—from ad agencies to media advisers to politicians and wannabe journalists, including bloggers, vanity-press authors, and people who pose as journalists—from police to fabricators.[7]

Ironically, most of these contenders want their particular message to look like news. They want it presented "as if" it were a factual, fair, and accurate account of their specific event, issue, or product. This is revealed in the form their messages take—advertorial, false news, fabricated stories, planted stories, or strategic leaks to select outlets. This tampers irresponsibly with the foundations of effective communication. To undermine, parody, plagiarize, manufacture, or fabricate that which makes news news (accuracy, credibility, balance) is to call into question almost every message within the news field. When the lines are thoroughly blurred between news, commentary, advertising, spin, and propaganda, then the public will react with its usual common sense and take everything, including the genuine article, with a grain of salt. This serves no one's interest. It will make it extremely difficult for governors to govern, for politicians to maintain the confidence of the public, and for journalists to maintain their credibility for providing useful, timely, and true information.

Endnotes

1. The *Calgary Herald* is a major daily newspaper in Canada. Its daily circulation weekdays in the 1980s averaged approximately 140,000.

2. Front-page editorials stand out in contrast to the usual editorial-page location for the official opinion of the newspaper. Putting this editorial on the front page signalled the critical nature of the NEP in the eyes of *Herald* editors.

3. See, for example, http://Calgarygrit.blogspot.com and http://freeAlberta.com for continuing rancorous references to the NEP.

4. Mulroney's media handlers were appalled in 1990 when he told *Globe and Mail* reporters that he was prepared to "roll the dice" with the nation's constitution to push through the Meech Lake Accord, which would have recognized Quebec as a "distinct society."

5. "Our guy (Mulroney) showed up (in the polls) as more popular than their guy (Turner)." Personal interview with a representative of the PC Party's Toronto-based ad agency, December 1988, Toronto.

6. Unsigned editorials are a journalistic conceit of mainstream English-language dailies in the U.K., the United States, and Canada. French-language newspapers, such as Montreal's *La Presse* or *Le Soleil* in Quebec City, carry similar institutional editorials but they are signed by the writer, often including a photo byline. As such, they take on a different, more personal, emphasis than the faceless formal editorial positions adopted by the *Globe and Mail*, the *Vancouver Sun*, or, my case, the *Calgary Herald*.

7. For example, Jayson Blair, the *New York Times* reporter, was exposed and fired in 2003 for making up stories, faking deadlines, and plagiarizing on a massive scale (Mnookin, 2004).

References

Bragg, Bob. 1980, 1981, 1983, 1988, 1995, 1997. *Calgary Herald*, Author's Byline Files.

Calgary Grit. Available at http://Calgarygrit.blogspot.com (accessed June 11, 2007).

Carey, James W. 1989. "A Cultural Approach to Communication." In *Communication as Culture: Essays on Media and Society*, ed. James W. Carey, 13–36. Boston: Unwin Hyman.

Committee to Protect Journalists. 2007. Available at www.cpj.org/killed/killed_archives/stats.html (accessed June 11, 2007).

Free Alberta. Available at http://freeAlberta.com(accessed June 10, 2007).

Mnookin, Seth. 2004. *Hard News: The Scandals at the "New York Times" and Their Meaning for American Media*. Random House.

Roberts, Soroya. 2005. "Lost in Translation." *Ryerson Review of Journalism*, March. Available at www.rrj.ca/print/539/ (accessed March 23, 2007).

Starowicz, Mark, executive producer. 1995. *Dawn of the Eye: The History of Film and TV News*, part 5, *The Electronic Battalions: 1975–1988*. Films for the Humanities and Sciences. CBC TV in association with the BBC and the History Channel.

University of Calgary. Applied History Research Group. Available at www.ucalgary.ca/applied history/tutor/calgary/energycrisis.html (accessed June 11, 2007).

Wahl, Otto F. 2003. *Media Madness: Public Images of Mental Illness*. 2nd ed. New Brunswick, N.J.: Rutgers University Press.

Walker, Rob. 2004. "The Hidden (in Plain Sight) Persuaders." *New York Times Magazine*, September 2004, 68–72.

Chapter 15
Spin Control: The Struggle over Access to Information

Alasdair Roberts

INTRODUCTION

Canada's Access to Information Act (ATIA) came into effect in 1983 (R.S.C. 1985, at c. A-1). The law recognizes the right of Canadians to obtain information from government institutions.[1] It establishes the procedures that must be followed in processing a request for information, including deadlines for response, and enumerates the conditions under which institutions are justified in withholding information. The law also created a new authority, the Information Commissioner, to investigate complaints about non-compliance with its requirements. If the Commissioner decides that a government institution has improperly denied a request for information and the institution continues to balk at disclosure, a remedy can be pursued in the Federal Court of Canada.

Before adoption, it was anticipated that federal institutions might receive about 100,000 requests for information under the ATIA every year (J. Roberts, 2001, pp. 32–33). This was a substantial overestimation of demand. Although the volume of requests has increased by about 7 percent per year, by 2005 the total number received was still only 25,207 (Figure 15.1). This total comprises several separate "information streams." The largest stream consists of requests from businesses, typically seeking information about inspection, regulation, and licensing activities, or about governmental procurement of goods and services (Table 15.1). The "information stream" generated by media requests is smaller and quite distinct. The plurality of these requests seek information about policy development and research, are more likely to receive broad public attention, and are almost always believed by officials to pose political risks for the government. Forming a similarly small but sensitive category of requests are those filed by opposition political parties. The volume is difficult to gauge because federal institutions do not distinguish such "partisan" requests in public reports (although they do internally). Perhaps 5 to 10 percent of all ATIA requests are partisan, although in some institutions the proportion can be substantially higher.

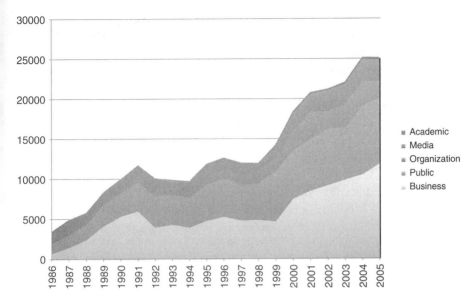

Figure 15.1 Number of Requests Filed by Source, 1986–2005

Based on data contained in annual reports filed by federal institutions under Section 72 of the Access to Information Act and tabulated by the Treasury Board Secretariat.

Table 15.1

	Business	Media	Org.	Other	ALL
Personnel management	1%	3%	4%	11%	5%
Procurement	32%	6%	21%	4%	17%
Budgeting & financial control	7%	12%	15%	12%	11%
Grants & contributions	2%	8%	17%	5%	6%
Inspection, regulation, & licensing	37%	13%	6%	14%	21%
Policing, criminal prosecutions, & corrections	4%	13%	3%	13%	8%
Research & policy development	5%	24%	21%	8%	11%
Other	12%	21%	14%	32%	20%
ALL	100%	100%	100%	100%	100%

Summing to 100 percent by source of request (Business, Media, Organization, Other). Based on an analysis of a sample of 663 ATIA requests drawn randomly from a list of requests received by federal institutions and logged in the Coordination of Access to Information Requests System (CAIRS) in 1999.[2]

By adopting the ATIA, Canada put itself in the vanguard of an international movement. Before 1982, only five other countries had adopted similar laws; today the total is almost 70 (Banisar, 2006, p. 6). In the intervening years, Canada was often looked to as a model of good practice—and with justification. Canada took the implementation of its disclosure law seriously, while many other countries did not. It created special offices to manage the inflow of requests, staffed these offices with trained professionals, and developed formal procedures to encourage prompt processing. At the same time, the Information Commissioner provided an easily accessible remedy in cases of maladministration. In many respects, the Canadian practice is superior to practice under the U.S. Freedom of Information Act (FOIA)—although the popular conception is often the reverse—and also superior to emerging practice under the more recently drafted U.K. FOIA.

However, the Canadian law is not without its problems. Indeed, it might be said to be in the vanguard in a second sense—as an illustration of difficulties that beset a mature access regime. One of the most serious of these difficulties is the growth of adversarialism in the administration of disclosure laws like the ATIA. Advocates of disclosure laws have underestimated the extent to which the conflict over government records is often precisely that—a *conflict*, precipitated by the clash of sharply opposed interests.

Disclosure laws regulate this conflict, and aim to change the terms of engagement in favour of non-governmental actors, but they cannot bring an end to conflict itself. On the contrary, government officials and non-governmental actors become increasingly adept at developing strategies that exploit or blunt the opportunities created by the law. There is no guarantee, of course, that the balance of forces will be preserved over time; one side may prove more skilled at developing new strategies than the other. Evidence suggests that departments and agencies in the federal government have developed techniques for managing sensitive requests that now undercut basic principles of the ATIA.

This chapter describes the various ways in which government agencies attempt to resist requests for information made by journalists and other citizens. It also explains why government officials engage in these kinds of resistance. It concludes by considering how much a law like Canada's Access to Information Act can actually achieve in terms of improving governmental transparency.

MODES OF RESISTANCE

The ATIA was launched with great expectations about its effect on the shape of Canadian governance. "This legislation," predicted Justice Minister Francis Fox in 1980, "will, over time, become one of the cornerstones of Canadian democracy." Fox anticipated that the law would "bring about a very major change of thinking within government":

> Simply put, the bill reverses the present situation whereby access to information is a matter of government discretion. Under this legislation, access to information becomes a matter of public right, with the burden of proof on the government to establish that information need not be released. (Drapeau & Racicot, 2001, pp. 161–62, 179)

The expectation that the ATIA could produce a "major change of thinking" about the release of information might be said to typify the idealist's view of what can be achieved by a disclosure law. Unfortunately, the idealists underestimated the resilience of our govern-

> **Income**: is the consumption and savings opportunity gained by an entity within a specified time frame, which is generally expressed in monetary terms.
>
> **Revenue**: is income that a company receives from its normal business activities, usually from the sale of goods and services to customers
>
> **Profit**: can be considered to be the difference between the purchase price and the costs of bringing to market whatever it is that is accounted as an enterprise (whether by harvest, extraction, manufacture, or purchase) in terms of the component costs of delivered goods and/or services and any operating or other expenses.
>
> **EBITSA** (Earnings before interest, taxes, depreciation and amortization): it measures all interest payments, tax, depreciation and amortization entries in the income statement are reversed out from the bottom-line net income. It purports to measure cash earnings canceling tax-jurisdiction effects, and canceling the effects of different capital structures.

to the access law are rare because they require legislative assent and typically attract a large amount of public attention, and are therefore politically costly. Absent crisis, they run a high risk of failure because they require a direct challenge to the principle of transparency.

A related but less risky technique consists of restricting the meaning, if not the actual language, of the ATIA. Throughout the 1990s, for example, the government challenged the Information Commissioner's authority to investigate alleged abuses of the ATIA and argued for more expansive interpretation of key sections of the law, such as the provision protecting Cabinet decision-making. In a long series of legal challenges, it also attempted to argue that the ATIA did not provide any right to records held within the offices of Cabinet ministers or the Prime Minister's own office. In 2001, the Chrétien government issued a formal notice that it considered many ministerial advisors to be exempt from the law; it then engaged Canada's Information Commissioner in prolonged and costly litigation to attain judicial support for its position (Treasury Board Secretariat, 2001; Roberts, 2002c).

INFORMAL METHODS OF RESISTANCE

Because these direct challenges to the right to information are done in the open, we sometimes think that they constitute the main forms of resistance to freedom of information law. This is far from being the case. Other changes in bureaucratic practice—in methods of record-keeping, processing freedom of information requests, and organizing delivery of services—also have the effect of undercutting the right to information. These effects may be more pervasive and substantial than the more easily observed challenges to the law itself.

Failure to Maintain Records

For example, the right to information may be subverted by corrosion of the quality of records kept by government institutions. Most disclosure laws do not recognize a right to information that has not been incorporated within a paper or electronic record; to put it another way, there is no right to information that is known to officials but not put down in a record. A disclosure law cannot be effective if records are incomplete or non-existent.

The widely held view is that disclosure laws like the ATIA cause officials to become more reticent in recording potentially controversial information. However, the evidence is not always supportive of this view. An early study of the Australian FOIA, based on interviews with government officials, found no significant impact on the frankness of official advice (Hazell, 1989, p. 204). A 2001 study by Canada's National Archives reached a similar conclusion. Archivists expected to find that the ATIA had had "a significant and negative influence on record-keeping" within the federal bureaucracy. However, the researchers were surprised to conclude from their research that there was "no evidence . . . that the Access to Information Act has altered approaches to record-keeping in the Government of Canada" (National Archives of Canada, 2001).

Canada's former Information Commissioner John Reid took on a more pessimistic view. In 2005 he expressed concern about a "troubling shift . . . to an oral culture" within senior levels of the public service, which he said constituted one of the main challenges to the effectiveness of the ATIA (Reid, 2005). In an earlier report the Commissioner had suggested that the federal government should adopt legislation that would create "a duty to create such records as are necessary to document, adequately and properly, government's functions, policies, decisions, procedures, and transactions" (Information Commissioner of Canada, 2001, p. 66).

The Gomery Inquiry, an investigation of corruption in federal advertising and sponsorship programs completed between 2004 and 2006, uncovered evidence to support the Commissioner's concern. A senior official responsible for management of the program at the heart of the controversy testified in 2004 that he had agreed with Cabinet office staff that they would keep "minimum information on the file" to avoid embarrassment through ATIA requests:

> There was a discussion around the table during the referendum year, 1994–95, when I worked very closely with the FPRO [Federal Public Records Office] and the Privy Council . . . We sat around the table as a committee and made the decision that the less we have on file, the better. The reason for that was in case somebody made an access to information request. I think, as I said back in 2002, a good general doesn't give his plans of attack to the opposition. (Standing Committee on Public Accounts, 2004)

Two caveats are needed when considering complaints about the rise of an "oral culture." The first is a matter of causality: the shift, to the extent that there is one, is probably not attributable only to the advent of disclosure laws. The decline of departmental budgets in many countries throughout the 1990s also contributed to a decline in proper record-keeping. A combination of other factors may be important as well—such as the increased pace of work, which may leave less time for thoughtful recording of departmental activities; the general decline of a print-based culture; and a similarly broad decline in respect for procedural formalisms (Scheuerman, 2004; Postman, 1986). The Canadian Commissioner's complaint about an "oral culture" is mirrored by concerns about the emergence of a "sofa culture" within the British government, documented by the Butler Review of Intelligence on Weapons of Mass Destruction in 2004. This is a culture in which "formal procedures such as meetings were abandoned [and] minutes of key decisions were never taken," which had apparently taken root well before the implementation of the United Kingdom's FOIA in 2005 (Oborne, 2004).

A second caveat relates to the impact of new information technologies on record production. In a sense, concern about the rise of an "oral culture" is profoundly mistaken. By sheer volume, modern bureaucracies generate more digital and paper records than ever before. For example, internal government databases now collect vast amounts of transactional data—such as information about inspections and regulatory or benefits decisions—that can be accessed under disclosure laws and used for "computer-assisted reporting" (Roberts, 2006, pp. 199–277). Similarly, electronic mail systems now capture interactions that had never been recoverable previously: conversations that once might have been undertaken in person or by telephone are now "a matter of record." The Canadian government's Chief Information Officer estimated in 2002 that its 150,000 public servants exchanged roughly 6 million email messages every working day, or about 1.5 billion messages a year (d'Auray, 2002).

On the other hand, journalists have complained that officials now routinely "RAD"—that is, "read and delete"—potentially sensitive emails (Lavoie, 2003; Weston, 2003). A recent and small survey of Canadian government officials whose email had been frequently targeted by ATIA requests found that a large majority had begun to write messages more carefully; used the telephone or direct conversation more often; and deleted email messages more quickly (Roberts, 2005c, p. 15). There is also evidence that some federal officials have begun to rely more heavily on BlackBerry messaging devices, which have the capacity to transmit messages without leaving a record of the transmission that is retrievable under the ATIA (Roberts, 2005b).

Manipulation of Records

Disclosure laws like the ATIA can also be subverted by the destruction or manipulation of government records. This is an uncommon but not unknown practice. In the late 1980s, federal officials destroyed tape recordings and transcripts of meetings in which public servants debated how to manage threats to public safety posed by contamination of the blood supply by HIV and hepatitis C a few days after receiving an ATIA request for the records (Information Commissioner of Canada, 1997). In 1997, another inquiry concluded that Canadian Defence officials had altered and attempted to destroy documents relating to the misconduct of Canadian forces in Somalia that were sought by journalists under the ATIA and by the inquiry itself (Somalia Commission of Inquiry, 1997). In 1998, the Canadian Parliament amended the ATIA to make it an offence for officials to "destroy, falsify or conceal a record" in an effort to thwart a request for information.

But in 2004, the Gomery Inquiry revealed yet another effort to manipulate records sought under the ATIA. A key issue explored by the inquiry was the manner in which officials had responded to ATIA requests filed by journalists attempting to cover the story. Testimony uncovered an instance in which officials had *created* expenditure guidelines for release in response to ATIA requests. The guidelines "had cosmetic values and purposes." In other words, they were intended to convey an impression of bureaucratic regularity regarding a decision-making process that was in fact deeply politicized (Gomery Commission, 2004b).

Special Procedures for Sensitive ATIA Requests

Another mode of resistance to the ATIA has been the development of sophisticated procedures within federal institutions for managing politically sensitive requests for information. These practices have been described by Ontario's Information Commissioner (who has witnessed the emergence of similar practices within provincial government) as "contentious issues management" procedures (Information and Privacy Commission of Ontario, 2005, p. 5). These procedures are not easily observed; indeed, for many years their existence was not widely known outside government. Yet they clearly have a significant effect in defining what the "right to information" means in practice. Elsewhere I have argued that they constitute part of a "hidden law" on access to information (Roberts, 2002a).

Within Public Works and Government Services Canada, the federal department at the centre of the scandal scrutinized by the Gomery Inquiry, the practice of isolating sensitive requests was highly routinized and described in a flowchart for the aid of departmental staff. Every week, a list of new ATIA requests would be sent to the Minister's office and the department's Communications Branch. In a weekly meeting, ministerial aides and communications staff would meet with ATIA staff to review the list and identify "interesting" requests (Roy, Gomery Commission, 2004a; Lloyd, Gomery Commission, 2004c, at 6547). An "interesting" request was "one where media attention had been paid to the issue or there [was] a potential for the Minister to be asked questions before the House [of Commons]." Requests from journalists or opposition parties were routinely classified as "interesting" (Lloyd, Gomery Commission, 2004c, at 6544). "Interesting" requests were tagged electronically in the tracking system used to manage the workflow of the ATIA office (Lloyd, Gomery Commission, 2004c, at 6559). This made it easier to generate lists of sensitive requests for oversight at a later date.

Particularly interesting requests required special handling by communications staff, whose task was to prepare a media strategy to anticipate difficulties following disclosure of information, which was also reviewed by ministerial staff before release. "We lost control . . . of the process once Communications had it in their process," the department's ATIA coordinator told the Commission,

> Once [the ATIA office] has completed the processing of the file we would send a package to Communications Branch . . . [T]hen they would circulate it to the [office whose documents had been requested] for media lines, or approval of media lines they had prepared. They would then circulate it to the deputy's office and the Minister's Office. When that was done we would get a coversheet back—it was a coversheet for their media lines—and that would be our notification that we could make the release. (Lloyd, Gomery Commission, 2004c, at 6549-51).

This process of review often produced significant delays in responding to requests: "Often we found that it would take about 20 days before we finally got the signoff from the Minister's Office so that we can make a release" (Lloyd, Gomery Commission, 2004c, at 6550).

These procedures were not unique to the Public Works department. Documents released in response to ATIA requests filed with other government departments in 2003 showed that several other federal institutions had adopted essentially the same routines. At Citizenship and Immigration Canada, for example, the ATIA office conducted a "risk assessment" of incoming requests to identify those that might be used "in a public setting to attack the Minister or the Department." A weekly inventory of requests from journalists and opposition political parties was prepared for review by ministerial and communications staff. Especially problematic requests were "amberlighted," a designation that triggered the production of a communications strategy and final review by ministerial staff. Other departments used a similar designation. In the Privy Council Office (PCO), for example, these especially difficult cases were known as "red files." According to the procedures manual for the PCO's ATIA office,

> Approximately once a week the [Office of the Prime Minister] is provided with a list of newly received requests. If they wish to see the release package of any requests they notify the [ATIA] Coordinator who passes on the information to the officer handling the request.

A check of the PCO's caseload in October 2003 suggested that about one-third of its caseload had been tagged as "red files." The majority of these were requests made by journalists or political parties (Roberts, 2005a; Rees, 2003).

These institution-specific routines were complemented by government-wide oversight practices. Public Works and Government Services Canada (PWGSC) operated, on behalf of central agencies in the federal government, a government-wide database known as the Coordination of Access to Information Request System (CAIRS). Treasury Board

Secretariat (TBS) policy required that institutions enter information about incoming ATIA requests into CAIRS within one day of receipt. The data on incoming requests entered into CAIRS again included the occupational code of the requester—such as "Media" or "Parliament." ATIA offices in all federal institutions were able to search the CAIRS database by several criteria, including occupation of requester. Evidence suggested that the search capacity of the software was used principally by Treasury Board Secretariat and Privy Council Office (Roberts, 2005a, pp. 8–9).

CAIRS has been described by officials as a tool to "facilitate the coordination of responding to requests with common themes" by federal institutions. However, reports generated from CAIRS could also be used by communications staff within PCO to guide their own oversight of politically sensitive requests. In 2002 a former director of research for the Liberal Party caucus complained that the PCO's "Communications Co-ordination Group" (CCG) had become an

> egregious example of bureaucratic politicization . . . The CCG . . . is made up of the top Liberal functionaries from ministers' personal staff, along with several of the PMO senior staff, and the top communications bureaucrats from the supposedly non-partisan Privy Council Office . . . While the CCG's mandate is supposedly to "co-ordinate" the government message, in practice much of the committee's time each week is taken up discussing ways to delay or thwart access-to-information requests. (J. Murphy, 2002)

A senior PCO official conceded in a 2003 *Toronto Star* report that PCO communications staff actively manage the government's response to sensitive requests received throughout government in order to ensure that "the department releasing the information is prepared to essentially handle any fallout" (Rees, 2003). For example, PCO communications staff insisted on reviewing responses to requests relating to the "grants and contributions" scandal of 2000 (Information Commissioner of Canada, 2000, pp. 15–18). "When Privy Council Office says they want to see a release package," a communications officer explained in an internal email released by Citizenship and Immigration Canada in 2003, "I am not at liberty to do anything but what they ask." The head of CIC's ATIA office agreed: "A request from PCO Comm is essentially a 'do it' for CIC" (Roberts, 2005a, pp. 8–9).

The problem of delay caused by the special procedures for sensitive requests that was noted in testimony before the Gomery Inquiry appears to be commonplace across government. An econometric study of processing time for 2,120 requests completed by Human Resources and Development Canada (HRDC) over three years (1999 to 2001) found that media and partisan requests took an additional three weeks for processing, even after other variables such as the size of the request and type of information requested were taken into account. The probability that processing times would exceed statutory deadlines also increased for media and party requests (see Roberts, 2002a). The Information Commissioner suggested in 2000 that one cause of such delays was the government's impulse during the "grants and contributions scandal" to "let its reflexive need to 'control' the story take precedence over the legal rights of access requesters to obtain timely responses. Ministers wanted to be out front of any access request—making a clean breast of any bad news before it hit the street and, when it did, being armed with an action plan" (Information Commissioner of Canada, 2000, pp. 15–18). A subsequent and larger study of processing patterns for 25,806 ATIA requests completed by eight federal institutions between 2000 and 2002 found similar delays for media or party requests in six of these institutions. At Citizenship and Immigration Canada, for example, media requests required an additional 48 days of processing time, and party requests an additional 34 days (see Roberts, 2005a, Tables 3 and 4).

Such delays suggest that a basic principle of the ATIA is widely and routinely flouted by federal institutions. The ATIA is supposed to respect the rule of equal treatment, a presumption that requests for information will be treated similarly, without regard to the profession of the requester or the purpose for which the information is sought. "The overriding principle," argue McNairn and Woodbury, is "that the purpose for which information is sought is irrelevant" (2004, Section 2.1 [a]). The 2002 report of the ATIA Review Task Force made the same point:

> [ATIA] Coordinators, or other officials with delegated authority, are administrative decision-makers when they decide on a right conferred by the Act . . . [T]heir decision has to be made fairly and without bias. Neither decisions on disclosure nor decisions on the timing of disclosure may be influenced by the identity or profession of the requester, any previous interactions with the requester, or the intended or potential use of the information. (Access to Information Review Task Force, 2000, p. 124)

A TBS study completed in 2001 also emphasizes that "It would be a substantial change in the principles of the Act to make the identity of the requester or the purpose of the request a relevant consideration" in processing requests for information (Treasury Board Secretariat, 2001, p. 10). Yet as a matter of practice, it is clear that the profession of the requester and the purpose for which information is sought *are* relevant considerations. There is an operating presumption that media and party requests should be regarded as sensitive and subjected to distinct procedures that often lead to lengthened processing time and a decreased probability of response within statutory deadlines.

Whether these requests are also prone to less fulsome disclosure decisions is more difficult to determine. There is no neat way of undertaking a statistical analysis of this question. The key issue is not whether a minister's office uses the final stage of the process—the review of the proposed disclosure package—as an opportunity to push for more restrictive disclosure decisions. The deeper problem is that the whole process may be permeated with an awareness that the minister's office has a special interest in the file. The office that holds the records—perhaps led by a civil servant four or five levels below the deputy minister—is told within days of a request's arrival that it is regarded as sensitive by ministerial staff. Over the next months, frontline officials and the ATIA office may engage repeatedly with communications staff, who may themselves raise questions about the boundaries of disclosure. It would be surprising if ministerial concerns had not been fully anticipated well before the disclosure package went to the minister's office for final review.

Pressure on ATIA Officials

Concern about the political damage that may be done by disclosure of official records may also drive senior officials to put other sorts of pressure on ATIA bureaucrats. During the Gomery Inquiry's hearings, evidence was given of the attempt by senior officials within PWGSC to persuade ATIA staff that a journalist's request for information should be interpreted restrictively and that the ATIA staff should attempt to lead the journalist into accepting a narrower definition of his ATIA request that would exclude especially sensitive information. Senior officials were attempting, an ATIA officer said, to "manage the issue." "There were quite a few meetings on this," said the ATIA officer, who consulted a lawyer three times for advice on how to respond to the internal pressures (Gomery Commission, 2004c, at 6576-98).

There is no doubt that ATIA staff *are* subject to continuing pressure from other officials to adopt restrictive understandings of an institution's obligations under the law, although it is difficult to gauge how intense this pressure may become. Only a few years after the law's adoption, a TBS survey found that many ATIA coordinators felt significant cross-pressures between their obligations under the law and career considerations within their department (see Treasury Board Secretariat, 1986). Coordinators, another study said, were the "meat in the sandwich" of the ATIA system (Mann, 1986). More recent studies show that these cross-pressures continue to operate. In 2002, an internal task force appointed to review the ATIA reported that it had a "number of very frank discussions" in which coordinators "talked about the stress involved in dealing with sensitive files and difficult requests" (Access to Information Review Task Force, 2002, p. 126). Some coordinators "deplored a perceived lack of accountability for compliance with the Act in some program areas and perceived lack of commitment to the spirit of the Act by some managers at all levels, including senior management" (Access to Information Act Review Task Force, 2000).

Shifts in Administrative Policy

There are also more prosaic ways in which bureaucracies can undercut the right to information. The failure to provide adequate resources for processing freedom of information requests may mean substantial delays in the disclosure of information. In many cases, the value of such information may be sharply diminished as a result of such delays. This is most obviously the case when the information is sought by journalists or opposition researchers for use in a current, but transient, policy debate.

The effect of under-resourcing in Canada's federal government became clear in the mid 1990s. Budgets for the administration of the ATIA were cut as part of a broader program of retrenchment in "non-essential" spending that followed the election of the Liberal government in 1993. The result was a significant lengthening of the time required for processing information requests. By 1997, Canada's Information Commissioner regarded the problem of delay as one of "crisis proportions." Paradoxically, the Commissioner's authority was also undermined by the cutbacks: the increased caseload within his office meant that the time required for resolution of delay complaints also grew (Roberts, 2002c). Under Canadian law, the Commissioner's own budget is set by the government as well. The Commissioner complained for several years that his enf

agencies to provic

Canada, 2004, Cl

Governme

A final mode of i
The ATIA requir
a list within the
drive to slim cen
quasi-governmen
sions were not in
organizations. Th
the destruction o
eral responsibiliti
no longer subject
of major airports
ity generators, m
similar way (Rob
elected Conserva
2006) partly reve
the ambit of the

REASONS I

Jews in the American Media

1. Sumner Redstone: CEA of Viacome, "world's biggest media giant"
2. Michael Eisner: major owner of Walt Disney
3. Warren Lieberford: pres of Warner Brothers
4. Neil Sharpiro: pres of NBC News
5. David Westin: pres of ABC News
6. Mel Karmazin: pres of CBS

Difference between media : Structure, Sourcing, Common owners & Demands of sudience

Structure of Newspapers

1. Seriousness, threshold or notice ability (ie: auto accidents, shark accidents, car chasing and smoking)
2. Clarify issues: one dimension, more appealing. Media shy away from serious issues
3. Cultural proximity: Quebec deals with Quebec and French issues.
4. Predictability
5. Continuity: if one media outlet makes an incident important, others then to jump on the same band wagon
6. Composition: the ability to connect the dots

The effect of freedom of information law has not been to establish a "culture of openness" in those countries that have had such laws for many years. It may well be that more information is released to journalists, opposition parties, or non-governmental organizations than ever before. But this may simply show that public officials respect the rule of law and are subject to legal processes that require disclosure. Even when disclosure is routinized—for example, by the "proactive" release of travel and entertainment expenses—this may not be a sign of cultural change within the public service. The establishment of new administrative routines in response to statutory requirements does not necessarily reflect a shift in official attitudes toward transparency.

On the contrary, experience suggests that the passage of time provides officials with the opportunity to develop a broader range of techniques for dulling the disruptive potential of new disclosure rules. Contests over official information are fought as fiercely as they were before the introduction of freedom of information law; it is simply that the terrain on which the battle is fought has shifted in favour of stakeholders outside government. Except in those areas where the contests over disclosure of information have been settled decisively, we are likely to see—as the Information Commissioner of Canada has recently said—a "stubborn persistence of a culture of secrecy" (Information Commissioner of Canada, 2005, p. 4). Not only do government officials become more adept in managing disclosure requirements, they become more articulate in expressing their reasons for resistance.

The Nature of Parliamentary Politics

One obvious defence of adversarialism rests in the nature of parliamentary politics. Partisan requests are often filed with the hope that they may produce information that will compromise the government's political position; similarly, stories generated by media inquiries may be used by opposition parties for the same purpose. Ministers and their staff argue that it is unfair to deny them the opportunity to anticipate how they may be called to account in Parliament and in other arenas.

"What we are talking about is power—political power," said Joe Clark, then leader of the opposition Conservatives, in 1978 (Osler, 1999). Clark made the observation as part of an argument in favour of broader dissemination of information—and thus of political influence—but the statement nevertheless conveys the hard realities that underlie the day-to-day administration of the ATIA. The same sentiment was conveyed in the 1977 Green Paper on Public Access to Government Documents. Secrecy, the discussion paper said, was partly rooted in

> the adversarial nature of party politics. Many of our social institutions proceed on an adversarial basis. Our court system, for example, is based on the belief that justice will be served by the clash of advocates presenting their case as strongly as possible. So, too, our political system is an adversarial process, based on the belief that the public interest will be served by both government and opposition parties presenting their views to public judgment as ably as they can. The effectiveness of this advocacy depends, at least to some extent, on the ability of parties to concert their plans in confidential discussions. *Government and opposition are a little like football teams who, in the huddle, prepare their action out of earshot.* (J. Roberts, 2001, p. 7; emphasis added)

Whether the metaphor is drawn from sports or the military (recall the comment during the Gomery Inquiry that *a good general doesn't give his plans of attack to the opposition*) the inference is the same: the ATIA is being used by actors whose aims are hostile to the government, and a strong defence is consequently justified.

Changes in Use of the Law

A second factor that may aggravate adversarialism is the rise in number and sophistication of sensitive ATIA requests. An ATIA official engaged in the overhaul of CIC's procedures for managing politically sensitive requests observed an internal email in 2002 that

> [ATIA] requests are more probing than they used to be. There are many more of them and their requests frequently involve far more, and more sensitive, records. The result is that ATI is much more complex than it was 10 years ago—more challenging for us and more threatening for government-side politicians.[4]

From the point of view of government as a whole, this observation is probably correct. It is difficult to measure the growth of partisan requests because this data is not publicly reported. However, it is undoubtedly true that the number of media requests has grown. In its last five years (Fiscal Year 1989 to Fiscal Year 1993), the Conservative government led by Prime Minister Brian Mulroney received a total of 4,823 requests from journalists; by contrast, the Liberal government received 12,535 media requests in the five years ending in Fiscal Year 2004.[5] Furthermore, there is anecdotal evidence that journalists have developed better understanding of bureaucratic routines and the law, enabling them to make more precise and less easily evaded requests. It may also be the case that partisans and journalists are more likely to "swarm" departments with ATIA requests once the department is affected by controversy, causing a quick surge in politically sensitive requests. For example, Human Resources and Social Development (HRDC) saw the number of ATIA requests from journalists alone jump from 36 in 1999 to 199 the next year, following the "grants and contributions" controversy.

More Complex Governing Environment

Resistance to the requirements of the ATIA is also driven by broader concerns among officials about the erosion of government's ability to govern effectively. This concern about the decline of "governability" is not entirely new or limited to Canadian policy-makers (see Roberts, 2006, Chapters 3 and 4). However, there are several reasons why concern for governability has increased over the past decade. Policy-makers perceive a decline in authority that is tied to processes of globalization and tighter fiscal constraints, and a surrounding environment that seems more complex and turbulent. In most advanced democracies, the number of interest groups has expanded, and so, too, have the number of external checks (such as auditors, commissioners, and ombudsmen) with authority to scrutinize the work of government. In Canada, Donald Savoie has observed that senior civil servants "have been confronting a work environment analogous to a perfect storm. They might as well be working in a glass house, given access-to-information legislation, several oversight bodies policing their work, and more aggressive media" (Savoie, 2003, p. 164).

A similar anxiety was expressed in a 1996 Organisation for Economic Co-operation and Development report, which observed that governments faced "intense pressure from

citizens, transmitted or provoked by the media, and demanding rapid responses."
Mechanisms for improving responsiveness—"policies of consultation with the public,
freedom of information, and transparency"—could be abused, the OECD report
suggested, blocking constructive governmental action. The report concluded that it was
important to resist "excessive pressure" from the media and pressure groups. Governments
needed "to pursue more active communication policies, to keep control of their agendas
and not just react passively to the pressure of events" (OECD, 1996, Session 2).

For those worried about the decline of governability, the changing role of the media
is often a matter for special concern. The structure of the media has clearly changed: traditional outlets have been undercut by new technologies so that there are now more
potential outlets for news, competing against each other in an accelerated news cycle.
"The objective circumstances in which the world of communication operates today are
radically altered," British prime minister Tony Blair said in 2007. "The media world is
becoming more fragmented, more diverse and transformed by technology" (Blair, 2007).
Added to these structural changes in the mass media is a perceived decline in the *attitude*
of the media toward governmental authority. In this view, as the Archbishop of
Canterbury has recently argued, journalists, too, often begin

> by assuming that the question to ask almost anyone . . . is the immortal: "Why is this
> bastard lying to me?" . . . [T]he effect is to treat every kind of reticence as malign . . .
> Exposing what is for any reason concealed becomes an end in itself, because the under-
> lying reason for all concealment is bound to be corrupt and mystificatory . . . [Politics
> is] reduced to a battleground where information is dragged out of reluctant and secre-
> tive powerholders. (Williams, 2005)

In Canada, this general concern about governability is aggravated by the ongoing
concern about constitutional issues. This was evidenced during the Gomery Inquiry:
One official recalled that his colleagues had made their decision to avoid record-keeping
"during the referendum year, 1994–95" (Standing Committee on Public Accounts, 2004)
when the threat to national unity seemed especially sharp. This concern was not new or
peculiar to the Liberal government. Between 1991 and 1993, the Conservative government also attempted to resist the release of public-opinion polls on constitutional matters
to journalists by arguing that disclosure could undermine "the very existence of the country as we have known it" (Canada v. Canada, 1993).

Perceptions of Unfairness

A final argument that is invoked by officials to justify their resistance to the ATIA is a sense
that the law itself is unfair in its design, by failing to block requests that serve no legitimate
interest or draw excessively on public resources. John Crosbie, who as Justice Minister was
responsible for the Act in its first years, gave voice to this argument when he dismissed the
ATIA as a tool for "mischief-makers" whose objective "in the vast majority of instances" was
to "embarrass political leaders and titillate the public" (Crosbie, 1997, p. 300).

It is indeed the case that disclosure laws, like any other laws, may be abused. In rare cases, officials may be subjected to requests for information whose aim is not to obtain information essential for the pursuit of some important purpose, but rather to harass government workers and obstruct government operations. Such requests are uncommon, a committee of senior officials told the ATIA Review Task Force in 2001, but "give access a bad name" (Access to Information Review Task Force, 2001b). The ATIA does not give federal institutions explicit authority to disregard such requests, as do some provincial laws. Ontario's Freedom of Information and Protection of Privacy Act, for example, denies the right to information if "the head [of an institution] is of the opinion on reasonable grounds that the request for access is frivolous or vexatious" (Ontario FIPPA, Section 10.1 [b]).[6]

More often, a request may serve a legitimate purpose but nonetheless draw disproportionately on public resources. The cost of processing a single ATIA request is not negligible: in 2000, a TBS study concluded that the annual cost of administering the ATIA was $24.9 million, or about $1,740 for each information request received that year (Treasury Board Secretariat, 2000). An individual may activate a request by paying only $5; certain additional fees may eventually be payable, but these will reflect only a fraction of the total cost of processing the request. There is, it must be made clear, a strong case for public subsidization of the ATIA system. However, many officials believe that the subsidy is too lavish, or inappropriately designed, and that requesters are not adequately deterred from making "broad, unfocussed requests and fishing expeditions" (Access to Information Act Review Task Force, 2001a).[7] This also undermines respect for the law within government agencies.

CONCLUSION: THE LIMITS OF TRANSPARENCY

In canvassing these defences of adversarialism I have not meant to suggest that they are necessarily complete or persuasive. These complaints must be weighed against compelling arguments in favour of transparency, and do not justify *sub rosa* practices that have the effect of undercutting rights granted by the ATIA itself. Nevertheless it is important to recognize that the arguments deployed by officials in defence of current practices are substantial; this implies that the practices themselves are unlikely to be easily changed.

This suggests the need for a more realistic perspective about the role of the law. Disclosure laws like the ATIA have often been promoted by policy-makers as tools for overturning the "culture of secrecy" within governments, putting in its place a "culture of openness"—a culture, as Australian High Court Justice Michael Kirby said in 1997, "which asks not why *should* the individual have the information sought, but rather why the individual *should not*" (Kirby, 2004; emphasis in original). Earlier I called this the idealist's view of disclosure law. It is widely held. Shortly after adoption of the Irish FOIA in 1997, for example, Information Commissioner Kevin Murphy observed:

> [The law] has been variously described as heralding "the end of the culture of public service secrecy" and as a "radical departure" into a brave new world of public service openness and transparency. I know that media people . . . may view such

> a statement as nothing more than hyperbole; nevertheless, it is a fact that the enactment of the FOI Act does mark a radical departure from one style or culture of public service to another. (Kevin Murphy, 1998)

The British FOIA adopted in 2000 has also been promoted as a tool to break down the "traditional culture of secrecy" and construct "a new culture of openness" (United Kingdom, 1997).

In practice, however, the "culture of openness" has proved elusive. The fortieth anniversary of the American FOIA in 2006 was not marked by a celebration of culture change, but by continued controversy over the Bush administration's efforts to narrow its obligations under the law (Podesta, 2003, pp. 220–36). Nor is there evidence of profound shifts in bureaucratic culture in Commonwealth jurisdictions that adopted similar laws in the late 1970s and early 1980s. In 2005, Information Commissioner John Reid marked the completion of his term by lamenting the "stubborn persistence of a culture of secrecy" within the Canadian government (Information Commissioner of Canada, 2005, p. 4). In 2002, the government's own Access to Information Task Force reached a similar conclusion about the durability of old values in federal institutions (Access to Information Review Task Force, 2002, pp. 157–65).

This is not to say that disclosure laws have failed as tools for obtaining information held by government institutions. On the contrary, government departments have often been compelled to disclose—to journalists, opposition parties, or non-governmental organizations—sensitive information that might never have been accessible previously. Every year, thousands of requests are filed that serve important public purposes: assuring fairness in the treatment of citizens and businesses; promoting better understanding of policy-making within government; and promoting a business environment that is regarded as stable and transparent. In many cases, institutions have developed new procedures for routine disclosure of information that is frequently requested under the law. Governments have become more open; but this does not mean that they have acquired a "culture of openness." It means only that the rules that govern the conflict over information have shifted in favour of openness, and that government officials (as a rule) ultimately recognize their obligation to submit to the rule of law.

Furthermore, the ATIA provides good value for money, even if particular requests may draw disproportionately on government resources. As I noted earlier, the annual cost of administering the law was about $25 million in 2000; it will have increased significantly since then, because of heightened demand and input costs. Nevertheless, a sense of proportion is needed. The federal government planned to spend $279 million on information activities—including advertising services; public relations and public-affairs services; and publishing, printing, and exposition services—in Fiscal Year 2008 (Government of Canada, 2007). The amount of money that is spent on the ATIA—what might be called *uncontrolled* information dissemination—is only a fraction of the total amount that is spent on *controlled* dissemination.

If a culture of secrecy persists after a quarter-century, what should we do about it? One approach, favoured in the report of the task force established to review the ATIA in 2000, is a renewed effort to create a "culture of access" (Access to Information Review Task Force, 2000, pp. 157–58). Another and perhaps more realistic view is one that recognizes that a "culture of openness" is unattainable. In certain areas, conflict over information will persist—and may actually intensify, either because of changes in the broader governance context or simply because the protagonists have become more adept at using the law and developing techniques to blunt its impact. Adversarialism is an unavoidable feature in the administration of the ATIA, particularly with regard to the roughly four or five thousand requests received annually that are thought to pose political sensitivities for the government of the day.[8] The aim of reform in this case is not to change organizational culture, or to deny the reality of conflict, but to construct rules of engagement between requesters and government officials that are transparent, fair, and properly enforced.

The law must also be amended to accommodate the new realities of governance. It is now a commonplace that our old conception of the public sector—in which the public's work was done primarily in government departments staffed by public servants—has become obsolete. The "public sector" has become a more variegated composite of governmental, quasi-governmental, and "private" actors, and there is good reason to think that this process of fragmentation will continue. A law that does not properly account for this fundamental change in the structure of governmental institutions will have declining relevance as a tool for providing an assurance of transparency in the performance of public work.

Media Journal Assignments

1. Access your provincial information privacy department to determine how freedom of information rules are applied to provincial government information. Imagine you are a journalist trying to obtain this information. How would these rules affect your job?

2. Access the annual reports of Canada's Privacy Commission and its provincial counterpart in your province. Has there been an increase or a decrease in the number of requests for information received by both offices? Does either report talk about the resolution of complaints from organizations or individuals dealing with the privacy acts? If so, what can you deduce from these complaints? Provide details where possible.

Endnotes

1. Strictly, the law gives a right of access to *records* in either paper or digital form. See Sections 3 and 4.3 of the Act.

2. The analysis is compromised by problems of under-reporting within CAIRS. For the full analysis, see Alastair Roberts, Jonathan DeWolfe, and Christopher Stack, "An Evidence-Based Approach to Access Reform," Policy Studies Working Paper 22 (Kingston: School of Policy Studies, July 2001).

3. The Federal Accountability Act (FAA) was introduced as Bill C-2 on April 11, 2006, and received royal assent on December 12, 2006. The FAA brought several recently established organizations (such as the Canada Foundation for Innovation and the Canada Millennium Scholarship Foundation) under the scope of the ATIA. However, organizations such as Nav Canada, Canadian Blood Services, and the Nuclear Waste Management Organization were not brought within the scope of the law. The FAA also extended coverage to many crown corporations and agents of Parliament that were already established at the time of the passage of the ATIA in 1982, but which had never been affected by

the law. The Conservative government did not honour its election promise to make several other reforms to the ATIA proposed by the Information Commissioner.

4. The comment was made in an email released in response to CIC ATIA request 2002-05225, p. 539.

5. Statistics provided by institutions in reports required by Section 72 of the ATIA, and consolidated by the Treasury Board Secretariat. The number of media requests rose between those two periods at a faster rate than queries from other types of requesters.

6. The institution must provide reasons for disregarding a request on these grounds (Section 27.1 [1]). Criteria for determining whether a request is "frivolous or vexatious" are elaborated in Provincial R.R.O. 1990, Regulation 460, Section 5.1. Such a request must be part of a "pattern of conduct that amounts to an abuse of the right of access or would interfere with the operations of the institution," or be "made in bad faith or for a purpose other than to obtain access." The decision to refuse a request may be appealed to the Information Commissioner.

7. See also the argument for fee reform in the TBS cost study: Treasury Board Secretariat, "Review of the Costs Associated with Administering Access to Information and Privacy (Atip) Legislation."

8. In fiscal year 2005 the federal government received 2,680 requests from the media. I assume that the federal government receives between 1,000 and 2,000 requests a year from opposition legislators and party researchers.

References

Access to Information Review Task Force. 2000. "Consultation—Access to Information Coordinators, October 19, 2000." Ottawa: Access to Information Act Review Task Force. Available at www.atirtf-geai.gc.ca/consultation2000-10-19-e.html (accessed September 14, 2008).

———. 2001a. "Assistant Deputy Ministers Advisory Committee—Highlights of Meeting, May 4, 2001." Ottawa: Access to Information Act Review Task Force. Available at www.atirtf-geai.gc.ca/adm_2001-05-04-e.html (accessed September 18, 2008).

———. 2001b. "Assistant Deputy Ministers Advisory Committee—Highlights of Meeting, October 4, 2001." Ottawa: Access to Information Act Review Task Force. Available at www.atirtf-geai.gc.ca/adm_2001-10-04-e.html (accessed September 18, 2008).

———. 2002. "Access to Information: Making It Work for Canadians: Report of the Access to Information Review Task Force." Ottawa: Access to Information Act Review Task Force. Available at www.atirtf-geai.gc.ca/report/report1-e.html (accessed September 18, 2008).

Banisar, David. 2006. "The Right to Know: Domestic and International Developments." In *Freedom of Information around the World 2006*, 6-32. London: Privacy International.

Blair, Tony. 2007. "The Changing Relationship between Politics and the Media in the 21st Century." London: Prime Minister's Office.

Canada v. Canada. 1993. Canada (Information Commissioner) v. Canada (Prime Minister), 1 F.C. 427.

Crosbie, John. 1997. *No Holds Barred*. Toronto: McClelland & Stewart.

d'Auray, Michelle. 2002. "Presentation to CIPS Breakfast: Annual Federal CIO Update." April 18. Ottawa: Office of the Chief Information Officer.

Drapeau, Michel & Marc-Auréle Racicot. 2001. *The Complete Annotated Guide to Federal Access to Information*. Toronto: Carswell.

Falconer, Lord Charles. 2004. "Address to the Society of Editors' Annual Conference." Department of Constitutional Affairs, October 18. Available at www.dca.gov.uk/speeches/2004/lc181004.htm (accessed May 17, 2005).

Gomery Commission. 2004a. "Transcript of Public Hearing, October 14, 2004." Ottawa: Commission of Inquiry to the Sponsorship Program and Advertising Activities.

———. 2004b. "Transcript of Public Hearing, October 14, 2004 (English Translation)." Ottawa, Canada: Commission of Inquiry into the Sponsorship Program and Advertising Activities.

———. 2004c. "Transcript of Public Hearing, November 23, 2004." Ottawa, Canada: Commission of Inquiry into the Sponsorship Program and Advertising Activities.

Government of Canada. 2007. Main Estimates, 2007–2008, Part II. Ottawa: Treasury Board Secretariat. Available at www.tbs-sct.gc.ca/est-pre/20072008/p2_e.asp (accessed September 18, 2008).

Hay, C. & D. Wincott. 1998. "Structure, Agency, and Historical Institutionalism." *Political Studies* 46: 951–57.

Hazell, Robert. 1989. "Freedom of Information in Australia, Canada and New Zealand." *Public Administration* 67 (2): 189–210.

Information and Privacy Commission of Ontario. 2005. "Annual Report 2004." Toronto: Office of the Information and Privacy Commissioner of Ontario.

Information Commissioner of Canada. 1997. "Annual Report 1996–1997." Ottawa: Office of the Information Commissioner.

———. 2000. "Annual Report 1999–2000." Ottawa: Office of the Information Commissioner.

———. 2001. "Annual Report 2000–2001." Ottawa: Office of the Information Commissioner.

———. 2004. "Annual Report 2003–2004." Ottawa: Information Commissioner of Canada.

———. 2005. "Annual Report 2004–2005." Ottawa: Office of the Information Commissioner.

Kirby, Hon. Michael. 1997. "Freedom of Information: The Seven Deadly Sins." Lecture to the British Section of the International Commission of Jurists. High Court of Australia, December 17. Available at www.hcourt.gov.au/speeches/kirbyj/kirbyj_justice.htm (accessed December 10, 2004).

Lavoie, Judith. 2003. "Civil servants fearful of FOI don't keep written record." *Vancouver Sun*, September 26, B3.

Mann, Bruce. 1986. "The Federal Information Coordinator as Meat in the Sandwich." *Canadian Public Administration* 29 (4): 579–82.

McNairn, Colin & C.D. Woodbury. 2000. *Government Information: Access and Privacy*. Release 1, 2000 ed. Toronto: Carswell.

Murphy, Jonathan. 2002. "Your candle's flickering, Jean." *Globe and Mail*, May 17, A15.

Murphy, Kevin. 1998. "Address on the Launch of the Freedom of Information Act, 1997." Dublin, Office of the Ombudsman, April 21. Available at http://ombudsman.gov.ie/21c6_156.htm (accessed December 3, 2004).

National Archives of Canada. 2001. "The *Access to Information Act* and Record-Keeping in the Federal Government." National Archives of Canada, August 2001. Available at www.atirtf-geai.gc.ca/paper-records1-e.html (accessed May 10, 2004).

Oborne, Peter. 2004. "The Sofa Revolution." *Tablet*, July 17. Available at www.thetablet.co.uk/reviews/192 (accessed September 4, 2008).

OECD. 1996. Organisation for Economic Co-operation and Development. "Ministerial Symposium on the Future of Public Services." Paris: OECD.

Ontario FIPPA. Ontario Freedom of Information and Protection of Privacy Act, Section 10.1 (b). Archives of Ontario Library.

Osler, Andrew. 1999. "Journalism and the FOI Laws: A Faded Promise." *Government Information in Canada* 17 (March 1999). Available at http://library2.usask.ca/gic/17/osler.html (accessed September 4, 2008).

Podesta, John. 2003. "Need to Know: Governing in Secret." In *The War on Our Freedoms*, ed. Richard C. Leone and Greg Anrig, Jr., 220–36. New York: Public Affairs.

Postman, Neil. 1986. *Amusing Ourselves to Death: Public Discourse in the Age of Show Business.* New York: Penguin Books.

Rees, Ann. 2003. "Red file alert: Public access at risk." *Toronto Star*, November 1, A32.

Reid, Hon. John. 2005. "Remarks to the House Committee on Access to Information, Privacy and Ethics." Office of the Information Commissioner of Canada, April 12. Available at www.infocom.gc.ca/speeches/speechview-e.asp?intSpeechId=111 (accessed August 16, 2005).

Roberts, Alasdair. 2001. "Statement to the MPs' Committee on Access to Information." Syracuse, N.Y.: Campbell Public Affairs Institute.

———. 2002a. "Administrative Discretion and the Access to Information Act: An "Internal Law" on Open Government?" *Canadian Public Administration* 45 (2): 175–94.

———. 2002b. "Canadian officials use September 11 as excuse to restrict access to information." *Winnipeg Free Press*, October 8, A19.

———. 2002c. "New Strategies for Enforcement of the Access to Information Act." *Queen's Law Journal* 27: 647–83.

———. 2005a. "Spin Control and Freedom of Information." *Public Administration* 83 (1): 1–23.

———. 2005b. "The Blackberry is the new poisoned fruit." *Ottawa Citizen*, November 26, B7.

———. 2005c. "The Insider." *Saturday Night*, October, 15.

———. 2006. *Blacked Out: Government Secrecy in the Information Age.* New York: Cambridge University Press.

Roberts, Alasdair, Jonathan DeWolfe & Christopher Stack. 2001. "An Evidence-Based Approach to Access Reform." Policy Studies Working Paper 22. Kingston: School of Policy Studies.

Roberts, John. 2001. "Green Paper on Legislation on Public Access to Government Documents." In *The Complete Annotated Guide to Federal Access to Information*, ed. Michel Drapeau and Marc-Auréle Racicot, 5–43. Toronto: Carswell. (Orig. pub. 1977).

Savoie, Donald. 2003. *Breaking the Bargain.* Toronto: University of Toronto Press,.

Scheuerman, William E. 2004. *Liberal Democracy and the Social Acceleration of Time.* Baltimore, Md.: Johns Hopkins University Press.

Somalia Commission of Inquiry. 1997. *Report.* Ottawa: Public Works and Government Services Canada. Available at www.dnd.ca/somalia/somaliae.htm (accessed April 23, 2003).

Standing Committee on Public Accounts. 2004. "Evidence." Ottawa: House of Commons.

Treasury Board Secretariat. 1986. "Review of Access to Information and Privacy Coordination in Government Institutions." Ottawa: Treasury Board of Canada Secretariat.

———. 2000. "Review of the Costs Associated with Administering Access to Information and Privacy (Atip) Legislation." Ottawa: Treasury Board of Canada Secretariat.

———. 2001. "*Access to Information and Privacy Acts* Implementation Report No. 78." Treasury Board of Canada Secretariat, March 30. Available at www.tbs-sct.gc.ca/gos-sog/atip-aiprp/impl-rep/impl-mise_e.asp (accessed September 28, 2003).

United Kingdom. 1997. "Your Right to Know: The Government's Proposals for a Freedom of Information Act." London: Stationery Office.

Weston, Greg. 2003. "Read and delete: Read it and weep." *Toronto Sun*, June 8, C4.

Williams, Rowan. 2005. "The Media: Public Interest and Common Good." Lecture delivered at Lambeth Palace, June 15. Available at www.archbishopofcanterbury.org/992 (accessed September 4, 2008).

Chapter 16

Framing Gomery in English and French Newspapers: The Use of Strategic and Ethical Frames

Anne-Marie Gingras, Shannon Sampert, and David Gagnon-Pelletier[1]

INTRODUCTION

There are few incidents in Canadian political history that can compare to the two-year saga of the Gomery Commission. In many ways it became Canada's political soap opera that played for audiences on television news replete with a cast of colourful characters. The Commission was formed under the guidance of Superior Court of Quebec Justice John Gomery at the behest of Prime Minister Paul Martin. Its mandate was to investigate the mismanagement of public funds in the Sponsorship Program and in Advertising Activities. However, for many Canadians, particularly for Quebecers, the Gomery Commission was much more than just a public administration exercise. While the Commission concentrated on the mismanagement of public funds, the relationship between the administrative and political branches of government, and the government's disregard for financial guidelines and for the administrative rules of the Treasury Board, what came into question was the integrity of the Liberal Party of Canada, and, by extension, all those who were promoting federalism.[2] These issues all deal with diverse dimensions of democracy: the independence of the civil service, the rule of law, the partisan system and its financing, and the values at the heart of our democratic system, such as integrity, responsibility, and accountability. The Gomery Commission was thus about governance and democracy.

This paper examines the media articulation of the Gomery Commission by comparing the coverage in French- and English-language newspapers during significant time periods within the hearing. The purpose of this study is to understand how the newspapers set the agenda for and framed their coverage of the Commission, and to explore the differences between French- and English-language treatments of it. Analysis of the newspaper coverage between the "two solitudes" shows that this was considered a major news story, with considerable time and resources spent on it. However, there were clear differences in *how* the issue was reported, both between French and English newspaper coverage and between individual newspapers generally. Moreover, for French-language newspapers, the federal sponsorship scandal was viewed as a moral issue, while for the English-language papers it was viewed much more strategically, with an emphasis on the political fallout from the testimony.

SETTING THE CONTEXT: THE FEDERAL SPONSORSHIP SCANDAL AND THE GOMERY COMMISSION

The federal Liberal government used its sponsorship program as a response to the 1995 Quebec referendum campaign in which Quebecers were asked if they wanted sovereignty after a formal offer of a political and economic partnership with the rest of Canada.[3] The campaign had been hard fought, with its last days marked by concerns within the federalist camp and the English-language media that there was a surge of support for Quebec sovereignty. The outcome of the referendum was extremely tight, with federalist forces winning by a very small margin: 50.6 percent of Quebecers voted to stay within Canada, while 49.4 percent voted for the sovereignists. These close results sent a shock wave throughout Canada, and the federal government responded by launching a high-stakes political-communication campaign through the establishment in 1997 of a new branch of Public Works and Government Canada, the mandate of which was to improve the federal government's visibility. The Communications Coordination Services Branch was set up specifically to "coordinate, promote, advise, and facilitate federal communications initiatives" (Auditor General of Canada, 2003, 3.5). The Sponsorship Program, put into effect after the 1995 referendum, was designed to establish a positive presence for the federal government in Quebec. Between 1997 and March 2003, the government spent about $250 million on sponsoring slightly less than 2,000 events. In total, 40 percent of the total expenditure ($100 million) went to communications agencies (Auditor General of Canada, 2003, 3.7). Eventually it became evident that the Sponsorship program was being promoted only in Quebec. Only when people from outside of Quebec became aware of the program were funds released to other provinces' programs (Auditor General of Canada, 2003, 3.17).

The Gomery Commission was formally set up in February 2004 to investigate the federal government's involvement in the Sponsorship Program. This followed an Auditor General's report that established that there were significant shortcomings at all stages of the contract-management process of the Sponsorship Program. A government-wide audit by Auditor General Sheila Fraser was conducted on all advertising and sponsorship activities from 1997 to 2001. In her report, released in November 2003, Fraser suggested that "the federal government ran the Sponsorship Program in a way that showed little regard for Parliament, the *Financial Administration Act*, contracting rules and regulations, transparency, and value for money" (Auditor General of Canada, 2003, 3.1).

Following the tabling of the Auditor General's report, Prime Minister Paul Martin called for a Commission of inquiry to investigate these findings. Quebec Superior Court Justice John Gomery was chosen to head up the investigation on February 10, 2004 (Perreault, 2006, p. 12), and the Commission of Inquiry into the Sponsorship Program and Advertising Activities was held in Ottawa from September 7, 2004, to February 14, 2005, and in Montreal from February 28 to May 30, 2005. During its 136 days of hearings, 172 witnesses were heard, producing 28,000 pages of transcripts and 7,000 boxes of documents filed as evidence (Perrault, 2006, pp. 193–94). The Commission also became a media event, with journalists from various news outlets assigned to cover it. As Gomery's media spokesman François Perreault points out in his behind-the-scenes look at the Gomery Commission, there would be as many as 40 reporters in the press room on the busiest days of the hearings (2006, p. 48). This paper analyzes how some of those reporters covered the hearings.

POLITICAL SCANDALS

Thompson defines *scandal* as "actions or events involving certain kinds of transgressions which become known to others, and are sufficiently serious to elicit a public response" (2000, p. 13). More specifically, political scandal deals with the "violation of due process" (Markovitz & Silverstein, cited in Thompson, 2000, p. 91). These definitions make it clear that scandal is both temporally and culturally contextual. As Esser and Hartung point out, "the public in one country is not excited or outraged by events that excite and outrage people in another country" (2004, p. 1048). In other words, what may be viewed as scandal in one country at any point in time is socially constructed. It also becomes clear that the definition of political scandal relies on an understanding of the exercise of political power and the rules and procedures by which that political power is yielded. Thus, a study of the press articulation of political scandal in Canada reveals much more than just the media's preoccupation with titillation and salacious detail; it also speaks quite clearly to how the media, and by extension the public, view the exercise of political power in Canada. Moreover, by comparing coverage in French- and English-language newspapers, our study can determine what, if any, cultural differences exist in the way scandal is viewed.

The media framed the controversy surrounding the federal sponsorship program as a scandal, and in many ways the coverage of the Auditor General's report and the Gomery Commission could be viewed as the media articulation of the shortcomings of the Liberal government in exercising its political power. Thompson outlines four phases of the mediation of political scandal. The first, the *pre-scandal phase*, is the phase in which information about the scandal is just becoming public but has not received a great deal of media attention, and it "may be characterized by gossip, rumour and hearsay" (Thompson, 2000, p. 74). In the sponsorship scandal, this pre-scandal phase was articulated in the coverage of the federal opposition parties that started to ask questions about the program in the House of Commons.

The second phase is the *scandal proper*. Thompson describes this phase as "the public disclosure of an action or event that sets in motion the process of claim and counter-claim which constitutes the mediated scandal" (Thompson, 2000, p. 74). In the federal sponsorship scandal, the Auditor General's report serves as the legitimization of the articulation of the shortcomings of the program as a scandal, and her findings brought the issue into the forefront. Thompson suggests that in this phase, the media "act as a framing device, focusing attention on an individual or an alleged activity and refusing to let go" (Thompson, 2000, p. 74).

The third phase in the mediation of a political scandal is considered the *culmination phase*. During this phase, the Gomery Commission took place and information about the federal sponsorship scandal was brought to a head. As Thompson points out, the culmination phase often contains a "dramatically staged event, such as a trial or a public hearing" (Thompson, 2000, p. 75), which becomes "endowed with all the trappings of symbolic power" (Thompson, 2000, p. 75). Indeed, Gomery presided over the hearings in both Montreal and Ottawa, flanked by two Canadian flags and surrounded in public by an entourage of high-profile career bureaucrats, making it a "media event" (Dayan & Katz, 1992, p. 2).

The final phase is the *aftermath*—"the period when the high drama of the scandal and its dénouement have passed, when journalists, politicians and others . . . engage in a reflection on the events and their implications" (Thompson, 2000, p. 76). The aftermath of the Gomery Commission was quite clear for the Liberals, who ultimately lost government to Stephen Harper's Conservatives. More importantly, Paul Martin's Liberals saw their support in Quebec drop, while support for the Conservatives surged. The Conservatives went from having no seats in Quebec to winning 10, while the Liberals dropped from 21 seats to just 13. This was perhaps the ultimate dénouement—the loss of traditional support for the Liberals in Quebec and the end of a 13-year reign over the Parliament of Canada.

METHODOLOGY

To evaluate how the scandal proper—the evidence that emerged during the hearings of the Gomery Commission—was covered in the press, we studied four of Canada's major newspapers that devote a great deal of resources to covering politics: the *National Post* and the *Globe and Mail*, the main English-language national newspapers; and *La Presse* and *Le Devoir*, the main French-language political newspapers in Quebec. All four of the newspapers are broadsheets, with the *Post*, the *Globe*, and *Le Devoir* publishing Monday to Saturday, and *La Presse* publishing seven days a week. *La Presse* is owned by Power Corporation of Canada, the *Globe* is part of the CTVglobemedia chain, and the *National Post* is part of Canwest MediaWorks, while *Le Devoir* is the only independent daily newspaper in Quebec. The *Post* and the *Globe* publish different papers for each of their regions across Canada, and the edition on which we relied was the national edition, which originated from Toronto. The *Post*, the *Globe*, and *La Presse* have high paid circulation rates, while *Le Devoir* is a smaller paper with significantly smaller circulation numbers. However, *Le Devoir* is considered Quebec's elite press and is seen as setting the political agenda for other French-language newspapers. The *Post* has an average daily paid circulation of over 206,000, compared to the *Globe* at over 337,000 and *La Presse* at 217,000. *Le Devoir* has an average daily paid circulation of 30,000 (Canadian Newspaper Association September, 2007).

Research on the differences between French- and English-language media in Canada is very limited. Early research suggested that there may be differences in how French- and English-language media set the agenda for news (see Halford et al., 1983; Elkin, 1975; Siegel, 1974). Halford, van den Hoven, Romanow, and Soderland wrote that the "nature of the event itself may well be crucial in determining whether or not there are significant differences in coverage by each linguistic media group." For example, national elections focusing on major party leaders tend to result in a more homogeneous media stance, while Quebec-specific events (the October 1970 FLQ crisis or the 1980 and 1995 referenda) generate distinct linguistic media agenda (Halford et al., 1983, p. 5).

In an article investigating views about the social and political roles of the media, Pritchard, Brewer, and Sauvageau found increasing gaps between English- and French-language journalists' assessment of the importance of journalistic functions. They write about the existence of a Canadian journalist's creed

> composed of five roles that a strong majority of journalists considered to be extremely important: accurately reporting the views of public figures, getting information to the public quickly, giving ordinary people a chance to express their views, investigating the activities of government and public institutions, and providing analysis and interpretation of complex problems. (2005, p. 290)

Their longitudinal study indicates that there have been shifts in the way journalists view their roles. Comparing 1996 to 2003, there was a decline among English-language journalists in rating the importance they attached to "accurately reporting the views of public figures, providing analyses of complex problems and giving ordinary people a chance to express their views." By comparison, French-language journalists only "exhibited a significant decline" in "getting information to the pubic quickly" (2005, p. 296). More precisely, 23 percent of the journalists who work for the English media accorded less importance to "accurately reporting the views of public figures," while this "role did not lose any ground among journalists in the French-language news organizations between 1996 and 2003." English-language journalists had become more skeptical toward business leaders, and the authors suggest that this may be because of the business and political scandals that were headline stories in English Canada between 1996 and 2003 (2005, p. 301).

On the other hand, French-speaking journalists were more worried about media concentration and more supportive of government action to limit concentration of the press (2005, p. 299). Pritchard et al. suggest that the "distinct professional culture of journalism in Quebec" may help to explain these concerns. They believe that the cohesive action of Quebec journalists' membership unions, such as their participation in the Fédération professionelle des journalistes du Québec (FPJQ), which "actively socializes journalists to the profession and its ideology" (Pritchard et al., 2003, p. 302), plays a role in lobbying government on media ownership issues.

Our study adds to the body of research on French and English media coverage by providing specific data on differences in the framing of a key political event. In his book *Inside Gomery*, François Perreault discusses the active role he played in ensuring that the media had the information they needed to follow the intricacies of the investigation. He suggests that, of all the Commission participants, he "had the greatest influence on the press. With a comment or suggestion, I could enhance a headline or improve an article, allowing certain reporters to set their work apart from the main lead story of the day" (Perreault, 2006, p. 54). Perreault talked about the balance journalists would have to strike in trying to cover Gomery with their own unique approach:

> In reality, all journalists struggled to extract newsworthy items from the same mass of raw material. In this way they resembled a team of medical specialists pouring over an X-ray and trying to agree on a diagnosis. With a touch of collegial humour, they established an informal "lead committee" to help pinpoint a common editorial line at the end of the day. They realized that given the mountain of evidence involved, this was the best way to achieve consistency in their reporting. The approach, colour or flavour of the story remained each reporter's prerogative when they sat down to write. The trust they placed in me had to do with my understanding of, and respect for, individual treatments, which writers would sometimes show me when they required clarification or further information (2006, pp. 54–55).

As our study is a content analysis of newspaper articles about the Commission rather than an investigation of the motivations and behaviours of the many actors and journalists involved in the reporting of it, it is impossible for us to evaluate Perreault's impact on the four newspapers studied. It does, however, shed some light on both the existence of pack journalism and the existence of diverse perspectives or diverse framings of the Gomery Commission.

This analysis focuses on six key time-periods in the life of the Gomery Commission. These were: (1) the testimony of Chrétien and Martin from February 7 to February 14, 2005; (2) the partial lifting of the publication ban on Chuck Guité's testimony from May 4 to May 11, 2005; (3) the coverage of the release of the report of the team of forensic accountants from May 24 to May 31, 2005; (4) the wrap-up of the inquiry from June 17 to June 24, 2005; (5) the tabling of the First Report from November 1 to November 8, 2005; (6) and, finally, the coverage following the tabling of the Final Report from February 1 to February 8, 2006.

AGENDA SETTING AND FRAMING

Since the media are the primary conduit through which the public learns about events, we were interested in the agenda setting and framing of the Commission inquiry by both the English- and the French-language newspapers. The media cover "events and, in choosing what to report and how to report it, shape their outcome" (Jamieson & Waldman, 2002, p. 95). Whatever "biases" or "reporting tendencies" each media outlet has, it seems clear that they can have an impact on the way the public sees the world. As David Taras suggests, denying the media's power to shape public perceptions and influence government is akin to arguing that "the earth is flat or that Tinkerbell and the Tooth Fairy are real" (Taras, 2001, p. 3). The media have the ability to "alert the public about which events are important and to set the context within which those events could be understood" (Taras, 2001, p. 30).

Agenda setting can be defined as the close connection between the content of a newspaper and the ideas of the reading public. This chapter does not study the effect of the newspaper coverage on the public's perception, but it does shed some light on how the media reported on the scandal proper. According to Stuart Soroka, sensational issues like a scandal are "media-driven." He believes that, while the public set the agenda on issues that relate to them personally and the government sets the agenda on policy issues, it is the media that set the agenda on sensational issues (Soroka, 2002, p. 21). In our evaluation, coverage of the Gomery Commission can be viewed as a sensational issue because it is seen as a political scandal. As Perrault outlines, various political parties tried to influence the media on how to cover Gomery, but based on the differences in coverage exhibited in this analysis, it becomes clear that these attempts were not entirely successful (for more details, please see Perrault, 2006).

The concept of framing suggests that no reality is totally objective. All political actors present their project from a particular perspective; all social actors do the same. In reporting facts and problems, the media select, organize, give priority to some aspects and not to others, and sort out information, all of which inevitably leads to emphasis on or favouring of certain standpoints. Framing is a perspective, an interpretation, a standpoint, a world view, or a narrative device. According to Todd Gitlin, "media frames are persistent patterns of cognition, interpretation, and presentation, of selection, emphasis, and exclusion, by which symbol-handlers routinely organize discourse, whether verbal or visual." He adds that "for organizational reasons alone, frames are unavoidable, and journalism is organized to regulate their production. Any analytic approach to journalism . . . must ask: What is the frame here? Why this frame and not another?" (Gitlin, 2003, p. 6). Since frames define the public debate by delineating the discourses available in the public sphere on an issue or event, finding out which frames are favoured by diverse media outlets helps us understand the overall picture of democratic conversation.

Framing leads to an understanding of journalism as socially constructed. As Gans points out, "Even if a perfect and complete reproduction (or construction) of external reality were philosophically or logistically feasible, the mere act of reproduction would constitute a distortion [or bias] of that reality" (Gans, 2004, pp. 304–5). So "reporting tendencies" are inevitable, as explained in sociology by the "social construction of reality," meaning that the world is socially constructed: any media report comes with a context (Whitney et al., 2004, pp. 94–111).

Studies conducted in Canada, the United States, and Australia indicate that journalists rely on the strategic or game frame when they cover elections (see, for example, Chapter 7 by Soroka and Andrew in this edition). This frame implies that politics is more about competition and strategy than it is about issues and nation-building. It leads to a very cynical view of the world by explicitly or implicitly presenting political actors as enemies working exclusively for limited partisan interests that always supersede any ideals or long-term vision. In this study, we explore whether the newspapers structured the Gomery Commission reports around the strategic perspective or whether they employed other frames, such as an emphasis on morality and ethics or an issue frame. Is every actor of the Gomery Commission seen as a potential winner or loser? We also investigate the differences between French newspapers in Quebec (*La Presse, Le Devoir*) and national English ones (the *Globe and Mail* and the *National Post*) in topics and frames. Did the Montreal and Toronto newspapers report the same story? Did they display a similar level of interest in the Gomery Commission? More specifically, were the Montreal papers more likely to use a moralist or ethical frame when reporting Gomery, given that the sponsorship program was all about mounting public relations campaigns to buy Quebec support for federalism?

AGENDA SETTING OF GOMERY

Both French-language papers published more stories covering Gomery than did the English language papers. *La Presse* published by far the most stories on Gomery, with a total of 159, while *Le Devoir* published 108. The *National Post* published slightly less with 106, and the *Globe and Mail* published 103 stories. The tabling of the first report garnered the most attention, with 33.6 percent of the overall coverage (160 stories). Coverage following the lifting of the publication ban on Chuck Guité's testimony came in second with 23.1 percent of the reports (110 stories), while Chrétien and Martin's testimony was also of interest (16.4 percent of the coverage or 78 stories). This is perhaps not surprising given the interest the media tend to give to government policy-making processes as they near their "finish line" and when a "'score' is highly consequential for one or both 'teams'" (Lawrence, 2000, p. 109). The release of the first report can be seen as the culmination of a government process.

The front page of any newspaper is the most prominent place a news story can appear and is always saved for news that is evaluated as the most important news of the day. To get a sense of the importance the newspapers placed on the stories coming out of the Gomery Commission, we need to analyze where the news items appeared. That the Gomery story was indeed an important news event for all four newspapers is demonstrated by the number of times it appeared on the front page, particularly for the *Globe and Mail* and *Le Devoir*. More than 20 percent of *Le Devoir*'s coverage of Gomery was situated on the front page (23 stories or 21.3 percent of its total coverage). The *Globe* also featured its coverage of Gomery prominently, placing it on the front page for 17.5 percent of its coverage (18 stories). The *National Post* ran 9 front-page stories (8.5 percent of its total coverage), and *La Presse* ran 17 (10.7 percent of its total coverage). The fact that the *National Post* ran the story less often on the front page than any other newspaper is surprising, particularly given the somewhat Conservative leanings of the newspaper, but this may also reflect the fact that this story in the English-language press was largely being driven by the work of two reporters at the *Globe and Mail*. Indeed, the Gomery Commission can in many ways be viewed as Canada's Watergate, with two dedicated reporters at the *Globe* breaking the story wide open in 2004. Daniel LeBlanc and Campbell Clark followed up on tips from an anonymous informer as they investigated the Liberals' involvement in the sponsorship program. The higher number of front-page articles in the *Globe and Mail* compared to the *National Post* reflects their work. *Le Devoir*'s decision to feature the story on the front page may be due to the fact that this newspaper is considered part of Quebec's elite press and has a strong interest in reporting on politics.

The one-week period following the partial lifting of the ban on Chuck Guité's testimony yielded the most front-page stories in all the papers. This was a particularly rich week for coverage for the media, as it included not only stories about the lifting of the ban, but also coverage of testimony by Michel Béliveau and Benoit Corbeil, Liberal insiders who testified about their involvement in the sponsorship scandal. In *Le Devoir*, 7 out of 18 front-page stories were in this time frame, while in *La Presse*, the story was in 7 out of 23 front-page stories. Three of the *Post*'s 8 front-page stories ran in this time period, compared with 4 of the *Globe*'s 18 front-page stories. This certainly suggests that for French-language papers, the testimony from Liberal insiders working in Quebec was a far more significant story than it was for newspapers in English Canada.

LEVELS OF MEANING: TOPICS AND FRAMES

The coverage of the Gomery Commission focused both on what was going on inside the hearing rooms in Ottawa and Montreal and on what was happening on Parliament Hill in response to the allegations made in the hearings. It was very clear that issues of ethics and accountability were the main topics for all the newspapers. The main topic of almost half of the stories had to do with ethics or accountability standards (48.3 percent or 230 stories). However, there was one significant difference found in the *Post*'s coverage. More than any of the other newspapers under study, the *National Post* ran stories on the impact of Gomery on the political parties should an election be held. It also ran more stories that referenced polling numbers, discussions about snap election calls, and the general impact the inquiry was having on party fortunes. These election musings made up 17 percent of its overall coverage (18 stories), compared to 10 percent in *Le Devoir* (11 stories), and less than 10 percent in the *Globe and Mail* (8.7 percent or 9 stories) and *La Presse* (8.8 percent or 14 stories). *Le Devoir* spent a great deal more time exploring the political responses of MPs and party leaders in its coverage of Gomery compared to the other papers. Almost a fifth of the stories in *Le Devoir* were about politicians' responses to the inquiry (18.5 percent or 20 stories). This compares to 8.8 percent (14 stories) in *La Presse*, 11.7 percent in the *Globe and Mail* (12 stories), and 13.2 percent (12 stories) in the *National Post*.

The differences among the papers in topic choice can be explained in a number of ways. First, as stated earlier, the media coverage of the Gomery Commission occurred in the third stage of scandal. Much of the information that was presented to the Commission during the hearings was not particularly "new" because it had been reported on earlier as the scandal became known. Thus, the newspapers may have been attempting to find a new angle from which to pursue the Gomery story. Because the prime minister at the time, Paul Martin, suggested he would hold an election after the release of the final Gomery report, the impact of the Commission's hearings on polling numbers for political parties had news value. As well, the work by LeBlanc and Clark at the *Globe* put that paper in the forefront of the scandal coverage for national English-language papers, forcing the *Post* to attempt to find an alternative space in which to make a name for itself and sell more papers. Clearly, the decision to focus on the strategic implications of Gomery on a potential election outcome was how the *Post* could differentiate itself from the *Globe* in its coverage. For the French-language papers, the fact that the Liberals in Quebec were expected to take a hit in popularity as a result of the scandal may have driven their coverage. Additionally, interviewing area MPs to get their reactions to the day's incidents in Gomery may have been one way to further localize the story.

We coded all of the stories about the Gomery Commission printed during the six time frames to determine the overriding frame of each story: strategic, moral, or issue. Stories determined to be dominantly strategically framed were stories that framed Gomery as a contest between winners and losers. They included stories about polling numbers, election predictions, and party tactics. Stories determined to be morally framed were those that discussed the moral or ethical implications of the federal sponsorship scandal. These included stories that suggested that the sponsorship program was morally corrupt. Finally, stories determined to be issue-framed related the actual proceedings of Gomery with little interpretation. They included transcripts of the Commission and announcements on scheduling.

The dominant frame for the coverage of Gomery was a strategic frame. In total, 52.4 percent (249) of the newspaper stories published were framed strategically, while 30.3 percent (144) had a moral frame and 17.3 percent (82) were issue-framed. What is interesting is that differences in the prevalence of the strategic frame were revealed by the comparison of the English- and French-language papers. The strategic frame was most dominant in the English-language newspapers and less dominant in the French-language papers. It was used in 71.4 percent of the stories (75) printed in the *National Post* and 62.1 percent of the stories in the *Globe and Mail* (64). The strategic frame was clearly present in the coverage of the French-language newspapers, but not to the same degree as in that of the English-language papers. *Le Devoir* used a strategic frame in 43.5 percent of its stories (47), while *La Presse* framed the issue strategically in 39.6 percent (63) of articles.

An example of the strategic frame can be found in a Mark Kennedy story from the *Post*: "The Conservative party is poised to win a minority government if an election is held now, but it can't count on public anger over the sponsorship scandal to guarantee victory at the ballot box, a new poll suggests" (Kennedy, 2005). In *La Presse* the strategic frame was found in this story, which ran on November 1, 2005, following the tabling of the first report: "The issue is how the Liberal Party will get out of this? In Quebec, this is quite clear. The Liberal Party will continue to bleed . . . Liberals have been afraid for months that the Gomery Report conclusions will give the opposition the necessary munitions to make the government fall" (Marissal, 2005).

In French-language newspapers, the use of moral and the issue frames was much more prevalent when compared to the English-language papers. The moral frame appeared in 32.4 percent (35) of *Le Devoir* stories and 39.6 percent (63) of the stories in *La Presse*. This compares to 26.2 percent (27 stories) in the *Globe* and only 18.9 percent in the *Post* (20 stories). This certainly suggests that the reaction to the details regarding the federal sponsorship program revealed in the Gomery Commission was different in Quebec than in the rest of Canada. Because the impetus for the implementation of the federal sponsorship program was national unity, the moralistic question of whether it was a prudent choice of action was more salient in Quebec. For example, *La Presse* quoted former Prime Minister Chrétien as he testified before the Commission:

> Mr. Chrétien described the post-referendum context in quasi-apocalyptic terms. "You remember the anxious moments that followed the referendum, the desperation of federalist forces, the many signs 'to sell' or 'to rent' during those years in Montreal? You remember those blocked windows in Montreal streets you saw every morning while coming to the Justice building, the feeling that there would be another referendum inevitably with a different result?" (Toupin, 2005)

Chrétien implied in his testimony that he felt morally obligated to implement the federal sponsorship program and would otherwise have risked economic fallout for Montreal.

The moral stance was used predominantly by Justice Gomery and others who focused on issues of integrity, responsibility, and accountability. As a story in *Le Devoir* points out, Justice Gomery's final report recommended a limitation of the Prime Minister's power, probably because the abuses inherent in the sponsorship scandal had been allowed to continue unabated for so many years. While senior bureaucrats, including deputy ministers, could have blown the whistle on the administration, they chose not to. In the article, *Le Devoir* indicates that Justice Gomery "goes so far as to ask himself whether a culture of intimidation was on the verge of having the edge over a culture of primacy of the law when there were political pressures on civil servants" (Myles, 2006).

The *Globe's* Leblanc also focused on the moral aspects of the story when reporting on the Commission wrap-up. Leblanc stated that there was not any evidence against Prime Ministers Jean Chrétien or Paul Martin in the sponsorship program; however, "former minister Alfonso Gagliano was 'ill-advised' to get so closely involved in the loosely defined initiative, federal lawyers will argue before the Gomery inquiry today" (LeBlanc, 2005).

The difference in the use of the issue frame among the papers was also interesting. Again, it was more prominent in the French-language papers when compared to the

English papers. Approximately 10 percent of the stories in both the *Post* and the *Globe* were stories about the facts of the Commission and the sponsorship program (9.4 percent or 10 stories in the *Post* and 11.7 percent or 12 stories in the *Globe*). This compares to 24.1 percent of *Le Devoir* articles (26) and 21.4 percent of *La Presse* stories (34), and suggests that French-language papers more often reported on the Gomery Commission with information provided with little journalistic interpretation. Moreover, the tendency of the French-language papers to provide more coverage about the process of the Commission itself suggests that those living in Quebec were given more detailed information on the inner workings of Gomery and the federal sponsorship scandal.

Both French-language papers relied on the issue frame during their coverage of two specific time periods: the tabling of the forensic accountant's report and the week following the lifting of the Guité ban. The majority of the stories written during those time periods in *Le Devoir* and *La Presse* were issue-framed. In total, there were 15 stories for those time periods that were issue-framed in *Le Devoir*, representing 13.8 percent of its overall total stories, while in *La Presse* there were 26 stories, representing 16.3 percent of its total stories. Here is how the issue frame was used in *Le Devoir*:

> The scandal is bigger than the public believed. The Sponsorship program cost tax payers $332 million, and not $225 million, as revealed by the Auditor General. After having examined 28 million pages of documents in 7,000 boxes, the Kroll, Lindquist, and Avey judicial accountants have tabled their bulky report to the Gomery Commission. From this ocean of numbers appears a troubling finding: the sponsorship abyss is surprisingly deep. . . . Although the program was created in 1996, Kroll has found that public funding was used to finance sponsorship activities as early as 1994. (Myles, 2005)

Details of the enormity of the work involved in hearing testimony at the Gomery Commission were then provided.

The story of the Gomery Commission was heavily mediated by commentators, particularly in the *Globe and Mail*. While the majority of the stories in all newspapers were news stories, the *Globe* had by far the highest percentage of stories that were either editorial or commentaries, while *La Presse* had the highest percentage of stories that were news stories. Slightly more than half of the stories in the *Globe* were news stories (53.4 percent or 55 stories), while 45.6 percent were editorials or columns (47 stories). In *La Presse*, 81.1 percent of the coverage of the Commission was found in news stories (129 stories), compared to 18.2 percent that were editorials or columns (26 stories). The *Post* had 68 news stories and 38 columns and editorials (64.2 percent and 35.8 percent of its overall coverage), while *Le Devoir* ran 71 news stories and 32 editorials and columns (65.7 percent and 29.6 percent of its overall coverage). The *Globe*, *La Presse*, and *Le Devoir* ran a small number of stories that were straight transcripts of the proceedings as well.

Why are the numbers of columns and editorials, particularly in the *Globe*, significant? Since the story had been discovered by Daniel Leblanc and Campbell Clark, it is likely that the paper wanted to keep the momentum and used columns and editorials to spark interest.

Columns and editorials are not expected to follow the journalistic rules of balance and fairness. They are expected to take a stance and signal to the reader an opinion or perspective. Media critics are concerned about the rise of punditry in the coverage of politics in Canada. Pundits can be defined as journalists who make their living by commenting on rather than reporting the news, and they find their work primarily as newspaper and magazine columnists. As Taras puts it, "their positions and credibility are established by their colourful views, their ability to goad and entertain their audiences and their credentials as veteran journalists who have special insights or information of some kind." Pundits wield "an enormous influence over public opinion and as individuals they are far more influential than any

> VNR (Video news release): is a video segment made to look like a news report, but is instead created by a PR firm, advertising agency, marketing firm, corporation, or government agency. They are provided to television newsrooms to shape public opinion, promote commercial products and services, publicize individuals, or support other interests.
>
> BCE-CTV deal remakes media landscape: by Iain Marlow (Sept 2010)
>
> - A merge of Canada's largest telecom carrier and the country's #1 broadcaster (CTV and BCE)
> - Bell Canada Enterprises acquired all of CTV's television assets, including: the CTV network, speciality cable channels such as TSN, Bravo and the Business News Network.
> - However, BCE will retain its current 15% of share of Canada's largest circulation national newspaper and its related websites.
> - The merge experiment was rejected, and in 2005 Micheal Sabia sold off the bulk of BCE's stakes.
> - The company was later remakes CTVglobalmedia to reflect Bell's diminished influence.
> - The largest move the departure of Teachers and Torstar, held 25% and 20% of CTVglobalmedia.
> - Thus, CTV, is almost entirely from BCE

The information presented in the opinion pieces is meant to interpret rather than simply impart information about the Gomery Commission. Its primary purpose is to engage and entertain, rather than provide an overview of the Commission outcomes.

Further, the framing of the editorials and columns in both the *Globe* and the *Post* remained dominantly strategic, while the same cannot be said about the columns and editorials in *La Presse* and *Le Devoir*, where the use of the moral frame increased significantly. More than 60 percent of the editorials or columns in *La Presse* were morally framed, and half of the editorials or columns in *Le Devoir* (16 stories each) were framed that way. For example, a high-profile columnist for *La Presse* wrote that the urgency to save Canada by selling federalism to Quebecers

> opened the door to mistakes and loss of control, particularly when the weight of incompetence is added. Let's think about Alfonso Gagliano. That is enough to create a climate favourable to waste and administrative mistakes, but also to unacceptable gestures. The result is a major scandal, although not from a financial point of view, because it has surpassed our level of tolerance by betraying the ideal of public service. (Dubuc, 2005)

In *Le Devoir*, the chief editorial writer assessed the first part of the work of the Gomery investigation with a clear moral frame:

> Those who created the Sponsorship Program have acted in total opacity. The ins and the outs have never ever been clearly presented to the members of the Cabinet . . . . The program being secret, risks of being called to account were limited, which opened the door to all abuses. In the hierarchical command chain, nobody asked questions. Nobody asked to see a bill. The responsibility of this is the burden of Chrétien, Pelletier, and Gagliano. The excuse of national unity could only serve to evade the issue. (Descôteaux, 2005)

While the attack by the English-language columnists may have been on the spending behind the sponsorship program, the French-language columnists denounced the fact that the program was simplistic in its attempts to deal with national unity.

CONCLUSION

This study shows that, while the main topics covered by newspaper reportage of the Gomery Commission hearings were ethics and accountability standards, the dominant frame was a strategic one; however, there were clear differences in how the English national newspapers covered the story as compared to the French-language papers. While the strategic frame was used in 71 percent of the stories in the *National Post* and 62 percent of the stories in the *Globe and Mail*, the numbers are more modest for the French-language newspapers: 43 percent in *La Presse* and 39 percent in *Le Devoir*. Conversely, the moral frame was much more prevalent in the French-language newspapers. It appeared in 32 percent of stories in *Le Devoir* and 39 percent in *La Presse*, compared to 26 percent in the *Globe and Mail* and 18 percent in the *National Post*. These numbers suggest that the English-language papers viewed the Gomery Commission more as a game with winners and losers, with less consideration of the ethical implications of the Liberal Party's actions. This was particularly true in the *National Post*. The moral outrage felt by French people in Quebec over what many viewed as a simplistic response to the issue of Quebec within Canada resonated in the French-language press, with the moral frame being used in a greater number of stories. Columnists emphasized three moral aspects of the scandal: the issues of buying Quebecers' affections by sponsoring sport and cultural events, of transgressing government policies and Treasury Board rules, and of setting up a diversion schema for financing the Liberal Party.

The implications of this are twofold. First, the use of a predominantly strategic frame in the English-language papers combined with a very small percentage of issue-framed articles makes us believe that their readers were provided with an incomplete vision of the implications of the findings of the Commission. The French-language press viewed this story differently from their English cousins and provided much more balanced coverage of the day-to-day testimony. The French-language newspapers told a more nuanced story of Gomery, with more news stories that were not mediated by columnists or journalistic interpretation, providing a richer overview of the main issues raised by the findings of the Commission.

Second, this research on framing sheds some light on the relationship between reporters on the one hand and columnists and editorial board members on the other. While the English press reporters covering the hearings in Montreal understood French, this was not the case for most of the Toronto pundits. Their ability to comment on the work of the Commission was thus very limited. Not only could they not understand the mainly French testimonies in the Montreal hearings, but they were also at loss to interpret their meaning in light of the political culture of Quebec. They had to rely on their reporters, and this second-hand information led them to stick to a single, oversimplistic vision of the story. Their frequent use of the strategic frame was an easy way to convey the story, and this was especially the case for the *National Post*.

Media Journal Assignments

1. Over a three-day period, monitor the way either your daily newspaper or an English Canadian national newspaper *frames* stories about government policy. Are you as a news reader provided with enough information about the policy to understand it? How does the framing of policy issues serve to highlight some elements of the story while obscuring or minimizing others?

2. Examine the *National Post* and the *Globe and Mail* over a three-day period to determine how much attention either paper gives to federal politics. Is the coverage substantive and in-depth? On what kind of sources do the papers rely for information? How does this shape what is written?

Endnotes

1. David Gagnon-Pelletier gathered and coded all data.

2. Boisvert and Desjardins (2006) go as far as to write that the resulting mistrust has extended to the whole political class.

3. The question was: "Acceptez-vous que le Québec devienne souverain, après avoir offert formellement au Canada un nouveau partenariat économique et politique, dans le cadre du projet de loi sur l'avenir du Québec et de l'entente signée le 12 juin 1995?"

References

Auditor General of Canada. 2003. *2003 November Report of the Auditor General of Canada*. Ottawa: Government of Canada.

Blatchford, Christie. 2005. "Forensic sleuths bolster Brault's credibility: Accountants deduce that the Groupaction boss, who said he paid kickbacks to the Liberals, had cash." *National Post*, May 25, A5.

Boisvert, Yves & Jean-Patrice Desjardins. 2006. "Les libéraux de Jean Chrétien: Des comportements inappropriés au détournement de la démocratie." *Éthique publique:Revue internationale d'éthique sociale et gouvernementale* 8 (1): 149–54.

Canada. 2005. Commission of Inquiry into the Sponsorship Program and Advertising Activities. *Who Is Responsible? Report of the Commission of Inquiry into the Sponsorship Program and Advertising Activities*. Ottawa: Commission of Inquiry into the Sponsorship Program and Advertising Activities.

Canadian Newspaper Association. Canadian Newspaper Circulation Data. Available at www.cna-acj.ca/client/cna/ult.nsf/ccsearch?OpenForm&nLoc=5.6 (accessed September 2007).

Cappella, Joseph N. & Kathleen Hall Jamieson. 1997. *Spiral of Cynicism: The Press and the Public Good*. New York: Oxford University Press.

Dayan, Daniel & Elihu Katz. 1992. *Media Events: The Live Broadcasting of History*. Cambridge: Harvard University Press.

Descôteaux, Bernard. 2005. "Il n'y a pas pire aveugle . . ." *Le Devoir*, February 12, B4.

Dubuc, Alain. 2005. "Les battements d'ailes du papillon." *La Presse*, February 9, A19.

Elkin, Frederick. 1975. "Communications Media and Identity Formation in Canada." In *Communications in Canadian Society*, 2nd ed., ed. B. D. Singer, 229–43. Toronto: Copp Clark.

Esser, Frank & Uwe Hartung. 2004. "Nazis, Pollution and No Sex." *American Behavioural Scientist* 47 (8): 1040–71.

Gagnon, Lysiane. 2005. "Ontario is the new Quebec." *Globe and Mail*, May 23, A13.

Gans, Herbert. 2004. *Deciding What's News: A Study of CBS Evening News, NBC Nightly News, Newsweek and Time*. New York: Random House. (Orig. pub. 1979.)

Gitlin, Todd. 2003. *The Whole World is Watching. Mass Media in the Making and Unmaking of the New Left*. Berkeley: University of California Press. (Orig. pub. 1980.)

Globe and Mail. 2005. "On the ethics watch." Editorial, November 5, A24.

Halford, Peter W., Adrien van den Hoven, Walter I. Romanow, & Walter C. Soderlund. 1983. "A Media Tale of Two Cities: Quebec Referendum Coverage in Montreal and Toronto." *Canadian Journal of Communication* 9 (4): 1–31.

Jacob, Steve. 2006. "La quête de transparence: Panacée ou placebo aux scandales politiques?" *Éthique publique: Revue internationale d'éthique sociale et gouvernementale* 8 (1): 165–69.

Jamieson, Kathleen Hall & Paul Waldman. 2004. *The Press Effect: Politicians, Journalists, and the Stories that Shape the Political World*. New York: Oxford University Press.

Kennedy, Mark. 2005. "Poll puts Tories ahead as party taps into anger: 36% support: Popularity driven by revelations from Gomery inquiry." *National Post*, May 4, A9.

Lawrence, Regina. 2000. "Game-Framing the Issues: Tracking the Strategy Frame in Public Policy News." *Political Communication* 17: 93–114.

Leblanc, Daniel. 2005. "Martin and Chrétien blameless, Ottawa says; Federal lawyers to address Gomery probe." *Globe and Mail*, June 17, A9.

———. 2006. *Nom de code: MaChouette; L'enquête sur les commandites*. Montreal: Libre Expression.

Marissal, Vincent. 2005. "La grippe aviaire du Parti libéral?" *La Presse*, November 1, A2.

Myles, Brian. 2005. "Le programme a finalement coûté 332 millions aux contribuables canadiens. Le PLC-Q aurait touché 2,6 millions des agences." *Le Devoir*, May 25, A1.

———. 2006. "La revanche des politologues. Le juge Gomery propose de restreindre les pouvoirs dévolus au cabinet du premier ministre." *Le Devoir*, February 4, B2.

Perreault, François. 2006. *Inside Gomery*. Toronto: Douglas & McIntyre.

Pritchard, David, Paul. R. Brewer, & Florian Sauvageau. 2005. "Changes in Canadian Journalists' Views about the Social and Political Roles of the News Media: A Panel Study, 1996–2003." *Canadian Journal of Political Science* 38 (2): 287–306.

Siegel, Arthur. 1974. "Canadian Newspaper Coverage of the F.L.Q. Crisis: A Study on the Impact of the Press on Politics." Ph.D. Dissertation, McGill University.

Soroka, Stuart. 2002. *Agenda Setting Dynamics in Canada*. Vancouver: University of British Columbia Press.

Taras, David. 2001. *Power and Betrayal in the Canadian Media*. Peterborough, Ont.: Broadview Press.

Thompson, John B. 2000. *Political Scandal: Power and Visibility in the Media Age*. Malden: Blackwell Press.

Toupin, Gilles. 2005. "Chrétien déplore les erreurs mais ne s'excuse pas. L'erreur aurait été de tout laisser l'espace des commandites au PQ." *La Presse*, February 9, A3.

———. 2006. *Le déshonneur des Libéraux; Le scandale des commandites*. Montréal: VLB Éditeur.

Whitney, D. Charles, Randall S. Sumpter, & Denis McQuail. 2004. "News Media Production. Individuals, Organizations, and Institutions." In *The Sage Handbook of Media Studies*, ed. D. McQuail, J. Downing, P. Schlesinger, and E. Wartella, 393–410. Thousand Oaks, Ca.: Sage.

Chapter 17
Covering Canada's Role in the "War on Terror"
Yasmin Jiwani

> When sovereignty becomes a stylized Rambo-on-steroids identity rather than the status of the nation-state, war is no longer a question of protecting national borders or national interests, but simply a matter of self-expression and self-constitution. (Mann, 2006, pp. 159–60)

INTRODUCTION

War stories allow a nation to project an image of itself vis-à-vis an "other." In such stories, the national self is inevitably valorized as heroic, worthy, and noble whereas the "other" is demonized, negated, or devalued. There is a definite gendered dimension to war stories. Heroes and villains are mostly male, while women are the victims needing rescue. As well, while military machinery and language is often coded as male—emphasizing the thrust, sturdiness, and precision of targets—the countries in which wars take place are often feminized, and the language used to describe military penetration is often highly sexualized (Agathangelou & Ling, 2004). In the process, victims worthy of rescue are identified and those deemed to be risks are killed or incarcerated. The discursive construction of war is indicative, then, of how we see ourselves (as projected by journalists and editors) and how, through this process, we define and redefine ourselves.

The media's role in constructing and projecting a national self cannot be underestimated. As Benedict Anderson (1983) and others have argued, the media are crucial conduits through which the discourse of a nation is produced and reproduced. Van Dijk (1993) has shown how media texts influence and inform common perceptions. Through talk, we reproduce the categories and meanings that are made available to us and that, over time, become part and parcel of our commonsensical stock of knowledge (Hall, 1990). Going back to Anderson's example, in a nation, people across the country may not know each other. In fact, nobody knows everyone in the nation, but we still adhere to the belief that we belong to a nation and that we are all Canadians. Not everyone, particularly those who are targeted as different, may evidence the same sense of belonging to the nation, nor will every individual be made to feel as if they are a part of it, but, more generally, the sense is that we are all members of the Canadian nation. As De Cillia et al. note,

> The idea of a specific national community becomes a reality in the realm of convictions and beliefs through reifying, figurative discourses continually launched by politicians, intellectuals and media people and disseminated through the systems of education, schooling, mass communication, and militarization, as well as through sports meetings. (1999, p. 153)

In a country the size of Canada, this sense of "nation-ness," of belonging to one country or one nation-state, is reproduced on a daily basis through a variety of rituals and practices. From the singing of the national anthem at symbolic gatherings, the carrying of the flag, and the requirement of a passport or other official documents to viewing Canadian television shows, reading Canadian publications, and voting in Canadian elections, one participates in the continual construction of the nation. The daily news provides us with a sense of being grounded in the nation, as we watch Canadian anchors and reporters discuss stories from different parts of the world using Canadian vernacular and from a Canadian perspective. Such a perspective is often regional, but is nonetheless subsumed within an overall framework of being a part of the nation-state. Richard Kaplan eloquently notes that "the news is a tale of the nation, which commemorates and commiserates in the nation's tragedies as well as its triumphs" (2003, p. 212).

In this chapter, I attend to the retelling of the story of the "War on Terror" in the Canadian press. I focus specifically on the *Globe and Mail*, one of Canada's two national dailies, which has a wide circulation and considerable public and political influence. Although historically there have been many wars on "terror" (Chomsky, 2001), the conceptual framing and rhetoric of the U.S. "War on Terror" can be traced to the days immediately following September 11, 2001.

The events of September 11 are etched in the memories of Canadians. Continual television replays of the planes crashing into the Pentagon and the Twin Towers of the World Trade Center in New York sent waves of shock and horror through everybody viewing them. New York became synonymous with America, and America had been hit by an unknown enemy (Silberstein, 2002). By the end of the day, President George W. Bush had identified that enemy as members of al Qaeda, a loosely formed group of terrorists headed by Osama bin Laden, a Saudi dissident. Bush's speech was carried by all the major Canadian networks and the complete text was reported in the *Globe and Mail* the very next day: "Today, our fellow citizens, our way of life, our very freedom came under attack in a series of deliberate and deadly terrorist acts." He went on to say, "We will make no distinction between the terrorists who committed these acts and those who harbour them" (September 12, 2001, p. A4).

Bush's speeches on that day and the days to follow were filled with binary oppositions congealing a sense of the noble, innocent, and democratic American nation-state under attack from "evil," heartless, and maniacal terrorists "out there." Kellner (2003), Nayak (2006), Silberstein (2002), and others have noted that the use of these

Manichaean oppositions in Bush's various speeches—good versus evil; freedom versus force; democracy versus totalitarianism—served to polarize the issue, and by delimiting the terms of the debate, failed to invoke a more concerted and rational response. Rather, the response became one of vengeance and revenge, with Bush as the Commander in Chief of a nation attacked without reason and provoked into retaliation.

In reporting on the events that unfolded on September 11 and immediately thereafter, the consensus appears to be that the American media by and large toed the patriotic line and failed to interrogate the issue in ways that would have shed light on the failure of the American security services as well as the Bush administration's role in either inciting or preventing the attack (Kellner, 2003). Where such critique was offered, it was quickly squelched, with heavy penalties for those who dared to speak out against the war on terror (Akram, 2002). As Judith Butler notes, "the binarism that Bush proposes in which only two positions are possible—'Either you're with us or you're with the terrorists'—makes it untenable to hold a position in which one opposes both and queries the terms in which the opposition is framed" (2004, p. 2).

Canadian retelling of the story concerning the war on terror began with the September 12 coverage. Before detailing this story, we need to contextualize Canada's position vis-à-vis the United States and the rest of the world. Unlike the United States, which is considered a superpower or "hyperpower" with considerable military and political might, Canada is regarded and sees itself as "a middle-power nation that is nicer and less aggressive than the United States" (Razack, 2004, p. 33). Indeed, as Sherene Razack aptly notes, "Never having been a colonial power or engaged in aggressive occupations (internal colonialism is once again ignored) Canadians are content to see themselves as playing a secondary, more innocent role in world affairs" (p. 33).

Notwithstanding the above, the criteria for newsworthiness also colluded in shaping how Canadian media reported on the "War on Terror." First, Canada's very proximity to New York was a major factor influencing the outcome. More importantly, Canadian media obtain much of their international news coverage from press feeds through international media organizations such as Associated Press (based in the United States), Reuters (based in the U.K.), and Agence France (based in Europe) (Rantanen, 2004). While some Canadian news organizations do send reporters and journalists out to the countries where the action is taking place, this is not always possible because of prohibitive costs. Hence, there is a heavy reliance on international news agencies. However, with regard to the coverage of September 11, there were other factors that also influenced how Canadian news organizations reported the story. These have to do with issues of cultural commonalities stemming from the shared cultural framework between the two countries, as evidenced by the use of a common language, economic dependencies and linkages, and the movement of people across borders. Consequently, there is a common framework of meaning. Added to this, criteria such as the suddenness of the event, its dramatic unfolding, the location of the event in an elite nation, and the involvement of other elite persons such as the President of the United States, all contributed to the media's amplified coverage (see Bennett, 2003).

Moreover, the attacks in New York occurred in a city where the major American media networks are concentrated. Hence, the visual footage, and the immediate interviews with survivors and those who had come to assist them, were broadcasted intensely and widely. In effect, as Nacos (2002) and Louw (2003) have argued, the attacks constituted "propaganda of the deed" in that they were intended to be highly publicized. Louw (2003) suggests that, for the terrorists, knowing that these acts would capture attention was one strategy by which they could alert the world to the vulnerability of a superpower like the United States, and, at the same time, avenge their own sense of injustice and recruit others who were disillusioned with American foreign policy and interventions abroad. Nacos (2002) prefers to call this "mass-mediated terrorism," which she defines as "violence for political ends against noncombatants/innocents with the intent to win publicity" (p. 19).

THE *GLOBE AND MAIL*'S RENDERING

In examining the *Globe and Mail*'s coverage in the week immediately after the events of September 11, several of the issues raised above are apparent. Using keywords that included World Trade Center, Taliban, Terror/Terrorism, Afghanistan, Attack, Islam, and Muslim, a search was conducted of the *Globe and Mail* database available in CD-ROM format in most libraries. Narrowing the search parameters further by adding other terms such as women, woman, gender, veil, burqa, and hijab resulted in 72 articles. Thereafter, the search was further narrowed down to 60 articles, by eliminating letters to the editor as well as stories that appeared in the sports section, the fashion section, and the section dealing with film and book reviews.

Within the duration of the week, the *Globe and Mail* had organized its coverage of 9/11 into four thematic categories: "Day of Infamy," "The Day After," "The Aftermath," and "The Brink of War." A fifth running category, "The War on Terror" began on September 22. These categorical headlines are interesting and informative as they reflected the positioning of the paper in terms of how it framed the stories. "Day of Infamy," for example, explicitly references Pearl Harbour as the one and only other time when the United States was attacked by a foreign power. The stories also covered the immediate fallout detailing the shock and horror of the event. "The Day After" and the "Aftermath" included stories that dealt with the survivors, victims, and the heroes who had assisted them, as well as stories about the backlash against Muslims in America and Canada. The "Brink of War" focused on preparations for war detailing the U.S. military might, the response of other nations to Bush's unilateralism, and the possible impact on Afghanistan.

While much of the coverage in this period dealt with the shock and horror of the attacks, my focus in the sections below deals with discourses of Orientalism, nationhood, backlash, and gender. In examining the stories, I carried out a close textual reading of each, paying particular attention to how different actors were framed and the kinds of explanatory frameworks that were privileged. My analysis is based on an informal discourse analysis (see van Dijk, 1993).

Edward Said's seminal work *Orientalism* (1978) outlines the predominant lens through which the West constitutes and interprets the East. He defines Orientalism as "a style of thought based upon an ontological and epistemological distinction made between 'the Orient' and (most of the time) 'the Occident'" (1978, p. 3). Said identifies four dogmas of Orientalism:

> one is the absolute and systematic difference between the West, which is rational, developed, humane, superior, and the Orient, which is aberrant, undeveloped, inferior. Another dogma is that abstractions about the Orient, particularly those based on texts representing a "classical" Oriental civilization, are always preferable to direct evidence drawn from modern Oriental realities. A third dogma is that the Orient is eternal, uniform, and incapable of defining itself; therefore it is assumed that a highly generalized and systematic vocabulary for describing the Orient from a Western standpoint is inevitable and even scientifically "objective." A fourth dogma is that the Orient is at bottom something either to be feared (the Yellow Peril, the Mongol hordes, the brown dominions) or to be controlled (by pacification, research and development, outright occupation whenever possible). (pp. 300–1)

These four dogmas are evident in the way that the news media report on events in the Middle East and in the way that these events are rationalized in popular culture (Jiwani, 2006; Karim, 2000; Said, 1981; Shaheen, 2001; Zelizer & Allan, 2002). They were also evident in the *Globe's* coverage, examined below.

Binaries between "Us" and "Them"

Immediately the day after, on September 12, popular *Globe and Mail* columnist Margaret Wente reiterated the Orientalist binaries that were encoded in George W. Bush's speech. This time, however, she added more of her own. She opined, "It only took a few men who hate America to hijack its own commercial airplanes and turn them into bombs. It only took a few to ram them into America's most potent symbols of financial and military might." She added,

> Those who are responsible are most likely men from remote desert lands. Men from ancient tribal cultures built on blood and revenge. Men whose unshakable beliefs and implacable hatreds go back many centuries farther than the United States and its young ideas of democracy, pluralism and freedom.
>
> Hard men, who hide out in desert bunkers and turn the instruments of Western technology—its computers and CD-ROMs and videotapes and airplanes—against the West. Men capable of flying Boeing 747s with pinpoint, deadly accuracy, and of giving up their lives for the greater glory of Allah, and of murder on a massive scale. (September 12, 2001, p. A1)

Wente's words not only contrast the "hard" men of the desert with the "innocent" and happily secular men of America, but they also evoke images of barbarism. The use of phrases such as "ancient tribal cultures built on blood and revenge" brings forth images of a primitive civilization driven by fanaticism. She underscores this in her statement about these men deploying Western technology with the "implacable determination of fanatics." Further, the notion of "ramming" planes into "potent" symbols of American might is suggestive of rape, of being violated. Bonnie Mann (2006) argues that

> The saturation of media space with films of the attack (the two erect towers penetrated then destroyed by the two planes over and over again) became the narrative vehicle that told the story of an extraordinary threat; the threat of the homosexual rape and simultaneous castration of the United States by a dark, brutal, and overwhelmingly masculine enemy" (p. 155).

This narrative may have been what Wente was drawing upon when she penned the above descriptions, but these are also narratives grounded in a tradition of Orientalism, where the East is always constructed as fixed, homogeneous, traditional, barbaric, irrational, hyper-emotional, and anti-modern (Said, 1978).

In a subsequent column on September 13 (2001, p. N3), Wente reiterated these same binaries, stating that "our world" is different and separate from 'their' world which is marked by "the rule of blood and sacred jihad."

The rhetorical question "Why do they hate us?" which underpinned many of the articles published during this week, had already been answered by Wente. But she was not alone in surmising that "they" hate us for our freedom, democracy, etc. Indeed, George W. Bush had made the same point in his address on September 12 and in subsequent speeches thereafter. However, what is most interesting is how this question segued into questions about Palestine and the Israeli experience of terror, a point I discuss further below.

On September 12, Marcus Gee (2001, p. N8) attempted to offer some analysis by drawing on the voices of experts to support his views. Beginning his article with a description of Palestinians celebrating the attack, Gee asks why so many people hate the United States. The latter's support for Israel quickly comes up as the answer. This is followed closely by a description of those who hate the United States for its backing of secular governments and those who decry Western decadence. Gee cites Yitzhak Sokoloff, an Israeli political analyst, whom he quotes as saying, "We're dealing with a culture that celebrates martyrdom and exults in the death of its perceived enemies." Gee then goes on to detail Osama bin Laden's particular grievances against the United States and ends with a quote from Mark Juergensmeyer's book on terrorism, *Terror in the Mind of God: The Global Rise of Religious Violence* (2000) (Gee, September 12, 2001, p. N8).

While this column might appear to be relatively straightforward and commonsensical, what is left out is an account of such grievances that situate it historically. Despite the abundance of scholars who are experts on Islam and the Arab world, and who also write and teach in English—in all parts of the West—none of these are quoted. Moreover, it is clear that an Israeli political analyst's view is used to proffer an explanation that "makes sense." Thus, what we end up with is an ideological reinforcement of the same binaries that are explicit in Wente's column. Here, we have an impression of a barbaric people that "exults in death" and "celebrates martyrdom." We also have a people who are heartless, as evidenced by the reference to Palestinians celebrating. In fact, the celebrating Palestinian story was repeated numerous times during the week-long coverage.

The *Globe* waited until September 13 before offering any substantive information on the terrorists themselves. In his lead, Paul Knox writes, "Some call it blowback. Some call it reaping what you sow" (September 13, p. A3). He then goes on to detail the nature of the blowback as stemming from Osama bin Laden's involvement in the fight against the Soviet occupation of Afghanistan, an occupation in which the CIA was also invested. However, rather than detail this investment or describe how the United States supported bin Laden and the Mujahedeen and thereby contributed to the formation of al Qaeda, Knox instead focuses on bin Laden himself as an individual, drawing attention to his fanaticism and his family life. So bin Laden is quoted as saying, "Allah ordered us in this religion to purify Muslim land of all non-believers and especially the Arabian Peninsula." Quoting those who knew him when he was younger, Knox states, "he frequented Beirut night clubs as a young man, drinking heavily and fighting over women with other men." Bin Laden is, then, a fanatical purist who was once a womanizer. Knox also provides details regarding the inheritance that bin Laden received upon his father's death in a helicopter accident (Knox, September 13, 2001, p. A3).

What is interesting about Knox's article is all that it neglects to report. As Douglas Kellner states, "bin Laden and the radical Islamic forces associated with the al Qaeda network were supported, funded, trained, and armed by the CIA and several U.S. administrations" (2003, p. 30). Further, bin Laden's elder brother died in a helicopter "accident" while flying in Texas, and there has been much speculation to date as to the cause of this accident. Moreover, the bin Laden and Bush families have long-standing ties in the ways in which their various business interests overlap, and both have heavy investments in the Carlyle group, "which heavily invests in the military-defence sector" (Kellner, 2003, p. 37). Robert Entman (2003) discusses this occlusion of the Saudi connection, demonstrating that, despite evidence to the contrary, the Bush administration's focused insistence on going after bin Laden and the Taliban became the mass media's main frame.

Bin Laden as "Evil Genius"

Aside from the one by Knox, there were several articles, including speeches by George W. Bush, that portrayed bin Laden as the "mastermind," "the evil" behind the attacks. In an insightful article, Samuel Winch (2005) describes how the construction of bin Laden as "evil genius" was a necessary ploy in the discourse of war. War, he argues, requires a worthy opponent. It would not seem fair to go after an opponent who is weak or who just happened to be lucky in striking out. Winch's analysis of coverage of bin Laden in major world newspapers over a four-year period shows a dramatic increase in the months following September 11. But despite the increase, the nature of the coverage—with the construction of bin Laden as an "evil genius"—remained the same. Winch argues that, aside from affirming the worthiness of an opponent and hence justifying extreme measures in warring such an opponent, the "evil genius" construction also serves another purpose: namely, to pre-empt failure. In other words, not being able to find or destroy Osama bin Laden is already factored into the equation. That aside, this construction of bin Laden also resonates with Orientalist notions of all that is Middle Eastern, as Middle Eastern/Arab/Muslim men are regarded as being brutal, devious, uncaring, and fanatical. Thus, it is not surprising to observe how this association with Islam and the Middle East spills over into a generalized backlash against Muslims, a theme I explore in the latter part of this chapter.

Heroes, Victims, Survivors, and Families

By far the greatest heroes of this "war" on America were the firefighters and the mayor of New York, Rudolph Giuliani. Giuliani was described as "presidential" and a "wartime mayor" (Houpt, September 13, p. A2). Then there was Michael Judge, a priest who worked with New York's fire department (Reguly, September 13, p. N4), and the firefighters, many of whom lost their lives (Wong, September 15, p. F4). There were other heroes as well. These included the resilient women who went to pray for the souls of the deceased (Cheney, September 17, p. A9), families searching for kin (Priest, September 15, p. A4), the stockbrokers who were lending assistance, the women and men who provided resources (Kelly et al., September 13, p. N4; Howlett et al., September 14, p. B1), as well as those who rescued others from the burning towers (Richer, September 15, p. F11). All these heroes were humanized and their stories were the personal-interest stories that made the telling and retelling of the events more bearable and emblematic of New York's/America's resilience and humanity.

Personal-interest stories featured the voices of those who were directly affected. Journalists mentioned "crying workers" and "bloodied office workers" desperately trying to make calls (Houpt, September 12, p. A9; Kelly, September 12, p. N4). First-hand accounts of those in the immediate vicinity or in the hijacked planes, of firefighters, and of others were heavily covered (Kesterton, September 13, p. A20). While the intense coverage of these stories gradually subsided to give way to other developments, they remained ever present as a constant reminder of the grief and horror caused by the attacks. More often, such stories were peppered with comments concerning the resilience of New Yorkers and nostalgic yearnings for the times before 9/11—before the "loss of innocence." At other times, they were accompanied by justifications for retaliation and anger. For example, commenting on his brother's reaction to the events of 9/11, columnist Ian Brown reported him as saying, "'I hope the Americans bomb the hell out of whoever did this. They're fucking animals." Toward the end of his column and reflecting on his change in perception and diminishing conviction with regard to the commonality of humankind, Brown wrote, "I will never see another devout, turban-wearing Muslim without wondering—. . . . was he part of it?" (September 12, p. N2). Such a statement from a columnist serves to rationalize and make commonsensical the fear and suspicion of those who look different and who are different by virtue of their race and religious beliefs. But in articulating such a viewpoint, the media render it acceptable. This becomes highly problematic when viewed against a backdrop of an extreme action that is unaccompanied by any kind of perspective or information concerning the motives or history behind such an attack.

What gets framed into a story, as Entman (2004) points out, captures our attention and thereby influences our decisions. What gets framed out is erased from consideration. What Brown also seems to forget is that Pakistanis, Indians, and Iranians were also working at the World Trade Center when it was attacked. They, too, were victims, and many of them were Muslims, a fact pointed out by Bush in one of his speeches to the nation.

Nationalist Discourses

News accounts not only told of people's fears of attacks occurring on Canadian soil, but also reaffirmed Canada's relationship with the United States. As one man interviewed by a journalist put it, "The U.S. and Canada have had a symbiotic relationship for so many years. This is like something happening to a member of the family" (Mitchell, September 12, p. N3). This motif was reiterated many times during the period of coverage examined. Many reporters accessed voices of the *vox populi*—the common man or woman on the street—gauging their responses to the events of September 11.

However, nowhere was this nationalist discourse more apparent than in the editorials of the *Globe and Mail*. The editorial represents the stand of the paper as a whole. It thus exercises more discursive weight than individual reports or columns. On September 13, the editorial focused on "The battle of ideas," arguing that all in the West should stand firm and in solidarity against terrorism and what it represents. Taking the moral high ground, the editorial argued that "[i]n the mind of the terrorist, the sins of the West are so great that they justify any outrage, even the deliberate murder of thousands of people whose only crime is to be American." It goes on with the following exhortation:

> To combat terrorism, people in Western countries need to challenge that poisonous world view. They must learn to stand together, not just around the national flag of the United States or Canada or France, but around the idea of the West. That means saying more forcefully than we have before that the values that are known as Western—democracy, freedom, individual liberty—are valid and sacred, not just for those who live in the West but for the rest of the world, too. (Editorial, September 13, 2001, A18)

Here, we see a nationalist discourse subsumed under the identity of the "West" and "Western" nations. That such nations have been involved in countless wars involving colonial and imperial missions is erased. Moreover, we see the same attributes—"democracy, freedom, individual liberty"—identified as the hallmarks of the West. Non-Western nations, by contrast, do not have these same attributes. What then happens to India, which is considered the largest democracy in the world? In a move to exonerate the United States's previous involvement and history in all such wars, or in eliminating popularly elected governments in different parts of the world (Herman & Chomsky, 2002), the editorial asks us to overlook this. These, as the extract below explicates, are "mistakes." Instead, "we" Westerners should take the moral high ground:

> But, whatever the sins and mistakes of the United States and its allies, terrorism is not our fault. It does not spring from Western oppression, and it is not justified by Western misdeeds. Because the United States bombed Cambodia in the 1970s or bombed Kosovo in 1999 does not make it all right to bomb the World Trade Center in return. Two wrongs do not make a right. No grievance, however deep, can excuse a resort to the deliberate slaughter of innocent people. (Editorial, September 13, 2001, p. A18)

Again, elevating the issue to a moral plane leaves little room for any countering or dissenting opinion. Christian ethics certainly come to mind in the argument that "two wrongs do not make a right." But what happens when we are faced with a magnitude of retaliation of the kind in which the United States subsequently engaged? The carpet bombing of Afghanistan, the fallout from the Gulf War, with an entire generation of children wiped out, leaves little room for those who are immediately affected to even begin to engage in a moral dialogue. My point is to underscore how this editorial, in taking up a moralistic tone and in defending Western values, undermined the extent and horrors of the wars that have been enacted in the name of colonialism and imperialism. As Judith Butler so eloquently put it, "Our own acts of violence do not receive graphic coverage in the press, and so they remain acts that are justified in the name of self-defence, but by a noble cause, namely the rooting out of terrorism" (2004, p. 6).

In her column on September 13 (N3), Wente takes this nationalist discourse further, arguing that "we" are the "same as" Americans and that "we" are civilized while "they" are not. Just as in the editorial, the nationalist discourse is intertwined and somewhat subsumed by a larger discourse—the West as the epitome of reason, democracy, tolerance, and the like. Wente's language, like that of the *Globe*'s editorial, utilizes a civilizational discourse anchored in the "clash of civilizations" thesis.

This thesis, articulated by Samuel Huntington (1993), has distilled and simplified a larger conflict into a rudimentary cultural framework, arguing that Islam and Confucianism are the two biggest threats to the West on grounds of cultural/religious differences (see Mamdani, 2004). Huntington's thesis falls short on various accounts, which others have critiqued with more acumen. Mamdani maintains that the conflicts are political but clothed in the language of culture. Tariq Ali (2002) argues that the clash of civilizations thesis basically masks perceived threats in religious guise, when in fact the real threats are economically rooted in inaccessibility of oil and the mass export of cheap Chinese goods. He advances the view that what we are witnessing in the world today is a "clash of fundamentalisms" (Ali, 2000).

Nationalist discourses also come through in stories about Canadian generosity. For example, in a report on business, Howlett et al. (September 14, p. B1) mention the support provided by Canadian corporations and the donations of funds by Canadian banks. In another such story, Canadians were urged to make charitable contributions (Cestnick, September 15, p. B12). There are references also to Canadians helping stranded passengers, offering their homes and providing assistance. Canadian benevolence and goodwill remain part of the national imaginary of the "peaceable kingdom" erasing Canada's complicity in this war and others (Razack, 2004).

Closely interwoven with the discourse justifying war is the theme of American patriotism. Wente (September 15, p. A21) railed about the anti-American sentiment that she came across in her friends and acquaintances and contrasted this to the staunch spirit of support that she found among those in the service sector. Johanna Schneller condemned the anti-Americanism that she constantly experienced (September 15, p. F11), stating that she was proud to be American when confronted with pictures of the devastation in New York.

Throughout the week-long period, there were a number of stories that dealt with displays of patriotism by Americans and demonstrations of solidarity by Canadians. American flags were a recurrent feature in such displays. In his column on September 13, Doug Saunders notes that Wal-Mart sold 88,000 flags on September 11, and that many other stores were sold out of flags. As Inderpal Grewal notes, "the flag was represented as the signifier of the truth of loyalty and national allegiance rather than as a signifier of multiple meanings which could also be used to conceal rather than to reveal" (2003, p. 549). However, allegiance to the nation was predicated on exclusion—identifying and targeting those who were not seen to belong. A woman interviewed by Doug Saunders was quoted stating, "We go opening doors to every country. That ain't gonna happen any more." (Saunders, September 13, 2001, p. N2)

In another story, Kelly et al. reported the comments of one of the women, Luz Medina, a nursing-home worker they interviewed: "All the Muslims. Send them back home. All their churches—they have to close them and send them people back. I don't like that people" (September 13, 2001, p. N4). Similarly, Alana Mitchell, in her coverage of anti-Muslim sentiments in the United States, quoted a 19-year-old male, one of the 300 who had marched to a mosque in a suburb in Chicago chanting "U.S.A.! U.S.A.!", as saying: "I'm proud to be American and I hate Arabs and I always have" (Mitchell, September 14, p. A1).

There were numerous examples of such statements, but some reporters also balanced the perspective by including opposing sentiments. For example, in his column, Doug Saunders quoted a man named DeWitt whom he interviewed as saying, "I think people are horribly misguided to dwell on those sorts of celebrations. It just propagates the situation" (Saunders, September 13, 2001, p. N2). But this is then quickly contrasted with a backlash statement by DeWitt's friend. The most interesting aspect of these backlash statements is that they are neither challenged nor condemned by the columnists commenting on them (in contrast to the moral tone of the other columnists reported thus far). This despite the fact that columnists have more room to manoeuvre, writing "soft stories" as opposed to the "hard stories" of journalists, who more often have to abide by rules regarding factual reporting (see Bird and Dardenne, 1988). Rather, the backlash seems justified, even rendered as a commonsensical reaction to the attacks.

Terror Unleashed

On the flip side of the jingoistic patriotism were stories featuring the terrorizing effect of the racial backlash on Muslims and Muslim communities. Take, for example, the case of Yasmin Hanidi, whose situation was described in a story by Alana Mitchell on September 12 (p. N3). Mitchell quoted the 44-year-old Toronto Muslim as saying, "You feel so scared. We can pray that the U.S. doesn't start a bloodbath."

Here, while the depiction at the start is sympathetic, locating Hanidi and underscoring her anxiety, the description ends on her anger and inability to escape from the East to the West. What the account suggests is that those who are not like the "angry men from the desert" leave such places and come to the benevolent and abundant West. There is no other information provided to contextualize this move; rather, we are left with a "common sense" notion that people migrate to better their circumstances and to escape from the turmoil that is "out there." What might have caused the turmoil and upheaval are left out of this account. Understandably, news accounts do not always provide context, nor are human-interest stories contextualized in such a way. But without a context to frame the issue, how one interprets Yasmin Hanidi's story is left to that storehouse of collective knowledge that itself is replete with stereotypes and half-truths, mixed with historical traces—what Stuart Hall calls that "rag bag of knowledge" generally called "common sense." Hall argues that "You cannot learn, through common sense, *how things are*: you can only discover *where they fit* into the existing scheme of things" (1979, pp. 325–26).

This "fit" came across clearly in the articles dealing with the backlash. In an article dated September 14, 2001, Alana Mitchell quotes several Muslim leaders about the escalating violence. In telling the story, Mitchell provides a context for the violence experienced by Muslims in the United States and then includes a quote from an American, Donald McClarty, concerned about his Muslim friend and his son. McClarty argues, "That's not right. A few fanatics caused this and the ordinary Arabs should be taken care of by everyone." This view, as Mitchell's article emphasizes, is not shared by all. Again, Mitchell's article quotes a Muslim woman who, along with her husband and eight children, spoke of her experience following the attack the previous Tuesday:

> "This was a mob," said the woman, who asked not to be identified out of fear. "We had people riding up and down our block shouting obscenities. 'Go home you bleeping ragheads, bleeping A-rabs, we're gonna get you,'" added the woman, who lives in Oak Lawn. "My husband and I stayed up all night guarding the windows," she added. "My husband is of Arab descent. He gave four years of his life in the U.S. Navy … to have some skinhead with an American flag screaming at your house." (Mitchell et al., September 14, 2001, p. A1)

In the same story, Mitchell recounts another, similar, occurrence that took place in Toronto: "The woman was waiting for a commuter train to take her home when another woman passed by. The passer-by said to the Muslim woman, 'If I had a gun, I would shoot you right now.'" The Muslim leaders interviewed for this story stated that the community felt as if it was under "siege" and the leaders advised their members to stay home (Mitchell et al., September 14, 2001, p. A1). The leaders pointed to the media as fanning the flames of Islamophobia and also to the parallels between their experiences and the internment of the Japanese in Canada during World War II. In these and other Canadian stories dealing with the backlash, Muslim men who were interviewed tended to be representatives of major Islamic organizations (see also Lewington and Peritz, September 15, 2001, p. A14).

What these stories suggest is that, despite distancing themselves from those who had perpetrated the attacks on September 11, Muslim communities were still targeted because of their shared religious identities with the perpetrators and their apparent difference from the American and Canadian publics. There was no acknowledgement that Muslims and other people of colour had also been killed in the attacks. Additionally, and as the first quotation from the terrorized Muslim woman demonstrates, there was little if any coverage of how Muslims themselves had served in American and Canadian institutions, with many of them born here and in the United States. That Muslims are part of Canadian and American society is thus erased, as is the reality that Islam is one of the fastest-growing religions in the United States and that Black Muslims have long been a part of American society and its history. Instead, these quotations suggest a victimized minority community that is different and apart from the society in which they live. As John Asfour, one of the elite voices interviewed in this story stated, "What do Canadian Arabs have to do with this tragedy? They have families, children and businesses to look after in this country they love" (Mitchell et al., September 14, 2001, p. A1). Patriotism becomes one way in which Muslims can "prove" that they are part of the country, but this patriotism is not always accepted at face value. As one Muslim man stated, "But if I say I feel the same as an American feels, nobody believes," [said] Mr. Hatem" (Wong & Reguly, September 17, p. A8).

The overwhelming sense of fear articulated by the leaders of various Muslim communities and the Muslim women whose experiences were reported underscores their victim status, as religious and racial minorities who are guilty by association. Such fears were well-founded. Various reports indicate that anti-Muslim hate crimes increased in the immediate aftermath of September 11 (Hamdani, 2005). Reem Bahdi notes that Muslim organizations had "recorded 110 incidents of harassment, threats, death threats, attacks on personal property, physical assaults, and attempts to burn down Islamic centres and places of worship in the two months following 9/11" (2003, p. 314).

These incidents were duly publicized through the various press conferences held by Muslim leaders and communities, with little if any promise for protection and understanding. Yet an editorial on September 17 (p. A18) again exhorts "Islamic groups in North America to raise the cry of alarm as soon as reports of a racist backlash begin." In part, the editorial recognizes that the more disenfranchised and alienated Muslims feel as a result of the backlash, the more likely they are to identify with the grievances articulated by groups such as al Qaeda. This perspective echoes Louw's (2003) argument that for al Qaeda, one of the audiences for the attacks in New York was the diasporic Muslim population, who would quickly recognize that the illusion of tolerance was simply that – just a veneer. (Editorial, September 17, p. A18). There is thus an instrumental motive here—Muslims should report the backlash because otherwise "we" will look bad and "they" could become anti-American. What about the rights of Muslims as citizens of this nation?

Grewal argues that

> the transnational figure of the "terrorist" suggests that such a figure is beyond redemption and thus is of such high risk to the nation and the state as to be incarcerated immediately or to be destroyed. The flip side of this danger is thus the "security" and happiness and freedom to be felt by the incarceration of such bodies designated as "risk producing." (2003, p. 539)

In the week following September 11, various articles mentioned the need for increased security around Canadian institutions and on airlines (Mickleburgh, September 17, p. A1). In an article dated September 17, Ingrid Peritz quotes several passengers at the Dorval Airport in Montreal. One stated, "We didn't take [security] that seriously before. Now we have to." (Peritz, September 17, 2001, p. B5).

The notion of Muslims, and, more particularly, Muslim men, as a risk to the nation was accompanied by the interrogation and detention of Muslim or Muslim-looking men. Kellner (2003) observes that, in the United States, over 1,200 Muslim men were arrested and detained in the month following the attacks. In Canada, as mentioned above, there were similar detentions and deportations. However, the beginnings of this profiling of Muslims as risks to the nation are evident in this early coverage. Rod Mickleburgh (September 17, p. A1) describes various incidents involving Middle Eastern men who were viewed with suspicion by paranoid passengers. As Badhi (2003) has argued, in the post-9/11 context, race and religion became the proxy for risk.

Muslim Women

Many of the backlash stories also made specific reference to the women and girls wearing the hijab (the Muslim headscarf) as being more likely to be targets of such hate. This theme was repeated in later coverage (Elmasry, September 14, 2001, p. A26.) The hijab (the headscarf) and the burka (the full body covering) have always been a source of irritation to, if not denigration by, Western authorities, and to that extent they have both fascinated and repulsed the media and Western writers. As Majid (1998), Macdonald (2006), Vivian (1999), and others have demonstrated, the veil or head-covering is a cultural symbol and not one anchored in Islam's religious text, the Qu'ran. However, different sects within Islam situated in different geographical regions of the world have adopted its use as a sign of allegiance to the faith. In the West, more and more younger women wear the hijab or burka in response to the racism and harassment they experience (Hoodfar, 1993).

Meyda Yeğenoğlu reasons that

> The veil attracts the eye, and forces one to think, to speculate about what is behind it. It is often represented as some kind of a mask, hiding the woman. With the help of this opaque veil, the Oriental woman is considered as not yielding herself to the Western gaze and therefore imagined as hiding something behind the veil. It is through the inscription of the veil as a mask that the Oriental woman is turned into an enigma. (1998, p. 44)

The quest then becomes one of "unveiling" Muslim women, to expose their "real" nature. This "real" nature is epitomized by Western notions of femininity, where the "'natural,' 'open,' and 'unveiled' body is constructed through regimes of internalized management (diet, exercise, plastic surgery) as stringent as those imposed from without by Victorian corsetry, [and] masked by a fetishisation of 'choice' as the confirmation of liberation and self-determining agency" (Macdonald, 2006, p. 13).

The veil, within the Western context, is then layered with multiple meanings. On the one hand, if worn by diasporic Muslims (those living in the West), it becomes a sign of not fitting in, of not assimilating, and thus invokes resentment and backlash. On the other hand, when worn by women in Afghanistan or in other parts of the Muslim world, the veil (hijab/burka) is taken to be a sign of religious oppression, and hence unveiling becomes part of the "rescue" narrative in which Western powers seek to liberate these oppressed women (Cooke, 2002).

Though seen as a sign of not assimilating or fitting into the Western dominant culture, the women who wore hijabs or burkas or who were attacked for doing so were most often constructed as victims, reacting to fear. With the exception of one case, their agency was limited in that they were rarely shown fighting back. Witness, for example, the experiences of Sharon Agemoler, a 26-year-old Muslim born and raised in Toronto: "It's safer for me and my family if I try to avoid anything" (Lewington & Peritz, September 15, p. A14). In contrast to Sharon Agemoler, a Muslim woman interviewed by Jan Wong and Eric Reguly in New York was quite assertive. Born and raised in the United States, a businesswoman who has been confronted with racial slurs, Jaezah Ahmed gives them an earful. "They get surprised and they back off" (September 17, 2001, p. A8).

The contrast between these two portrayals is striking. The first woman, Agemoler, is Canadian, whereas Ahmed is American. The reporters for both stories are Canadian. The only difference is that reporter Jan Wong is a woman of colour. Is it that the other journalists could not find an example of an assertive Muslim woman or was it that they never looked beyond the stereotypical constructions of Muslim women as passive victims of oppressive cultures? That aside, the victimized status of Muslim women acts as double signifier. Not only are the women in the cases cited above victims of the backlash, they are also portrayed as victims of their cultural/religious traditions.

The "Good" Muslim versus the "Bad" Muslim

Mohamed Elmasry's article concerning the stereotyping and stigmatization of Muslims appeared on September 14 in the *Globe*'s section titled "Facts & Arguments." Thus, it reflects an individual submission by an outsider—not necessarily a journalist, columnist, or regular writer—setting it apart from the rest of the coverage. However, Elmasry's intervention in the mediated discourse thus far is interesting on two accounts: first, it represents a Muslim voice that is not confined to a few quotable quotes framed by a reporter; second, and more relevant to this discussion, is the implicit distinction he makes between "good" Muslims and "bad" Muslims. This is a discursive device that was also used by George W. Bush and Tony Blair when they attempted to stem the tide of the rising anti-Muslim sentiments in America and Britain, respectively. Mahmud Mamdani notes, "good Muslims are modern, secular, and Westernized, but bad Muslims are doctrinal, antimodern, and virulent" (2004, p. 24). For Elmasry, it is this distinction that needed to be clarified in the name of Islam. Taking the Qu'ran as his point of departure, Elmasry argues that Muslims such as those who attacked New York "should know better." He then argues that "we live in fear of being found guilty by association because of North America's prevailing ignorance about our faith." In this statement, Elmasry seems to be advocating education as a panacea for ignorance. Hate crimes are then seen as emanating from ignorance rather than the racialization of difference. Timothy McVeigh, who bombed the Murrah Federal Building in Oklahoma City (1995), was never regarded as a "bad" white in contrast to other good whites (Volpp in Bahdi, 2003, p. 312). Neither were his actions attributed to ignorance, which could then be treated with a requisite amount of education.

Another good Muslim was Ahmed Shah Massood, who had fought against the Taliban in Afghanistan. In an obituary, Massood, assassinated by the Taliban, was described as a "legendary guerrilla commander" and the one credible force in the anti-Taliban movement. His past history showed that he had successfully fought against the Soviet occupation and that he was a recognized leader. However, the obituary is quick to note that despite his supposedly progressive stance, his "reasonable" character, regarding women's equality, Massood's own wife is veiled as a result of custom (Bearak, September 17, 2001, p. R7).

The quotation marks around "reasonable" immediately raise the question as to whether he was indeed the "good" Muslim. There is no mention in this article of how the United Front differed from other competing groups that had similarly mistreated and subjugated women (as had, for example, the Northern Alliance), nor of why the issue of women had suddenly become important after years of being ignored by the media (Kolhatkar, 2002).

The Israeli–Palestinian Connection

Throughout the corpus of the stories examined, Palestinians came across as "bad" Muslims. There were numerous references to Palestinians celebrating in Ramallah upon hearing of the attacks on the Twin Towers and the Pentagon. Similarly, various columnists accessed voices of Israeli experts. Israel was vindicated: Americans could now feel what the Israelis were experiencing on a daily basis (Adams, September 14, p. A17). Interestingly, while Israeli experts holding high, credible, and often elite positions were quoted directly, for the Palestinian side, such quotes only came from the local people on the street—a cab driver, a woman, and Islamic clerics. This differentiation between the kinds of voices that are accessed and the over-reliance on elite voices from one side leads to a privileging of expert voices, since their voices carry more authority (van Dijk, 1993). Moreover, voices from the *vox populi*, as in the Palestinians on the street, are often positioned at the end of the article, while those of expert voices are usually positioned near the top of the story (see MacKinnon, September 15, p. A7). Articles that showed the plight of the Palestinians were often organized under a lead that cast suspicion on Palestinian motives, as, for example, Paul Adam's article (September 14, p. A17), which ran under the lead "Leaders try to contain the damage caused by images of people celebrating the attack." The "good" Muslims among the Palestinians are those who feel revulsion at what happened in New York; the "bad" Muslims are those who celebrated. However, the grief and sympathy expressed by all Arabs was also portrayed as suspect. In a story such as "Arab world's leaders walking a tightrope" (MacKinnon, September 15, p. A7), we get the sense that any articulation of grief, condolence, or sympathy expressed by Arab leaders is suspect in that it is based on a fear of retribution rather than an authentic expression of sorrow.

In all of these columns, the issue of retaliation is legitimized and the war becomes a "just war" (September 13, p. N3). As Norman Spector writes, Canada is the peaceable kingdom, but not for long; Spector takes us on a journey to Israel, where we witness once again the intransigence and recalcitrance of those who are not willing to side with the West. The need for force to quell these insubordinate others is justified, according to Spector. He argues, "In our triumph over Nazism, we did not shy away from bombing Dresden. We used nuclear weapons in bringing Japan to heel" (September 13, p. A19). We can see here the ideological preparation for war, the justifications that are used to legitimize retaliation, and the persuasive rhetoric used to convince readers that any amount of force is necessary, even if it involves nuclear warfare. The issue of going to war is not so much debated as simply presumed (see Hall et al., 1978).

The justification of war was not only articulated in terms of "liberating" a people or imposing a democracy, but also on the grounds that the attacks waged were unfair. Witness this account by Ian Brown in which he invokes the familiar Orientalist constructions of Muslims as "others" in his account of the death of 100,000 Iraqi soldiers in the Gulf War:

> No one in a sane or even reasonable state of mind thinks that military deaths suffered in a war Saddam started himself justify any sort of terrorism, or the killing of innocent civilians in an office tower in New York.
>
> But those deaths begin to explain how the people in a hot, dry, hungry, repressed and defeated country have come to hate the people in a glittering, wealthy, irrepressible city of silver towers on the other side of the Earth. (September 15, 2001, p. F6)

What Brown fails to point out is that approximately 300,000 children were killed in that first Gulf War in 1991, and they were not killed by Iraqis (see Ali, 2002, p. 300). That aside, whether the lives lost are those of civilians or soldiers, should it matter? Washburn reasons that "War stories are told with the flourish of explicit moral discourse. Trade stories are told with the patient repetition of words suggesting, but nor directly stating, that the rival nation is unreasonable and unfair" (quoted in Altheide, 2007, p. 288).

The other rationale for war was more implicit and woven around the discourse of Canadian dependence on and fraternity with the United States. In a column dated September 18, Paul Sullivan writes about Canada's relationship with the United States, stating that our peaceable state of affairs has been made possible by the "United States and its military." (September 18, 2001, p. A15).

In other words, the United States has kept "us" safe from despots and dictators, and hence "our" security and prosperity are intertwined. "We" look up to the United States, and we are under its benevolent protection. But we are "ineffable"—we don't speak about or make support so explicit. To drive the point home, Sullivan castigates an anti-war email he received from Vancouver Status of Women, claiming that he hadn't received a similar email about the ruthless treatment of women under the Taliban regime. Support for America, then, comes through in the chastisement of the anti-war movement and the harnessing of Afghan women's oppression under the Taliban.

It was not until September 17 that the *Globe* ran an article about the impact of the United States's impending war on Afghanistan on the population there. Under the category "Brink of War," Geoffrey York's article details the panic erupting in Afghanistan as thousands attempted to flee the U.S. bombing (September 17, p. A1). York describes the situation of Jamila Salim and her escape from Kabul. Her account details the brutality of the Pakistani and Taliban border guards, and how, by bribing the police, she was able to get herself and her family into Peshawar. In the meantime, York explains, the United States and Pakistan were attempting to seal the borders. York provides a gripping image of the fear- and panic-stricken refugees.

York then goes on to describe the dire predictions of international relief agencies. The few other stories that mention Afghanistan do so within a discussion about preparations for war and the United States's military might. Again, in these stories, there is no debate about the utility or futility of such a war. Instead, the war is already presumed. The media not only define a situation but also set the limits of the terms of debate—and in this first week, there was little to no debate.

CONCLUSION: EXPLANATORY FRAMEWORKS

But what happened on Tuesday . . . was about hatred. Hatred of America's insistence on individualism, its blasé freedoms, its naiveté. Passionate hatred, full of certitude. (Schneller, September 15, 2001, p. F11).

Indeed, the flip side to the world's appetite for the American Life is a dark mix of emotions: envy, resentment and hatred. (Cernetig, September 17, p. A13)

The media, as Hartley (1982), Gitlin (1979), and others have demonstrated, proffer explanatory frameworks that "make sense." In so doing, they frame out certain information and frame in, or give privileged attention to, other kinds of information. The *Globe's* primary explanation of the events of 9/11 focused on the hate and resentment felt by others. The emphasis on emotions (hate, resentment, anger) displaced the focus so that critical issues regarding United States foreign policy were hardly, if ever, brought up. When these issues were mentioned, they were never historicized or contextualized. I can recall only one statement that, aside from a couple of *vox populi* quotes, critically challenged the prevailingly emotive frame of hate using similar emotively charged words. This statement was made in the *Guardian* newspaper in Britain and then reprinted in the *Globe* (Cernetig, September 17, p. A13). Even here, the impact of the statement was overshadowed by the focus on "envy, resentment and hatred."

The lack of a critical perspective in the retelling of this story was, undoubtedly, influenced by the shock and horror of the attacks and Canada's cultural and geographic proximity to the United States. Nevertheless, as crucial agents in shaping public discourse and facilitating critical debate and discussion, the media have a responsibility of informing citizens. Instead, the analysis of the coverage detailed here, though limited to a one-week time span, reveals that war was a foregone conclusion and that "envy, resentment and hatred" were the driving force underpinning the attacks. The week's coverage also showed that the seeds of all that followed September 11, 2001, were sown in such a way that they legitimized the "risk/security" discourse, paving the way for the "necessity" of security certificates and increased surveillance, as well as detention and deportation of those considered to be risks to the nation. The trope of victimized women was harnessed not only to reflect on the Taliban's barbarism but also to point out that those who do not fit in will be vulnerable to attacks. Similarly, the "good" Muslim/"bad" Muslim dichotomy served to separate those who were on "our" side from those who were opposed to "us." The nationalist discourse clearly positioned Canada as allied with the United States in many different ways.

However, that said, we cannot assume that audiences are all dupes. Many turned to alternative sources on the internet rather than simply relying on the mainstream press. Moreover, there was a concerted effort at the grassroots level by the anti-war movement that galvanized considerable opposition to the impending war. Nevertheless, in the weeks that followed, we saw the cultivation of many of these seeds of fear as well as the full brunt of the "collateral damage" inflicted on Afghanistan.

Media Journal Assignments

1. Examine your local newspaper's coverage of Canadian soldiers' involvement in Afghanistan over a three-day period. Do you feel the portrayal promotes an "us-versus-them" mentality? Should the media be supporting this dichotomy or critiquing it? Why or why not?

2. Van Dijk (1993) posits that headlines act as cognitive organizers—they organize the information so that we get a sense of how the story should be read. Go over the headlines of the newspaper articles in the References section for this chapter and see if you arrive at the same conclusions as Jiwani has.

3. Over a one-week period, examine how either the *National Post* or the *Globe and Mail* conceptualizes the Canadian self-image. Do the newspapers actively construct an image of Canada as separate from the United States?

References

Agathangelou, A.M. & L.H.M. Ling. 2004. "Power, Borders, Security, Wealth: Lessons of Violence and Desire from September 11." *International Studies Quarterly* 48 (3): 517–38.

Akram, S.M. 2002. "The Aftermath of September 11, 2001: The Targeting of Arabs and Muslims in America." *Arab Studies Quarterly* 24 (Spring–Summer): 61–118.

Ali, T. 2002. *The Clash of Fundamentalisms: Crusades, Jihads and Modernity.* London and New York: Verso.

Altheide, D.L. 2007. "The Mass Media and Terrorism." *Discourse & Communication* 1 (3): 287–308.

Anderson, B. 1983. *Imagined Communities: Reflections on the Origin and Spread of Nationalism.* rev. ed. London: Verso.

Bahdi, R. 2003. "No Exit: Racial Profiling and Canada's War against Terrorism." *Osgoode Hall Law Journal* 41 (2/3): 293–316.

Bennett, L.W. 2003. *News: The Politics of Illusion.* 5th ed. White Plains, N.Y.: Longman.

Bird, E.S. & R.W. Dardenne. 1988. "Myth, Chronicle, and Story: Exploring the Narrative Qualities of News." In *Mass Communication as Culture: Myth and Narrative in Television and the Press*, ed. J. Carey, 67–87. Beverley Hills, Cal.: Sage.

Butler, J. 2004. *Precarious Life: The Powers of Mourning and Violence.* London and New York: Verso.

Chomsky, N. 2001. "An Evening with Noam Chomsky: The New War against Terror." Technology and Culture Forum at MIT. October 18. Available at http://web.mit.edu/tac/past/2001-2002/index.html (accessed August 21, 2008).

Cooke, M. 2002. "Saving Brown Women." *Signs* 28 (1): 468–70.

De Cillia, R., M. Reisigl, & R. Wodak. 1999. "The Discursive Construction of National Identities." *Discourse & Society* 10 (2): 149–73.

Entman, R.M. 2003. "Cascading Activation: Contesting the White House's Frame after 9/11." *Political Communication* 20 (4): 415–32.

Gitlin, T. 1979. "News As Ideology and Contested Area: Toward a Theory of Hegemony, Crisis and Opposition." *Socialist Review* 9 (6): 11–54.

Grewal, I. 2003. "Transnational America: Race, Gender and Citizenship after 9/11." *Social Identities* 9 (4): 535–61.

Hall, S. 1979. "Culture, the Media and the 'Ideological Effect.'" In *Mass Communication and Society*, ed. J. Curran, M. Gurevitch, and J. Woollacott, 315–47. London: E. Arnold in association with The Open University Press.

———. 1990. "The Whites of their Eyes: Racist Ideologies and the Media." In *The Media Reader*, ed. M. Alvarado and J.O. Thompson, 9–23. London: British Film Institute.

Hall, S., C. Critcher, T. Jefferson, & B. Roberts. 1978. *Policing the Crisis: Mugging, the State, Law and Order.* London: MacMillan Press.

Hamdani, D. 2005. *Triple Jeopardy: Muslim Women's Experience of Discrimination.* Canadian Council of Muslim Women. Available at www.ccmw.com/documents/Triple_Jeopardy.pdf (accessed August 21, 2008).

Hartley, J. 1982. *Understanding News.* London and New York: Methuen.

Herman, E.S. & N. Chomsky. 2002. *Manufacturing Consent: The Political Economy of the Mass Media*. New York and Toronto: Pantheon Books, Random House. (Orig. pub. 1988.)

Hoodfar, H. 1993. "Veil in Their Minds and on Our Heads: The Persistence of Colonial Images of Muslim Women." *Resources for Feminist Research* 22 (3/4): 5–18.

Huntington, Samuel. 1993. "The Clash of Civilizations." *Foreign Affairs*. Available at http://history.club.fatih.edu.tr/103%20Huntington%20Clash%20of%20Civilizations%20full%20text.htm (accessed September 11, 2008).

Jiwani, Y. 2006. *Discourses of Denial: Mediations of Race, Gender and Violence*. Vancouver: University of British Columbia Press.

Jurgensmeyer, Mark. 2000. *Terror in the Mind of God: The Global Rise of Religious Violence*. Berkeley: University of California Press.

Kaplan, R.L. 2003. "American Journalism Goes to War, 1898–2001: A Manifesto on Media and Empire." *Media History* 9 (3): 209–19.

Karim, H.K. 2000. *Islamic Peril*. Montreal: Black Rose Books.

Kellner, D. 2003. *From 9/11 to Terror War: The Dangers of the Bush Legacy*. Lanham, Boulder, New York, Oxford: Rowman & Littlefield.

Kolhatkar, S. 2002. "The Impact of U.S. Intervention on Afghan Women's Studies." *Berkeley Women's Law Journal* 17: 12–30.

Louw, P.E. 2003. "The 'War against Terrorism': A Public Relations Challenge for the Pentagon." *Gazette: The International Journal for Communication Studies* 65 (3): 211–30.

Macdonald, M. 2006. "Muslim Women and the Veil: Problems of Image and Voice in Media Representations." *Feminist Media Studies* 6 (1): 7–23.

Majid, A. 1998. "The Politics of Feminism in Islam." *Signs: Journal of Women in Culture and Society* 23 (2): 321–61.

Mamdani, M. 2004. *Good Muslim, Bad Muslim: America, the Cold War and the Roots of Terror*. New York: Pantheon.

Mann, B. 2006. "How America Justifies Its War: A Modern/Postmodern Aesthetics of Masculinity and Sovereignty." *Hypatia* 21 (4): 147–63.

Nacos, B.L. 2002. *Mass-Mediated Terrorism: The Central Role of the Media in Terrorism and Counterterrorism*. Lanham, Boulder, New York, Oxford: Rowman & Littlefield.

Nayak, M. 2006. "Orientalism and 'Saving' U.S. State Identity after 9/11." *International Feminist Journal of Politics* 8 (1): 42–61.

Rantanen, T. 2004. "European News Agencies and Their Sources in the Iraq War Coverage." In *Reporting War: Journalism in Wartime*, ed. S. Allan and B. Zelizer, 301–14. Oxon and New York: Routledge.

Razack, S.H. 2004. *Dark Threats and White Knights: The Somalia Affair, Peacekeeping, and the New Imperialism*. Toronto: University of Toronto Press.

Said, E.W. 1978. *Orientalism*. New York: Vintage Books.

———. 1981. *Covering Islam: How the Media and Experts Determine How We See the Rest of the World*. New York: Pantheon Books.

Shaheen, J.G. 2001. *Reel Bad Arabs: How Hollywood Vilifies a People*. New York: Olive Branch Press.

Silberstein, S. 2002. *War of Words: Language, Politics and 9/11*. London and New York: Routledge.

van Dijk, T.A. 1993. *Elite Discourse and Racism*. Vol. 6. Newbury Park, CA: Sage.

Vivian, B. 1999. "The Veil and the Visible." *Western Journal of Communication* 63 (2): 115–39.

Winch, S.P. 2005. "Constructing an 'Evil Genius': News Uses of Mythic Archetypes to Make Sense of Bin Laden." *Journalism Studies* 6 (3): 285–99.

Yeğenoğlu, M. 1998. *Colonial Fantasies: Towards a Feminist Reading of Orientalism*. Cambridge and Melbourne: Cambridge University Press.

Zelizer, B. & S. Allan, eds. 2002. *Journalism after September 11*. London and New York: Routledge.

Articles from the *Globe and Mail*

Adams, P. 2001. "The aftermath: The world reacts: Palestinians massage their message." *Globe and Mail*, September 14, A17.

Bearak, B. 2001. "Rebel led fight against the Taliban: Ahmed Shah Massood." *Globe and Mail*, September 17, R7.

Brown, I. 2001. "Day of infamy: New York: This is the way the world changed." *Globe and Mail*, September 12, N2.

———. 2001. "The aftermath: The things we can't get out of our minds." *Globe and Mail*, September 15, F6.

Bush, G.W. 2001. "U.S. reaction: Complete text of President Bush's national address." *Globe and Mail*, September 12, A4.

Cernetig, M. 2001. "The brink of war: American dream shows its dark side." *Globe and Mail*, September 17, A13.

Cestnick, T. 2001. "Tax matters: A time to consider the true meaning of charity." *Globe and Mail*, September 15, B12.

Cheney, P. 2001. "The brink of war: 'A very strange, unusual time.'" *Globe and Mail*, September 17, A9.

Editorial. 2001. "The battle of ideas." *Globe and Mail*, September 13, A18.

———. 2001. "What we stand for." *Globe and Mail*, September 17, A18.

Elmasry, M. 2001. "Neighbours as collateral damage." *Globe and Mail*, September 14, A26.

Gee, M. 2001. "Day of infamy: Celebrating the misery of 'the head of the snake.'" *Globe and Mail*, September 12, N8.

Houpt, S. 2001. "Day of infamy: Wall Street in Ruins: Sun blotted out by smoke and soot." *Globe and Mail*, September 12, A9.

———. 2001. "The day after: City unites behind Giuliani; Outgoing mayor described as more presidential than the President." *Globe and Mail*, September 13, A2.

———. 2001. "The aftermath: The human toll: Rescue workers show strain of grisly task." *Globe and Mail*, September 14, A14.

Howlett, K. 2001. "The day after: U.S. brokers need time to heal." *Globe and Mail*, September 13, B1.

Howlett, K., R. Blackwell, E. Church, & A.Willis. 2001. "The aftermath: Corporate camaraderie emerges." *Globe and Mail*, September 14, B1.

Kelly, D. 2001. "Day of infamy: Eye witness: 'I can't get to anyone I love. I hate this.'" *Globe and Mail*, September 12, N4.

Kelly, D., P. Brethour, K. Cox, C. Freeze, I. Wallace, Associated Press et al. 2001. "The day after: Heroes 'No retaliation can take this pain away'; Horrors." *Globe and Mail*, September 13, N4.

Kesterton, M. 2001. "The day after: One day in September." *Globe and Mail*, September 13, A20.

Knox, P. 2001. "The day after: The blowback that made bin Laden an enemy of U.S.: The prime suspect." *Globe and Mail*, September 13, A3.

Lewington, J. & I. Peritz. 2001. "The aftermath, day of mourning: Canadian Muslim won't go out alone." *Globe and Mail*, September 15, A14.

MacKinnon, M. 2001. "The aftermath: The world reacts: Arab world's leaders walking a tightrope." *Globe and Mail*, September 15, A7.

Mickleburgh, R. 2001. "The brink of war: Hairpins, paper clips seized from travellers." *Globe and Mail*, September 17, A1.

Mitchell, A. 2001. "Day of infamy: Canada apocalypse now: Canadians fear the horror, south of the border has people coast to coast braced for the worst, 'We can't escape anywhere in the world today.'" *Globe and Mail*, September 12, N3.

Mitchell, A., with reports from Reuters, Associated Press, James Rusk, Sean Fine, and Kevin Cox. 2001. "The aftermath: Arab Canadians duck to avoid harassment." *Globe and Mail*, September 14, A1.

Peritz, I. 2001. "The brink of war: Air travel: Patience is new price of flying." *Globe and Mail*, September 17, B5.

Priest, L. 2001. "The aftermath, the rescue efforts: Relatives hope against all odds." *Globe and Mail*, September 15, A4.

Reguly, E. 2001. "The day after: Heroes; Horrors." *Globe and Mail*, September 13, N4.

Richer, S. 2001. "The aftermath, first person: The man who went down instead of up." *Globe and Mail*, September 15, F11.

Saunders, D. 2001. "The day after: Faith, hope and fear." *Globe and Mail*, September 13, N2.

Schneller, J. 2001. "The aftermath first person: let me raise a flag to the ash-grey sky: I am an American." *Globe and Mail*, September 15, F11.

Spector, N. 2001. "The day after: Goin' down the Israeli road to thwart terror." *Globe and Mail*, September 13, A19.

Sullivan, P. 2001. "The brink of war: The West: Coming together in Lotusland." *Globe and Mail*, September 18, A15.

Wente, M. 2001. "Day of infamy: U.S. will never be the same." *Globe and Mail*, September 12, A1.

———. 2001. "The day after: We're all Americans now." *Globe and Mail*, September 13, N3.

———. 2001. "Counterpoint: They had it coming?" *Globe and Mail*, September 15, A21.

Wong, J. 2001. "The aftermath: Day of morning: Little is silent in New York." *Globe and Mail*, September 15, A12.

———. "The aftermath lives: Two portraits of courage." *Globe and Mail*, September 15, F4.

Wong, J. & E. Reguly. 2001. "The brink of war: New York's agony: Attacks spawn racial backlash." *Globe and Mail*, September 17, A8.

York, G. 2001. "The brink of war: Afghans run for border." *Globe and Mail*, September 17, A1.

GLOBE AND MAIL ARTICLES

Please note: The *Globe and Mail* provided permission to reprint quotations of 25 words or less from *Globe and Mail* articles for free. Longer quotations required payment for the rights to print the articles with the additional requirement that the articles be printed in their entirety. The full text of these articles follows.

Day of Infamy: U.S. will never be the same
Column: Wednesday, September 12, 2001, A1, Margaret Wente

8:45 a.m., Eastern Daylight Time. A crack in the centre of the world. Someone took revenge on America, and America was helpless.

Nothing there will ever be the same again.

A nation at the height of power, peace and prosperity, blessed by every fortune, whose enemies, it seemed, were as harmless as a few far-off fluffy clouds on a blazing blue September day.

A nation that yesterday looked infinitely vulnerable.

It only took a few men who hate America to hijack its own commercial airplanes and turn them into bombs. It only took a few to ram them into America's most potent symbols of financial and military might. America's sense of its own security exploded with those towers in a cloud of smoke and dust.

Americans will never feel quite so safe again. Nor will any of the rest of us, who looked to them to keep us safe, too.

Their defences were completely useless. Their intelligence and security machine, fuelled by billions of dollars and the best high-tech devices ever invented, could not keep the bad guys out. They slipped through with ease, and struck the nation in its heart.

The skyline of the capital of the world has a gaping wound where the towers once stood; a scar that will last forever.

The slaughter of civilians had always happened somewhere else. Now the horror has come home.

Who did these things? All indications point to a sacred jihad from the Middle East. Maybe it was Saddam Hussein, exacting his blood revenge at last. Or Osama bin Laden, the millionaire fanatic who hates America for sending troops to Saudi Arabia during the war in the Persian Gulf, and for supporting Israel. "Blood, blood and destruction, destruction," he commanded in a videotape to his followers last fall. To kill Americans is holy.

Those who are responsible are most likely men from remote desert lands. Men from ancient tribal cultures built on blood and revenge. Men whose unshakable beliefs and implacable hatreds go back many centuries farther than the United States and its young ideas of democracy, pluralism and freedom.

Hard men, who hide out in desert bunkers and turn the instruments of Western technology— its computers and CD-ROMs and videotapes and airplanes—against the West. Men capable of flying Boeing 747s with pinpoint, deadly accuracy, and of giving up their lives for the greater glory of Allah, and of murder on a massive scale. Men who've mastered all the modern Western technocratic skills, and who deploy them with the implacable determination of fanatics.

Men whom most Americans, in their innocent and happy secularism, can scarcely comprehend and hardly ever gave a thought since that nearly bloodless cartoon war in the gulf.

That innocence is now gone.

For a decade now, these terrorists have been America's greatest threat. Its military muscle could have obliterated them long ago, but the will was never there. The tradeoffs were judged to be too great. Mr. Hussein and Mr. bin Laden are experts at survival. They are hard to catch, and surround themselves with men armed with guns and rocket launchers. Americans would not have been able to stomach too much loss of life to catch these men and the possibility of failure and political embarrassment was too great.

And no one wanted to create another Islamic martyr.

Everything will change now, will tip and destabilize in ways far beyond knowing.

The Middle East, the world's economy, the American intelligence establishment, its entire defence strategy, the way it fights its foes. Millions of people of Islamic faith unfairly tarnished by the terrorism of a few.

We have ahead the test by fire of a presidency.

We will have agonizing stories of human suffering, too many to bear. We will have the dead, and countless families shattered, and grief and mourning beyond measure.

But the wounds to America, though terrible, are very far from mortal.

"Americans will persevere," said one New York woman yesterday, staring hard into the camera. She had seen people die before her eyes. That was her message to us and to the men who did this.

Shock and disbelief and grief will give way to anger and resolve.

The fanatics and the terrorists will not prevail. The wider Arab world will not rally to support them, and America will not be driven away. Americans will persevere.

But everything has changed, and the world will never go back to the way it used to be, before the madness began, at 8:45 a.m. Eastern Daylight Time.

The battle of ideas
Editorial: Thursday, September 13, 2001, A18

The new war against terrorism that must follow this week's events in the United States will require many changes in the way that target nations conduct themselves, from tightened airport security to more aggressive international policing. But perhaps the most important change will be intellectual. If we are to win this war—and win it we must—all of us must brace for a battle not just of arms, but of ideas.

The central idea behind most of modern terrorism is that the West, as an entity, is oppressing the rest of the world. The West oppresses the world's poor by raking off the world's wealth through its multinational corporations and leaving scraps for everyone else. The West oppresses the world's non-Christian religions by spreading corrupting secular values such as individualism and sexual liberation. The West oppresses the world's other cultures by polluting them with shallow Hollywood movies and American television shows. All this is laid at the feet of the Western nations, especially the United States.

In the mind of the terrorist, the sins of the West are so great that they justify any outrage, even the deliberate murder of thousands of people whose only crime is to be American.

To combat terrorism, people in Western countries need to challenge that poisonous world view. They must learn to stand together, not just around the national flag of the United States or Canada or France, but around the idea of the West. That means saying more forcefully than we have before that the values that are known as Western—democracy, freedom, individual liberty—are valid and sacred, not just for those who live in the West but for the rest of the world, too. These values are universal and, by rights, they should apply to every man and woman on Earth.

That may seem obvious. But for many of those who live in the West, it is not. Though almost everyone condemns terrorism, many people harbour a grudging sympathy for the anti-Western world-view that underpins it. Just as British liberals in the 1930s admired the Soviet Union for challenging Western capitalism and imperialism, many Westerners today admire Third World liberation movements that challenge globalization and "U.S. hegemony." Whenever a new terrorist horror occurs, we are urged to look at the root causes and examine our own responsibility for them.

But, whatever the sins and mistakes of the United States and its allies, terrorism is not our fault. It does not spring from Western oppression, and it is not justified by Western misdeeds. Because the United States bombed Cambodia in the 1970s or bombed Kosovo in 1999 does not make it all right to bomb the World trade Center in return. Two wrongs do not make a right. No grievance, however deep, can excuse a resort to the deliberate slaughter of innocent people.

It was wrong in the Cold War to argue that there was a moral equivalency between the crushing oppression in the Communist bloc and the misbehaviour of the United States. It is wrong today to say that there is a parallel between Western wrongs and terrorist mayhem. To say so is to lend terrorism a legitimacy that it does not deserve. Any movement that sends its young men to die in a suicide attackis illegitimate on its face.

Let's be clear. When terrorists attacked the United States this week, they did not just attack buildings and people. They attacked our deepest ideals. The least we can do in response is to agree that those values are worth fighting for.

The Aftermath: Arab Canadians duck to avoid harassment
International News, Friday, September 14, 2001, A1, Alana Mitchell

With reports from Reuters, Associated Press, James Rusk, Sean Fine and Kevin Cox

Saying they are under siege in their own country, Arab Canadians are shunning school, work, travel and even the streets to avoid escalating harassment from fellow citizens angry over catastrophic attacks on the United States.

"We are seen as the enemy within," said Jehad Aliweiwi, executive director of the Canadian Arab Federation. "A lot of people feel it's probably a time to stay at home."

In the United States, anti-Muslim sentiment reached hysteria as investigations began to point to a connection between the Middle East and the attacks in New York and Washington.

The situation was so heated that both U.S. President George W. Bush and his father, former president George Bush, called for tolerance for Arab Americans and Muslims. The elder Mr. Bush took pains to explain that Muslims believe "in a God of love and mercy." Some Islamic centres in the United States have been fired on. Mosques have been vandalized.

On Wednesday night, police turned back 300 marchers—some waving U.S. flags and shouting "USA! USA!"—as they tried to march on a mosque in the Chicago suburb of Bridgeview.

Three demonstrators were arrested. There were no injuries and demonstrators were kept blocks from the closed Muslim house of worship.

"I'm proud to be American and I hate Arabs and I always have," said 19-year-old Colin Zaremba, who marched with the group.

As he waited to get on a plane at Halifax airport yesterday to continue his interrupted journey home, Donald McClarty of San Francisco spent some time on the phone telling a Muslim friend that he should consider keeping his son home from school for a few days.

"I'd hate to think that some racist act would happen to a seven-year-old boy because there are a lot of people out there who are going to blame all this on the Muslims or the Arabs," he said.

"That's not right. A few fanatics caused this and the ordinary Arabs should be taken care of by everyone." A Muslim woman said she, her husband and their eight children endured a night of terror in the aftermath of Tuesday's attack.

"This was a mob," said the woman, who asked not to be identified out of fear. "We had people riding up and down our block shouting obscenities. 'Go home you bleeping ragheads, bleeping A-rabs, we're gonna get you,'" added the woman, who lives in Oak Lawn.

"My husband and I stayed up all night guarding the windows," she added. "My husband is of Arab descent. He gave four years of his life in the U.S. Navy . . . to have some skinhead with an American flag screaming at your house."

Police were investigating scores of other threats against Americans of Middle Eastern background from coast to coast.

In Toronto, Imran Yousuf, spokesman for the Canadian Muslim Civil Liberties Association, said his organization, which represents Muslims whose families stem from Arab countries and other parts of the world, is considering pleading with its members to keep out of sight until tensions ease.

And in the United States, Altaf Ali of the Council of American-Islamic Relations urged people to avoid going out.

"Right now, we are encouraging Muslim families to stay home for a few days until this issue cools down a bit. . . . Emotions are running very high at the moment," he said.

In Canada, the Islamic Supreme Council and Muslims Against Terrorism have set up hot lines in Toronto and Calgary for victims of threats. The groups are urging police and governments to help keep Muslims safe from hate crimes.

Included in the types of harassment across Canada are vicious e-mails calling Arabs "vermin," violent telephone messages, attacks on mosques in many parts of the country and personal threats.

Women and girls tend to be more heavily targeted, especially if they wear the traditional Muslim head scarf, Mr. Yousuf said. Some employers are arranging for Muslim and Arab workers to be escorted to and from their premises, he said.

"We are now in a state of siege," said Mr. Aliweiwi, adding that the Arab and Muslim communities feel they are surrounded by an intensifying "sea of hate."

Mr. Yousuf got a horrifying call yesterday from a woman who works in downtown Toronto. The woman was waiting for a commuter train to take her home when another woman passed by. The passerby said to the Muslim woman: "If I had a gun, I would shoot you right now."

The Muslim woman said she was terrified. Eventually, she got home and called the police.

"She was in shock. You would probably want to run for your life," Mr. Yousuf said.

He said the association has reports from Muslim parents saying that they are keeping their children at home. Some Muslim schools across Canada have closed, including one in Calgary that shut for two days and another in Montreal.

The Edmonton Islamic School remained open but kept the pupils inside at recess.

"Some people are actually saying: 'Let's pack our bags,'" Mr. Aliweiwi said.

John Asfour, president of the Canadian Arab Federation, said he believes newspapers, radio stations and television outlets are fanning the flames of hatred against Arabs.

"It seems to be that some media outlets are taking it on as a holy campaign against Arabs and Muslims," he said. "What do Canadian Arabs have to do with this tragedy? They have families, children and businesses to look after in this country they love."

Dr. Asfour, who has a PhD in modern English literature from McGill University, said the widespread discrimination Arabs are experiencing is akin to what the Japanese felt during the Second World War.

Toronto Mayor Mel Lastman made the same connection yesterday.

After he signed a condolence book in the lobby of City Hall, the mayor recalled the "mistake" of the ill treatment and internment of Japanese-Canadians after the 1941 attackon Pearl Harbor, and said that the city should not repeat that experience.

"Don't go around hurting people. Don't go around allowing your kids to hurt other kids. No hate literature," he said.

The Aftermath: The things we can't get out of our minds
Focus: Saturday, September 15, 2001, F6, Ian Brown

'Are they trying to pass a phone back and forth? What are they saying to each other - goodbye, I love you, it's okay? Do they know each other?' An essay by IAN BROWN

For myself, I remember the towers burning, black smoke creeping like a thick poison up toward the vents. I remember the screams on the videotape as the first tower collapsed. I remember the reports of that little kid calling his mother to say he couldn't breathe, and goodbye.

Everybody does, everybody always will. This is who we are, at least these days—a collection of reactions. According to the always-entertaining CNN instant poll, 48 per cent of us are "angry" about the attacks on America. Only 26 per cent of us, apparently, feel "shock" or "sorrow."

But there are other numbers and details I can't get out of my mind, for reasons I am afraid to understand. I'm beginning to think this means something. I'm beginning to think there are no winners in this war, and that the pictures on the television have been telling us this all along.

For instance, there were the body bags. On Wednesday, the rescuers in New York City put out a call for 30,000 of them. That's a lot. The usual order, according to Mike Grimm, vice-president of Evident Crime Scene Products of Union Hall, Va., is "30 to 40 body bags at a time."

So the whole body-bag industry has been in a panic ever since the attacks. The last time it saw this kind of demand was in 1999, when 14,000 people died in an earthquake in Turkey. The bags run $280 for a box of 24, are advertised as having "features" such as the Loop Lock Zipper and names like Super Duty Transport Bags. The largest manufacturer, Centennial Industries, manufactures 60,000 a year in chlorine-free polypropylene and three different colours. But they don't anticipate a shortage at Centennial, I was told, because New York won't need full-size units.

I know this is morbid. But the numbers themselves become an obsession, or at least a distraction. By the end of the week, they even began to improve. Estimates of the number of dead in Washington and in New York—and they were estimates at best—began to fall, from 30,000 to 10,000, at one point even to 5,000. That 5,000 dead could bring even some relief describes the immensity of the tragedy.

Stick with the numbers and they will tell you secrets, maybe even reveal the truth. Five thousand dead, for instance, is better than 10,000 dead. But fewer dead also complicates the response of the Americans, makes their—our—global antiterrorist cause less cut-and-dried, less forceful and righteous.

Because there are other numbers too. In June, 1991, the U.S. military estimated that more than 100,000 Iraqi soldiers died in the Gulf War. Many human-rights groups peg the figure much higher, and the civilian toll higher still. But we can agree that the Iraqis lost four World Trade Centers worth of soldiers alone. The United States, on the other hand, lost 148 men in that war.

That is one reason why Saddam Hussein this week claimed America was reaping the seeds of evil it had sown. No one in a sane or even reasonable state of mind thinks that military deaths suffered in a war Saddam started himself justify any sort of terrorism, or the killing of innocent civilians in an office tower in New York.

But those deaths begin to explain how the people in a hot, dry, hungry, repressed and defeated country have come to hate the people in a glittering, wealthy, irrepressible city of silver towers on the other side of the Earth.

But what I really can't get out of my mind is that picture of people leaning out of the World Trade Center, 90 storeys up in the air. Do you know the one I mean? The entire photograph consists of a few floors, high up one side of one of the towers.

I know a lot of numbers about the towers, too: Tower 1 suffered immediate airplane damage from floors 96 to 103, whereas Tower 2's hit took out levels 87 to 93. Tower 2's hit was worse: It needed only 56 minutes to fall, whereas Tower 1 lasted an hour and 40 minutes. It took 50 minutes to walk down from anywhere above the 51st floor.

This picture, though, is another story altogether. Out of what once were windows, people are leaning out and up, or out and down. Their short arms are reaching, but for what, we can't tell. They're talking, leaning up and down to one another from one floor to the next, close but not close enough. They're trapped.

They don't look like they're panicking, not really, but they're a long way away. In their midst, a woman in black pants and a gold top is standing on the window sill. She appears to be thinking of jumping.

I've been staring at this picture for days now.

What are those people high up the side of that burning building saying to one another? Are they saying, "Goodbye, baby," or "I love you," or "It's okay, it's okay, just hang on, we'll be all right"? How long did that fantasy last? Are they trying to pass a cellphone back and forth, so everyone can call husbands and children? Do they know each other?

And, worst of all, how frightened must they be? I find it hard to think of how frightened they must be.

Some of the pictures I couldn't forget were eminently forgettable. The first time I turned on the television to watch CNN, I actually hit the shopping channel instead. To this day, I can't picture that footage of the fireball in the tower without seeing another kind of footage as well: Three fat white dames sitzing their feet in some useless electrical contraption. I wonder how many they sold. I wonder what Afghanistan would make of them.

Sometimes it is just words that obsess me. The phrase everything is different now, for instance. There are other words too: Assassin. Suicide.

According to long-established polls, 60 per cent of Americans believe that God speaks directly to them. Fortunately, they don't then strap themselves into stolen planes and drive themselves into the sides of building in Baghdad or Jiddah in the hope of becoming divine assassins.

To do that, you need help. According to the Oxford English Dictionary, an Assassin, formally speaking, was "a member of the Nizari branch of Ismaili Muslims, when the newly established sect ruled part of northern Persia (1094-1256). They were renowned as militant fanatics, and were popularly reputed to use hashish before going on murder missions."

The origin of the word assassin, in fact, dates to the middle of the 16th century, from the French version of the medieval-Latin assassinus,which in turn derives from the Arabic word hasisi, or hashish-eater. The routine was well established: Young men in their 20s would be given the drug in copious amounts, and then led into beautiful tents filled with silken pillows and magnificent feasts and voluptuous women. When they came to, they were told they'd been to Paradise.

All a man had to do to return there was to fulfill his killing mission, whereupon he would be rewarded with 15 virgins. "I'm not sure about the number," Dr. Isaac Sakinofsky, a Toronto psychiatrist, told me. "But it's more than one."

And then there was that other kind of suicide, that photograph of a man who jumped from the trade centre. You know that picture too, don't you? He's upside down, head first, the position that makes you fall fastest, his body as straight as a pin, save for one crooked knee. Was that intentional? Did he want to fall as fast as he could? Was he blown out of a window? Probably not, given the time of day he fell; he probably jumped.

How could he jump out of a 110-storey building? Maybe it was easy. Psychologists are already suggesting that under the circumstances, such a leap would be "a healthy response."

"It may well have been a suicide," John Violante, a psychologist at the Rochester Institute of Technology, explained to me the other day. "You could say it was a suicide prompted by an attempted murder. But I wouldn't call it suicide. I would call it an individual facing certain death, trying to give himself a choice, the time and manner of his death."

Twenty-four-thousand gallons of jet fuel were burning in those buildings, at temperatures estimated at 800 degrees Centigrade. Aluminum and gold alloys melt at roughly that point, by which time lead is pure liquid.

Would you rather fly to your death, or burn to it? From a height of 110 storeys, a 200-pound adult would reach a terminal velocity—the steady speed achieved by an object falling through air—of about 150 miles an hour. You would be in the air for roughly 20 seconds. Twenty seconds, about as long as it takes to recite your name, address, city, province, telephone number, the names of your children. And a little extra time.

Would you hold your breath? Would you scream? Would you sing? What would you think about? (Provided you stayed conscious, which isn't guaranteed.) Would you try to watch the world one last time, to see sunlight and faces in windows streaming by?

I think—I want to think, anyway—that I would try to picture my children. In those circumstances, or in one of the planes that went down, they're the only image that would bring me peace. I would probably think of my daughter, my first born. I would fix her bright face in the eye of my mind, and I would keep thinking of her until blackness came. That way—and I know this sounds primitive and ancient—that way, if there is some form of consciousness after death, I would be where I could rest.

Or perhaps that hope is not so primitive. After all, on Friday at the Washington Memorial Service, George W. Bush justified any future invasion of a foreign country to strike back at terrorism on the grounds that it was God's will.

Perhaps it makes sense that we can't get these ideas out of our heads. In a way, they were already there.

A burning tower, after all, is an ancient image. The symbol the terrorists chose to strike isn't just an icon of capitalism; it's a symbol that is pre-biblical, maybe even prehistoric. There are towers everywhere: Gilgamesh, Babel, Babylon, Watts, of London, of Pisa, of David. It's a long list.

There is even, to my surprise, a Tower in the Tarot, the 16th card. It's a burning tower; people wearing crowns, powerful people, are shown falling to the ground. It refers, usually, to man's pride and vanity—to the imminent sudden destruction of a lifestyle, to sudden change and release and downfall and revelation, to the "ego fortress" that we build around our "true beautiful selves," that we intend as protection but which "actually serves as a prison," as my local Tarot reader informed me.

It's a card that could describe Islamic funadamentalist assassins and American fundamentalist capitalists too.

In 1939, Carl Jung—a fan of the Tarot himself—started to dream about waves and rivers of blood. He had thought he was going crazy until the Second World War began. He was simply dreaming the collective consciousness of his day.

We didn't dream those burning towers last week, though they often seemed like a reverie. Instead, the television dreamed them for us. Rivers of blood can't be far behind.

APPENDIX Putting It into Practice: A Primer on Content and Discourse Analysis

Content analysis uses objective and systematic counting and classification procedures to produce a quantitative description of the symbolic content in a text (Neuman, 2000, p. 293). *Content* refers to words, meanings, pictures, symbols, ideas, themes, or any message that can be communicated. A *text* is anything written, visual, or spoken that serves as a medium for communication. Content analysis is used in media research because it is non-reactive. *Reactivity* is the threat to validity that arises when subjects are aware that they are being studied. Because media texts have already been produced, there is no danger of them being affected or influenced by content analysis. As well, content analysis facilitates comparisons across texts (and different kinds of texts), and generates results that are:

- *valid* (the study measures what it intends to measure);
- *rigorous* (categories are precisely defined);
- *reliable* (measures are applied consistently); and
- *replicable* (the project can be replicated by another researcher).

Content analysis does have its weaknesses. It is labour-intensive, as a lot of care and attention is needed to create a coding framework (see below) and carry out the coding and data analysis. Moreover, measurement is tricky; how you count counts. Researchers need to determine how to deal with message frequency, replication, and intensity. Sometimes the researcher must grapple with how to count what's not there—what isn't being communicated by a text. The researcher must consider the validity of the texts, as the purpose of and intended audience for the communication can shape its messages. Context must be considered, as words and phrases have different meanings in different contexts. Perhaps most importantly, content analysis can reduce the text to its component parts, thus obscuring overall meanings and messages. This is why some researchers combine content analysis with discourse analysis, as is the case with Chapters 4, 8, and 15. **Discourse analysis** examines the ways in which language is used to construct meaning. Social and political understandings are constituted through discourse, thus interpreting texts is an important way of revealing power relations. Because discourses are "agents of knowledge, analyzing them can help reveal the "everyday knowledge" that is communicated via the media or political actors, including social movement organizations (Jäger, 2002, p. 37). Dominant discourses are revealed, critiqued, and problematized through discourse analysis, which relies heavily on discourse theories (too complex to be enumerated here). In very simplistic terms, content analysis identifies the manifest content of texts, while discourse analysis reveals what the messages signify in the context within which they are communicated and understood. In Chapters 12 and 17, discourse analysis is used exclusively by the authors.

When should you consider using content or discourse analysis of texts? The following aspects of political communication can be analyzed with these methods:

- **How** political actors (politicians, governments, citizens, civil society organizations) communicate (rhetoric, style, mode) (see http://pcl.stanford.edu/campaigns/index.html)
- **What** political actors communicate (ideas, goals, social norms, values)

As well, a wide range of political texts can be analyzed—everything from news stories to election advertisements, campaign brochures, government documents, policy or position papers, protest signs, songs, and slogans. However, neither content analysis nor discourse analysis can reveal how audiences interpret political communication; in other words, these methods do not get at media effects. Experimental designs have been coupled with content analysis to explore the effects of media agenda setting, priming, and framing (Iyengar, 1996).

A PRIMER ON CONTENT ANALYSIS: STEPS AND PROCEDURES

1. Determine a research question and hypotheses:
   - What do you want to know, and why?
   - What does the relevant literature say?
   - What is your precise question?
   - What are the likely answers?
   - Which hypothesis (or hypotheses) do you want to test?
   - Which concepts will you need to define and measure?
   - How does the literature suggest you should define and measure the concepts?

2. Choose the texts and unit of analysis:
   - **Texts**—the communications sources most appropriate for answering your question
   - **Unit of analysis**—the amount of text that is assigned a code equal to one case:
     - Is it a newspaper article, or part of an article (e.g., a headline)?
     - Is it the entire political speech, or each individual paragraph?
     - Is it the entire television newscast, or each individual news story?

3. Choose the **population**—the cases you will actually analyze:
   - Census—all of the texts on a certain subject over a specified time period
   - Non-random sample—a selection of texts based on clear and justifiable criteria:
     - All news stories mentioning the party in the headline.
   - Random sample—texts that are randomly selected based on a sampling interval:
     - Randomly selecting 1,000 out of 40,000 possible texts by choosing every fortieth case.

4. Determine measures:

- How will you measure your concepts? What are the particular elements or characteristics in the text that you will look at? What will you look for?
- *Frequency*—counting whether something occurs and, if it does, how often
- *Type*—the meaning of messages in or the structure of the content along some continuum or classification scheme
- *Intensity*—the strength or power of a message in a direction (e.g., minor or major)
- *Space*—the number of words or volume of space devoted to a message (e.g., length of direct quotations, in words or seconds)

5. Determine variables and values:

- *Structural variables*—focus on the structure of the communication (how it is said), e.g., placement of a news story in a newspaper or type of news story
- *Substantive variables*—focus on the substantive content of a communication (what is said), e.g., how an actor is evaluated in a news story (positively, negatively, neutrally, not evaluated)

6. Develop a codebook with

- A *coding frame*—a list of items (variables) you plan to count, and how you plan to count them (values):
  - Variables must measure the concepts in your hypotheses.
  - Values must be **mutually exclusive** and **collectively exhaustive**.
- *Coding notes*—your plan should include consistent rules for coding the texts so that you have clear criteria for judgment

7. Test and retest the coding frame:

- Resolve any coding issues and record your decisions.
- Ensure that everyone is coding consistently.

8. Create a coding sheet:

- This is where you will record the values for each case.

9. Code all of the cases in your sample.

10. Conduct data entry and analysis:

- Create an SPSS or Excel file for your data.
- Enter the data.
- Run and print your frequencies and fix any errors in data entry.
- Analyze your data—what have you found? What does it mean? Here you come full circle, as you will make reference to your literature review when making sense of your data.

A PRIMER ON DISCOURSE ANALYSIS

(NOTE: This is adapted very loosely from Jäger, 2002 and Cappella and Jamieson, 1997.)

1. Identify the "discourse plane"—the types of texts to be examined (e.g., political advertisements, country music, hip-hop videos, newspaper articles).
2. Determine the "discourse strand"—the exact texts that will be analyzed.
3. Identify the character of the discourse strand—what type of communication is it? Where does it appear? Who is the intended audience? What format does it normally take?
4. Conduct a detailed analysis of a selection of the texts ("discourse fragments") by summarizing the

   a. Author(s)
   b. Text "surface"—or "syntactical structures" (format, structure, layout). For newspaper articles, these include headlines, lead paragraphs, quotations, conclusions (see van Dijk, 1991 for a discussion of the semantic roles of the structures of newspaper stories).
   c. Thematic structures—the central themes or arguments of the text
   d. Scripts (standard storylines that create narrative tension) or frames (narrative devices that tap into existing knowledge)
   e. Rhetorical devices—stylistic choices that convey themes and meanings such as forms of argumentation, symbols, images, sources
   f. Ideological assertions or claims (e.g., about human nature, power, political values and goods)

SAMPLE CODEBOOKS

Codebook from Chapter 8, "Covering Muslim Canadians and Politics in Canada: The Print Media and the 2000, 2004, and 2006 Federal Elections," Yasmeen Abu-Laban and Linda Trimble.

Variable #	Variable name	Values and Value labels
1	caseid	
2	election	1. 2004 2. 2004 3. 2006
3	paper	1. *National Post* 2. *Globe and Mail* 3. *Vancouver Sun* 4. *Calgary Herald* 5. *Edmonton Journal* 6. *Ottawa Citizen*
		(continued)

Variable #	Variable name	Values and Value labels
		7. *Toronto Star*
		8. *Montreal Gazette*
4	date	**(dd/mm/yy)**
5	location	***What is the location of the story?***
		1. Front page
		2. Front section
		3. Op/Ed section
		4. Special election section/page
		5. Other (specify)
		9. Unable to determine location
6	storytype	***What type of story is it?***
		1. Hard news/feature
		2. Editorial
		3. Standing head stories (in brief, etc.)
		4. Column by newspaper columnist
		5. Guest columns—op/ed
		6. Other (specify)
7	report	***Who is writing the story?***
		1. Journalist for the newspaper
		2. Columnist for the newspaper
		3. Someone identified with the Muslim community
		4. Other commentator (not associated with Muslim community)
		5. No byline (editorial or wire service, e.g., "CP")
8	headline	***Is Muslim or Islam* in the headline?***
		1. Yes
		2. No
9	leadp	***Is Muslim or Islam* in the lead paragraph?***
		1. Yes
		2. No
10	locat	***What is the location of the first mention (in the story) of Muslim or Islam?***
		1. Top 30 percent of story
		2. Middle 30 percent
		3. Bottom 30 percent

(continued)

Variable #	Variable name	Values and Value labels
11	import	**What is the role of Muslim Canadians in the story?** 1. Tangential (mentioned only; listed among other groups) 2. Integral (main focus of story) 3. Important, but not the main focus
12	topic	**What type of election issue/public policy is discussed in the story?** 1. Domestic (e.g., same-sex marriage) 2. Foreign policy/security 3. Electoral game—who's winning, voting, strategy, support, polls, etc. 4. Other—specify
13	religious	**Are Muslim Canadians identified only as a religious group?** 1. Yes 2. No
14	voters	**Are Muslim Canadians identified as voters (voting bloc)?** 1. Yes 2. No
15	power	**If Muslim Canadians are identified as a voting bloc, are they framed as having power/influence over electoral outcome?** 1. Yes 2. No 9. N/A (not identified as a voting bloc)
16	turnout	**Is the electoral turnout rate of Muslim Canadians discussed in the story?** 1. Yes 2. No
17	candidates	**Does the story identify/discuss individual Muslim Canadian candidates?** 1. Yes 2. No

(continued)

Variable #	Variable name	Values and Value labels
18	Cdn	**Are Muslims <u>explicitly</u> identified as Canadian citizens?** 1. Yes 2. No
19	conserv	**Are Muslim Canadians framed as socially conservative (e.g., patriarchal)?** 1. Yes 2. No
20	homogen	**Are Muslim Canadians framed as a homogeneous group?** (Article does not discuss any aspect of community diversity/heterogeneity.) 1. Yes 2. No
21	extreme	**Are Muslim Canadians framed as extremists/radicals?** (with use of words like extreme, fanatic, hard-line, fundamentalist, militant, violent) 1. Yes* 2. No *If yes, record the words/phrases for the discourse analysis.
22	eval	**How are Muslim Canadians evaluated in the story?** 1. Positively* 2. Negatively* 3. In a balanced or neutral fashion 4. N/A (not evaluated; tangential to story) *Record any words/phrases of positive or negative evaluation for the discourse analysis.
23	speak	**Are Muslim Canadians speaking for themselves/their communities in the story? [e.g., quoted, cited]** 1. Yes 2. No

Codebook from Chapter 4, "Belinda Stronach and the Gender Politics of Celebrity," Linda Trimble and Joanna Everitt.

(NOTE: This codebook is from the analysis of national newspaper coverage of the defections.)

Variable #	Variable name	Values and Value labels
1	caseid	**Case identification**—by initials of defector and newspaper, number, e.g., BSGM1
2	defection	**Who is the defector?** 1. Belinda Stronach 2. David Emerson
3	paper	**Name of newspaper** 1. *Globe and Mail* 2. *National Post* 3. *Toronto Star* 4. *Winnipeg Free Press* 5. *Vancouver Sun* 6. *Edmonton Journal* 7. *Montreal Gazette*
4	date	**Day of story**—day
5	location	**Location of story in paper** 1. Front page 2. Front section 3. Business section 4. City section/Metro/Local 5. Style/Lifestyle section 6. Sports section 7. Other (specify) 8. Unknown/unable to determine
6	storytyp	**Type of story** 1. Hard news 2. Editorial 3. Column or opinion piece 4. Other (specify) 5. Unknown/unable to determine
7	sexrept	**Sex of reporter/columnist** 1. male 2. female 3. both (co-authored) 4. Don't know (wire service; editorial; no author identified; can't tell from author's name)
8	storyln	**Length of story (number of words)**

(continued)

Variable #	Variable name	Values and Value labels
9	defechdln	**Is the defector (Stronach or Emerson) named in the headline?** 1. Yes 2. No
10	headname	**If the defector is named in the headline, how is she/he named?** 1. First and last name 2. Last name only 3. First name only 9. N/A—not named in headline
11	headpm	**Is Peter MacKay named in the headline?** 1. Yes 2. No 9. N/A—Emerson defection
12	head1	**Who is named first in the headline?** 1. Belinda Stronach 2. David Emerson 3. Peter MacKay 4. Paul Martin 5. Stephen Harper 6. Other (specify in variable 30) 9. N/A—None of these political actors mentioned Coding notes: actor must be named directly (not by position)
13	headrel	**Is the Stronach/MacKay relationship mentioned in the headline?** 1. Yes 2. No 9. N/A—Emerson defection
14	defhl	**Is the defection the main topic of the headline?** 1. Yes 2. No
15	defectionh	**How is the defection evaluated in the headline?** 1. Positively 2. Negatively 3. Neutrally 9. Not evaluated in headline *(continued)*

Variable #	Variable name	Values and Value labels
16	defectorh	*How is the defector evaluated in the headline?* 1. Positively 2. Negatively 3. Neutrally 9. Not evaluated in headline
17	impacth	*How is the impact of the defection evaluated in the headline?* 1. Positively 2. Negatively 3. Neutrally 9. Not evaluated in headline
18	story1	*Who is named first in the story?* 1. Belinda Stronach 2. David Emerson 3. Peter MacKay 4. Paul Martin 5. Stephen Harper 6. Other 9. N/A (no political actor named)
19	snamed	How many times is **Stronach** named in the story (including the headline)?
20	enamed	How many times is **Emerson** named in the story (including the headline)?
21	mnamed	How many times is **Paul Martin** named in the story (including the headline)?
22	hnamed	How many times is **Stephen Harper** named in the story (including the headline)?
23	mknamed	How many times is **Peter MacKay** named in the story (including the headline)?
24	defquote	If the **defector is quoted** in the story, count the number of words quoted.
25	mtopic	*Is the defection the main topic of the story?* 1. Yes 2. No

(continued)

Variable #	Variable name	Values and Value labels
26	storyrel	*Is the Stronach/MacKay relationship mentioned in the story?* 1. Yes 2. No 9. N/A (Emerson defection)
27	defections	*How is the defection evaluated in the story?* 1. Positively 2. Negatively 3. Neutrally 9. Not evaluated in the story
28	defectors	*How is the defector evaluated in the story?* 1. Positively 2. Negatively 3. Neutrally 9. Not evaluated in story
29	impacts	*How is the impact of the defection evaluated in the story?* 1. Positively 2. Negatively 3. Neutrally 9. Not evaluated in the story

DISCOURSE ANALYSIS QUESTIONS (STRONACH AND EMERSON DEFECTIONS)

For each description and evaluation analyzed, indicate whether it occurs in the headline or the news story, and record who said it.

1. If the Stronach/MacKay relationship is mentioned, how is it described?
2. How is the defector (Stronach or Emerson) described? Evaluated?
3. How is the defection described and evaluated? What is said about the impact of the defection (e.g., on Canadian politics, political parties, citizen attitudes, etc.)?
4. From articles about Stronach's defection, record any rhetorical devices, images, descriptions, metaphors, frames, and inferences that signal the following aspects of "celebretization":

   a. Popularization (indications that celebrity status led to media visibility and prominence)

   b. Personalization (sexualization, private relationships, private life, style, and aesthetics)

References

Cappella, Joseph N., & Kathleen Hall Jamieson. 1997. *Spiral of Cynicism: The Press and the Public Good*. New York: Oxford University Press.

Iyengar, Shanto. 1996. "Framing Responsibility for Political Issues." *Annals of the American Academy of Political and Social Science* 546 (July): 59–70.

Jäger, Siegfried. 2002. "Discourse and Knowledge: Theoretical and Methodological Aspects of a Critical Discourse and Dispositive Analysis." In *Methods of Critical Discourse Analysis*, ed. Ruth Wodak, 32–62. London: Sage.

Neuman, W. Lawrence. 2000. *Social Research Methods: Qualitative and Quantitative Approaches*. 4th ed. Toronto: Allyn & Bacon.

van Dijk, Teun. 1991. *Racism and the Press*. London: Routledge.

Index

E